MATCH-ADTC

Modular Approach to Therapy for Children with Anxiety, Depression, Trauma, or Conduct Problems

Bruce F. Chorpita, PhD
University of California, Los Angeles

John R. Weisz, PhD, ABPP
Harvard University and Judge Baker Children's Center

Before You Get Started:
How to Use MATCH-ADTC

What Is MATCH-ADTC?

Modular Approach to Therapy for Children with Anxiety, Depression, Trauma, or Conduct Problems (MATCH-ADTC) is a collection of 33 independent therapeutic procedures that can be flexibly arranged to guide a course of individualized, evidence-based therapy for children, addressing not only their main problems, but also any accompanying issues or challenges.

Flowcharts

The five flowcharts in the first section of this manual guide the selection and arrangement of the therapy procedures. The first flowchart ("Main") asks you to determine the primary focus of the child's problems. That focus, which can include anxiety, depression, traumatic stress, or conduct problems, points to one of four detailed flowcharts that correspond to each of these areas. Each of these detailed flowcharts outlines an order and logic for choosing modules from the program.

Core practices. The four problem-area flowcharts emphasize the core evidence-based practices pertaining to that problem area. For example, the anxiety flowchart follows a progression from engagement, to psychoeducation, to self-monitoring, to exposure, and then to review and termination.

Handling interference. Each flowchart also features a collection of recommended procedures that can be applied if interference arises that somehow challenges or threatens the application of the core procedures. In that sense, the course of therapy can take a "detour" and apply other evidence-based procedures in order to get back on track for treatment. For example, when treating a child for depression, you might determine that a reward program must be established to increase motivation to complete the exercises regarding negative thoughts. If so, you can use the reward module to address that challenge before returning to the core procedures for depression.

Termination. Each problem-area flowchart ends with instructions to return to the main flowchart in order to assess whether another significant problem remains, which could then be targeted directly by using another problem-area flowchart that corresponds to the remaining problem.

Therapy Modules

The next section of the manual presents the therapy procedures themselves. The steps of each procedure are outlined in a two-column format, with a checklist on the left side and detailed descriptions on the right. The detailed descriptions, which provide specific strategies for approaching the steps of the procedure, are intended for therapists who are just getting to know the program. More experienced users who have implemented the steps before might simply refer to the checklist for prompts.

Some modules offer "Special Cases" information at the end, which explains how to adapt the material for particular clinical presentations (e.g., how to adapt the module for practicing feared items in the case of panic disorder), thus extending the applicability of many modules to a wider variety of specific problem types.

There is also a special module, "MATCH Essentials," which presents material that is common to almost every other procedure, such as how to set an agenda or assign and review homework. In order to avoid having these descriptions appear in every individual module, they appear in the "MATCH Essentials" module only.

Worksheets, Handouts, and Records

The third and final section of the manual contains all of the supplemental materials required for each therapy procedure: *worksheets*, which are exercises usually completed by the child, *handouts*, which are informational brochures and tips for caregivers, and *records*, which are forms used for tracking ratings of emotions or behaviors.

MATCH in Action

A key part of implementing MATCH is the application of ongoing assessment to measure progress toward goals. Accordingly, almost all therapy modules recommend a minimum amount of ongoing assessment (e.g., weekly mood, fear, or behavior ratings). This assessment can be supplemented with other measurement, and ongoing review of outcomes should guide decisions about which modules to choose next, when to move ahead, and when to complete a course of treatment (as indicated in the flowcharts). Given the high degree of flexibility of this program as well as the many recommendations for adapting or individualizing each procedure, treatment can take many different paths for different children. Nevertheless, with careful application, all children should receive the appropriate evidence-based procedures designed to address their challenges and help them make the changes they need to improve their lives.

Contents

Worksheets, Handouts, and Records   163

Quick Calming

Presenting a Positive Self

Cognitive Coping - BLUE

Cognitive Coping - TLC

Plans for Coping

Engaging Parents

Learning About Behavior

One-on-One Time

MATCH Flowcharts

MATCH

Main Flowchart

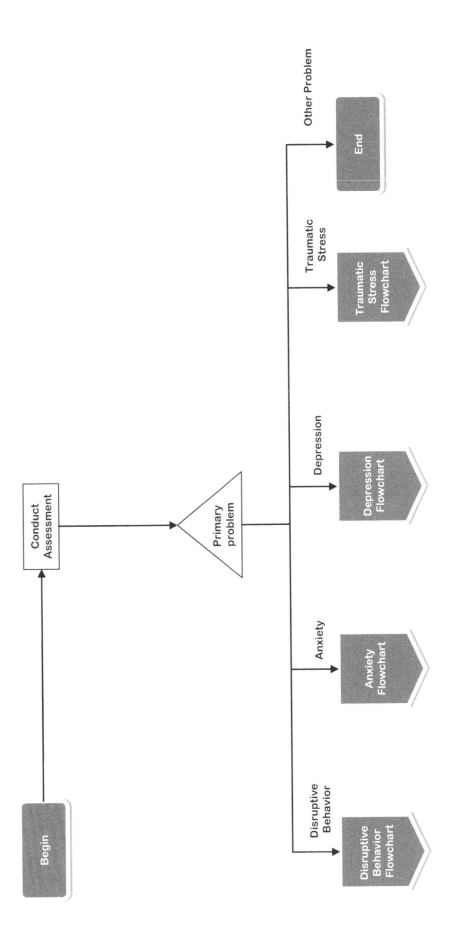

Anxiety

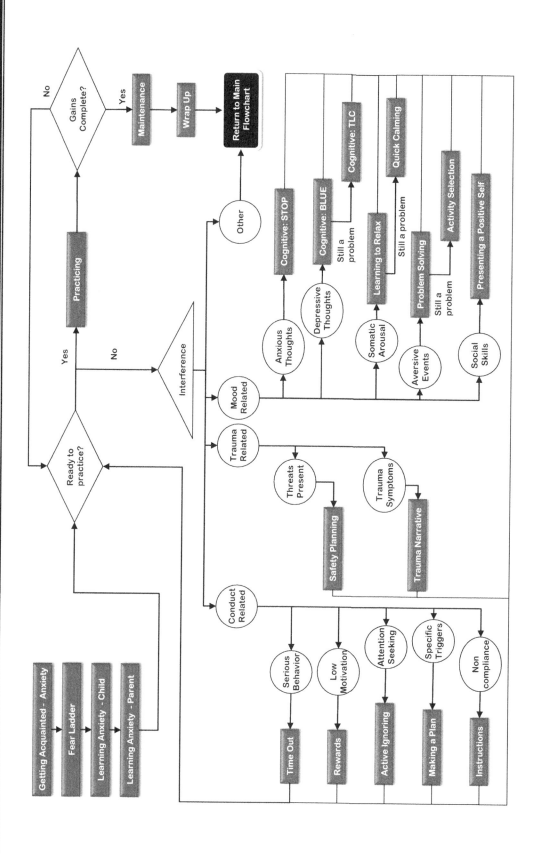

Depression

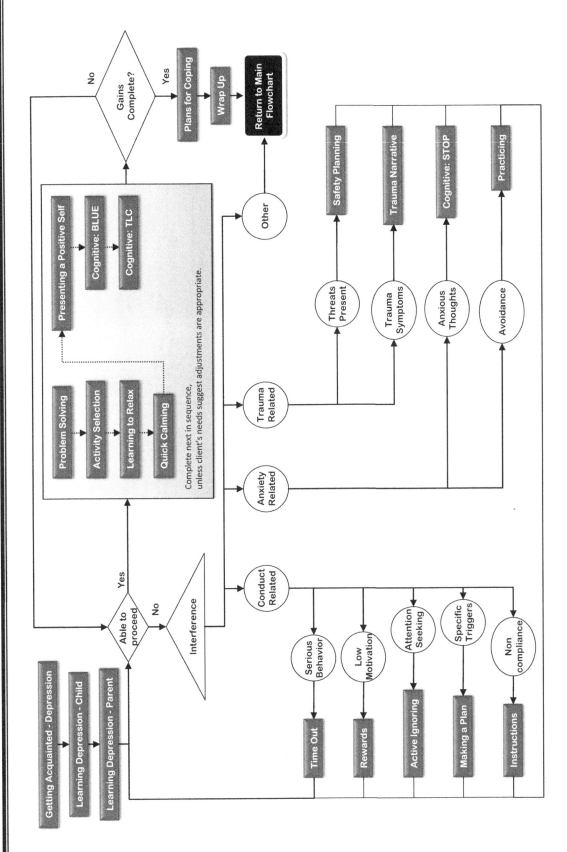

Traumatic Stress

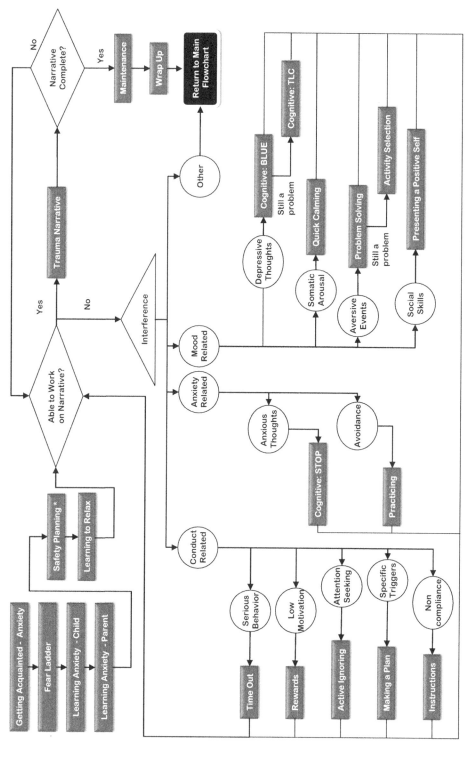

* Safety Planning can be moved to the end (before maintenance) if safety issues are not urgent

Conduct Problems

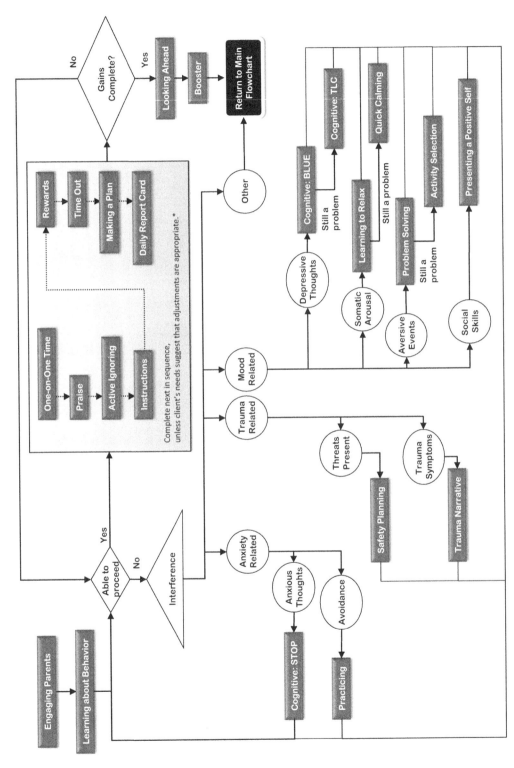

* Daily Report Card should always be preceded by Rewards

Therapy Modules

MATCH

MATCH Essentials

Setting an Agenda

Always start the session by setting an agenda together. You should not jump straight into teaching the new material, nor should you begin with an open ended check-in. Instead, begin with a brief overview of the material to be covered, breaking it into a few main steps. Then ask the child or parent if he or she has other items to add to the agenda. If there has been a crisis of the week (COW), put that into the agenda at the beginning. Set an appropriate time limit on your discussion of the COW so that you can transition to the other items on your agenda, or if more fitting, to a review of material already learned that might apply to this COW. Always try to make room at the end of the session for the "Leave 'Em Laughing" activity, and mention this activity when setting the agenda.

Reviewing Practice Assignments

Always remember to review practice assignments that were assigned in a previous session, no matter how small. Forgetting to review assignments sends the message that practice is not important, just the opposite of what you want to convey. In fact, practice is the most important part of learning new skills.

If the assignment was completed, be sure that the child or parent understands the basic ideas and objectives that it was intended to convey. Be highly supportive in your comments and provide plenty of praise, even if there were problems or there was only partial completion.

Discuss whether completion of the practice assignment felt successful. If it did, review what skills, behaviors, or insights were related to that success. If the practice was felt to be unsuccessful, suggest different interpretations of the outcome or see whether the child or parent can find a silver lining. This is also a good time to emphasize the importance of persistence. Especially with parenting skills, it often takes a few tries before things start to work smoothly.

If the practice assignment was not completed at all, determine what factors might have prevented it from getting done, and work together to develop a plan to address any barriers. Possible solutions might include a reminder phone call to the home about the practice during the week, asking the child or parent to place a reminder sticky note in a prominent place at home, or working with the parent to develop a specific plan that allows the child and parent to do the practice together at home during the week. Sometimes it can help to have the child or parent pick the specific day and time that they will complete the practice (e.g., after dinner but before bath time on Tuesday), so that it is "on the schedule."

Being Socratic

Another essential skill is being Socratic, which means to teach by asking questions rather than by explaining. There is usually a lot of material to teach, and if you find yourself doing most of the talking, you are probably not being Socratic. Instead, you should think of the concept or idea that you want to explain, and then ask guiding questions until the child or parent articulates that concept or idea. For example, rather than saying, "Maybe you should try again," you could ask, "What do you think you should do next?", "What would happen if you tried again?", or "What happens to people when they give up?" to see if you can get the right answer. If the answer isn't right, keep asking questions to steer the child or parent toward the desired insight. Being Socratic can feel slow and even tedious for the therapist, but it is much more interesting for the child or parent and far more likely to lead to enduring new beliefs and ideas for them.

Getting Acquainted - Anxiety

Goals

- The child will feel more comfortable through introductory get-acquainted activities
- The child will understand basic information about the treatment of anxiety
- The child will learn about the importance of confidentiality, take-home assignments, and regular attendance
- The child will know how to use the *Fear Thermometer*

Materials

- *Fear Thermometer*
- Materials from recent assessment (if available)
- Pens, pencils, markers

⧗ *If time is tight: Begin to build the therapy alliance and learn more about the child.*

Main Steps	*Remember to start by setting an agenda together.*
☐ **Warm Up**	Try to get a conversation going at a pace that suits the child. It is often helpful to make sure that formal treatment does not begin too quickly, since anxious children tend to be avoidant, generally fearful or wary, and typically not familiar with questions about their feelings. Try to refrain initially from asking a lot of personal questions of the child.
☐ **ACTIVITY** *Ice Breaker*	An ice breaker activity is a good idea to build a therapeutic alliance. The appropriate activities will depend on the child's age and interests, so you should prepare beforehand, trying to obtain enough prior information about the child to plan a uniquely tailored ice breaker. The exercise may be as simple as engaging in a discussion with the child centered on three things about him or her that are unusual or interesting. Art materials may also be helpful if the child enjoys drawing or if you feel that the child might find a nonverbal means of connecting easier at first.

☐	**ACTIVITY** *Personal Facts Game*	To introduce your need to gather information, and the idea that this information is important to you, it might be helpful to play a "Personal Facts" game. In this game, both you and the child supply answers to the same questions, such as "What is your middle name?", "How old are you?", "How many brothers and sisters do you have?", or "What is your favorite activity?" Keep in mind that including questions about favorite TV shows, heroes, and superheroes can provide information that will be helpful later in treatment. After giving answers, you and the child might quiz each other. It is important that you recall the details accurately as this conversation is one of the child's first attempts to share personal information with you. It will also be helpful throughout the treatment if you are comfortable with the child's asking personal information about you and with providing answers to appropriate questions.
☐	**Provide Overview and Rationale**	Provide the child with a brief overview of the program, and explain that this program is a joint effort between the therapist and the child. Provide an overall review of the ways the program is designed to help the child.
☐	**Discuss Goals**	Begin to discuss the goals for treatment. Explain that the main principle of the work you will be doing together is that it is possible to reduce feelings of anxiety in challenging situations by changing how one copes with and responds to those situations. Let the child know that during your work together, you might focus on skills that involve the ways he or she responds to anxiety, thinks about things, or both.
☐	**Encourage Participation**	Invite the child to ask questions about treatment. Continue to re-open this invitation periodically until the child begins to share his or her questions and concerns. Stress to the child that information from his or her point of view is very important. Emphasize that you're interested in what the child sees and thinks about various situations. Value should be placed on the child's point of view.
☐	**Describe Treatment Structure**	Lay out the structure and sequence of the treatment program. Be sure to cover the following points: • the activities that will happen in the various sessions (e.g., role-playing, practicing new skills) • the importance of regular attendance (because each session builds on the contents of the previous ones, and the entire program is needed to maximize the chances of success) • the worksheets, which contain practice assignments for him or her to do each week between sessions
☐	**ACTIVITY** *Fear Thermometer*	Have the child do a rating for his or her current level of fearfulness. You may need to practice once or twice with sample anchors to make sure the child is giving accurate ratings. Ask the child what the number he or she chose means, in order to be sure he or she understands the concept. Ask the child to indicate, using the *Fear Thermometer*, how afraid he or she would be of several other situations (i.e., eating his or her favorite dessert, riding on a roller coaster, being in a strange place by him or herself) in order to make sure that the child feels comfortable using this scale. It is particularly important that the child be able to use the full range of the scale, not just the ends.
☐	**Praise**	Praise the child for his or her good work during this first session.

Leave 'Em Laughing

End the session on a fun note, with a game, activity, or other exercise that will leave the child feeling really good about the work you have done together today.

Share with Parent (if possible)

At the end of the session, if a parent is available, it can be helpful to brief him or her on the materials covered.

☐ **Consider Privacy**	Before bringing the parent into the room, it is important to ask the child if there is anything that he or she told you today that he or she does not want you to tell the parent. Be sure to honor the child's confidentiality within the appropriate limits of safety.
☐ **Review Concepts**	Have the child explain to the parent what concepts he or she has learned in the session. You can add information as necessary.
☐ **Review Fear Thermometer**	For this session the parent should also be introduced to the *Fear Thermometer*. Let the parent know that he or she and the child will be asked at each session to rate the child's current level of anxiety with respect to specific events and situations. Explain that the *Fear Thermometer* will be an important tool during treatment to gather information on the child's anxiety and the types of things that cause the child's fearfulness to increase or decrease. The parent should understand that the *Fear Thermometer* is a tool that takes a global rating of their child's anxious feelings. Ask the parent to use it to rate the child's fear under various circumstances.

Example script

If your child was at home watching his favorite movie, how scared or nervous would he be then? How scared or nervous would he be if he was on a really scary rollercoaster ride? How about if he was about to make a speech in front of the whole school?

Ask the parent what the number means, in order to be sure he or she understands the concept.

How's Your Style?

- Did you praise often?
- Did you review often, by asking questions?
- Did you simplify the steps as needed?
- Did your pace match that of the child or family?
- Did you stay on track?

Fear Ladder

Goals

- The child will identify situations that make him or her anxious
- The child will describe his or her reactions to signs of anxiety
- Together you will produce a list of feared items that will guide the practice exercises for subsequent modules

Materials

- *Fear Ladder* (blank and unrated)
- *Fear Thermometer*
- *Learning Your Anxious Feelings* worksheet (if panic is a major focus)
- Index cards
- Assessment materials from recent assessment (if available)
- Access to photocopier or computer with printer

⧗ *If time is tight:* Construct a list of situations that provoke anxiety in the child, and note what factors might make the situations easier or harder.

Main Steps	*Remember to start by setting an agenda together.*
☐ **Introduce the Ladder Concept**	Let the child know that you want to find out some more about his or her specific fears or worries by constructing a list or "ladder" of anxiety-provoking situations. You will want to learn more about the types of situations that trigger anxiety, how the child reacts to anxiety, and how the child responds to the anxiety-provoking situations.
☐ **Encourage Openness**	Point out that it is important to be as honest and as thorough as possible when making a list of fears. This part of the program is one of the most important parts of working together, and the better you do on this task together, the better the program is likely to work.
	Example script
	The work we are going to do today is really important. I know you can do really well with this, and the more you can help me learn about your anxious feelings, the more successful we will be in making those feelings go away...
☐ **Review *Fear Thermometer***	Review the *Fear Thermometer* if needed. You may need to practice once or twice with examples to make sure the child can provide accurate ratings. Remember that it is better if the child can use the full range of the scale and not just the extremes.

☐ **Begin Making List**	Work together to establish a list of feared situations within the primary domain of concern (if the child has multiple domains of anxiety, you can always develop another *Fear Ladder* at a later time). For example, if the primary problem is panic disorder, the list should contain only items or triggers related to feelings of panic. If social phobia is the primary concern, the list should contain only items related to social or evaluative fears. As you agree on each item generated by the child or by you, write it down on an index card and put it aside.	
	Example script	
	Let's try to think of as many parts of this problem as we can that make you feel afraid, scared, or nervous. What are some of the things that you can tell me?	
☐ **Develop the List**	Staying within the selected area, identify as many feared situations, cues, sensations, or obsessions as possible. Try to generate a diversity of items while sticking to the domain that will be the target of treatment. For a specific phobia or discrete social phobia, try to identify as many variations of the particular stimulus as possible.	
☐ **Provide Support**	If the child finds it difficult to be specific about his or her anxiety, try to ask the child to imagine an actual situation while you observe his or her behavior for signs of anxiety. To introduce the procedure, model the process by imagining yourself in an anxiety-provoking situation while describing each step. The child can then be invited to "tag along" as you repeat the imagining process with another situation and, finally, to imagine him- or herself in an anxiety-provoking situation, with you providing prompts as needed.	
☐ **Get Enough Items**	If you do not have at least 10 items, consider the following: (a) go back through the assessment or intake materials together to identify other items the child may have forgotten (e.g., many structured interviews will have checklists for symptoms and cues) and/or (b) try to come up with some variations of items already identified. This latter approach can be done by changing small features of the stimulus/situation (e.g., more/fewer people around, stimulus more/less proximal, escape more/less difficult).	
☐ **Get Ratings**	Once you have at least 10 items (the more the better), read them one by one to the child, each time getting a rating using the *Fear Thermometer*. Write down the rating on the index card.	
☐ **Get a Range**	Once the child has rated each card, sort the cards in order of the fear ratings. If you have gaps in the ratings associated with each cards (2 or 3 point span with no items), go back to earlier steps, trying to generate items that fall into the missing scale points. The aim is to have a range of items differing in intensity.	
☐ **Praise**	Praise the child for doing well on this important task. Explain that you will now meet alone with his or her parent for a few moments and then you will meet with everyone together.	
☐ **Prepare with Parent**	Meet with the parent alone. Shuffle the cards so that they are no longer in the order of the child's ratings. Make sure the parent is familiar with the *Fear Thermometer*.	

☐	**Get Parent Ratings**	Without letting the parent know the child's ratings, read each item and get a parent rating. Write down parent ratings on the card for each item, making sure to distinguish these ratings from the child ratings (e.g., circle all the parent ratings). If two parents are present and disagree with each other, have them work together to come up with a number they agree on.
☐	**Look for Missing Items**	Ask the parent if there are any other objects or situations he or she feels that you or the child omitted. Write those items down on cards, and get parent ratings for those as well.
☐	**Bring Everyone Together**	Bring the child into the session (everyone should be together at this point). If the parent has added any new items, get fear ratings from the child for those final items.
☐	**Select Items**	Select the items that will go on the ladder and will be used to guide later practice exercises. Choose 10-12 items that (a) translate relatively easily into exposure or role play exercises and (b) suggest a logical sequence or progression of these exercises. Seek input from the parent or child when you are unclear about specific properties of an item being considered (e.g., how readily can it be practiced, is it too similar to another item we already have on the ladder, etc.). In some rare cases, you will be forced to choose fewer than 10 items, but first be sure you have been as thorough as possible on earlier steps.
☐	**Sort into Themes**	If there is a very large number of cards, it helps to sort them into piles by "themes" when creating the ladder. For example, with social anxiety, try to put all the cards related to assertiveness together, then all the cards related to speaking in public, then all the cards related to conversations, etc. The number within each pile can then be reduced by taking out things that are too similar in content or severity. For example, it is best to keep things within a theme that are different in severity rating or different enough in content to be important for later practice exercises.
☐	**Praise Everyone Again**	Praise the child again, thank the parent, and let them know that you will need a few moments to prepare the child's *Fear Ladder*.
☐	**Create Unrated *Fear Ladders***	Copy the final items (but not the ratings) onto a *Fear Ladder* form. You can do this by hand or by typing them on the computer. Items should be listed from highest to lowest intensity, according to the child's ratings. Make about 20 copies of the form.
☐ ⬆	**PRACTICE ASSIGNMENT** *Fear Ladder*	Give an unrated *Fear Ladder* to the child and another to the parent. Ask the child and his or her parent to choose one day during the coming week to fill in ratings for each of the items. Make sure that the child and his or her parent complete the *Fear Ladder* on the same day and write the date on the form, but do not consult with one another. It can be helpful to give the child a *Fear Thermometer* to take home to use as a guide when completing the *Fear Ladder*.
☐	**Record Today's Ratings**	After the session has ended, select two more unrated *Fear Ladders*, date them, and enter today's child and parent ratings from the index cards. Save the additional copies for future sessions.
		Each session you will distribute an unrated, dated copy of the *Fear Ladder* to the child and parent (if available), asking them to provide ratings. The parent and child should work independently to complete the forms, just as they did when the ladder was constructed. Take the completed forms with you into the session, as they will provide useful information for the formulation of practice exercises.

Leave 'Em Laughing

End the session on a fun note, with a game, activity, or other exercise that will leave the child feeling really good about the work you have done together today.

Special Cases

Generalized Anxiety	The items on the ladder for generalized anxiety disorder should focus as much as possible on feared *consequences* of the worry. For example, it is better to have an item such as "getting a bad grade" than "worrying about schoolwork." This is because the treatment program will be directly targeting the fears about the *consequences*.
Panic	A child with panic disorder may not be able to differentiate among the various physical sensations of a panic attack in order to provide accurate rankings. Therefore, you may need to conduct an interoceptive assessment to create the *Fear Ladder*. Explain to the child that you want to have a better understanding of what his or her panic attacks are like, so that you can practice together learning that panic attacks are uncomfortable, but not dangerous, and work together to complete the *Learning Your Anxious Feelings* worksheet.
Obsessions and Compulsions	Children with obsessive-compulsive disorder (OCD) tend to produce longer *Fear Ladders*. It is useful to have a list of both the feared stimuli and the behavioral responses the child currently engages in to neutralize the fear (compulsions). Practice will involve repeated exposure to the feared situations without engaging in the ritualized neutralizing behaviors (e.g., touching something dirty without being able to wash hands until the fear has abated).
Posttraumatic Stress	For a child with posttraumatic stress, the *Fear Ladder* may include "trauma reminder" items that have been inaccurately associated with the traumatic event (for example, all playgrounds for a child abused on a playground, or all men for a child whose assailant was male). However, actual people and places involved in the traumatic event that may truly be dangerous are not included. Keep in mind that these "trauma reminders" can be addressed using the *Fear Ladder* after the trauma narrative has been completed, and the specific memories of the traumatic event, which go in the narrative, need not be included on the *Fear Ladder*.

How's Your Style?

- Did you praise often?
- Did you review often, by asking questions?
- Did you simplify the steps as needed?
- Did your pace match that of the child or family?
- Did you stay on track?

MATCH
Protocol

Learning About Anxiety - Child

Use This:

To teach the child how anxiety works and to introduce concepts needed for treatment.

For Child

Goals

- The child will understand how anxiety works and will have a rationale for exposure practice
- The child will be optimistic about his or her situation
- The child will be interested in participating in and learning more about treatment

Materials

- *Fear Thermometer*
- *Fear Ladder* (2 unrated copies)
- *Anxious Feelings and Thoughts* worksheet
- Picture book, magazine, or other material depicting someone scared
- *Learning About Anxiety* worksheet

⧖ *If time is tight*: Teach the child about how unwanted anxiety can be similar to a false alarm and how gathering clues and practicing can help reduce unwanted anxiety.

Main Steps	Remember to start by setting an agenda together and by reviewing any practice assignments.
☐ **Obtain Weekly Ratings**	Using the 0 to 10 scale of the *Fear Thermometer*, obtain *Fear Ladder* ratings from both the child and his or her parent (if available).
☐ **Review Definitions and Vocabulary**	Meet with child alone. State that you will be talking about anxiety today, and begin by asking the child for their definition of anxiety. Elicit other words that might mean the same thing as anxiety. Praise the child's definitions and incorporate them into your own.
☐ **ACTIVITY** *Body Map*	Explain to the child that anxiety has three parts to it. One part is what we feel in our bodies (i.e., sensations), like feeling out of breath, having a racing heart, having our muscles become all tense, becoming shaky or sweaty, or having "butterflies."
	Introduce the *Anxious Feelings and Thoughts* worksheet (use only the girl or the boy drawing, as appropriate). Using questions (and pointing to areas if necessary), have the child label each area that feels different for him or her during anxiety.
	Examples: • *Can you mark places on this drawing where you feel things when you are anxious or scared?* • *Do any other places ever get those feelings when you are scared?*

☐	**ACTIVITY** *Thought Bubbles*	Explain that the second part to anxiety is what we think when we are anxious. To make sure that the child understands what a thought is, use the third page of the **Anxious Feelings and Thoughts** worksheet, or draw some of your own characters with empty "thought bubbles" over their heads. Try to get examples of some anxious thoughts the child has had recently, and write those in the bubbles.
☐	**ACTIVITY** *Finding Anxious Behavior*	Explain that the third part to anxiety is what we do when we are anxious, such as running away from the things that make us scared. Go through a book, magazine, or other materials together to see if the child can find an example of someone behaving in a way that looks anxious.
☐	**Normalize**	Explain that anxiety is an emotion that all people experience. Reassure the child that all people have fears and anxieties (including adults, heroes, and brave people). You can explain that even you get anxious about things sometimes, being sure to give an appropriate example.
☐	**Introduce the Alarm Concept**	Ask the child if he or she can name different kinds of alarms (e.g., fire alarms, burglar alarms). Ask the child what alarms do (i.e., warn us that something bad or dangerous might be about to happen). Praise the child's efforts to come up with examples of alarms and what they do.

Example script

That's right! Alarms protect us from harm by letting us know when danger might be near.

Explain that anxiety is the body's alarm system, a very special one. It is so well-designed that it actually has two parts to it. The first is a warning that danger might be coming, and the second tells us the danger is here.

Example script

So anxiety acts as our own alarm system, and it has two parts. The first part tells you that something bad might be about to happen. It is just like a yellow warning light that says "be careful now." Have you ever felt like you knew something bad was going to happen? Yes, that was the "yellow light" part of your alarm. The second part of our alarm system tells us that the danger is here right now. That part is like a red light that says, "Oh no!" or "Let's get out of here!"

Make sure to explain that people's alarms are not just for warning about fires or robbers. People can feel alarms about teasing, tests at school, taking a trip, getting sick, and lots of other things.

☐	**Quiz About Alarms**	Make sure that the child understands the difference between the "yellow light" and the "red light" stages of the alarm system by asking him or her to state in his or her own words what you have just discussed. Give some examples, as follows:

Example script

If I were really scared of lightning, and I heard it start to rain, what kind of alarm would I have? Would that be a yellow light or a red light? What if lightning struck nearby? What kind of alarm would I feel then?

☐	**Show How Anxiety Can Be Good**	Ask the child whether he or she thinks anxiety is good or bad. Ask the child to explain why. Praise any response, and then go on to ask whether anxiety can really be both good *and* bad.

Example script

You: So, do you think anxiety is a good thing or a bad thing?

Child: Um, bad.

You: OK, so can you tell me what makes you think anxiety is bad?

Child: It feels bad.

You: Right! Sometimes too much anxiety can make us feel really bad inside, and nobody likes that. But can anxiety sometimes be a good thing, too? How might anxiety be good for us?

Ask the child what would happen if we did not have anxiety. Illustrate this point by asking the child what would happen if they tried to cross the street without looking (i.e., we might get hit by a car). See if you can get the child to say that anxiety can protect us from dangerous situations or from getting hurt.

☐	**Discuss False Alarms**	Ask the child if he or she knows what a false alarm is. If the child is unable to answer this question, explain that false alarms are when alarms go off, but there is actually nothing bad happening, such as when a car alarm goes off, but there is really no one stealing the car.

Test to see if the child understands the difference between a false and a real alarm. It may help to draw a picture of a house with a smoke alarm going off and no fire and another house with a fire. Ask which one is the real alarm and which one is the false alarm.

Explain that anxiety—people's alarm system—can have false alarms, too. That is when people get scared or anxious when there is really no danger. It is when people begin to have a lot of false alarms that their anxiety has gotten out of control, and it is in these cases that anxiety becomes harmful.

☐	**Set Goal to Reduce Excess Anxiety Only**	Tell the child that one of the goals in working together will be to get rid of the extra anxiety (that does not help), not the good anxiety (that does help). We do not want to get rid of the alarms altogether. We just want to stop having so many false alarms.
☐	**Set up Tests**	See if the child can explain how to tell if an alarm is real or false. First, give an example of something like a fire alarm at school.

Example script

*How do the **teachers** know that there is no fire and everyone can go back inside? Did someone check for fire?*

Then ask how the child could test out whether his or her own "anxiety alarms" are real ones or false ones.

Example script

What could you do when your anxiety alarm goes off to see if the danger is real? How could you find out if there is anything to hurt you?

Encourage the child to give answers that suggest one needs to check or test to see if the alarm is real. Make sure the child understands that this would mean going toward the scary thing or situation sometimes, just like one has to go look at one's car when a car alarm goes off.

☐	**Explain the Importance of Practice**	Explain that conducting these tests of whether alarms are real or false is why practice is so important. Ask the child why they think practice, in any area, might be important (answer: to improve).

Example script

You: What if I tried to teach you how to play soccer, and I told you everything about soccer—what the rules were, how people score points, and why people get penalties. After I told you everything there is to know about soccer, would that help you to play soccer really well?

Child: Probably not.

You: Why not?

Child: 'Cause I need to learn how to kick the ball and stuff like that.

You: That's right, you need to get good at kicking and running, right? How do people get good at those things?

Child: Practice.

You: Right!

Other examples can be incorporated into the above discussion that are more applicable to the child, such as playing an instrument, learning to swim, or better yet, something the child is already skilled at and about which the child is not anxious.

☐	**Relate Practice to Anxiety**	Explain how the same principles that apply to learning how to play soccer are true for anxiety. By practicing situations that make the child a little anxious, he or she can learn to test and control the false alarms. Use questioning to arrive at the idea that practice can be gradual, and that small steps will be required until bigger ones can be taken. It can help to reverse roles and ask the child how to help you with a false alarm, picking an example that involves an area of relatively little anxiety for the child (e.g., his or her pet, high places, being teased).

Example script

You: So, you're a good swimmer. Let's say I'm really scared of going in a pool—even in the shallow end where I can touch the bottom and even though I can swim. How would you help me?

Child: I would tell you not to be afraid of the pool.

You: But how would you convince me to go in?

Child: Maybe I'd go in first and show you.

You: Good! That might help me. Now, what if I was still too afraid to jump in where you are? What else could you do?

Child: I'd tell you to go in by the steps first, where it's really shallow.

You: That's great! I think I could do that!

☐	**Introduce Monitoring**	Finally, introduce the idea of monitoring, which is just like gathering clues or evidence.

Example script

Now, working on anxiety can be a bit like solving a mystery. What do detectives look for when solving a mystery? That's right—clues! So, just like two detectives, we are going to gather clues to help us learn more about your anxiety. Sometimes when you're practicing things to help with anxiety, I will need you to write down some things (or tell your parents some things to write down). This will help us solve the mystery!

☐ ⌂ PRACTICE ASSIGNMENT *Learning About Anxiety*	Give the child the *Learning About Anxiety* worksheet to complete at home. Explain that you will go over it together the next time you meet.

Leave 'Em Laughing

End the session on a fun note, with a game, activity, or other exercise that will leave the child feeling really good about the work you have done together today.

Share with Parent (if possible)

At the end of the session, if a parent is available, it can be helpful to brief him or her on the materials covered.

☐ Consider Privacy	Before bringing the parent into the room, it is important to ask the child if there is anything that he or she told you today that he or she does not want you to tell the parent. Be sure to honor the child's confidentiality within the appropriate limits of safety.
☐ Review Concepts	Have the child explain to the parent what concepts he or she has learned in the session. You can add information as necessary.

Helpful Tips

- If this is too much material, it can be covered in two (or more) sessions. The most important concepts are the false alarm idea and the importance of practice and monitoring.
- If a child finds it difficult to discuss his or her own experiences, introduce concepts in the abstract or by referring to other people, rather than focusing on the child's own experience. What do other people do when they are scared? How do you know your little sister is scared?

Special Cases

Generalized Anxiety	A child with generalized anxiety may never experience many "red light" alarms, but can have a "yellow light" that seems to be always on. It can be helpful to talk about what kinds of things the yellow light comes on for—if it is saying "be careful!" why might that be? What kinds of things is it saying could go wrong? Be sure to point out that people's yellow light can come on for all sorts of little things, like homework, teasing, or being on time, not just serious danger.
Panic	For a child with panic disorder, the "alarm" metaphor can be used to describe what happens when the child begins to notice sensations in his or her body (sweaty palms, heart beating, rapid breathing). The panic attack itself is really a "red light" alarm for the child, whereas the worry about having another panic attack may be more of a "yellow light" alarm. The false alarm of a panic attack may feel to the child very similar to a real alarm (having a heart attack, going crazy), so this may be a good time to identify the core fear the child has attached to the panic attacks.

Obsessions and Compulsions	For a child with OCD, the obsessions can be described as an alarm that keeps going off, all the time, for no reason (like when a smoke alarm has a bad battery). Because the alarm is so distressing, the child tries to turn it off by doing something in response (compulsions). However, the more he or she tries, the louder the alarm becomes and the more often it goes off. This is a good time to identify the behaviors that the child has developed to try and "turn off the alarm."
Posttraumatic Stress	For a child with PTSD, explain that sometimes when we have experienced a real alarm, people, places, sounds or memories that remind us of the scary experience can make us feel like the experience is happening all over again. This is actually a false alarm, but it can feel very real in the moment.

How's Your Style?

- Did you praise often?
- Did you review often, by asking questions?
- Did you simplify the steps as needed?
- Did your pace match that of the child or family?
- Did you stay on track?

MATCH
Protocol

Learning About Anxiety - Parent

Use This:

To introduce the parent to the planned course of treatment for his or her child's anxiety.

For Caregiver

Goals

- You will continue to establish rapport with the parent
- The parent will understand confidentiality issues
- The parent will understand the nature of anxiety and its expression in youth
- The parent will understand how the treatment plan addresses anxiety
- The parent will know the importance of completing worksheets and practice assignments
- The parent will understand the importance of regular attendance for sessions

Materials

- *Fear Thermometer*
- *Fear Ladder* (2 unrated copies)
- *Parent Interview* (if necessary)
- *Helping Your Child Succeed* parent handout
- *Understanding Anxiety* parent handout
- Materials from recent assessment (if available)

> ⧖ *If time is tight: Develop the parent's enthusiasm about the treatment program, especially practice, and learn more about the child's specific difficulties with anxiety from the parent's perspective.*

Main Steps	Remember to start by setting an agenda together and reviewing any practice assignments.
☐ **Obtain Weekly Ratings**	Obtain the *Fear Thermometer* and *Fear Ladder* ratings from both the child (if available) and his or her parent.
☐ **Discuss Confidentiality**	Start by discussing the confidentiality of what the child says in treatment. Point out that you plan to regularly share the main ideas discussed in each sessions, but that keeping some details of what the child says confidential will likely be helpful to the child. Of course, any issues that lead you to be concerned about the child's safety or the safety of others would be disclosed to the parent. Finally, tell parents that in most cases they have a right to access their child's record, so that any suggestions you make are merely helpful guidelines that do not restrict those rights.

☐ **Discuss What Does Not Work**	Begin with a brief discussion of what does **not** work for anxiety. For example, telling a child "just relax," or explaining that their anxiety is unnecessary or does not make sense will not help. Also, with the exception of problem solving around everyday worries, "talking it out" is generally not considered to help in the long run. Another common approach, "getting to the origin of the fears" has not been show to help reduce anxiety, either.
	Example script
	Have you ever been really worried about something and had someone tell you "just relax?" Did it make you relax? Why not? That's right, it is not that simple! You see, one of the things we have learned is that just talking about worries or telling people to relax doesn't really show them how to get started. So what we would like to try will be a bit different than just "talking it out" or saying, "just relax."
☐ **Manage Expectations**	Explain to the parent that this means you will not be "talking it out" with the child nor will you be "searching for the root of the fears." It is important that parents understand that those types of approaches are not likely to help.
☐ **Discuss What Can Work**	Follow this with an explanation of what can work. The one skill that has been shown more than any other to help anxiety problems in children is practice. Ask the parent to give an example of how someone who is scared of something could get used to it by practicing.
	Example script
	Have you ever known someone who was scared to fly in airplanes? How would they get over that fear?
	Be sure to point out that practice involves getting used to something and learning that it is safe. Praise the parent for good examples.
☐ **Describe Your Role**	Explain that your job, then, is not really to be just a listener, but to be a coach. Use an example from sports or exercise to explain how the coach's job is to:
	• make sure practice is goal-directed (children are not asked to stand around with a basketball during practice, they are asked to dribble or shoot baskets);
	• ensure that practice is safe (coaches make sure that children are properly warmed up and don't do anything that could lead to injury);
	• maintain enthusiasm (coaches often give pep talks, especially when practice is hard or things are not going well).
	This is what you will do as a therapist: plan, organize, supervise, troubleshoot, and give feedback about practice. If things are getting in the way of practice, your job is to help make practice easier.

☐	**Describe Parent's Role**	Explain that another important goal is for the parent to become the coach as quickly as possible. To the extent possible, the parent will be asked to learn how to do all the practice exercises with the child, and to learn how to fix problems that come up. As soon as the parent can start to take over, the therapist backs away a bit, providing support only when needed. Eventually, the family will be able to do all the practice without help and won't need the therapist anymore. Remind parents that all this represents an active approach to treatment, and that children always do better when their parents participate actively.

> **Example script**
>
> *So, remember, your child and I won't just be talking about how she feels each week. I am going to teach her skills to practice. Eventually, I'd like you to help with the practice and work as a coach for your child to continue to improve these new skills.*

☐	**Introduce Alarm Concept**	As you did with the child, point out that anxiety is an emotion that all people experience, and that it works as the body's natural alarm. Usually, that alarm is helpful and protects us from danger. Ask the parent to imagine what someone would do if he or she felt no anxiety (the parent should be guided to provide an answer suggesting that a person could not avoid danger, which would be bad). Then point out that, in their child's situation, the alarm is a little too sensitive—it goes off too easily. Thus, the goal of therapy is to make sure that their child is better able to tell what fears are real and what dangers are only false alarms. The goal is not to help the child get rid of all his or her anxiety, but rather to have her experience anxiety only when it is appropriate.
☐	**Check In**	Answer any questions at this point, and try to frame your answers within the alarm model of anxiety reviewed so far.
☐	**Acknowledge the Parent's Perspective**	Explain to the parent that in order to facilitate conducting practices with their child in future sessions, you would like to get some more specific information about the child's anxiety and overall functioning.

> **Example script**
>
> *One of the things that will help me the most in working with your child will be getting your perspective on her anxiety and the kinds of things that happen for your child when she experiences anxiety. Because you are really the expert on your child, your perspective on how things have been going for her will be very valuable.*

☐	**Conduct** *Parent Interview*	If you do not have detailed background about the child, administer the *Parent Interview*, writing down those details that you think will be helpful for informing future practice exercises.
☐	**Review and Clarify**	At the end of this process, you should review what appear to be the child's main issues and areas of concern, and ask the parent to let you know which parts seem right and which parts don't.

☐	**Validate the Parent**	Remind the parent of his or her invaluable role in the child's treatment program and the unique perspective he or she brings. As much as possible, you should build the parent's enthusiasm and increase his or her motivation to participate in the child's treatment.
☐	**Cover the *Helping Your Child Succeed* Handout**	At this point, go over the *Helping Your Child Succeed* handout together. Be sure to stop and answer questions as you go along.
☐	**Go over Rules for Practice Assignments**	Discuss the purpose of practice assignments between sessions, and plan together how and when the child will be able to work on them. Later in the treatment, you might need to ask for the parent's assistance in getting the child to complete the practice assignments, so it is wise to set the stage for this possibility at the outset.
☐	**Set up Communication**	Ask if the parent minds your calling the child at home to remind him or her to do the practice. To facilitate ongoing contact, you should exchange phone numbers with the parent, and make sure the parent has a phone number to call in the event of an emergency.
☐	**Review and Questions**	Make sure you leave time for discussion of any questions or concerns the parent may have.
☐	**Provide *Understanding Anxiety* Handout**	Provide the parent with the *Understanding Anxiety* handout to take home, and finally, thank the parent enthusiastically for making the time to talk with you.

Helpful Tips

- Therapists should be careful when discussing commitment and motivation with families, so as to avoid suggesting that the family is "not interested" in their child's progress. Many families are motivated for their child to improve, but do not have the time or resources to help. A better approach is to describe that treatment must be an important goal for both the parent and the child using the words "high priority" instead. Parents should be encouraged to inform their therapist if they are not finding enough time to practice outside of session, as well as to discuss any other difficulties they are having with treatment as such difficulties arise.

How's Your Style?

- Did you praise often?
- Did you review often, by asking questions?
- Did you simplify the steps as needed?
- Did your pace match that of the parent?
- Did you stay on track?

Practicing

Goals

- The child will practice exposure to feared items or situations
- Over the course of several attempts, the child will show decreased ratings for these items or situations
- The child will understand the relationship between the practice performed and the decreased anxiety

Materials

- *Fear Thermometer* and *Fear Ladder* (2 unrated copies, for anxiety/trauma), *Feelings Thermometer* (for depression), or *Behavior Rating Scale* (for disruptive behavior)
- *Practice Record* (Start-and-Stop or Before-and-After)
- *Practice* parent handout

> ⧖ *If time is tight*: *Have the child practice an anxiety-provoking situation, successfully handle the anxiety produced by that situation, and experience a reduction in fear.*

Main Steps	*Remember to start by setting an agenda together and reviewing any practice assignments.*
☐ **Obtain Weekly Ratings**	If the main focus is traumatic stress or anxiety, use the 0 to 10 scale of the *Fear Thermometer* to obtain *Fear Ladder* ratings from both the child and his or her parent. If the main focus is depressed mood, use the *Feelings Thermometer* to take a rating. If the main focus is disruptive behavior, take a parent rating with the *Behavior Rating Scale*.
☐ **Introduce Practicing**	If this is the first time starting exposure practice, review with the child that this phase of treatment will involve practicing in order to build new skills for coping with anxiety. If you have covered the Learning About Anxiety Module with the child, you can tie in concepts already covered.
☐ **Select an Item**	Assist the child in choosing a situation from his or her *Fear Ladder*, easy ones at first, harder ones later. If the child has no *Fear Ladder* (i.e., anxiety is not the main target), pick the feared situation you currently wish to address.
☐ **Define Goals**	Ask the child to visualize the situation and define overt behavioral goals for that situation (e.g., starting a conversation, being separated from his or her mother). If necessary, discuss and modify the goal so that it is not so hard that the child will refuse. Remember that small steps are OK, and "not being anxious" is not allowed to be a goal.

☐	**ACTIVITY** *Let's Practice*	To the extent possible, practice the exposure together. If the exposure will involve discrete trials of behaviors such as holding one's breath or asking someone a question, it is best to use the *Before-and-After Practice Record*. For extended or continuous behaviors, such as standing in a dark room, giving a speech, or touching a feared object, it is best to use the *Start-and-Stop Practice Record*. Date the *Practice Record*, and write the name of the practice item in the leftmost empty space. During discrete exposure practices, take fear ratings only before and after each trial. During continuous exposure practices, take a rating when you start, then take additional fear ratings at one about minute intervals during the exercise (intervals can be longer if the exposure might run longer than 10 minutes), and take a final rating as you stop. Repeat the exposure until the fear rating is a 3 or less for items starting at a 5 or above, 2 or less for items starting at 4 or below, or until 30 minutes has elapsed. When finished, draw one line to connect the values within each trial and another line to connect the "before" or "start" values across trials.
☐	**Review the Practice**	Praise the child for his or her hard work. If fear ratings decreased during the practice, ask the child what happened to his or her anxiety. Ask if the feared consequences occurred or if anything bad happened. Use the *Practice Record* to demonstrate that anxiety did indeed go down over time.
☐	**Praise Even if Ratings Did Not Decrease**	If the fear did not decrease, point out that the child endured the anxiety without quitting and that the feared consequences did not occur. **Example script** *You did a great job! And did anything really terrible happen to you? Nice job being so brave!*
☐	**Repeat Practice**	If there is time, repeat the practice exercise again after a short break. Ask the child if he or she noticed whether the practice gets easier with repetition.
☐ 🏠	**PRACTICE ASSIGNMENT** *Practice at Home*	If the child has never practiced at home before, explain the *Practice Record* and its use. Assign exposure practice to be completed during the week by filling out a new *Practice Record*. Typically, the child should be asked to practice on at least 4 different days that week. On the *Practice Record*, write the items selected and the appropriate instructions (e.g., stop when ratings come down to a …). Remind the child that filling out the *Practice Record* is just like gathering clues—the ratings will help us learn what's happening. If the *Practice Record* is too difficult for the child to use, have a parent assist. It may be necessary to give the parent a demonstration of how to use the form by doing a "mini-practice" together.

Leave 'Em Laughing

End the session on a fun note, with a game, activity, or other exercise that will leave the child feeling really good about the work you have done together today.

Share with Parent (if possible)

At the end of the session, if a parent is available, it can be helpful to brief him or her on the materials covered.

☐	**Consider Privacy**	Before bringing the parent into the room, it is important to ask the child if there is anything that he or she told you today that he or she does not want you to tell the parent. Be sure to honor the child's confidentiality within the appropriate limits of safety.
☐	**Review Concepts**	Have the child explain to the parent what concepts he or she has learned in the session. You can add information as necessary.
☐	**Show off Success**	When the child has completed a practice exercise or activity successfully, this is a good time to repeat it with a parent there to see. During the practice, you can model to the parent how to encourage and praise the child's behaviors.
☐	**Give Parent Handout**	Give the *Practice* handout to the parent. Make sure the parent is familiar with the concepts so that he or she can assist the child at home if needed.

Helpful Tips

- Practice should progress from easy items to more challenging items across sessions.
- If ratings do not come down within practice trials, the practice trials may need to be longer.
- If ratings come down within practice trials but not between practice trials, the practice trials may be too far apart. Consider making them more frequent.
- You can add new items to the *Fear Ladder* if they arise.
- If a practice is too unusual or difficult, one option is to role-play or act it out first.
- If the exposure is being conducted with a child who has already received sessions with cognitive techniques (e.g., STOP), then you should have the child precede each practice exercise by stating first their anxious thoughts and then coming up with other coping thoughts. Following the practice, review with the child which thoughts came true, the anxious thoughts or the coping thoughts ("So which thing came true?").

Special Cases

Panic	You will be using the *Fear Ladder* you created from information gathered in the interoceptive assessment. Remind the child that the goal of practicing these feelings is to learn the difference between a real and a false alarm, and to get used to the feelings so that they no longer provoke panic attacks. When starting the practice, ask the child to focus on his or her physical sensations and to give a cue (e.g., raise a hand) when they notice the feared feelings. Start taking ratings at that point, and remind the child to focus on the fear and not to distract themselves. Continue each exercise for at least 30 seconds once the sensation is noticed. After the practice, it can be helpful to ask the child to also give a rating of how strong the feelings were (not just an anxiety rating). Point out that the feelings may not become less strong, but the anxiety about them should decrease over time.

Obsessions and Compulsions	For a child with OCD, be sure to explain the importance of refraining from special behaviors or rituals used to "turn off the alarm" (compulsions). Some compulsions may be hard to detect, such as the child's looking at something, mental counting, etc. You can check on this by asking the child periodically about whether he or she has urges to perform the ritual and to rate the urge. The urge to perform the ritual often decreases as time elapses following the exposure. Once the urge and the fear have subsided, it may be appropriate to allow some form of the ritualized behavior (for example, allowing a child to briefly wash hands when the exposures have involved touching something truly dirty).
Posttraumatic Stress	For children with posttraumatic stress, you should have first completed the trauma narrative. If the child has a remaining list of "trauma reminders" (situations, people, or places that have become linked to the traumatic memories) on the **Fear Ladder**, you can practice those together with this module. Be sure that the content of the **Fear Ladder** is innocuous (based on false alarms) and does not actually present any danger to the child.

How's Your Style?

- Did you praise often?
- Did you review often, by asking questions?
- Did you simplify the steps as needed?
- Did your pace match that of the child or family?
- Did you stay on track?

Maintenance

Use This:

At the end of a course
of treatment for anxiety
or traumatic stress to
consolidate gains and
prepare for termination.

For Child

Goals

- The child will recognize that gains have been made and receive praise for his or her hard work in treatment
- The child will be able to review the main points covered in previous sessions, identify his or her new skills, and explain how to apply them to real life problems and conditions
- The child will understand that even though some concerns may remain at this point, continued practice after therapy has ended will lead to further improvement over time
- The parent will make plans to help the child maintain and build on newly acquired skills

Materials

- *Fear Thermometer*
- *Fear Ladder* (2 unrated copies)
- *What's New* worksheet
- *Maintaining Success* parent handout
- Paper and pencils for written exercises

> ⧗ *If time is tight:* Demonstrate to the child that gains have been made, ensure that practice will continue after meetings with the therapist are over, and reassure the child that if he or she continues to practice after treatment has ended, continued improvements are expected.

Main Steps	Remember to start by setting an agenda together and reviewing any practice assignments.
☐ **Obtain Weekly Ratings**	Using the 0 to 10 scale of the *Fear Thermometer*, obtain *Fear Ladder* ratings from both the child and his or her parent (if available).
☐ **Introduce Maintenance**	Discuss and review some of the basic concepts that the child has learned during treatment and how this new understanding fits his or her experiences. Ask the child why he or she is doing better, and help him or her to see that many of the gains are due to hard work and practice.
☐ **ACTIVITY** *Summary Picture or Narrative*	Some children may benefit from working on a drawing to symbolize their progress through treatment, such as creating a multi-panel cartoon that involves the progression from difficulty coping with feelings or worries to successfully coping with challenging or stressful situations, with some scenes of the practice in between.

☐	**Review the Importance of Continued Practice**	Discuss the importance of continued practice in everyday life. Encourage the child to continue to practice using his or her new skills, and convey confidence in his or her ability to apply his or her new skills successfully. You can return to analogies of sports, exercise, or playing a musical instrument, etc. to make the point that without regular practice, people can get "rusty." Ask how the child thinks he or she will continue to challenge him- or herself day to day with "mini practice" exercises.
☐	**Quiz Child on New Applications of Skills**	Discussing with the child how he or she will use the skills he or she has learned with challenging events in the future should be a highly interactive portion of the session, with lots of input from the youth as to which specific ways of applying his or her new skills and tools will be likely to really work.
☐	**Predict Challenges**	Prepare the child for the realistic possibility that there could be a return of sad feelings, worries, or fears. Experience and previous research tells us that lapses are common among individuals who have experienced anxiety or depression. The message to the child should be that this is all very normal and common, that almost no one can expect to have no bad feelings ever. Even though old feelings can come back sometimes, now there are new skills in place to deal with them.
☐	**ACTIVITY** *What's New?*	Complete the ***What's New?*** worksheet by having the child first write all of the things that were difficult in the left column. These things can be items taken from the ***Fear Ladder***, but can also be quality of life domains as well (e.g., family time, friends, hobbies).
		Then, read each item to the child and ask, "has this gotten better for you?" If the child answers yes, have him or her cross it out and rewrite it in the second column. At the end of the exercise, most or all of the things should be under the right column.
		If any remain under the left column, ask the child how he or she plans to apply to these things the same skills that worked for everything else. Some of these items can also be worked on at home and reviewed together in the final sessions as the child continues to work on the list.
☐	**Plan the Last Sessions**	Discuss with the child the structure of the next few sessions. Suggest that during the next few sessions, you will be reviewing the practice exercises that the child is working on outside of session and engaging in continued practice exercises with the child during sessions. Sessions may become further apart and will end after a few more meetings together.
☐	**Prepare for Final Session**	As you get closer to the "wrap up" module, work with the child to plan a special fun activity for the final session. This can involve snacks, playing a game, making a good-bye card, or going for a walk (these interests and activities will differ widely by child and by age).

Leave 'Em Laughing

Continue the tradition of ending the session with an enjoyable activity—something that you and the child pick out as the most fun way for the child to end his or her time with you. Try to leave extra time for these activities in the later sessions.

Share with Parent (if possible)

At the end of the session, if a parent is available, it can be helpful to brief him or her on the materials covered.

☐	**Review Concepts**	Bring the parent in to meet with you. Discuss the same issues that were reviewed with the child with respect to:

- the specific skills and tools that the child has acquired during the course of treatment
- how these newly acquired skills and tools fit the child's real-life everyday problems and concerns
- the fact that the child's gains and progress during treatment are the result of the child's hard work and practice during treatment
- the importance of continued practice

☐	**Review *What's New?* Worksheet**	Review the ***What's New?*** worksheet that you have just completed. This should create an opportunity for the parent to comment on the changes that have been made and to offer ideas about continued goals and objectives.
☐	**Praise and Give Credit**	Praise the child in front of the parent, and praise the parent for his or her efforts as well. Make sure to point out that the progress was due primarily to the child and family's efforts, not to the therapist. It is important that the child takes responsibility for the success that was experienced and attributes gains to his or her own effort.
☐	**Review Lapse vs. Relapse**	Discuss the difference between a "lapse" and a "relapse." Explain that lapses are natural, and involve minor steps backward. This discussion can involve the ***What's New?*** worksheet by telling the child that some of the things in the right column might try to drift back to the left side. Remind the child that if minor steps backward occur, these lapses can simply be worked on with additional practice exercises. Lapses are more common during stressful times, and it is perfectly normal for some anxiety or depression to return now and then. Remind them again that the goal was not to get rid of all anxiety, just to reduce it to tolerable levels. A "relapse" would mean that things went all the way back to where they started. Relapse is highly unlikely if the child's new skills are applied early when a lapse is detected.

> **Example script**
>
> *If you start to feel scared or worried, it's important that you do not jump to the conclusion that you are back at square one. Remember, all of the skills you learned during treatment will always be a part of you. All you need to do is use them when anxiety starts to bother you.*

☐	**Review Plan for Last Sessions**	Talk with the family about how you will gradually be decreasing the number of sessions. Future meetings will involve a "check up," progress review, and question-and-answers every two or three weeks. These meetings will eventually go down to once a month and then finish. For some children, reducing the frequency of meetings may go quickly if they are successful at maintaining gains and continuing to practice and if the parent is feeling comfortable with progress. For other children, the sessions may need to be tapered more gradually to allow time to establish independence and confidence with the new skills.
☐	**Provide Handout**	Give the parent the ***Maintaining Success*** parent handout.
☐	**Problem Solve**	Review any lingering concerns that the parent may have, and use questioning to have the child and parent articulate a plan for how to approach new problems, being sure to incorporate the new skills learned during treatment.

Helpful Tips

- During the maintenance phase of treatment, it is often helpful to assure the child and his or her parent that they can contact the therapist in between sessions if problems arise.

Special Cases

Posttraumatic Stress	For children with PTSD, prior to working on termination, the last few sessions of treatment will include at least one conjoint parent-child session, to allow the child to read the narrative in its entirety to the parent. Prior to the child sharing the narrative with the parent, the following conditions should be met: the child should be comfortable reading the narrative aloud, and the parent should have already heard the narrative in parts and be able to tolerate hearing it and make supportive comments to the child. The child should be praised heavily after sharing the narrative with the parent. The child may also have additional questions and/or topics to discuss with the parent (e.g., the parent's thoughts and feelings about the trauma). Practice these questions/discussions with the child prior to conjoint sessions. The goal for these conjoint sessions is open communication between the child and parent. Other topics may include attributions about the trauma, healthy sexuality, healthy relationships, and/or maintaining safety. The review of the narrative and resulting discussion should precede the other parts of this module.

How's Your Style?

- Did you praise often?
- Did you review often, by asking questions?
- Did you simplify the steps as needed?
- Did your pace match that of the child or family?
- Did you stay on track?

Cognitive - STOP

Goals

- The child will learn to identify feelings that may be signs of anxious thinking
- The child will learn how different thoughts can lead to different ways of feeling and acting
- The child will begin to recognize his or her self-talk (expectations, automatic questions, and attributions) in anxiety-provoking situations
- The child will learn four steps to modify anxious self-talk into coping self-talk

Materials

- *Fear Thermometer*
- *Fear Ladder*
- *STOP* worksheet
- Pen/pencil

⏳ *If time is tight*: *Provide the child with the 4-step plan to use when feeling anxious and teach the STOP acronym.*

Main Steps	Remember to start by setting an agenda together and reviewing any practice assignments.
☐ **Introduce Concepts**	Explain to the child that you will be spending the session talking about different kinds of feelings that children have and how to identify those feelings in themselves and in other people. Let the child know you will introduce a way to stop bad feelings. The technique is called "STOP," and will involve several steps that you will discuss together.
☐ **Introduce *STOP* Worksheet**	Show the child the **STOP** worksheet, and point out the stop sign in the upper left hand corner, explaining that here it refers to the first step. Go through the first two pages of the **STOP** worksheet to elicit ideas about feelings from the child, ask the child how he or she would be able to tell if someone else is experiencing these feelings, and find out when he or she has those feelings.

| ☐ Explain Purpose of Anxious Feelings | Next, discuss with the child the idea that there are often many reasons that can explain nervous feelings in a person's body. This should be tied in with what was learned in the Learning About Anxiety module. |

> **Example script**
>
> *Remember all these feelings are part of the alarm system that is meant to help you when there is danger. Why do you think these people have these feelings?*

Using as many questions as possible, point out that the alarm makes your heart beat faster, makes you breathe faster (so you might feel out of breath), and makes you sweat so you can cool off if you need to run away. You get butterflies or stomachaches because your stomach stops working on food so your body can concentrate on the danger. Feeling shaky or dizzy or blushing is often from all the increased energy that your body generates. Make sure the child sees that most of these feelings are things that people get when they exercise hard, and suggest that feeling scared gets your body ready for some hard work in case you need to get out of trouble.

| ☐ Introduce the First Step: "Scared" | Point out that the first step in overcoming scared or anxious feelings is to know when you are feeling that way. Ask the child the first thing he or she notices when he or she becomes frightened or scared. We call this step "Scared," and the first letter in STOP is also the first letter in scared. Refer back to the stop sign on the worksheet. |

| ☐ Introduce the Next Step: "Thoughts" | Point out that the next step in overcoming scared or anxious feelings is to work on the thoughts that make children feel upset. Tell the child that you will be teaching him or her how to identify and deal with these thoughts to make him or her feel better. Explain that anxious thoughts can be unpleasant and even scary, but that there are tools to handle them. |

| ☐ Explain How Thoughts Are Guesses | Complete page 3 of the worksheet together, making sure that the child has a clear understanding of what a thought is, and how thoughts are distinguished from feelings. Introduce the idea that children's thoughts can cover a range of different topics, but that thoughts often include guesses about the future. Elicit some predictions of the future from the child to make sure that the child understands this concept, and praise him or her for such efforts. For some children, the idea of a fortune teller or crystal ball may be helpful. |

> **Example script**
>
> *You: Have you ever heard of a crystal ball?*
>
> *Child: Uh huh.*
>
> *You: In stories that you've read or movies that you've seen, what does a crystal ball do?*
>
> *Child: People look into them and they can see the future.*
>
> *You: Right! People look into them and make guesses about the future. Sometimes those guesses are right, and sometimes they are wrong. That's just how your own thoughts can work. Your thoughts tell you what might happen in the future.*

☐	**Illustrate that Guesses Are Not Always Right**	Go on to page 4, and discuss the "roller coaster" picture to illustrate that not everyone makes the same guesses or has the same thoughts about a situation. Some children guess good things will happen, and other children may guess that bad things will happen. Check to see if the child understands the idea that thoughts, which are guesses, can be wrong. If the child makes this connection, you can then point out how a wrong guess is a lot like a false alarm.
☐	**Make Connection Between Thoughts, Feelings, and Actions**	Once the child has provided examples of good and bad guesses, discuss with the child the ways in which different thoughts can lead to different feelings and actions. Use the example on page 4 to demonstrate how two different thoughts in the same situation can result in quite different feelings and actions.

Example script

What would the girl do in this situation? What would the boy do? Who wants to go on the roller coaster? Why?

☐	**Connect "Thoughts" with "STOP"**	Point out that the second letter in STOP stands for "thoughts." Inform the child that this is the second step in learning to overcome scared or anxious feelings: noticing anxious thoughts. Ask the child to name some ways that recognizing thoughts might help when feeling anxious or scared.
☐	**Introduce the Next Step: "Other Thoughts"**	Tell the child that the next letter in STOP stands for "other thoughts." Mention that you are going to see whether it is possible to make other guesses about a scary situation. Go over page 5, and ask if the child is able to come up with realistic other thoughts about how the bad things will not come true (e.g., "I bet there will be other new kids" or "It's OK not to know the answer"). Ask the child how having these other thoughts might make someone feel in a scary situation (e.g., "would you feel better or worse?").
☐	**Counter Your Own Thoughts**	Complete page 6, and discuss with the child about what to do in particular situations to better cope with his or her own scared or worried feelings.

☐	**Apply the Steps to Examples**	Discuss how the steps covered so far can help in everyday situations that are scary.

> **Example script**
>
> *Therapist: Let's imagine that you are at school and the teacher calls on you. You think you know the right answer, but you are afraid you could be wrong. What would you do?*
>
> *Child: I might just not say anything.*
>
> *Therapist: Let's remember the first step. What is the S for? So would you feel Scared? How would you know?*
>
> *Child: Well, I would probably turn red, and get all hot, and I would feel my heart beating.*
>
> *Therapist: Right! Now what does the T stand for? What kinds of thoughts would you have? What guesses are you making?*
>
> *Child: I'm guessing the teacher will be mad if I say the wrong thing.*
>
> *Therapist: OK. Now let's look at the third step. What are some Other thoughts that you might have that would make this situation less scary?*

☐	**Praise and Repeat**	Praise the child for his or her efforts in this exercise. If time allows, ask the child to work through another situation in which he or she might feel anxious or scared, indicating how he or she would use each step on his or her own. Provide praise again.
☐	**Introduce the Final Step: "Praise"**	Inform the child that now you will review the last step in helping to overcome scared and anxious thoughts. Tell the child that this step is called **Praise**, and discuss the last page of the ***STOP*** worksheet. Ask the child for some examples of children doing well at a task, and ask the child to suggest some things these children could tell themselves after doing so well (e.g., "it was hard but I did it—nice job!" or "I was really brave this time!"). It is OK to write some of these down on the last page of the ***STOP*** worksheet.
☐	**Review the Plan**	Indicate to the child that he or she has just learned a plan that can help to cope with scared or anxious feelings. Point out that it is often difficult to remember all of the steps when feeling scared or nervous, and remind him or her that the first letter of each step spells out the word STOP.
☐	**ACTIVITY** *STOP*	Choose a mildly anxiety-provoking item from the child's *Fear Ladder*. Describe the situation for the child and ask him or her to walk you through what he or she would do in that situation, using the steps from the STOP acronym. If the feared situation involves a social interaction, you should role play with the child and walk him or her through all four steps in the plan.
☐	**Praise and Prompt Self-Praise**	After the child has successfully demonstrated the STOP steps in role-play, praise the child and remind him or her to praise him- or herself when practicing these steps in the future.
☐ 🏠	**PRACTICE ASSIGNMENT** *STOP* **Worksheet**	The practice assignment for this week is for the child to complete the ***STOP*** worksheet if it was not finished in session. Let the child know that you will review this worksheet together the next time you meet.

Leave 'Em Laughing

End the session on a fun note, with a game, activity, or other exercise that will leave the child feeling really good about the work you have done together today.

Share with Parent (if possible)

At the end of the session, if a parent is available, it can be helpful to brief him or her on the materials covered.

☐	**Consider Privacy**	Before bringing the parent into the room, it is important to ask the child if there is anything that he or she told you today that he or she does not want you to tell the parent. Be sure to honor the child's confidentiality within the appropriate limits of safety.
☐	**Review Concepts**	Have the child explain to the parent what concepts he or she has learned in the session. You can add information as necessary.

Helpful Tips

- Once children have used STOP, they should be encouraged to go through the four steps each time an exposure exercise or a reading of a trauma narrative is performed. For example, you can ask the child before starting an exposure practice about how he or she will know if he or she feels scared. Then ask about what some scared thoughts might be, and write those down. Next, have the child generate some other thoughts that might be more realistic and reassuring. At that point, suggest that the child recite some of those other thoughts to him- or herself during the practice. Complete the exposure exercise, and then remember to praise and to encourage self-praise. These steps should be used for practice at home as well as those done together.

- To facilitate some children's ability to identify and label feelings, it can help to use pictures of people, showing different expressions that reflect different emotions. Discuss what type of feeling each person might be experiencing. Pictures illustrating different feelings and emotions can often be found in magazines or in illustrated children's storybooks.

- When working with younger children, it can be helpful to create a "Feelings Dictionary" by cutting out from magazines pictures that display physical responses to emotions, mounting them on paper, and binding them together in a booklet created by the child.

How's Your Style?

- Did you praise often?
- Did you review often, by asking questions?
- Did you simplify the steps as needed?
- Did your pace match that of the child or family?
- Did you stay on track?

Wrap Up

For Family

Goals

- The child will review skills learned and discuss how to apply them to anticipated future challenges
- The child will prepare a "commercial" or advertisement for the child's treatment program
- The child will engage in a fun activity that leaves the child feeling positive and successful about the progress that he or she has made
- The parent will make plans to help the child maintain and generalize his or her newly acquired skills
- The child and/or parent will ensure that practice will continue after meetings with you are over and plan for using specific skills in the future

Materials

- *Fear Thermometer* and *Fear Ladder* (2 unrated copies, for anxiety/trauma), *Feelings Thermometer* (for depression)
- Any useful worksheets from previous sessions

⧗ *If time is tight: Review the skills and tools that the child has acquired during treatment and celebrate the gains that have been made together.*

Main Steps	Remember to start by setting an agenda together and reviewing any practice assignments.
☐ **Obtain Weekly Ratings**	If the main focus is traumatic stress or anxiety, use the 0 to 10 scale of the *Fear Thermometer* to obtain *Fear Ladder* ratings from both the child and his or her parent. If the main focus is depressed mood, use the *Feelings Thermometer* to take a rating.
☐ **Assess Child's Feelings About Termination**	In a positive way, check in to get a sense of how the child is thinking and feeling about termination.
	Example script
	Well, here we are at our last meeting. I am really impressed with the good work you've done in our meetings and in the practice assignments. And I have really enjoyed getting to know you in these meetings. How about you—how are you feeling about finishing up?
☐ **Address Any Concerns**	Explore any issues that the child brings up about termination, answer any questions, and make sure that you devote sufficient time to address concerns that the child may have. Be sure to frame the discussion in a positive manner, pointing out the gains that have been made and that are expected to continue.

☐	**Review Main Points and How They Apply**	See if the child can review the main points of treatment, highlighting specific skills or tools that he or she has learned during the course of treatment. Get examples of how these skills or tools fit the child's real-life everyday problems and concerns.
☐	**Emphasize Continued Use of Skills**	Emphasize to the child the importance of continuing to practice applying his or her new skills, and to persevere in the face of challenges.
☐	**Predict Challenges**	At this time, you should point out that there will probably be some failed attempts to apply new skills and tools in the future, and there may even be an occasional return of sad feelings, worries, or fears. This information is not intended to frighten or worry the child, but rather to establish realistic expectations and to avoid feelings of panic, failure, or disappointment when challenges inevitably arise. Experience and research tell us that occasional lapses are likely among individuals who have experienced anxiety or depression.

Example script

Kids who go through this program and get better find that it doesn't solve all their problems, and sometimes they feel bad again. But what's different now is that you have new skills to use if any problems come back. Let's think more about what skills you might want to use in the future.

The message to the youth should be that lapses are normal and common, that almost no one can expect to have no bad feelings ever. But one needn't worry when one has good skills and strategies to use when sad feelings or worries arise. Reassure the child that by using the strategies and skills that he or she has acquired in treatment, he or she can have more control over those bad feelings than before, and make them go away faster than before.

☐	**Plan Solutions**	If you have not done so in previous sessions, plan how the child will use the tools and skills he or she has learned during treatment to deal with possible difficult situations and events in the future (i.e., those events or situations most likely to elicit symptoms of anxiety or depression). This part of the session should be highly interactive with lots of input from the child as to which specific ways of applying the skills will be likely to really work.

☐ **ACTIVITY** *Commercial*	This exercise involves working together with the child to record a "commercial" for the child's treatment program. This activity is useful both for improving the child's memory of the skills that he or she has learned during treatment and for personalizing the program. Encourage the child to star in his or her own videotaped or audio-taped advertisement for the program. Examples of what can be included are:

- A review of the main concepts that the child has learned during treatment. Have the child summarize the main ideas of the treatment program as he or she remembers them.
- What is good about the treatment program—e.g., why other kids would benefit from learning and being able to use the skills that the child has learned.
- "Greatest hits of practice." Have the child discuss one or two of the most effective practice assignments that he or she has completed. Be sure that the child talks about the effect of the practice assignment on his or her mood.

First, have the child rehearse the commercial while you serve as an "audience member," offering support and encouragement. Next, if possible, video or audio tape the commercial for the child. If possible, view or listen to the commercial with the child and parent during the final portion of the session. The tape can be sent home with the child and parent, or a copy can be made and sent to them.

☐ **ACTIVITY** *Celebration*	During the very last session, engage in a fun activity with the child (typically planned during the previous session), such as having a "party" with snacks and drinks, playing a game, making a good-bye card, going for a walk (these interests and activities will differ widely by child and by age). This opportunity can focus on upcoming positive events for the child (e.g., an approaching birthday, an upcoming social event with peers, summer vacation, a special trip, a promotion to a new grade with the chance to make new friends). The general idea is to make this a celebration with a "positive future" orientation.

Share with Parent (if possible)

At the end of the session, if a parent is available, it can be helpful to brief him or her on the materials covered.

☐ **Consider Privacy**	Before bringing the parent into the room, it is important to ask the child if there is anything that he or she told you today that he or she does not want you to tell the parent. Be sure to honor the child's confidentiality within the appropriate limits of safety.
☐ **Review Concepts**	Try to allow the child to do as much of the talking as possible. Discuss these same issues that were reviewed with the child with respect to:

- the specific skills and tools that the child has acquired during the course of treatment
- how these newly acquired skills and tools fit the child's real-life everyday problems and concerns
- the fact that the child's gains and progress during treatment are the result of the child's hard work during treatment
- the importance of continued practice of his or her new skills

 Say Your Goodbyes and Thank the Family	Thank the parent for his or her help and support during treatment. Let the parent know that you have enjoyed getting to know him or her, and that you are now passing the baton along, as formal treatment is ending. Point out that the progress was due primarily to the child and family's efforts, not to your own. It is important that the child takes responsibility for the success that was experienced and attributes gains to his or her own effort.

Helpful Tips

- For many children, the review of concepts and the planning of the celebration activity may have been going on for several sessions already. In those cases, it might be possible to move more quickly through the first steps of this module and spend more time on the commercial or celebration. Even when moving quickly, it is usually hard to perform the commercial and the celebration in the same session.

- Another way to commemorate the child's success is to write a letter or card to the child, detailing all of his or her progress and your happiness at his or her success in treatment. It does not need to be long or elaborate, but it should be genuine. The letter should be something that the child will keep and can look at to remember what treatment was like and what he or she learned from treatment. You may choose to present the letter in the final session or to send it soon afterwards as a transitional experience for the child.

- Another idea is to provide the child with a few stamped envelopes, addressed to you at your workplace. You can invite the child to send a note every now and then to let you know how things are going for him or her. This gesture allows the child to leave the last session knowing that contact with you and the clinic has not ended completely, and provides him or her with an opportunity to stay in touch.

- In order to assist the child in his or her continued application of newly acquired skills to everyday situations, you might wish to make extra copies of any worksheets they would like to use regularly. The child and parent can then use these worksheets to resume formal practices if challenges arise after treatment has ended. This is particularly important if you feel that the child has made good use of the practice assignments throughout treatment.

- Although video or audio taping equipment may not always be available, the exercise of creating and presenting a "commercial" for the treatment program is a valuable component of the final session with the child. By making a clear statement in favor of the program, the child is more likely not only to remember his or her statement, but also more likely to believe in it. If it is not possible to record a commercial, consider having the child develop an advertisement or brochure that the child can present and explain to you, and possibly his or her parents, in order to help the child remember and understand the main points of his or her treatment program.

- In addition to engaging in fun activities with the child during the last session, you might also consider awarding a certificate of completion for his or her participation in the program.

- If the child or parent is particularly concerned about ending treatment, you can plan to check in over the phone at a schedule that seems appropriate.

How's Your Style?

- Did you praise often?
- Did you review often, by asking questions?
- Did you simplify the steps as needed?
- Did your pace match that of the child or family?
- Did you stay on track?

Getting Acquainted - Depression

Use This:

At the beginning of depression treatment to establish a relationship and a plan.

For Child

Goals

- The child will feel more comfortable through introductory get-acquainted activities
- The child will understand how the program can meet his or her goals
- The child will learn about the importance of confidentiality, take-home assignments, and regular attendance
- The child will know how to use the *Feelings Thermometer*

Materials

- *Feelings Thermometer*
- *Daily Feelings Record*
- Materials from recent assessment (if available)
- Pens, pencils, markers

⧗ *If time is tight: Begin to build the therapy alliance and learn about how the child shows depressive symptoms.*

Main Steps	*Remember to start by setting an agenda together.*
☐ **Warm Up**	Try to get a conversation going at a pace that suits the child. It is often helpful to make sure formal treatment does not begin too quickly, since depressed children may be irritable, anxious, and not familiar with questions about their feelings. Try to refrain initially from asking a lot of personal questions of the child.
☐ **ACTIVITY** *Ice Breaker*	An ice breaker activity is a good idea to build a therapeutic alliance. The appropriate activities will depend on the child's age and interests, so you should prepare beforehand, trying to obtain enough prior information about the child to plan a uniquely tailored ice breaker. The exercise may be as simple as engaging in a discussion with the child centered on three things about him or her that are unusual or interesting. Art materials may also be helpful if the child enjoys drawing or if you feel that the child might find a nonverbal means of connecting easier at first.

☐	**ACTIVITY** *Personal Facts Game*	To introduce your need to gather information, and the idea that this information is important to you, it might be helpful to play a "Personal Facts" game. In this game, both you and the child supply answers to the same questions, such as "What is your middle name?", "How old are you?", "How many brothers and sisters do you have?", or "What is your favorite activity?" Keep in mind that including questions about favorite TV shows, heroes, and superheroes can provide information that will be helpful later in treatment. After giving answers, you and the child might quiz each other. It is important that you recall the details accurately as this conversation is one of the child's first attempts to share personal information with you. It will also be helpful throughout the treatment if you are comfortable with the child's asking personal information about you and with providing answers to appropriate questions.
☐	**Provide Overview and Rationale**	Explain that this program is a joint effort between the therapist and the child, focused on feelings—especially feelings we don't like that can keep us from doing the things we want to do and should be doing.
		Tell the child that everyone has times when they feel bad, sad, gloomy, or grouchy, and that it's OK to feel bad sometimes. However, not everyone knows what to do to stop feeling that way, and sometimes they get "stuck" feeling bad. Getting stuck in the bad feelings can stop us from enjoying friends, getting our schoolwork done, and doing other things that would be good for us. Note that by working with you in session, the child will be learning ways to get "unstuck" so that he or she can do the things he or she really values and wants to be doing.
		You might ask the child if he or she can remember times when he or she got stuck in bad feelings (bad, sad, gloomy, grouchy) and those bad feelings stopped him or her from doing something fun (like hanging out with a friend) or important (like schoolwork).
☐	**Child's Perspective and Goals**	Ask if this sounds like what the child thought you would be working on together. If not, find out what the child had expected and see if you can identify common ground between goals of treatment and the child's expectations.
		Ask if the child has specific goals that he or she wants to work on in therapy. Help the child to word the goals in a way that can relate to improving mood.
☐	**Encourage Participation**	Invite the child to ask questions about treatment. Continue to re-open this invitation periodically until the child begins to share his or her questions and concerns. Stress to the child that information from his or her point of view is very important. Emphasize that you're interested in what the child sees and thinks about various situations. Value should be placed on the child's point of view.

☐	**Describe Treatment Structure**	Lay out the structure and sequence of the treatment program. Be sure to cover the following points: • the activities that will happen in the various sessions (e.g., role-playing, practicing new skills) • the importance of regular attendance (because each session builds on the contents of the previous ones, and the entire program is needed to maximize the chances of success) • the worksheets, which contain practice assignments for him or her to do each week between sessions • Parent meetings and the limits of confidentiality
☐	**ACTIVITY** *Feelings Thermometer*	Have the child provide a rating for his or her current mood. You may need to practice once or twice with sample anchors to make sure the child is giving accurate ratings. Ask the child what the number he or she chose means, in order to be sure he or she understands the concept. Ask the child to indicate, using the *Feelings Thermometer*, how his or her mood would be in several different situations (i.e., spending time with a favorite friend, after a disappointing grade, etc.) in order to make sure that the child feels comfortable using this scale. It is particularly important that the child be able to use the full range of the scale, not just the two endpoints.
☐ ⬆	**PRACTICE ASSIGNMENT** *Daily Feelings Record*	The practice assignment for this week involves having the child practice making ratings of his or her mood each day during the coming week. Give the child a *Daily Feelings Record*. Ask the child to make one rating each day by circling a number on the thermometer and to write what happened that day to make him or her feel that way. Remind the child that you will often take ratings with the *Feelings Thermometer* to gather clues and evidence about his or her feelings. Let the child know that at the next session, you will review his or her ratings together and talk about any changes that might have occurred in his or her mood over the week.
☐	**Praise**	Praise the child for his or her good work during this first session.

Leave 'Em Laughing

End the session on a fun note, with a game, activity, or other exercise that will leave the child feeling really good about the work you have done together today.

Share with Parent (if possible)

At the end of the session, if a parent is available, it can be helpful to brief him or her on the materials covered.

☐	**Consider Privacy**	Before bringing the parent into the room, it is important to ask the child if there is anything that he or she told you today that he or she does not want you to tell the parent. Be sure to honor the child's confidentiality within the appropriate limits of safety.
☐	**Review Concepts**	Have the child explain to the parent what concepts he or she has learned in the session. You can add information as necessary.

☐ Review *Feelings Thermometer*	For this session, the parent should also be introduced to the *Feelings Thermometer*. The parent should understand that the *Feelings Thermometer* is a tool that takes a global rating of the child's mood. Discuss that this tool will be used throughout the treatment to monitor the child's good and sad feelings. Explain to the parent how the *Feelings Thermometer* works. For practice in the session, ask the parent to use it to rate the child's mood under different circumstances (some good, some bad).

> **Example script**
>
> *If your child just did really well on an exam at school, what would his or her Feelings Thermometer rating be? What would the rating be if your child got into a disagreement with a best friend at school?*

Then have the parent rate the child's current mood. Ask the parent what that specific rating means, so you can be sure the concept is clear.

Helpful Tips

- Children often describe their depression as "tired," "bored," "cranky," "worried," or "mad," as well as sad. Be sure to use the same language the child uses in describing his or her mood.

- Some children will have surprising insight, others relatively little, into what it is like to feel good and what it is like to feel bad. Use gentle encouragement, plus your own modeling, to draw out the child if he or she is reticent or reluctant to elaborate on ideas. It can also be helpful to refer to other people's experiences of feeling sad or down, just to get the child to talk about feelings.

How's Your Style?

- Did you praise often?
- Did you review often, by asking questions?
- Did you simplify the steps as needed?
- Did your pace match that of the child or family?
- Did you stay on track?

Learning About Depression - Child

For Child

Goals

- The child will understand the nature of depression
- The child will learn that individuals can control their mood by changing **how they act** and **how they think**
- The child will be optimistic about his or her situation and the likelihood of improving
- The child will be interested in participating in and learning more about treatment

Materials

- *Feelings Thermometer*
- *Thinking-Feeling-Doing* worksheet
- *How I Show My Feelings* worksheet

> ⧖ *If time is tight: Teach the child about the Thinking-Feeling-Doing model of depression and how gathering clues and practicing skills can help reduce unpleasant moods.*

Main Steps	*Remember to start by setting an agenda together and by reviewing any practice assignments.*
☐ **Obtain Weekly Ratings**	Using the 0 to 10 scale of the *Feelings Thermometer*, obtain ratings from both the child and parent (if available).
☐ **Review Definitions and Vocabulary**	Ask the child to describe how he or she knows when he or she is in a bad mood. What emotions are experienced during these times? Elicit other words (e.g., mad, grouchy) that might describe the symptoms of depression the child experiences. Praise the child's definitions and incorporate them into your own.
☐ **Introduce the Feeling-Thinking-Doing Triangle**	Explain to the child that depression has three parts to it: what we **feel** (using the child's language), what we **think**, and what we **do**.
☐ **ACTIVITY** *The Feeling-Thinking-Doing Triangle*	Cover the first page of the *Feeling-Thinking-Doing* worksheet. Use questions to gather information from the child's own life to demonstrate how thoughts, feelings, and behaviors are often connected and can result in both pleasant and unpleasant emotions. Examples: • *Is there a time recently when you felt (sad/mad/upset)?* • *What happened that started those feelings? What did you think in your head?* • *How did you feel?* • *What did you do in response to those thoughts or feelings?*

☐	**Normalize**	Remind the child that everyone feels sad or bad sometimes; the important thing is knowing what to do in order to get "unstuck" from these feelings so we can get on with the things we need to be doing. If possible, use an example from this child's life (from previous session)—some activity the child values that he or she doesn't do when "stuck" in bad feelings. As an alternative, or in addition, you may use an example from your own life, or that of "another kid I know."
☐	**Introduce the Toolbox Concept**	Ask the child if he or she knows what a toolbox is. Ask him or her to describe what sorts of things are in a toolbox (e.g., hammers, screwdrivers, wrenches). Point out that toolboxes have tools to solve all sorts of different problems, because not all tools work in every situation. Praise the child's efforts to come up with examples of tools and how they are used. Explain that people feel sad/down/upset for lots of different reasons, and show their feelings in lots of different ways. You have lots of tools that can be helpful to the child in improving his or her mood. Part of your work together will be trying out different tools in order to find out which ones work best.
☐	**Learn About the Child's Tools**	Ask the child what "tools" he or she use to improve a bad mood already. What are things he or she has tried in the past that have helped, even just a little bit?
☐	**Explain the Importance of Practice**	Explain that trying out new tools that we are not used to can be strange at first, like learning how to use anything new. Ask the child to think of a time when they practiced to become good at something that was difficult at first. Examples could include riding a bike, playing an instrument, learning to use an electronic tool, learning to use chopsticks, etc.
☐	**Relate Practice to Mood**	Explain how the same principles that apply to learning how to do anything new also apply to changing mood. By practicing using different tools, the child will get better at controlling his or her mood in order to have fewer unpleasant moods and less interference with things he or she wants to be doing. Use questioning to arrive at the idea that practice can be gradual, and that small steps will be required until bigger ones can be taken. It can help to reverse roles and ask the child how to help you learn to use something that they are very good at, such as an iPod or a video game. **Example script** *You: How would you explain this game to me?* *Child: I would explain the rules and how to use each of the control buttons.* *You: But it seems really hard to me. I don't think it works for me. How can I get to be as good as you?* *Child: I'd tell you to learn one little step at a time. Also, if you practice it will get easier.* *You: Great! That's exactly the same as practicing ways to change your feelings!*
☐	**Explain About "How Feelings Look"**	Explain that since all people look, act, and feel differently when they are sad/mad/upset, you would like to get a better understanding of what the child "looks and feels like" when he or she is feeling this way.

☐ **ACTIVITY** *How I Show My Feelings Worksheet*	Complete the worksheet with the child, asking for more information to better understand the child's presentation of depression, including the triggers that provoke positive or sad feelings, the bodily response to such feelings (e.g., increased or decreased energy, changes in appetite or sleep), the outward appearance that accompanies the feelings (e.g., downcast eyes, slumping body), the thoughts that go along with the feelings (e.g., "I'm no good" or "The world sucks"), and the behavioral display involved (e.g., talkative and seeking others out vs. quiet and withdrawn).	
	To make this as engaging as possible, you could do a form of "Feelings Charades," asking the child to show you his or her reactions and then recording the correct responses in the worksheet. You can also model disclosure by answering each question yourself.	
☐ **Explain the Importance of Monitoring**	Introduce the idea of monitoring, which is just like gathering clues or evidence.	

Example script

Now, figuring out the kinds of things that lead us to have good or bad feelings can be like solving a mystery. What do detectives look for when solving a mystery? That's right—clues! Just like two detectives, we are going to gather important clues to help us learn more about the kinds of things that affect your feelings. Whenever you practice something here in session or at home for practice, I will ask you to fill in a Feelings Thermometer, like we did in session today. These ratings will tell us important things to help solve the mystery of what kinds of things make you have positive feelings, and what kinds of things make you have negative feelings.

☐ 👆 **PRACTICE ASSIGNMENT** *Thinking-Feeling-Doing*	Give the child the *Thinking-Feeling-Doing* worksheet to complete page 2 during the upcoming week. Ask the child to pick a time when he or she felt bad and to write on the sheet. The child should then write what he or she thought, felt, and did and come up with alternative thoughts, feelings, and behaviors relevant to that example.

Leave 'Em Laughing

End the session on a fun note, with a game, activity, or other exercise that will leave the child feeling really good about the work you have done together today.

Share with Parent (if possible)

At the end of the session, if a parent is available, it can be helpful to brief him or her on the ideas covered in the session, and the materials as well.

☐ **Consider Privacy**	Before bringing the parent into the room, it is important to ask the child if there is anything that he or she told you today that he or she does not want you to tell the parent. Be sure to honor the child's confidentiality within the appropriate limits of safety.
☐ **Review Concepts**	Have the child explain to the parent what concepts he or she has learned in the session. You can add information as necessary.

Helpful Tips

- For children who are high-energy, you can make the activities more engaging by using interactive games such as charades, or by drawing the "Thinking-Feeling-Doing" triangle on a large piece of paper and letting the child illustrate it.

- If the child enters the session in a bad mood, or seems tired, lethargic, or uninterested, this is an opportunity to introduce a "mood booster." Use the *Feelings Thermometer* to take a brief mood rating, spend a few minutes engaging in a pleasant activity, then re-rate the mood. Be sure to highlight for the child this important point: *what you do changes how you feel*.

- Check in on goals: Does the child feel that he or she is making progress? How does the material you covered today relate to the goals you set together?

How's Your Style?

- Did you praise often?
- Did you review often, by asking questions?
- Did you simplify the steps as needed?
- Did your pace match that of the child or family?
- Did you stay on track?

<table>
<tr><td>MATCH
Protocol</td><td colspan="2"># Learning About
Depression - Parent</td><td>

Use This:

To introduce the parent to the planned course of treatment for his or her child's depression.

</td></tr>
</table>

Goals

- You will continue to establish rapport with the parent
- The parent will understand confidentiality issues
- The parent will understand the nature of depression and its expression in youth
- The parent will understand how the treatment plan addresses depression
- The parent will understand the importance of the child's worksheets and practice assignments
- The parent will understand the importance of regular attendance for sessions

Materials

- *Feelings Thermometer*
- *Parent Interview for Depression*
- *Understanding Depression* parent handout
- Materials from recent assessment (if available)

⧗ *If time is tight: Help the parent build enthusiasm about the treatment program, and learn more about the child's specific difficulties with depression from the parent's perspective.*

Main Steps	*Remember to start by setting an agenda together and reviewing any practice assignments.*
☐ **Obtain Weekly Ratings**	Using the 0 to 10 scale of the *Feelings Thermometer*, obtain ratings from both the child and parent (if available).
☐ **Discuss Confidentiality**	Start by discussing the confidentiality of what the child says in treatment. Point out that you plan to regularly share the main ideas discussed in each session, but that keeping some details of what the child says confidential will likely be helpful to the child. Of course, any issues that lead you to be concerned about the child's safety or the safety of others would be disclosed to the parent. Finally, if the parent disagrees with this plan, collaborate to establish clear guidelines about the types of information that will be shared.

☐	**Discuss the Nature of Childhood Depression**	Begin this discussion by asking for the parent's ideas of what depression is and how it is affecting his or her child.

Example script

Many people have different thoughts about what depression is and what depression looks like.

How would you describe depression? How would you describe your child's depression?

Frame the discussion around the depressive symptoms identified by the parent. Include the following points: (1) the difference between a transient sad mood and the more enduring nature of depression, (2) the fact that depression in children and teens may sometimes show up as irritability rather than the sadness seen in adults, and (3) the fact that different children may show the depression in very different ways.

☐	**Note Your Need for the Parent's Perspective**	Explain to the parent that in order for this program to be most effective, you need to get his or her perspective on the child's depression and overall functioning.

Example script

As we were just discussing, depression can look very different in different children. What about your child? Because you are the true expert on your child, it would help me a lot to learn from you just what your child is like when he is feeling depressed.

☐	**Conduct *Parent Interview for Depression***	Administer the ***Parent Interview for Depression*** writing down those details that you think will be helpful for informing treatment. Get as much specific information about the child's mood and functioning as possible.
☐	**Review and Clarify**	At the end of this interview, you should review what appear to be the child's main issues and areas of concern, and ask the parent to let you know which parts seem right and which parts don't.
☐	**Validate the Parent**	Remind the parent that his or her role in the child's treatment will be a key to success. Build the parent's enthusiasm and work to increase his or her motivation to participate in the child's treatment.

☐	**Provide Rationale for Treatment**	Review with the parent the notion that our behaviors and our thoughts greatly influence the way we feel.

Example script

Our thoughts and our actions are very closely related. Was there ever a time when you had a job to do, and you felt pretty negative about it—like you wouldn't be able to do well at it? What did that do to your performance on that job? Exactly! Your negative thoughts about yourself and your future performance probably made it a lot harder to do well on the job. In much the same way, children who are depressed can feel down about themselves, and that can lead them to have problems developing close relationships and doing well in school or sports, which can lead to even more feelings of sadness. Part of changing this negative cycle for your child will be to work on his thoughts and his actions that are leading him to feel depressed.

Review with the parent the goals for treatment: to gradually change the child's negative thoughts and behaviors through special coping techniques and consistent practice, and to teach the child new ways to cope with sad or upset feelings, so that the child won't feel as depressed and will have the skills needed to feel better.

☐	**Introduce Toolbox Concept**	Talk about the "toolbox" notion of treatment; the goal is to teach the child a number of specific coping skills, then to work with the child to figure out which specific skills will work well for him or her for which specific problems.

Example script

As we discussed earlier, depression is different for each individual. That also means that different children will need different things—different coping skills—to help them feel better. One of the main goals in treatment will be to give your child a toolbox, or a set of coping strategies. We'll teach your child several different strategies, find out which ones work best for him, and then have the child practice those specific coping strategies until they are easy for your child to use when he feels sad or down.

☐	**Describe Parent's Role**	Encourage the parent to support the child's treatment by joining the child and therapist at the end of every session and by helping the child use the skills.

Example script

*So, remember, your child and I won't just be talking about how he feels each week. I am going to teach him skills to learn and practice, skills that **you** can help with, too. We are doing it this way because we know that when parents help, it makes a big difference for kids.*

☐	**Go over Rules for Practice Assignments**	Discuss the purpose of practice assignments and plan together how and when the child will be able to work on them. Later in the treatment, you might need to ask for the parent's assistance in getting the child to complete the practice assignments, so it is wise to set the stage for that possibility in this initial conversation.

☐	**Set up Communication**	To facilitate ongoing contact, exchange phone numbers with the parent, and make sure the parent has a phone number to call in the event of an emergency.
☐	**Review and Answer Questions**	Leave time for discussion of any questions or concerns the parent may have about treatment. Encourage questions from the parent; these can help you make sure that the parent understands what you have said and how treatment is going to work.
☐	**Provide the *Understanding Depression* Handout**	Give the parent the *Understanding Depression* handout to take home, and thank the parent **enthusiastically** for taking the time to talk with you.

Helpful Tips

- Depending on how thorough the child's initial assessment was, you might wish to modify the *Parent Interview for Depression* to obtain more detailed information.

- When discussing parental commitment and motivation with respect to the child's treatment, be careful to avoid suggesting that the family is "not interested" in their child's progress. Many families are motivated for their child to improve, but do not have the time or resources to help. A better approach is to describe that treatment must be "a high priority" both for the parent and the child. Encourage the parent to inform you if he or she is not finding enough time to assist and support his or her child with the completion of practice exercises outside of session, and also to discuss any other difficulties that may arise with treatment.

- It is often useful to conduct a **home visit** or **school visit** to gain additional information about the child. If you plan on visiting the home or school, discuss the purpose of the **home visit** (as you schedule it) and the **school visit**. For the **school visit**, identify an appropriate school contact, and request the parent's written permission for you to make such contacts.

How's Your Style?

- Did you praise often?
- Did you review often, by asking questions?
- Did you simplify the steps as needed?
- Did your pace match that of the child or family?
- Did you stay on track?

Problem Solving

Goals

- The child will know the five steps for effective problem solving
- The child will know how to generate a variety of ideas and possible solutions prior to evaluating them or acting on them
- The child will know how to apply these problem solving skills to real problems in his or her life

Materials

- *Fear Thermometer* and *Fear Ladder* (2 unrated copies for anxiety/trauma), *Feelings Thermometer* (for depression), or *Behavior Rating Scale* (for disruptive behavior)
- *Five S-T-E-P-S to Problem Solving* worksheet
- *Helping Your Child Solve Problems* parent handout

⧖ *If time is tight: Teach the child a procedure for solving problems using the S-T-E-P-S acronym.*

Main Steps	*Remember to start by setting an agenda together and reviewing any practice assignments.*
☐ **Obtain Weekly Ratings**	If the main focus is traumatic stress or anxiety, use the 0 to 10 scale of the *Fear Thermometer* to obtain *Fear Ladder* ratings from both the child and his or her parent. If the main focus is depressed mood, use the *Feelings Thermometer* to take a rating. If the main focus is disruptive behavior, take a parent rating with the *Behavior Rating Scale*.
☐ **Introduce Problem Solving**	Discuss the fact that we all have problems every day. Note that solving them can make us feel good or keep us out of trouble, and not solving them can make us feel bad or get us in trouble. Let the child know you will be talking about a new way to solve problems, called "S-T-E-P-S."
☐ **Discuss Types of Problems**	Discuss some examples of problems people often deal with on a daily basis. Use examples the child is likely to have experienced and that can be solved through direct action. This can be done by using calculated self-disclosure; that is, share with the child *appropriate* information about problems you have encountered and how you solved them.

☐	**Introduce Problem Solving S-T-E-P-S**	Describe each part of problem solving S-T-E-P-S:

S: Say what the problem is. State the problem as specifically as possible.

T: Think of solutions. Brainstorm at least three solutions without judging their feasibility or quality at this point.

E: Examine the solutions. Identify the pros and cons of each suggested solution, including the likely consequences of each.

P: Pick one and try it out. Use the pros and cons to choose the best solution.

S: See if it worked. What was the outcome? If it didn't work, choose another solution to try.

☐ **ACTIVITY** *Solve a Problem Using S-T-E-P-S*

Present the child with a fun problem to solve that can be solved in the session together. Write down the process in terms of the problem solving S-T-E-P-S, and then point out to the child that you followed a process to solve the problem and that this is how S-T-E-P-S can be used. Example fun problems include:

- Problem: move an object from one part of the room to another without using hands
- Problem: keep a balloon in the air for 60 seconds without hands
- Problem: Move from one chair to another without letting feet touch the ground

Alternatively, use a problem from your own life and enlist the child as a helper to work through the problem-solving S-T-E-P-S.

☐ **Apply S-T-E-P-S to Child's Life**

Help the child identify a problem from his or her life that the two of you can work on using the problem solving S-T-E-P-S procedure. Practice using S-T-E-P-S to address a relatively simple problem in the child's life. Provide the child with the *Five S-T-E-P-S to Problem Solving* worksheet and help him or her to apply each part of the strategy to the identified problem.

☐ **Review Problem Solving S-T-E-P-S**

With the worksheet out of sight, discuss this new problem-solving strategy with the child to ensure that he or she (a) knows when it might be helpful to use the S-T-E-P-S strategy, (b) understands how to use this strategy, and (c) knows each of the five parts of S-T-E-P-S.

Example script
You: So, when would someone want to use these S-T-E-P-S?
Child: Well, when they're feeling bad about a problem, or feeling like they're stuck.
You: And if they felt like they had a problem or couldn't figure something out, what would you tell them to do?
Child: To think about their problem and some ways to try to solve it by going through the S-T-E-P-S.
You: Great. But what if they're not familiar with solving problems by using S-T-E-P-S? How would you get them started? What would be the first thing that they would need to do?
Child: Well, they would need to start by saying what the problem is...
You: Perfect! Then what? (continue asking similar questions, walking the child through the problem solving process)

| ☐ ⬆ PRACTICE ASSIGNMENT *Practice at Home* | Ask the child to practice using problem solving S-T-E-P-S on his or her own. The child should identify a problem in his or her life and fill out a *Five S-T-E-P-S to Problem Solving* worksheet for that problem at home. The child should then try one of the solutions and tell you how it worked in the next session. Remind the child to bring the completed worksheet to the next session for discussion. |
| | Be sure to help the child pick a relatively simple problem for this practice assignment, rather than something big or complicated. Appropriate problems might include resolving a disagreement with a parent over a minor matter or with a friend about what to do over the weekend. |

Leave 'Em Laughing

End the session on a fun note, with a game, activity, or other exercise that will leave the child feeling really good about the work you have done together today.

Share with Parent (if possible)

At the end of the session, if a parent is available, it can be helpful to brief him or her on the materials covered.

☐ Consider Privacy	Before bringing the parent into the room, it is important to ask the child if there is anything that he or she told you today that he or she does not want you to tell the parent. Be sure to honor the child's confidentiality within the appropriate limits of safety.
☐ Review Concepts	Have the child explain to the parent what concepts he or she has learned in the session. You can add information as necessary.
☐ Introduce S-T-E-P-S	For this session, the parent should also be introduced to the problem solving S-T-E-P-S. The parent should understand that this is a tool to solve problems that arise in the child's life.
☐ Encourage Monitoring and Praise	Ask the parent to be on the lookout for times when the child uses problem-solving S-T-E-P-S over the upcoming week and to support the child with praise for trying to solve problems.
☐ Give Parent Handout	Give the *Helping Your Child Solve Problems* handout to the parent. Make sure the parent is familiar with the concepts so that he or she can assist the child at home if needed.

Helpful Tips

- If the child is reticent or having difficulty identifying a problem, you may use a story to illustrate a problem and then have the child apply the S-T-E-P-S to that problem. Alternatively, some children may be able to apply the S-T-E-P-S to a problem of someone they know or are close to, such as a friend or family member. The primary goal of this module is to teach the child a new skill for solving problems—not necessarily to solve a specific problem at hand. Eventually, this skill can be used to address problems specific to the child, even if the child is not ready at this point to discuss his or her unique problems during the session.

- Check in on goals: Does the child feel that he or she is making progress? How does the material you covered today relate to the goals you set together?

Special Cases

Depression	If the child enters the session in a bad mood, or seems tired, lethargic, or uninterested, this is an opportunity to introduce a mood booster: take a brief mood rating using the **Feelings Thermometer**, spend a few minutes engaging in a pleasant activity, and then take another mood rating. If the activity was successful, highlight to the child that what we do changes how we feel and then move on to covering the problem solving skill.

How's Your Style?

- Did you praise often?
- Did you review often, by asking questions?
- Did you simplify the steps as needed?
- Did your pace match that of the parent?
- Did you stay on track?

<table>
<tr>
<td>MATCH
Protocol</td>
<td colspan="2"># Activity Selection</td>
<td></td>
</tr>
</table>

For Child

Goals

- The child will learn the relation between the things we do and how we feel, emphasizing the link between positive activities and feeling good
- The child will identify 10 activities that he or she can do to improve his or her mood
- The child will schedule activities that make him or her feel good

Materials

- *Fear Thermometer* and *Fear Ladder* (2 unrated copies for anxiety/trauma), *Feelings Thermometer* (for depression), or *Behavior Rating Scale* (for disruptive behavior)
- *Doing Something Fun to Feel Better* worksheet
- *Ten Things I Can Do to Feel Better* worksheet
- *Scheduling Time for Fun* worksheet
- *Activity Selection* parent handout
- Pencils, crayons, markers

> ⧖ *If time is tight:* Convey the link between activities and feelings and help the child brainstorm a list of 10 activities that he or she could do to feel better.

Main Steps	*Remember to start by setting an agenda together and reviewing any practice assignments.*
☐ **Obtain Weekly Ratings**	If the main focus is traumatic stress or anxiety, use the 0 to 10 scale of the *Fear Thermometer* to obtain *Fear Ladder* ratings from both the child and his or her parent. If the main focus is depressed mood, use the *Feelings Thermometer* to take a rating. If the main focus is disruptive behavior, take a parent rating with the *Behavior Rating Scale*.
☐ **ACTIVITY** *Doing Something Fun to Feel Better*	1. Induce a negative mood with the child by describing a stressful situation. An example would be: *Close your eyes and imagine that you are having a terrible day. You are late to school, and you forgot your homework! At lunch, you spill your drink on your clothes, and a bunch of kids laugh at you. When you get home, your mom makes you clean your room, and you miss your favorite TV show.* 2. Have the child rate his or her mood at the top of the *Doing Something Fun to Feel Better* worksheet. 3. Engage in a fun, high-energy activity with the child (e.g., hula-hooping, playing Nerf basketball) for a few minutes, until the child is having fun. 4. Have the child do the second mood rating on the *Doing Something Fun to Feel Better* worksheet.

☐	**Debrief the Activity**	Briefly discuss with the child the effect of the activity on his or her mood ratings. Explain how low mood was related to thinking about something sad. Note how doing something for only a few minutes can improve mood. If the child's mood rating went up after the activity, note how well this activity worked for the child; if the child's mood rating remained the same or declined after the activity, discuss possible reasons for this (e.g., child didn't like activity, too little time).

Example script

*So we just did something really quick and it raised your mood by 2 points! You went from a 5 to a 7! That's great! And I bet hula-hooping isn't even one of your favorite activities! What's an activity that you really **love** doing? What do you think your rating would be if you were doing **that** instead?*

☐	**Discuss Connection Between Feelings and Actions**	Discuss how what we do—our activities—can affect our mood, or how we feel. Explain that doing activities we enjoy can make us feel good and that doing activities we do not enjoy (or doing **nothing**) can make us feel bad (or **bored**). Have the child think of a time when he or she felt sad, did nothing, and continued to feel bad as well as a time when he or she felt sad, did something fun and felt better.

Example script

So what we do affects how we feel. When we are in a good mood, we probably want to do a lot of fun things. But when we are in a bad mood, we may not want to do anything fun, and then we may just stay in a bad mood. Can you think of a time when you were in a bad mood or were upset, and you didn't do anything (or maybe you decided not to do something fun) and you stayed in a bad mood? What about a time when you felt bad, did something fun, and then felt better?

☐	**Discuss Four Types of Activities**	Discuss with the child four types of activities that can improve mood and have the child list some examples for each activity:

- **Activities that I have enjoyed before:** explain how doing things we usually like makes us feel better
- **Activities with someone I like:** emphasize how doing something with someone we like or would like to know better is a great way to build relationships and improve mood
- **Activities that keep me busy:** explain how scheduled activities, help us stay busy and in a good mood. Have the child identify some of his or her interests and link those interests to clubs, groups, or teams (e.g., Scouts, choir, basketball, drama) the child can join
- **Activities that help someone else:** emphasize how helping others can make us feel good

☐	**Complete *Ten Things I Can Do to Feel Good* Worksheet**	Help the child complete the *Ten Things I Can Do to Feel Good* worksheet. Make sure the activities include the four types of activities previously discussed and are (1) simple, (2) free, (3) available almost any time, and (4) virtually guaranteed to make the child feel good. Make sure the list includes activities that require energy and activities the child can do on his or her own. Examples include playing with a pet, riding a bike, reading a book, talking to a friend, helping a family member or friend, drawing, and painting fingernails.

☐	**Begin** *Scheduling Time for Fun* **Worksheet**	Explain to the child that staying busy—having plans to do fun things—is a great way to improve your mood or to keep your mood high. Help the child brainstorm one fun activity he or she can do every day, and fill in the first column of the *Scheduling Time for Fun* worksheet. Work with the child to write—in the left column—one specific activity he or she will plan to do on each day and note when that activity is planned (e.g., after school, after dinner). Refer to the *Ten Things I Can Do to Feel Better* list if you need to come up with enough ideas to fill the week. Try to make sure that the activities include at least one that uses energy, at least one that is with another person, and at least one that helps someone else (e.g., help clear the table and do dishes after dinner).
☐ ⬆	**PRACTICE ASSIGNMENT Complete Worksheet**	Explain to the child that the practice assignment for this week is to complete the *Scheduling Time for Fun* worksheet. Instruct the child to do the activity the two of you have written down (or a substitute activity if necessary) each the day in the coming week. Each day the child should write down what the activity was and as well as his or her *Feelings Thermometer* ratings both before and after the activity.

Leave 'Em Laughing

Close with some really funny, or enjoyable activity—something that will leave the child either laughing or feeling great. Possibilities: America's Funniest Home Videos, tell some funny jokes, play a board game that the child really loves.

Share with Parent (if possible)

At the end of the session, if a parent is available, it can be helpful to brief him or her on the materials covered.

☐	**Consider Privacy**	Before bringing the parent into the room, it is important to ask the child if there is anything that he or she told you today that he or she does not want you to tell the parent. Be sure to honor the child's confidentiality within the appropriate limits of safety.
☐	**Review Concepts**	Have the child explain to the parent what concepts he or she has learned in the session. You can add information as necessary.
☐	**Show off Success**	When the child has completed a practice exercise or activity successfully, this is a good time to repeat it with a parent there to see. During the practice, you can model to the parent how to encourage and praise the child's behaviors.
☐	**Give Parent Handout**	Provide the parent with the *Activity Selection* parent handout. Be sure that the parent is familiar with the concepts so that the he or she can assist the child in using the new concepts and tools introduced in the therapy sessions.

Helpful Tips

- If you have a hard time coming up with ideas, here are **10 possible activities** you could try: (1) toss a ball back and forth, (2) play trash can basketball (crumble up a piece of paper to make a ball and use the trash can as the goal), (3) hula-hoop, (4) jump rope, (5) run/hop in place, (6) do jumping jacks, (7) play a quick game/computer game, (8) play an instrument (maracas, tambourine), (9) play Simon Says, and (10) draw a picture.

- If the child is having difficulty generating activities for the ***Ten Things I Can Do to Feel Good*** worksheet, offer suggestions based on your earlier session with the parent—when the parent identified activities that improve this child's mood. In addition, you may suggest activities that most children would enjoy (e.g., playing a game with a friend, practicing dribbling and shooting a basketball, playing with a pet).

- If the child lists passive activities like sleeping or watching TV, accept these answers and write them down. However, make sure to include some activities that require energy (e.g., riding a bike, shooting baskets) or that are more engaging (e.g., reading, painting).

- If the child enters the session in a bad mood, or seems tired, lethargic, or uninterested, this is an opportunity to introduce a mood booster: take a brief mood rating, spend a few minutes engaging in a pleasant activity, then re-rate the mood. If the rating improves, be sure to highlight to the child that what you do changes how you feel.

- The practice assignment for this session—and the ***Scheduling Time for Fun*** worksheet—can be used again, multiple times. If this child is one who tends to drift into bad moods—or lethargy— at home between sessions, it may be helpful to add the structure of regular weekly planning, looking to the week ahead and planning one mood-enhancing activity for each day of the week, using the ***Scheduling Time for Fun*** worksheet.

- Check in on goals: does the child feel that he or she is making progress? How does the material you covered today relate to the goals you set together?

How's Your Style?

- Did you praise often?
- Did you review often, by asking questions?
- Did you simplify the steps as needed?
- Did your pace match that of the child?
- Did you stay on track?

Learning to Relax

Goals

- The child will understand that staying calm and relaxing are good ways to affect the way we feel—especially when we are stressed out or tense
- The child will identify somatic cues that show when he or she is tense
- The child will learn how to do self-calming through deep breathing, deep muscle relaxation, and guided imagery

Materials

- *Fear Thermometer* and *Fear Ladder* (2 unrated copies for anxiety/trauma), *Feelings Thermometer* (for depression), or *Behavior Rating Scale* (for disruptive behavior)
- *Learning to Relax* worksheet (2 copies)
- *Relaxing at Home* worksheet
- *Self-Calming Through Relaxation* parent handout
- Relaxation audio file for the child to keep, downloadable at http://relax.practicewise.com (you can email it, burn it on a CD, or show the child where to download it)
- MP3 audio player (any type that has good sound quality; this could be your computer)
- Pens, pencils, markers

> ⧗ *If time is tight:* Convey the idea that staying calm and relaxing are good ways to affect the way we feel, and use the audio recording to teach the child how to do deep muscle relaxation.

Main Steps	Remember to start by setting an agenda together and reviewing any practice assignments.
☐ **Obtain Weekly Ratings**	If the main focus is traumatic stress or anxiety, use the 0 to 10 scale of the *Fear Thermometer* to obtain *Fear Ladder* ratings from both the child and his or her parent. If the main focus is depressed mood, use the *Feelings Thermometer* to take a rating. If the main focus is disruptive behavior, take a parent rating with the *Behavior Rating Scale*.
☐ **Discuss Feeling Stressed & Feeling Bad**	Tell the child that the way our body feels when we are worried, sad, or stressed out involves muscle tension. When we feel upset or worried, some parts of our body become tense or tight, and that tension makes our body feel uncomfortable. Discuss with the child times when he or she has felt uptight, tense, or stressed, particularly focusing on the physical feelings he or she has experienced at those times.

☐	**Introduce Deep Muscle Relaxation**	Introduce the child to the idea that learning to make our bodies relax can help combat stressful feelings and the tension that goes with those feelings. If we can make our bodies feel relaxed, we are taking an important step toward coping with bad feelings. In addition, it helps to breathe slowly and calmly; and it also helps to picture, in our minds, a calm, peaceful place.

Example script

Sometimes when we feel sad, worried, or stressed, our bodies feel tense or tight. Today we are going to practice a way to get our bodies to relax. We are going to play a recording that teaches how to do something called Deep Muscle Relaxation. It teaches how to tense and relax different muscles in the body until we begin to feel more relaxed all over. (Demonstrate this concept by tightening and relaxing your fist, and having the child do the same.) *In addition, the recording will teach us to slow down our breathing—to take deep breaths and let the breath out slowly. And it also teaches us to imagine a calm, peaceful place, and to picture that place in our mind while we relax. People who use this recording feel much calmer and more relaxed after using it.*

☐	**ACTIVITY** *Deep Muscle Relaxation & Guided Imagery*	Cue up the audio recording, but before you play it, do the following:

1. Work with the child to create an image or a story of a very stressful day or a stressful situation, thereby inducing a negative mood.
2. Have the child complete the top half of the **Learning to Relax** worksheet—rating his or her mood while thinking about the imaginary stressful situation, and also describing how he or she feels physically while thinking about the stressful situation.
3. Make the room more comfortable (e.g., you may dim the lights).
4. Have the child sit comfortably in a chair with feet on the floor and arms at his or her side. The child can also close his or her eyes (or look at a boring spot on the floor or wall, if closing eyes makes the child uneasy or uncomfortable).
5. Play the relaxation audio file.
6. Have the child finish filling in the **Learning to Relax** worksheet.

☐	**Discuss the Relaxation Exercise**	Discuss the relaxation exercise with the child. Did the child's rating and physical feelings change, as shown on the worksheet? Did the child feel more relaxed? What did the child like/dislike? What was most helpful?

Make sure to explain:

- the big difference between a relaxed body and a tense one
- how slowing one's breathing and paying attention to it can help relax the body
- how tensing and relaxing muscles helps relax the body
- how picturing a calm, relaxing place can make the experience even more relaxing
- how calming it can be when we combine all three of the things the recording teaches—i.e., slowing down our breathing, tensing and relaxing our muscles, and imagining a calm, peaceful place.

☐	**Repeat the Relaxation Activity**	If time permits, repeat the relaxation activity with the child. Note that relaxing and calming ourselves is a skill that we can get better at the more we practice. Use the recording to practice relaxation one more time. Then discuss with the child what he or she noticed the second time that was different from the first. Ask the child which activities seemed easier to do the second time than the first.
		Tell the child that you are going to give him or her the recording to use for this week's practice assignment. Encourage the child to use it anytime he or she feels tense, uptight, angry, or even just sad.
☐	**Reinforce Relaxation**	Reinforce and further develop the child's awareness of how and when relaxation might be useful. Help the child identify situations in which relaxation could be helpful and most needed.
☐ 🏠	**PRACTICE ASSIGNMENT** *Relaxing at Home*	Give the child a copy of the relaxation audio file for practice (you can email it, burn it on a CD, or show the child where to download it). Explain to the child that he or she should practice *twice* during the week and should complete the *Relaxing at Home* worksheet. Review this worksheet with the child to make sure he or she understands how to do the practice assignment and how to fill in the sheet. Discuss the mechanics of how the relaxation practice will work by identifying when and where the child can practice.

Leave 'Em Laughing

Close with some really funny or enjoyable activity—something that will leave the child either laughing or feeling great. Possibilities: America's Funniest Home Videos, tell some funny jokes, play a board game that the child really loves.

Share with Parent (if possible)

At the end of the session, if a parent is available, it can be helpful to brief him or her on the materials covered.

☐	**Consider Privacy**	Before bringing the parent into the room, ask the child if there is anything he or she told you that you should not tell the parent. Be sure to honor the child's confidentiality within appropriate limits of safety.
☐	**Review Concepts**	Have the child explain to the parent what concepts and skills he or she has learned in the session. You can add information as necessary.
☐	**Show off Success**	When the child has completed a practice exercise or activity successfully, this is a good time to repeat it with a parent there to see. During the practice, you can model to the parent how to encourage and praise the child's behaviors.
☐	**Give Parent Handout**	In addition, give the parent the *Self-Calming Through Relaxation* parent handout and explain that you have provided the child with a copy of the relaxation audio file. The main goal of this part of the session is to familiarize the parent with the concepts (and provide a good review for the child), so the parent can assist the child in using his or her new relaxation skills.

Helpful Tips

- Be creative! Use your imagination to find ways to help the child understand relaxation.
- If the child is having difficulty describing physical sensations, have the child imagine and describe a stressful situation (a test, giving a speech), or play a stressful game in the session

(e.g., Jenga, Operation). Have the child describe his or her anxious feelings and muscle tension during this activity.

- To demonstrate the physiological effects of self-calming, you can take the child's temperature (using paper temp-a-dots) and/or pulse prior to and after relaxation. For most people, temperature rises slightly, and pulse slows, as they become more relaxed.

- Check in on goals: Does the child feel that he or she is making progress? How does the material you covered today relate to the goals you set together?

Special Cases

Depression or Conduct Problems	If the child enters the session in a bad mood, or seems tired, lethargic, or uninterested, this is an opportunity to introduce a mood booster: take a brief mood rating using the **Feelings Thermometer**, spend a few minutes engaging in a pleasant activity, and then take another mood rating. If the activity was successful, highlight to the child that what we do changes how we feel and then move on to covering the relaxation skills.
Generalized Anxiety	Relaxation techniques can be beneficial for children with generalized anxiety, particularly when the child can't fall asleep. In such cases, the recording may be used just prior to bedtime to help the child relax enough to fall asleep.
Posttraumatic Stress	For children who have posttraumatic stress symptoms or have experienced trauma, it may not be helpful—and it may increase distress—to darken the room, or have the child lie on the floor or a couch, or to ask the child to close his or her eyes, because these procedures may trigger distressing memories of past trauma. Instead, have the child slouch in a chair and look down at an uninteresting place, perhaps the floor.

How's Your Style?

- Did you praise often?
- Did you review often, by asking questions?
- Did you simplify the steps as needed?
- Did your pace match that of the child or family?
- Did you stay on track?

Quick Calming

For Child

Goals

- The child will understand that learning to stay calm and relaxed can have a positive effect on the way he or she feels—especially when stressed out or tense
- The child will learn Quick Calming, a relaxation technique to use when time is short, when in a public place, or when caught off-guard by a stressful situation

Materials

- *Fear Thermometer* and *Fear Ladder* (2 unrated copies for anxiety/trauma) or *Behavior Rating Scale* (for disruptive behavior)
- *Feelings Thermometer*
- *Anxious Feelings and Thoughts* worksheet (from the Anxiety section of MATCH)
- *My Relaxing Place* worksheet
- *Quick Calming Practice* worksheet
- *Quick Calming* parent handout

> ⧖ *If time is tight:* Convey the idea that staying calm and relaxed can have a positive effect on the way we feel. Teach the child a brief relaxation strategy that can be used in public places where he or she may not be able to use deep muscle relaxation techniques.

Main Steps	Remember to start by setting an agenda together and reviewing any practice assignments.
☐ **Obtain Weekly Ratings**	If the main focus is traumatic stress or anxiety, use the 0 to 10 scale of the *Fear Thermometer* to obtain *Fear Ladder* ratings from both the child and his or her parent. If the main focus is depressed mood, use the *Feelings Thermometer* to take a rating. If the main focus is disruptive behavior, take a parent rating with the *Behavior Rating Scale*.
☐ **Review the Purpose of Relaxation**	Ask the child to explain the relationship between muscle tension, stress, and negative feelings. Work with the child to generate an explanation that learning to relax our bodies can help us feel better emotionally. If the child previously did the relaxation training session with the audio file, recall how the instructions helped the child relax, and how the child's overall feelings (e.g., Thermometer ratings) improved.

☐	**Explain Purpose of Quick Calming**	Explain to the child that some stressful situations are public or unexpected, and it can be difficult to use elaborate relaxation methods—as in the audio file instructions—at those times. Provide examples of stressful situations in which you might need to relax but don't have a lot of time or there are other people around (e.g., just before an exam, just before you have to give a report in front of your class, just after an argument with a friend that has left you angry and your heart pounding).
☐	**ACTIVITY** *Develop "Quick List"*	To help the child understand when it would be helpful to use the Quick Calming technique, ask the child to come up with some examples of times he or she may be stressed, tense, or uptight in public places, or when time is limited. Provide help, if the child needs it, reminding the child of situations he or she has discussed with you in which stress levels are likely to be high.
☐	**Introduce Quick Calming**	Tell the child that what you are going to work on today is a way to do **Quick Calming**, and that it involves three steps (they spell "ReST"):

- <u>Re</u>lax your muscles
  - ○ Relax the muscles, especially those that feel most tense
- <u>S</u>low your breathing
  - ○ take slow, deep breaths and exhale slowly each time
- <u>T</u>hink of a peaceful place
  - ○ Picture a peaceful place and imagine that you're relaxing there

Tell the child the basic idea is that we can get good at doing these three things, and then—when we are in a stressful situation, we do these three things over and over again until we feel calmer, or until we have to take some action (e.g., take the test that is stressing us out, or shoot the free throw in basketball). Remind the child of some examples of stressful situations on the list the two of you just generated (above).

☐	**Identify Areas of Chronic Muscle Tension, Using a "Body Map"**	Help the child identify areas in the body where muscles most often feel tight in times of stress. First, ask the child to imagine a situation in which he or she often feels stressed out (e.g., starting a test, arguing with parents, or other situations from the list the child gave you, above). Ask the child where his or her body feels tense in such stressful situations. If you have not done so in a prior session, select one of the first two pages of the *Anxious Feelings and Thoughts* worksheet and use it to "map" the feelings in the child's body (use only the girl or the boy drawing, as appropriate). Using questions (and pointing to areas if necessary), have the child mark each area on the body where he or she often feels muscle tension. Get as much information as possible, for example:

- *Can you mark places on this drawing where your muscles feel tight and tense when you are stressed out?*
- *Do any other places ever get those tight and tense feelings?*

Point out that when doing Quick Calming, it helps a lot to focus on these tense areas of the body, trying to really get those areas relaxed.

☐	**Introduce Slow, Deep Breathing**	Tell the child that the second part of Quick Calming is slow, deep breathing. Explain that when people feel stressed or anxious, they often take short, shallow breaths which only make them feel *more* stressed. Discuss that taking slow, deep breaths from the stomach can help to slow the breathing, to calm the body, and to improve mood.
☐	**ACTIVITY** *Slow, Deep Breathing*	Teach the child how to take slow, deep breaths. Have the child get comfortable in the chair with feet on the floor and arms at his or her side. Ask the child to take a slow, deep breath from his or her stomach. (his or her hand will move when inhaling). After 1-2 seconds, the child should exhale, even slowly than when inhaling. An example follows:
		Now, we are going to learn how to do deep breathing. Take a slow deep breath in through your nose, and feel the breath go down through your chest and all the way down into your stomach. You will feel your chest rise first, and then feel your stomach rise, like a balloon is being blown up. When you breathe in, the hand on your stomach should move out. Hold your breath there for a moment, and then slowly let your breath out. When you breathe out, your hand will move in. You will feel your stomach go down, like the air is going out of a balloon. Let's try it a few times together.
		Explain to the child that this kind of slow, deep breathing is what he or she will do during Quick Calming. He or she probably won't have a hand on the stomach, but everything else should be the same during Quick Calming.
☐	**Introduce Guided Imagery**	Tell the child that the third part of Quick Calming is picturing a peaceful place. Explain that just thinking about or imagining a peaceful, relaxing place can help us feel calm.
☐	**ACTIVITY** *My Relaxing Place*	Complete the **My Relaxing Place** worksheet together. Have the child describe his or her favorite relaxing place (e.g., the beach, bedroom) in detail. Focus on how that place looks, smells, feels, tastes, and sounds. Tell the child that he or she should make a **good mental picture** of this special peaceful place and how it looks, smells, feels, sounds, and tastes—because this is the picture the child will hold in mind during Quick Calming.

☐	**ACTIVITY** *Quick Calming* *Practice*	Lead the child through three rounds of Quick Calming practice. First, have the child imagine being in one of the stressful situations you discussed earlier (e.g., just before a math test or before shooting a free throw). Hold up the *Feelings Thermometer*, and see if—with a few tries—the child can imagine the stressful situation strongly enough to report a low ("Bad" or "Very Bad") rating on the Thermometer.

If imagining a situation doesn't generate a low rating, try rehearsing a stressful situation together. For example, you might ask the child to get ready to take a Nerf basketball shot (imagining it is during a big game), or prepare to read a difficult tongue-twister aloud three times fast. Or you might play a quick game that is stress-inducing.

Once you have gotten to a relatively low *Feelings Thermometer* rating, write it down. Then have the child do Quick Calming for two minutes. Before starting, remind the child that the three steps of Quick Calming spell **ReST**. See if the child can remember the three steps.

Once the child begins the practice, you should periodically remind the child of the three steps (in bold, below), using a soft voice:

- **Relax your muscles** (sit in a relaxed posture, with hands resting loose on the lap or thighs; notice tension in any specific muscle groups and try to relax those muscles)
- **Slow your breathing** (take slow, deep breaths and exhale slowly each time)
- **Think of a peaceful place** (bring to mind the mental picture of that peaceful place you identified previously)

After the two-minute practice has ended, ask the child for another *Feelings Thermometer* rating and write it down. Then repeat the Quick Calming exercise a second and a third time, obtaining *Feelings Thermometer* ratings after each time.

☐	**Discuss Activity**	After the three rounds of practice, discuss the effect of Quick Calming on the child's feelings, and Feelings Thermometer ratings. If the child's ratings showed improvement after successive Quick Calming practices, note how well Quick Calming worked; if the child's rating remained the same or got worse after the activity, discuss possible reasons for this (e.g., the exercise was too brief to do the trick, or Quick Calming is a skill that needs practice before it can work really well).
☐	**ACTIVITY** *Quick Calming in* *Public*	If time remains, arrange for one in-session practice of Quick Calming in a public place. You might have the child go to the clinic waiting room and practice Quick Calming; afterward, you can debrief, noting how the child did the calming privately, so that no one else in the room knew he or she was doing it (just like kids in school would not know if the child were using Quick Calming). Remember to take Feelings Thermometer ratings before and after this 'public' practice of Quick Calming.

☐	**Review Quick Calming Steps**	Praise the child for doing a good job on the activities, and explore how he or she can use this technique in real-life situations. Explore options for making it easier to do well. Some basic concepts to communicate in this discussion: • Recognizing tense muscles in the body and relaxing them helps calm us down • Taking slow, deep breaths and exhaling slowly can help us get even calmer • Picturing a favorite peaceful place can add a lot to the calming experience
☐	**Anticipate Difficulties**	Briefly review some common difficulties that people experience when using Quick Calming techniques: • **Distracting thoughts**: Everyone has these. When these thoughts come up, the child should just gently refocus attention on his or her breathing and picture his or her relaxing place. • **Physical reactions and sensations**: Most people have little muscle twitches and tingling sensations when they do Quick Calming. It's not a problem, and there may be fewer twitches and tingles the more the child practices Quick Calming.
☐ 🏠	**PRACTICE ASSIGNMENT** *Quick Calming at Home*	Ask the child to find a time during the coming week to practice Quick Calming in a public place. Show the child the *Quick Calming Practice* worksheet, and go over it with the child. Briefly review the Quick Calming steps, and remind the child to make a rating on the *Feelings Thermometer* both before and after practicing. Also remind the child that Quick Calming is a skill that will improve with practice.

Leave 'Em Laughing

Close with some really funny or enjoyable activity—something that will leave the child either laughing or feeling great. Possibilities: tell some funny jokes, play a board game that the child really loves.

Share with Parent (if possible)

At the end of the session, if a parent is available, it can be helpful to brief him or her on the ideas and skills covered.

☐	**Consider Privacy**	Before bringing the parent into the room, it is important to ask the child if there is anything that he or she told you today that he or she does not want you to tell the parent. Be sure to honor the child's confidentiality within the appropriate limits of safety.
☐	**Review Concepts**	Have the child explain to the parent what concepts and skills he or she has learned in the session. You can add information as necessary.
☐	**Show off Success**	When the child has completed a practice exercise or activity successfully, this is a good time to repeat it with a parent there to see. During the practice, you should model to the parent how to encourage and praise the child's behaviors.

☐ Give Parent Handout	In addition, give the parent the *Quick Calming* parent handout. The main goal of this part of the session is to familiarize the parent with the concepts (and provide a good review for the child), so the parent can assist the child in using his or her new relaxation skills.

Helpful Tips

- If the child is having difficulty describing a relaxing place, have him or her draw a picture of the place.
- Check in on goals: does the child feel that he or she is making progress? How does the material you covered today relate to the goals you set together?

Special Cases

Depression	If the child enters the session in a bad mood, or seems tired, lethargic, or uninterested, this is an opportunity to introduce a mood booster: take a brief mood rating using the *Feelings Thermometer*, spend a few minutes engaging in a pleasant activity, and then take another mood rating. If the activity was successful, highlight to the child that what we do changes how we feel.
Conduct Problems	If you are using this technique with a child with conduct problems and he or she has not been introduced to the *Feelings Thermometer*, you will need to introduce it at the start of this session.

How's Your Style?

- Did you praise often?
- Did you review often, by asking questions?
- Did you simplify the steps as needed?
- Did your pace match that of the child or family?
- Did you stay on track?

Presenting a Positive Self

For Child

Goals

- The child will learn that being positive and optimistic can improve mood and have a positive effect on relationships with others.
- The child will practice positive-self skills in session

Materials

- *Fear Thermometer* and *Fear Ladder* (2 unrated copies for anxiety/trauma) or *Behavior Rating Scale* (for disruptive behavior)
- *Feelings Thermometer*
- *My Negative Self and My Positive Self* worksheet
- *Practicing My Positive Self* worksheet (2 copies)
- *Presenting a Positive Self* parent handout

⧗ *If time is tight:* *Discuss how the way we present ourselves impacts us and others. Use role plays to help the child experience the benefit of positive self skills. Compile a list of things the child can do to show a positive self.*

Main Steps	Remember to start by setting an agenda together and reviewing any practice assignments.
☐ **Obtain Weekly Ratings**	If the main focus is traumatic stress or anxiety, use the 0 to 10 scale of the *Fear Thermometer* to obtain *Fear Ladder* ratings from both the child and his or her parent. If the main focus is depressed mood, use the *Feelings Thermometer* to take a rating. If the main focus is disruptive behavior, take a parent rating with the *Behavior Rating Scale*.
☐ **Introduce Positive Self**	Tell a story (ideally about yourself) that illustrates the value of showing a positive self.

Example script

*I remember one time when I woke up feeling gloomy and grouchy, and I went through my whole day acting negative. When I did this, I noticed that I started feeling worse, and also that other people seemed not to be enjoying being with me very much. So, the next time I woke up feeling gloomy and grouchy, I **decided** to make myself go through my day with a positive attitude. I tried things like dressing in my favorite outfit and showing other people how much I was enjoying being with them. As the day went on, I noticed that making myself present a positive self actually made me start feeling better; and other people seemed to enjoy being with me, too.*

☐	**Review Main Ideas**	In telling the story and discussing its meaning, convey three main ideas:

- Presenting a negative, gloomy exterior to the world can make us feel bad, and can also make other people uncomfortable and less likely to spend time with us.
- Showing a positive self to the world can make us feel better, and can also make other people more comfortable and more likely to spend time with us.
- Showing a positive self is a skill, like sports, dancing, or math. It involves specific kinds of behavior that people can practice and improve when they do practice.

☐	**Model Negative vs. Positive Self**	Begin the discussion by noting the things YOU do to convey a negative and positive self. For example, you might say—**and demonstrate for the child**— that when you show a **Negative Self**, you have...

- Poor eye contact and posture
- Negative facial expression
- Sad or irritable tone of voice
- Say negative things about your experiences, others, and the world

In contrast, to illustrate your **Positive Self,** you might say—**and demonstrate for the child**—that when you are being positive, you show...

- Direct eye contact and upright posture
- Pleasant facial expressions
- Clear, pleasant tone of voice
- Say positive things about your experiences, others, and the world

☐	**ACTIVITY** *Demonstrate Negative vs. Positive Self*	Have **two** role-play conversations with the child in which you first display your negative self, then your positive self. Make the experience funny by exaggerating your negative self. Ask the child: which of these people was more pleasant to interact with? What differences did he or she notice in your behavior, expressions, etc.?
☐	**Develop Description of Child's "Positive" and "Negative" Selves**	Use the *Presenting My Negative Self and My Positive Self* worksheet to generate a list of specific behaviors the child uses to show a negative and a positive self.

☐	**ACTIVITY** *Role Play* *Negative vs.* *Positive Self*	Have the child do two role plays, acting out the behaviors listed on the worksheet. [If you have access to video-recording equipment, you can use it to record the two role plays and play each back for the child, to prompt a discussion about negative and positive self; this make these particular role plays especially effective.] The first role play is **Negative Self**. First practice with the child, coaching him or her to show the behaviors listed in the Negative Self column of the worksheet, as you read items from the interview below. Have the child provide a *Feelings Thermometer* rating before and after the role-play. Then do the role play by conducting the following interview:

- *Please tell your name, age, where you live, and where you go to school.*
- *Now just talk about yourself. Tell what you are like, what your interests or hobbies are, anything else people should know about you.*
- *Now tell me how you feel about your school, and what some of your classes are like.*
- *Tell me about some of the kids you know, and what they are like.*
- *Tell me about some of the things you do with other kids, outside of school.*
- *Now please tell me about your family or who you live with, what they are like, and what kinds of things you do with them.*
- *Finally, please tell me what you would do if you had a million dollars?*

Use the same interview script to guide the child through a **Positive Self** role-play. First, coach the child in a practice session, prompting and encouraging him or her to display the positive self items written on the worksheet. Have the child provide *Feelings Thermometer* ratings before and after this role-play.

☐	**Discuss Experience of Positive vs. Negative Self**	Discuss the child's experience of the role-plays, including how the child felt after acting so negative/positive, how he or she might feel after acting that way all day, and how other people would react to these two styles of self-presentation. Review the child's *Feelings Thermometer* ratings for evidence of how self-presentation affects mood.
☐	**ACTIVITY** *"Real World"* *Positive and* *Negative Self*	If time permits, arrange for the child to go outside the therapy room and try his or her positive self out on a third person. For example, after practicing once or twice with you, the child might choose to walk to the clinic receptionist, flash a big smile, and say something like "May I have the key to the restroom?" or "How late is the clinic open today?" or "I like that pin you are wearing." When the child comes back into the office, you can discuss how it felt to try this positive self, how the person responded, and how it feels now that the experience is over. Alternatively, the third person could be the child's parent. (It is wise to prepare the receptionist or parent before the session, so that he or she will be sure to respond to the child in a positive way.)

It may also be helpful to role play a time when the child can show his or her positive self in the real world, such as when he or she comes home from school after a difficult day, or when talking with an authority figure.

☐ 🏠 **PRACTICE ASSIGNMENT** *Positive Self at Home*	The child will practice using his or her positive self two times, and will complete the *Practicing My Positive Self* worksheet as part of this practice. So, give the child two copies of this worksheet. Decide with whom the child will practice presenting his or her positive self each time, and write this on the worksheets. Work with the child to pick a person who is likely to give a positive response. The child is to record *Feelings Thermometer* ratings before and after each Positive Self practice during the week.

Leave 'Em Laughing

End the session on a fun note, with a game or other activity that will leave the child feeling really good about the work you have done together today.

Share with Parent (if possible)

At the end of the session, if a parent is available, it can be helpful to brief him or her on the materials covered.

☐ **Consider Privacy**	Before bringing the parent into the room, it is important to ask the child if there is anything that he or she told you today that the child does **not** want you to tell the parent. Be sure to honor this.
☐ **Review Concepts**	Then, have the child bring the parent into the room. Have the child explain to the parent what concepts he or she learned in the session. You can add information as necessary.
☐ **Encourage Monitoring and Praise**	Ask the parent to be on the lookout for the child's presentation of his or her positive self. Encourage the parent to praise and support the child in using this new tool.
☐ **Give Parent Handout**	In addition, give the parent the *Presenting a Positive Self* parent handout. Familiarize the parent with the concepts (and provide a good review for the child) so the parent can assist the child in using new concepts and skills introduced in this session.

Helpful Tips

- If the child has not already been trained in the use of the *Feelings Thermometer*, it will be important to introduce that skill before going through the activities in this session.

- When helping the child identify behaviors that convey a negative-self and positive-self, be sensitive to cultural, familial, and developmental differences in the interpretation of body language and verbal behavior.

- Be careful to avoid any impression that you are criticizing any child's "depressed" self. Instead, the exercises should be presented in the context of exploration and curiosity. That is, you really do want to know what the child thinks about these two different role plays, and what he or she thinks the consequences of positive and negative behavior may be for how we feel and how others feel about us.

- Try not to imply that "showing a positive self" is the same thing as "faking it." Instead, the key idea is that we all have the capacity inside us to behave in lots of different ways; the positive ways seem to make us feel better, and to make other people feel better about being with us.

- It is important that the child's positive-self be likely to elicit a positive response both from peers and from adults. You want to avoid creating a positive-self profile that might seem arrogant or obnoxious to adults, even if it is likely to evoke a positive reaction from peers. Instead of "I'm great at soccer!" the child might say "I love soccer"—i.e., positive, but not arrogant. Likewise, avoid coaching the child to behave in a way that adults might like but that his or her peers may find "nerdy" or socially undesirable.

- If you intend to use a third person, either a parent or co-worker, it is wise to prepare this person ahead of time, to ensure that the child receives a favorable response to showing his or her "positive self."

- If the child enters the session in a bad mood, or seems tired, lethargic, or disinterested, this is an opportunity to introduce a **mood booster**: take a brief mood rating, spend a few minutes engaging in a pleasant activity, then re-rate the mood. If it is successful, be sure to highlight to the child that *what we do changes how we feel*.

- Check in on goals: Does the child feel that he or she is making progress? How does the material you covered today relate to the goals you set together?

How's Your Style?

- Did you praise often?
- Did you review often, by asking questions?
- Did you simplify the steps as needed?
- Did your pace match that of the child or family?
- Did you stay on track?

Cognitive Coping - BLUE

Use This:

To identify and revise unrealistic negative thoughts in order to improve mood.

For Child

Goals

- The child will understand the relationship between thinking and feeling
- The child will be able to identify unrealistic negative thoughts
- The child will learn to evaluate the evidence that supports or does not support the negative thoughts
- The child will learn to generate more realistic thoughts

Materials

- *Fear Thermometer* and *Fear Ladder* (2 unrated copies for anxiety/trauma) or *Behavior Rating Scale* (for disruptive behavior)
- *Feelings Thermometer*
- *Changing B-L-U-E Thoughts* worksheet
- *Double Bubbles on My Own* worksheet (2 copies)
- *Changing B-L-U-E Thoughts* parent handout
- Sunglasses
- Pencils, pens, markers

⏳ *If time is tight: Make the connection between what we think and how we feel and help the child identify and change unrealistic negative thoughts.*

Main Steps	*Remember to start by setting an agenda together and reviewing any practice assignments.*
☐ **Obtain Weekly Ratings**	If the main focus is traumatic stress or anxiety, use the 0 to 10 scale of the *Fear Thermometer* to obtain *Fear Ladder* ratings from both the child and his or her parent. If the main focus is depressed mood, use the *Feelings Thermometer* to take a rating. If the main focus is disruptive behavior, take a parent rating with the *Behavior Rating Scale*.
☐ **Introduce Connection Between Thoughts and Feelings**	Explain to the child that today's session will focus on how our thinking can change our feelings, and on learning how to examine and change thoughts in order to feel better.

Example script

Imagine that you get a bad grade on a test. How you think about this situation can affect how you will feel about it. One way of thinking about this might be "Oh no, I've failed. I'm always going to fail. This means I'll never get anywhere in life. I'm probably the biggest idiot in the whole school." Another way to view the situation is, "I'm sorry I made a bad grade, but I know I can study more next time and do better." How would you feel after having these thoughts? What would you do?

☐	**ACTIVITY "B-L-U-E" Glasses**	Ask the child to imagine he or she is wearing dark sunglasses (better yet, <u>provide</u> sunglasses), and to describe how things appear to him or her. Are things clear or blurry? Are colors accurate? Do things appear as they really are?
		Having negative thoughts can be like seeing the world through dark glasses. It makes it harder to see the world the way it really is (the colors, etc.), and it affects our mood (makes us feel more down/sad). Discuss what it is like to take off the dark glasses, and talk about the similarity between seeing more clearly and thinking more realistically.
☐	**Introduce B-L-U-E**	Introduce the child to the acronym B-L-U-E, looking at the *Changing B-L-U-E Thoughts* worksheet, and provide some examples of each type of thought, asking the child for suggestions.
		B **Blaming myself**: Taking too much personal responsibility for negative events
		L **Looking for the bad news**: paying attention only to the negative information and ignoring the positive information.
		U **Unhappy guessing**: Expecting bad outcomes when we don't really know how things will turn out.
		E **Exaggerating**: Making a things seem worse than they really are
☐	**Relate B-L-U-E to the Child's Life**	Ask the child to give examples of some unrealistic negative thoughts he or she has had, and apply the correct B-L-U-E label to those thoughts. Be sure to come with your own examples of BLUE thoughts, in case the child can't think of any. (If the child *does* offer negative thoughts, but they don't fit one of the BLUE categories, don't worry about fitting them into BLUE; instead, just say something like, "Yes, that does sound like a pretty unrealistic thought")
☐	**Make a Connection Between Thoughts and Feelings**	Explain that when thoughts are overly negative and unrealistic, they can result in bad moods or actions (like giving up or arguing). Discuss with the child the way that different thoughts can lead to different feelings and actions, using one of the examples on page 1 of the *Changing BLUE Thoughts* worksheet.
☐	**Explain That Thoughts Can Be Untrue**	Ask the child if he or she has ever had thoughts that later turned out to be incorrect. Gather some examples, or offer some of your own. Point out that when we are in a bad mood, we are more likely to have negative thoughts, *but just because we think it doesn't mean it's true.*
☐	**Illustrate "Just Because I think it Doesn't Mean It's True"**	Go back to the example on page 1, and choose one of the B-L-U-E thoughts you and the child wrote there. How can we know whether that thought is accurate or not? One way is to evaluate the evidence. Are there are any other ways to think about the situation—ways of thinking that are more realistic and might improve feelings?
		Example script
		So in this example, how does the kid know that [negative thought] is true? Is there any other way of looking at the situation? What would you tell someone in this situation who had this B-L-U-E thought?
		And by the way, what if some negative thoughts actually are true? How bad would that be? For example, maybe I won't ever be as good a skater as my sister. Is that a big deal? Not really!

☐	**Introduce and Practice Double Bubbles**	Use the *Changing B-L-U-E Thoughts* worksheet to practice evaluating **B-L-U-E** thoughts and generating more realistic **TRUE** thoughts (e.g., "If I practice hard I will improve," "The whole team made mistakes today, not just me."). Ask the child why the negative thought may be unrealistic, and to come up with more realistic **TRUE** thoughts.
☐	**Counter Your Own Thoughts**	Complete one copy of the *Double Bubbles on My Own* worksheet with examples from the child's own life, discussing with the child the evidence that supports or does not support the **B-L-U-E** thought, as well as alternative interpretations of events (i.e., **TRUE** thoughts).
☐	**Praise and Repeat**	Praise the child for his or her efforts in this exercise. If time allows, ask the child to work through another situation in which he or she might have negative **B-L-U-E** thoughts, and examine the evidence in order to come up with more realistic **TRUE** thoughts. Provide praise again.
☐ ☝	**PRACTICE ASSIGNMENT** *Changing Thoughts at Home*	The child's practice assignment for the week is to fill in a second *Double Bubbles on My Own* worksheet, for a B-L-U-E thought he or she has during the upcoming week. Tell the child to write the B-L-U-E thought he or she had in the B-L-U-E bubble, and write a more realistic TRUE thought in the TRUE bubble, and to mark on the *Feelings Thermometers* how each thought made the child feel. Tell the child that you will review the worksheet together the next time you meet.

Leave 'Em Laughing

End the session on a fun note, with a game, activity, or other exercise that will leave the child feeling really good about the work you have done together today.

Share with Parent (if possible)

At the end of the session, if a parent is available, it can be helpful to brief him or her on the materials covered.

☐	**Consider Privacy**	Before bringing the parent into the room, it is important to ask the child if there is anything that he or she told you today that he or she does not want you to tell the parent. Be sure to honor the child's confidentiality within the appropriate limits of safety.
☐	**Review Concepts**	Have the child explain to the parent what concepts he or she has learned in the session. You can add information as necessary.
☐	**Encourage Monitoring and Praise**	Ask the parent to join the child in "detective work" by being on the lookout for examples of unrealistic negative thinking and successful counter-thinking over the upcoming week. Encourage him or her to praise and support the child in using this new tool!
☐	**Give Parent Handout**	In addition, give the parent the *Changing B-L-U-E Thoughts* parent handout. The main goal of this part of the session is to familiarize the parent with the concepts (and provide a good review for the child), so the parent can assist the child in using his or her new coping skills.

Helpful Tips

- If the child has not already been trained in the use of the *Feelings Thermometer*, it will be important to introduce that skill before going through the activities in this session.

- To make your discussion of thoughts less abstract and more concrete for the child, examples are very helpful. Such examples can involve thought bubbles attached to drawings or cartoons, stories of people thinking very negative thoughts, or illustrations that come to mind from television programs, movies, or books.

- If the child is reluctant to discuss his or her own negative thoughts, or can't think of any, you can choose to discuss "another kid I know," or give appropriate examples from your own life.

- Make sure the child understands that these 4 types of cognitive errors are only examples, and that there are other forms of negative, unrealistic thinking beyond those in the B-L-U-E list.

- A variety of interactive games can be played to increase engagement in this session—indeed, to make it genuinely fun for the child. Some ideas include: asking the child to ring a bell (or say "beep") every time the therapist voices a B-L-U-E thought, and asking the child for a more realistic TRUE thought each time; if you do this, you will want to slip B-L-U-E thoughts into the conversation for the child to catch—e.g., "Oh, forgot to tell you something—I'm a terrible therapist!"). Or you might come up with hypothetical situations and ask the child to come up with as many realistic TRUE thoughts as possible in response to the therapist's negative B-L-U-E thoughts.

- If the child enters the session in a bad mood, or seems tired, lethargic, or uninterested, this is an opportunity to introduce a **mood booster**: take a brief mood rating, spend a few minutes engaging in a pleasant activity, then re-rate the mood. Be sure to highlight for the child that *what we do changes how we feel*.

- Check in on goals: Does the child feel that he or she is making progress? How does the material you covered today relate to the goals you set together?

How's Your Style?

- Did you praise often?
- Did you review often, by asking questions?
- Did you simplify the steps as needed?
- Did your pace match that of the parent?
- Did you stay on track?

Cognitive Coping - TLC

Goals

- The child will **think of friends** that he or she can talk problems over with
- The child will **look for the "silver lining"** in order to identify good things that are made possible because of bad situations
- The child will learn how to **change the channel** to get his or her mind off bad things that have happened, by thinking of something else

Materials

- *Fear Thermometer* and *Fear Ladder* (2 unrated copies for anxiety/trauma) or *Behavior Rating Scale* (for disruptive behavior)
- *Feelings Thermometer*
- *Coping Through TLC* worksheet
- *Using TLC When Bad Things Happen* parent handout

> ⧖ *If time is tight: Illustrate that talking things over with friends, looking for silver linings, and distracting ourselves are ways we can make ourselves feel better even if we can't change what is making us feel bad directly.*

Main Steps	Remember to start by setting an agenda together and reviewing any practice assignments.
☐ **Obtain Weekly Ratings**	If the main focus is traumatic stress or anxiety, use the 0 to 10 scale of the *Fear Thermometer* to obtain *Fear Ladder* ratings from both the child and his or her parent. If the main focus is depressed mood, use the *Feelings Thermometer* to take a rating. If the main focus is disruptive behavior, take a parent rating with the *Behavior Rating Scale*.
☐ **Introduce TLC**	Explain that the focus of today's session will be good things to do when bad things happen. Indicate to the child that you will discuss three good things to do to help him or her feel better: T **Talk to a friend:** Think things over with someone I trust. L **Look for the silver lining:** Figure out a good thing that comes out of my bad situation. C **Change the channel**: Stop thinking about things that make me feel bad. Get my mind on something else.

☐	**ACTIVITY** *Tell a Story*	Begin your discussion of these three strategies with a story of a child having a bad experience that leaves him or her feeling down. You should feel free to select any illustration that you think would fit the child well and capture his or her interest. The idea is to present the scenario (the protagonist has had a difficult or upsetting experience) and then note that we all have bad things happen to us, things that bring us down—and that there are at least three things that almost everyone can do to feel better, when such bad things happen. Tell the child that today we are going to talk about those three things.
☐	**Introduce "Think of a Friend"**	Explain that the "T" in TLC stands for **Think of a Friend.** Discuss with the child that seeking support from a friend or family member can be helpful even when the situation cannot be changed, because simply having someone to listen, understand, and provide additional suggestions/perspectives can help you feel better.
☐	**Brainstorm a List of Friends**	Identify a list of people the child can talk to when something bad happens and write this list down on page 1 of the *Coping Through TLC* worksheet. The list should include several people, and at least two adults.
☐	**Introduce "Look for the Silver Lining"**	Discuss with the child what it means to look for a silver lining. Ask if the child has ever looked at a dark cloud and seen a bright light around the edges (show the picture in the *Coping through TLC* worksheet). Note that this is called the "silver lining," and that the saying is "Every dark cloud has a silver lining." Note that the same kind of thing is often true in everyday life.
		Example script
		Sometimes we come across bad situations we can't change or control. What are some examples from your life? In these cases, we have a situation we don't like—a kind of "dark cloud"—but often the bad situation has a good side, too—something good that is made possible by the bad situation. And figuring out what that good thing is can make us feel better. Let's try some examples...
☐	**Continue Worksheet**	Work on completing page 2 of the *Coping through TLC* worksheet with the child in session.
☐	**Introduce "Change the Channel"**	Introduce the third *TLC* skill: *Changing the Channel.* Illustrate this skill by using either the **White Bear Activity** or the **Rock and Candy Activity**, below.
☐	**ACTIVITY** *White Bear*	Illustrate the concept of *changing the channel* by asking the child to think about a white bear. Tell him or her to really focus on the bear. Wait about 30 seconds and tell the child "Do NOT think about the white bear." Wait another 30 seconds, then ask the child to tell you how much he or she thought about the white bear after you asked him or her to stop. Next, introduce a distracting activity, such as a preferred game. Spend a few minutes engaged in this distracting activity, and then ask the child again how much he or she thought about the white bear. Make the point that it's hard to just stop thinking about something—it's much easier to just distract ourselves with other thoughts.

☐	**ACTIVITY** *Rock and Candy*	As another way to illustrate this point, give the child a small rock. Tell the child to put the rock in his or her shoe. Have the child stand up, then ask what the experience is like for him or her. Ask about both feelings and thoughts (e.g., irritation, thoughts about discomfort, thoughts about how mean the therapist is, etc.) and get a *Feelings Thermometer* rating from the child. Then give the child a piece of candy and tell the child to put the candy in his or her mouth and describe *that* experience. Ask the child how he or she feels and what she or he thinks when focusing on the taste of the candy. Note that it's hard to just stop thinking about a bad experience—the rock; it's much easier to distract yourself by focusing on a good experience—in this case, the candy.
☐	**Relate Distraction to Mood**	Make explicit that it is very difficult to simply "stop thinking" about something that is bothering you—but thinking about bad things again and again can make us feel bad. Sometimes you need to do something completely different in order to get your mind off your bad mood for a little while. Elicit examples of times where the child "replayed" negative thoughts. **Example script** *When I asked you to just stop thinking about the white bear, you thought about it a lot, right? But when we played a game, you stopped thinking about it altogether! Can you think of a time when you could not get your mind off of something bad or upsetting? What do you think you could have done to distract yourself?*
☐	**Continue Worksheet**	Work with the child to identify distracting activities the child can use to stop ruminative-depressive thoughts. The activities should be realistic and rewarding for the child, acceptable to parents, and likely to work well in disrupting the child's ruminative thoughts.
☐ ⬆	**PRACTICE ASSIGNMENT** *TLC Worksheet*	For the practice assignment, the child should use page 4 of the *Coping Through TLC* worksheet to write down something that happened that made him or her feel bad, and complete a *Feelings Thermometer* to show how he or she felt when the bad thing happened. Next, the child should write down one of the three **TLC** skills he or she can use to feel better, and try that skill out, then re-rate his or her mood.

Leave 'Em Laughing

Close with some really funny or enjoyable activity—something that will leave the child either laughing or feeling great. Possibilities: America's Funniest Home Videos, tell some funny jokes, play a board game that the child really loves.

Share with Parent (if possible)

At the end of the session, if a parent is available, it can be helpful to brief him or her on the materials covered.

☐	**Consider Privacy**	Before bringing the parent into the room, it is important to ask the child if there is anything that he or she told you today that he or she does not want you to tell the parent. Be sure to honor the child's confidentiality within the appropriate limits of safety.

☐ **Review Concepts**	Have the child explain to the parent what concepts he or she has learned in the session. You can add information as necessary.
☐ **Give Parent Handout**	In addition, give the parent the ***Using TLC When Bad Things Happen*** parent handout. The main goal of this part of the session is to familiarize the parent with the concepts (and provide a good review for the child), so the parent can assist the child in using his or her new coping skills.

Helpful Tips

- The take-home message for the child in discussing the **TLC** skills is that he or she can cope with situations that can't be changed, not only by changing his or her thoughts but also by using the three skills taught in this session: seeking social support, identifying something good caused by a bad situation, and ending rumination by using distraction.

- When helping the child identify people on the first page of the worksheet, try to make sure that at least two of the people on the child's list are adults. A close relationship with a caring adult is a predictor of positive outcomes for youth facing a variety of risk conditions; thus, your effort to help the child identify such persons may be of lasting value.

- If the child enters the session in a bad mood, or seems tired, lethargic, or uninterested, this is an opportunity to introduce a **mood booster**: take a brief mood rating, spend a few minutes engaging in a pleasant activity, then re-rate the mood. If it is successful, be sure to highlight for the child that what you do changes how you feel.

- Check in on goals: Does the child feel that he or she is making progress? How does the material you covered today relate to the goals you set together?

How's Your Style?

- Did you praise often?
- Did you review often, by asking questions?
- Did you simplify the steps as needed?
- Did your pace match that of the child or family?
- Did you stay on track?

Plans for Coping

For Child

Goals

- The child will review all the skills he or she has learned with you
- The child will identify the specific coping skills that are most effective for him or her
- The child will learn not to give up when trying to cope with problems or feel better
- The child will learn that when one skill isn't working, he or she can try another

Materials

- *Feelings Thermometer*
- *My Favorite Skills for Feeling Good* worksheet
- *Following My Plans* worksheet
- *Practicing My New Skills* worksheet (2 copies)
- *Plans for Coping* parent handout
- Pens, pencils, markers

⧗ *If time is tight: Ask the child to identify his or her three favorite coping skills and emphasize that if one skill doesn't work, it is important to try another.*

Main Steps	*Remember to start by setting an agenda together and by reviewing any practice assignments.*
☐ **Obtain Weekly Ratings**	Using the 0 to 10 scale of the *Feelings Thermometer*, obtain ratings from both the child and parent (if available).
☐ **ACTIVITY** *My Favorite Skills for Feeling Good*	Have the child identify some situations where he or she feels sad, gloomy, upset, stressed, or tired. Then encourage the child to identify as many as possible of the coping skills you have covered in previous sessions (or key phrases used to name the skills). Encourage the child and provide hints when necessary. Praise the child for remembering the skills and for all of his or her hard work in previous sessions.
	Ask the child what his or her three favorite skills are. You can help by encouraging the child and providing hints and reminders of the skills he or she liked best or used most. Complete the *My Favorite Skills for Feeling Good* worksheet while discussing the child's three favorite skills and how he or she has used these skills and can use them in the future.
☐ **Review Toolbox Concept**	Emphasize that, for each person, some of the coping strategies will work better than others. Review the toolbox metaphor with the child, explaining that each coping skill the child has learned is a tool, and different problems require different tools. Describe the child's three favorite skills as the child's best "tools" for solving problems and for coping with bad feelings.

☐	**Introduce Idea of Perseverance**	Discuss with the child the importance of not giving up when dealing with a challenging situation. Stress that it is important for the child to keep trying new solutions until he or she has succeeded.

Example script

When trying to solve problems, it is important to not give up if one skill doesn't solve the entire problem. Today, I want to talk about why it is important to keep trying your coping skills. Sometimes you may need to use 2 or 3 of the tools in your toolbox to solve a problem, or to feel better.

☐	**Explain** *Following My Plans* **Worksheet**	Review and help the child fill in the *Following My Plans* worksheet. The child's favorite skill should be written in the first box under "Try Plan A;" the second-favorite skill goes under "Try Plan B," and the third-favorite skill under "Try Plan C." Emphasize that when the child encounters difficult or challenging situations, it is important to use Plans A, B, <u>and</u> C, and keep trying, rather than giving up.

☐	**ACTIVITY** *Practicing My New Skills*	Ask the child to rehearse a situation with you in which the child acts as a therapist and you are a person with a problem. The goal is to have the child coach you through a Plan A, Plan B, and Plan C sequence.

Procedures:

1. Write the following problem under "what's making me feel bad" on one copy of the *Practicing My New Skills* worksheet: "*I got into a fight with my best friend, and I know that we won't be friends ever again. I feel terrible and don't feel like doing anything.*" Say the problem aloud to the child.
2. Write your *Feelings Thermometer* rating in the appropriate space on the worksheet.
3. The child should have you come up with a goal rating for the *Feelings Thermometer* rating you would *like to have*. Write that on the worksheet.
4. You and the child should copy the child's top three skills from the *Following My Plans* worksheet onto the *Practicing My New Skills* worksheet. These should be written under "Plan A," "Plan B," and "Plan C."
5. The child should name the first skill, explain how the skill will help you, and explain to you how to do it. If the child does not explain the skill to you, ask, "What does that mean?" or "How do I do that?"
6. You should then act out the skill (e.g., slow your breathing, do S-T-E-P-S, try a fun activity).
7. The child should ask you what your rating is after each step in the plans. Your ratings should improve but not reach the goal.

These procedures should continue until the last plan has been demonstrated. Your final rating should equal or surpass your goal rating, and you should praise the child for helping you solve your problem and improve your mood.

☐ ⟨⟩ **PRACTICE ASSIGNMENT** *Practicing My New Skills* **Worksheet**	Give the child the second copy of the *Practicing My New Skills* worksheet. Have the child identify a situation in session, write that situation at the top of the sheet, write down a rating of his or her feelings when thinking about the situation, and write down a goal rating. Then have the child write in his or her three favorite skills as Plan A, B, and C on the sheet. Provide help as needed, using the *My Favorite Skills for Feeling Good* worksheet if needed. The child should also fill in the second column "How this will help" for each plan.
	At home, the child should try out each plan—A, B, and C—and complete the column on the right side of the sheet. Walk the child through the steps to be sure that he or she understands how to do the assignment.

Leave 'Em Laughing

Close with some really funny, or enjoyable activity—something that will leave the child either laughing or feeling great. Possibilities: America's Funniest Home Videos, tell some funny jokes, play a board game that the child really loves.

Share with Parent (if possible)

At the end of the session, if a parent is available, it can be helpful to brief him or her on the materials covered.

☐ **Consider Privacy**	Before bringing the parent into the room, it is important to ask the child if there is anything that he or she told you today that he or she does not want you to tell the parent. Be sure to honor the child's confidentiality within the appropriate limits of safety.
☐ **Review Concepts**	Have the child explain to the parent what concepts he or she has learned in the session. You can add information as necessary.
	Emphasize the importance of perseverance and making plans, so that if one coping approach doesn't do the trick, the child is ready to try another approach. Explain that the parent is in a unique position to help the child apply the coping skills to real-life situations as they arise because the parent (a) knows many of the new skills his or her child has learned, (b) knows the child well, and (c) is in close touch with the child's daily life.
☐ **Give Parent Handout**	Provide the parent with the *Plans for Coping* parent handout. Be sure that the parent is familiar with the concepts so that the he or she can assist the child in knowing how to persevere in the face of challenges.

Helpful Tips

- There are lots of forms to complete for this session, so make the session fun, engaging, and interactive for the child! Be creative!
- Have fun with the role-play! As appropriate, challenge the child by saying "I don't think that is going to work!" or "Nothing can help me!" to really test the child's knowledge of the skills, and the child's willingness to be persistent. Also, exaggerate when acting out the skills—the child will love it and you'll have lots of fun.
- Remember to emphasize the concept of "Plan A, Plan B, Plan C" in any sessions you do with the child after this one and in any practice assignments after this one.

- If the child enters the session in a bad mood, or seems tired, lethargic, or uninterested, this is an opportunity to introduce a **mood booster**: take a brief mood rating, spend a few minutes engaging in a pleasant activity, then re-rate the mood. If the rating improves, be sure to highlight to the child that what you do changes how you feel.

- Check in on goals: Does the child feel that he or she is making progress? How does the material you covered today relate to the goals you set together?

How's Your Style?

- Did you praise often?
- Did you review often, by asking questions?
- Did you simplify the steps as needed?
- Did your pace match that of the child or family?
- Did you stay on track?

MATCH Protocol

Safety Planning

Goals

- The child will understand how to maintain his or her personal safety
- The child, parent, and therapist will develop a plan to ensure safety in the present and future
- The child and parent will understand and follow the safety plan

Materials

- *Fear Thermometer* and *Fear Ladder* (2 unrated copies, for anxiety/trauma), *Feelings Thermometer* (for depression), or *Behavior Rating Scale* (for disruptive behavior)
- Educative materials as needed (pamphlets, dolls, videos)

> ⧗ *If time is tight: Your main objective is to develop a plan for the child's present and future safety.*

Main Steps	Remember to start by setting an agenda together and reviewing any practice assignments.
☐ **Obtain Weekly Ratings**	If the main focus is traumatic stress or anxiety, use the 0 to 10 scale of the *Fear Thermometer* to obtain *Fear Ladder* ratings from both the child and his or her parent. If the main focus is depressed mood, use the *Feelings Thermometer* to take a rating. If the main focus is disruptive behavior, take a parent rating with the *Behavior Rating Scale*.
☐ **Minimize Self-Blame**	There is a risk that children will interpret your plan to teach safety skills as evidence of their having failed to respond appropriately to the traumatic event (e.g., "I did not do the proper things to keep myself safe; this was my fault"). To minimize this risk, start out by normalizing and validating the child's previous responses to trauma, and praise him or her for doing what he or she knew to do at the time.
☐ **Review Basic Facts and Vocabulary**	Review basic facts related to the type of trauma the child experienced (for example, statistics related to sexual abuse, natural disasters, etc.). Ensure the child has the appropriate vocabulary to discuss the trauma (for example, children who have been sexually abused may need to review anatomical names for body parts). This may require some outside research on your part to prepare to cover this material.

☐	**Teach Child to Detect Danger**	Discuss with the child how to detect actual danger cues ("true alarms") in his or her environment. Because not all danger has external cues (e.g., smelling smoke), you should also discuss what sorts of feelings we have when we are in danger. These could include physiological cues (sweating, heart racing) or affective cues (guilt, anger, worry). This may include rehearsal or role plays in which the child acts out a scenario he or she might face.
		Example script
		Let's say you believe someone in your family is angry and about to start a fight. Let's talk about how you would know that is about to happen? What clues are there, and how would you feel?
☐	**Discuss Body Ownership**	If the trauma involves sexual abuse, discuss body ownership with the child, noting that some parts of the body are private. Clarify the difference between "good touch" and "bad touch," and note that any touching that makes the child feel uncomfortable can be a sign to use the safety plan.
☐	**Develop Safety Plan**	Working together, write down steps the child can take in the future to ensure safety. For situations in which steps can be taken to minimize or appropriately confront the danger, the plan should incorporate such steps (for example, not leaving candles lit to prevent fires, learning how to operate a fire extinguisher). For situations in which the danger cannot always be addressed directly, such as those involving abuse or domestic violence, the emphasis should be placed on identifying safe places and people to whom the child can turn in order to report these events.
		The written safety plan can include: (a) identifying safe people to talk with about dangerous or uncomfortable things, (b) identifying safe places to go when something dangerous is happening, (c) calling 911, or (d) planning how to ask for help (which can even involve writing a script together). The plan should involve sequential steps, such that if the first step does not work, the child has a "back up plan."
☐	**Address Secrets**	If the nature of the trauma could involve the child being asked to keep it a secret, review the difference between "safe" and "unsafe" secrets.
		Example script
		Safe secrets are secrets that we don't keep forever, and that are fun—like planning a party or a present that you know someone will really like. Unsafe secrets are secrets that kids are asked to keep from parents and never tell anyone about. These are secrets that kids don't want to keep, and don't feel comfortable keeping. Unsafe secrets include things like someone asking you to keep "bad" touches a secret.
☐	**ACTIVITY** *Rehearse Plan*	Practice the plan together by imagining an unsafe scenario. Ask the child first to identify the signs of danger and then to name the safety plan steps that would be taken. Be sure to ask lots of questions ("What would you try next?" "What if that person didn't answer the phone?" etc.) to ensure that the child has a firm understanding of the plan and when to use it. Provide plenty of praise.

Leave 'Em Laughing

End the session on a fun note, with a game, activity, or other exercise that will leave the child feeling really good about the work you have done together today.

Share with Parents (if possible)

At the end of the session, if a parent is available, it can be helpful to brief him or her on the materials covered.

☐	**Consider Privacy**	Before bringing the parent into the room, it is important to ask the child if there is anything that he/she told you today that he/she does not want you to tell the parent. Be sure to honor the child's confidentiality within the appropriate limits of safety.
☐	**Review Concepts**	Have the child present the safety plan to the parent. Encourage the parent to suggest additions to the plan, to practice the skills at home with the child, and to alert others who may be involved (for example, neighbors or relatives).

Helpful Tips

- Depending on the family situation, a parent may be involved in the entire session, including rehearsing their responses to the child's safety plan.
- There are many excellent books and videos/DVDs available for education about personal safety. However, since children learn best via interactive discussion and role plays, make sure that these materials are integrated into more active presentation of safety skills and planning.

How's Your Style?

- Did you praise often?
- Did you review often, by asking questions?
- Did you simplify the steps as needed?
- Did your pace match that of the child or family?
- Did you stay on track?

Trauma Narrative

Goals

- The child will understand the reason for creating a story about the traumatic event
- The child will initiate or add to a written narrative about the traumatic event
- Through relaxation and repeated exposure to the narrative, the child will learn to control anxious responding to traumatic cues
- The child can find ways to challenge blaming or catastrophic thoughts related to the event
- The parent will understand the progress being made using these strategies

Materials

- *Fear Thermometer* and *Fear Ladder* (2 unrated copies, for anxiety/trauma), *Feelings Thermometer* (for depression), or *Behavior Rating Scale* (for disruptive behavior)
- *Start-and-Stop Practice Record*
- Writing materials (e.g., pen and paper, computer)

> ⏳ *If time is tight*: *Make sure the child understands the rationale and adds some new content to the trauma narrative.*

Main Steps	Remember to start by setting an agenda together and reviewing any practice assignments.
☐ **Obtain Weekly Ratings**	If the main focus is traumatic stress or anxiety, use the 0 to 10 scale of the *Fear Thermometer* to obtain *Fear Ladder* ratings from both the child and his or her parent. If the main focus is depressed mood, use the *Feelings Thermometer* to take a rating. If the main focus is disruptive behavior, take a parent rating with the *Behavior Rating Scale*.

☐	**Introduce Rationale**	If this is the first time performing this module, explain the general rationale of creating a trauma narrative. Many people find it difficult to think about or discuss their bad experiences. However, when one tries to avoiding thinking or talking about them, the memories may come back unexpectedly, and in a way that is especially vivid and upsetting. In order to develop control over these memories, it is important to discuss them, a little at a time, in order to become used to the feelings those memories generate.
		Example script
		Have you ever fallen down and scraped your knee? When you scrape your knee, sometimes dirt and germs get caught in the wound and it can get infected. That's why it is so important to clean out a cut when it happens, even though doing so can hurt a bit at first. Over time, cleaning it allows the scrape to heal, even though it might leave a little scar. If you ignore the scrape, it gets worse or doesn't heal properly. By talking about the scary thing that happened to you, a little bit each week, we can make sure that you are able to heal from this event, and over time the feelings will fade so that it doesn't feel as fresh and scary as it does right now.
☐	**Create Feeling of Safety**	Reassure the child that although you plan to write about or discuss some of the events that happened, you are there to assure their safety and comfort, and to provide support if he or she begins to feel too uncomfortable.
☐	**Introduce *Fear Thermometer* (if necessary)**	If the child has not yet been introduced to the fear thermometer, introduce it here, pointing out how it will be used to monitor the degree of fear and to help you know if things are getting too uncomfortable. If the child is already familiar with the fear thermometer, you may skip the fear thermometer activity immediately below.
☐	**ACTIVITY *Fear Thermometer***	Have the child give a rating for his or her current level of fearfulness. You may need to practice once or twice with sample anchors to make sure the child is giving accurate ratings. Ask the child what the number he/she chose means, in order to be sure he or she understands the concept. Ask the child to indicate, using the *Fear Thermometer*, how afraid he or she would be of several other situations (i.e., eating his/her favorite dessert, riding on a roller coaster, being in a strange place by him- or herself) in order to make sure that the child feels comfortable using this scale. It is particularly important that the child be able to use the full range of the scale, not just the ends.
☐	**ACTIVITY *Relaxation***	Review and practice the skills learned in the **Relaxation** module (if the child has already covered **Secret Calming** and finds that relaxation approach preferable, then review and practice that approach instead). This should take approximately 10 minutes. Use the *Fear Thermometer* or *Feelings Thermometer* to rate the child's emotional state before and after relaxing.

☐ Develop Narrative	Once the child is in a relaxed state, begin writing or adding to the narrative.
	If the child is just starting the narrative, it is often useful to begin with a non-traumatic chapter (e.g., some content about him- or herself, where he or she lives and with whom). Over the course of multiple sessions, the writing will involve the traumatic event itself. As this happens, encourage the child to describe the context surrounding the event, for example their relationship with the perpetrator, or the day before the event occurred, etc. Provide praise to the child throughout this process.
	Until the narrative is complete, do not challenge any negative or catastrophic thoughts reported by the child; simply record them and note that these may be areas to revise at a later time.
	Example script *Let's go back to the day you woke up because you smelled smoke in your house. Where were you when you woke up? What did you see around you? What did you hear/smell/feel? What did you think inside your head? What happened next? What was the worst moment?*
☐ Encourage Thoroughness	While the child is writing, encourage him or her to write all the memories, as well as the thoughts and the physical sensations that accompany them.
☐ Provide Reassurance and Elicit Coping Skills	If the child seems overwhelmed, remind him or her that these are only feelings. They are not related to something that is happening right now, but something that happened to him or her in the past. If the anxiety becomes too elevated, you may also prompt the child to use relaxation to establish control over these feelings.
☐ Develop the Final Chapter	Once the traumatic event has been described in its entirety (usually after several sessions of writing), it is useful to have an additional final section of the narrative in which the child describes the ways in which he or she has changed, or how his or her life is different now, as well as advice he or she would give to other children.
☐ Practice Reading	When the child is finished writing for the day, ask the child to read everything that he or she has written so far, from the very beginning of the narrative. If the child is hesitant, you can offer to read it aloud. If there is time, ask the child to repeat reading the narrative.
	Typically, the child will experience less emotional and physiological activity after each repetition, but if not, you can also ask the child to use his or her relaxation skills.
☐ Take Ratings	Use the *Fear Thermometer* or *Feelings Thermometer* before and after each reading to quantify the degree of anxiety within each session. If the child experiences a decrease in ratings, point this out to him or her as evidence that he or she is making progress. If using the *Fear Thermometer*, you may record ratings on the *Start-and-Stop Practice Record*.

☐ **Address Cognitions**	Once the narrative is complete (no more content being added) and has been read aloud over several sessions, determine whether the child has any lingering blaming thoughts ("it was my fault") or overestimations of recurrence ("I know it will happen again"). If so, you may introduce (or review, if covered already) the appropriate **Cognitive** module to address these beliefs (e.g., BLUE or STOP). Review specific examples of problematic thoughts in the narrative with the child, and determine whether they are accurate and helpful. Ask the child to identify the types of thoughts present (e.g., "blaming") and to provide alternatives. At this point, the narrative can also be edited to reflect the child's more accurate beliefs. **Example script** *Can you see any thoughts in this paragraph that are not accurate or helpful? What about here, where you thought, "If I had woken up earlier I would have been able to save my cat from the fire?" Please help me understand a little better. Was there a way you could control when you woke up?*
☐ **ACTIVITY** *Relaxation*	Once again, practice the skills learned in the **Relaxation** or **Secret Calming** module. Use the *Fear Thermometer* or *Feelings Thermometer* to rate the child's emotional state before and after relaxing.

Leave 'Em Laughing

End the session on a fun note, with a game, activity, or other exercise that will leave the child feeling really good about the work you have done together today.

Share with Parent (if possible)

At the end of the session, if a parent is available, it can be helpful to brief him or her on the materials covered.

☐ **Consider Privacy**	Before bringing the parent into the room, it is important to ask the child if there is anything that he or she told you today that he or she does not want you to tell the parent. Be sure to honor the child's confidentiality within the appropriate limits of safety.
☐ **Review Concepts**	For this part of the session, you will want to meet with the parent alone. With the child's permission, share what has been written in the narrative today. Prepare the parent by first discussing his or her own experience of the trauma verbally. Because this experience can often be emotional, be sure that you leave adequate time to restore the parent's composure. Discuss his or her reactions to the narrative and provide support, explaining that repetition of the narrative will help to reduce the acute feelings associated with the traumatic event. The complete narrative will be shared with the parent and the child during the final session.

Helpful Tips

- It is best if you keep the trauma narrative with the child's records in your office rather than send it home with the child each week. Among other things, doing so will safeguard the privacy of the narrative and prevent it from being lost or misplaced.

- When writing the narrative, some children may easily recall information, while other children may require gentle prompting from you. Some children may also want you to do the writing, which is allowable.

- Younger children may provide drawings to accompany the narrative, and all children should be given the opportunity to decorate or personalize their narrative if they wish.

- For children who have experienced multiple or repeated traumas, it may be more helpful to create a "timeline" or "life story" rather than focusing on specific isolated events.

How's Your Style?

- Did you praise often?
- Did you review often, by asking questions?
- Did you simplify the steps as needed?
- Did your pace match that of the child or family?
- Did you stay on track?

Engaging Parents

Goals

- You will begin to establish rapport with the parent
- The parent will outline the main challenges and goals
- The parent will understand basic information about the treatment
- The parent will identify ways to address barriers to his or her active participation
- The parent will understand the *Behavior Rating Scale*

Materials

- *Challenges and Goals Interview*
- *What Can Help* handout
- *Thinking Ahead* worksheet
- *Behavior Rating Scale*
- Materials from recent assessment (if available)
- Pens, pencils, markers

⌛ *If time is tight*: Do what you can to make sure you have another session after this one.

Main Steps	*Remember to start by setting an agenda together.*
☐ Conduct *Challenges and Goals Interview*	Administer the *Challenges and Goals Interview*, writing down those details that you think will be helpful for planning future work together. Convey an attitude of empathy, support, and interest. You may already have some of this information from a prior assessment, so focus on trying to get new information and establishing priorities. You may need to guide the parent to organize the challenges into a list or to identify the greatest priorities if there are too many issues. If the parent dwells on any one problem at length, prompt him or her that you have noted that problem and would like to see if there is another to add to the list. When identifying goals, try to establish goals related to each of the challenges listed, and ensure that intermediate steps are identified for goals that might be difficult.
☐ Review and Clarify	Repeat back to the parent what appear to be the child's main problems or challenges and your understanding of the parent's goals for seeking services. Ask the parent to let you know which parts of your understanding seem right and which parts seem wrong.

☐	**Validate the Parent**	Emphasize to the parent that he or she provides the perspective of a caring adult who knows the child much better than you ever will. Remind the parent of his or her invaluable role in the treatment process and the unique perspective he or she can bring. Acknowledge that the parent is the "true expert" on his or her child and that you therefore really depend on what he or she has to say.
☐	**Check in about Prior Experiences**	Check in with the parent about past experiences in treatment. Ask the parent what has worked well for his or her family in the past as well as what strategies were less helpful. Encourage the parent to express any general concerns he or she has about agency procedures or the therapy process. Try to become aware of parental perceptions that may favorably or unfavorably impact the course of treatment.
☐	**Manage Expectations**	Explain that during this treatment program you will not be "talking it out" with the child and you will not be "searching for the root of the child's behavior problems." In fact, in most cases, you will not even spend the majority of your time meeting with the child at all, because that is unlikely to provide the type of help that is needed.
☐	**Discuss What Can Work**	Point out that one approach known to be particularly helpful is to work primarily with a parent, focusing on specific skills known to be helpful in managing children's behavior. Emphasize that you will (a) work together to establish or strengthen a number of powerful skills in the parent for increasing his or her child's positive behavior, and (b) work together to figure out which specific skills work best.

Example script
One of our biggest goals in working together will be to give you a toolbox, or a set of skills to use when managing your child's behavior. We'll start by learning some new strategies or working with some that you may already know, and seeing how we can improve them. Then we will try to learn which ones work best with your child.

☐	**Describe Your Role**	Explain that your job will not be to spend a lot of time with the child, nor to be a passive listener to the parent. Instead your role will be more like a coach. Explain that a coach's job is to:

- make sure practice is aimed at specific goals (you will not ask parents to practice things that don't move them towards their goals)

- ensure that practice is not too hard or too easy (you will work to make sure that parent and child develop skills at an appropriate pace)

- maintain enthusiasm (coaches often give pep talks, and you will work to make sure that the parent stays motivated and interested, especially when times get challenging)

This is what you will do as a therapist: plan, organize, supervise, troubleshoot, and give feedback about new skills. If things get in the way of learning or using those skills, your job is to address those barriers.

☐	**Describe Parent's Role**	Explain that another important goal is for the parent to become the coach as quickly as possible. The parent will be asked to learn how to use these new tools and techniques with the child, and to learn how to fix new problems that come up. As soon as a parent can start to take over, the therapist backs away a bit, providing support only when needed. Eventually, family members will be able to use all of their new skills and strategies without help and won't need the therapist anymore. Remind the parent that all this represents an active approach to treatment, and that children always do better when parents participate actively in treatment.
☐	**Cover the** *What Can Help* **Handout**	At this point, go over the ***What Can Help*** handout together. Be sure to stop and answer questions as you go along. The parent should be given this handout to take home.
☐	**Cover the** *Thinking Ahead* **Worksheet**	Next, complete the ***Thinking Ahead*** worksheet. Your goal is to identify any potential barriers to treatment participation and to identify corresponding solutions in advance. The parent should get a copy of the completed handout to take home.
☐	**Introduce** *Behavior Rating Scale*	Introduce the parent to the ***Behavior Rating Scale***. The ***Behavior Rating Scale*** is a tool to help take a global rating of the child's behavior. Explain to the parent how the scale works (e.g., higher numbers represent better behavior), and ask the parent to use it to rate his or her child's behavior under various circumstances. Let the parent know that he or she will be asked for a rating of his or her child's behavior at the beginning of each treatment session. Ratings will be used to guide discussion and to measure how the child's behavior is changing.
☐	**Obtain a Rating**	Have the parent rate his or her child's behavior for this week. Ask the parent what the number he or she chooses means, in order to be sure he or she understands.
☐	**Address Agency Ground Rules**	Before finishing, discuss any "deal-breaker" policies if they exist in your agency (e.g., what happens if families cancel less than 24 hours in advance, no-show, etc.) so that such procedures do not come as a surprise to parents later.
☐	**Answer Questions**	Answer any questions at this time and thank the parent for his or her participation.

Leave 'Em Laughing

End the session on a positive note with the parent by perhaps talking about things that are unrelated to his or her child, or discussing an area of interest you have in common with the parent. Also, the parent might be feeling overwhelmed by the challenging tasks he or she is undertaking; it can sometimes be helpful to leave a few minutes at the end of the session for the parent to share concerns or the challenges he or she has faced with the child since the previous session. The end of each session should be used to praise the parent's efforts and to convey support and encouragement.

Share with Child (if possible)

At the end of the session, if the child is available, it can be helpful to brief him or her on the materials covered.

☐	**Review Concepts**	Explain to the child that there will be some changes in communication in the family that are meant to be helpful for everyone. You can tell the child that for the time being, you will be working with his or her parent to help everyone in the family develop better ways to communicate with one another and to solve problems that might come up at home. Use this time to answer any questions that the child might have, and to indicate that you will be checking in with him or her each week after meeting with his or her parent.

Helpful Tips

- Some parents may be surprised at, or resistant to, the idea that you will be working mainly with them, expecting instead that you would mainly talk to the child. Such parents may perceive that the focus on parents implies that they are being blamed for their child's problems. Dealing with such concerns skillfully in the first meeting can go a long way toward ensuring that parents get engaged and continue to participate in treatment. Consider the following approaches:

  o One approach is to note that overcoming conduct problems is different from overcoming other problems, such as anxiety or depression. In the case of conduct problems, experience over the past fifty years has shown that working with parents is especially effective. One reason may be that monitoring the child's conduct has to be done mostly at home and in other places where the child lives his or her everyday life—not in the therapist's office. Parents are the most important people in the child's life, and the most influential. The child might spend, at most, an hour per week with the therapist, but *many more* hours every week at home with parents. So it makes sense that most of the solution to conduct problems needs to be based at home, and with the parents.

  o Another point that can be helpful is to note that this particular child has special needs that require special steps. You might say: *Suppose, for example, that you bought a car and you found that it wouldn't start if you just turned the key in the ignition. Instead, you have to turn the key while pushing a special button on the steering wheel and wiggling the gear shift. You could insist that the car* should *start when you turn the key, and you would be right. However, the reality is that for this particular car you have to do something special to make it work right. In a similar way, different children need different procedures to help them be their best. Your child may not be just the* standard model *child who responds to standard good parenting procedures. Instead, special parenting procedures may be needed to help your child be his or her best. That's why so much of our time will be spent with just us together—working on those special procedures needed to help your child be his or her best.*

- Therapists should be careful when discussing commitment and motivation with families, so as to avoid suggesting that the family is "not interested" in the child's progress. Many families are motivated for their child to improve, but do not have much time or have limited resources. A better approach is to describe that treatment must be an important goal for the parent using the words "high priority" instead. Parents should be encouraged to inform their therapist if they are not finding enough time to practice outside of session, as well as to discuss any other difficulties they are having with treatment as such difficulties arise.

- For parents who seem resistant to committing time to therapy, ask them to consider how much time and energy they are currently spending engaged in conflict with their child, or managing the consequences of their child's misbehavior in school with peers. Let them know that this approach will take time now to save them time later.

How's Your Style?

- Did you praise often?
- Did you review often, by asking questions?
- Did you simplify the steps as needed?
- Did your pace match that of the parent?
- Did you stay on track?

Learning About Behavior

For Caregiver

Goals

- You will begin to establish rapport with the parent and enlist support in the treatment process
- The parent will understand four factors relevant to children's disruptive behavior
- The parent will identify how the factors may be relevant to their child and family
- The parent will understand the role of consequences in changing behavior

Materials

- *Behavior Rating Scale*
- *Four Factors* worksheet
- Pens, pencils

> ⧗ *If time is tight*: Help the parent understand that children's behavior has many causes, is not anyone's fault, and can be modified by addressing some of those causes.

Main Steps	Remember to start by setting an agenda together.
☐ **Obtain Weekly Ratings**	Obtain the **Behavior Rating Scale** rating from the parent.
☐ **Get Parent's Perspective**	Invite the parent to discuss *what causes* he or she believe lead to their child's misbehavior. Show great interest in what the parent says, and write down each of the parent's ideas. Keep track of these ideas for application to the four factor model later in this session.
☐ **Introduce Four Factor Model**	Thank the parent for his or her ideas. Note that the parent's ideas include a number of different causes of the child's conduct problems. Point out that this is very consistent with what lots of experts have found: Child conduct problems usually have LOTS of different causes. Note that these causes are often grouped into four categories, and that you will spend the next several minutes reviewing each of these. Introduce the *Four Factors* worksheet, and inform the parent that you would like his or her help in brainstorming examples of how those four factors might relate to his or her child's behavior.

☐ **Describe Factor 1: Children**	Review the following child characteristics as part of the first factor, using the parent's examples and ideas wherever possible:

- **Psychological Characteristics**: Explain to the parent the notion of *temperament*: the basic building blocks of the child's personality, which includes activity level, attention span, irritability, ease of getting along with others, response to stimulation, desire for routines, etc. Almost like eye color, these aspects of a child appear to be inborn to a great extent, and they are usually noticeable before the child's first birthday. Some of these temperamental features can be quite positive—a cheerful disposition, for example; but others—such as short temper—can bring children into conflict with their caregivers at a very early age. The impact of inborn temperament illustrates why parents should not blame themselves for all of the child's behavior problems.

- **Physical or Developmental Characteristics**: Give an example of how the child's physical appearance, motor coordination, strength, stamina, or skill with language and reasoning can impact how others react to him or her, whether positive or negative.

Example scripts

Imagine a child who is well-coordinated and good at games and sports. This can be a major strength, helping the child earn the respect of other kids and be accepted by them, and this could help the child get along well with others. On the other hand, imagine a child who is clumsy. This child may have more accidents than most kids, may not be good at games or sports, and may be teased or rejected by other kids. This could lead the child to argue with other kids, get angry with them, or even get into fights.

Imagine a child who is good with words. When there is conflict with other kids, or with parents, this child can solve problems calmly by talking through them. On the other hand, imagine a child who is not very good with words. When other kids tease this child, or when an argument starts, this child doesn't know what to say. So, instead of talking, this child hits, and then gets into trouble. Even at home this child may act out with bad behavior, partly because he or she is not so good at talking things over with parents.

☐ **Add to Worksheet**	Get examples from the parent about such strengths and difficulties for his or her child, and write them in the appropriate box on the *Four Factors* worksheet. Get specific examples (e.g., if the parent states that his or her child is "not accepted by his peers," ask the parent to indicate what specific child characteristics might be responsible).

☐ **Describe Factor 2: Parents**	Discuss how a parent may also have inherited temperamental characteristics, physical features, predispositions to particular emotional states, or other characteristics that can be either strengths or challenges for them as parents.

Example script

In the same way that children have different characteristics, different parents naturally have different personalities and temperaments, too. Parents' personalities and temperaments can help or hurt their ability to work effectively with difficult child behaviors. For example, some parents get frustrated quickly if they don't get a good night's sleep, whereas other parents might not have that problem. Some parents are more sensitive to shouting and loud noise, whereas others might not be. Some parents get nervous easily, whereas others always seem calm.

☐ **Add to Worksheet**	Get examples from the parent about his or her own helpful and challenging characteristics, and write these in the appropriate box on the *Four Factors* worksheet. Emphasize to the parent that the intent of this form is to make parents more aware of the "fit" between their own and their child's characteristics, and to take particular note of where conflict between the parent and their child might be made better or worse by a good or bad fit.

Example script

A child who tends to be loud and very active may not fit so well with a parent who doesn't like loud noises and prefers a calm, orderly household. Or a parent who tends to "tell it like it is" may not fit so well with a child who is very sensitive to criticism. Can you see any places in what we've talked about so far where there is not a perfect fit?

☐ **Describe Factor 3: Consequences**	Tell the parent that almost all behavior is affected by its consequences, or the events that follow that behavior. Children will do what works for them (e.g., gets them rewards, gets them out of doing things they don't like). Thus, one of the other factors to pay attention to is the consequences associated with the child's positive and negative behaviors.

Example script

You: Lots of what children do happens for a reason. Usually that reason has to do with what the child does or does not get after he or she does something. Children, like everyone else, will do things that are rewarding or get them out of things that they don't like. Sometimes those can be good behaviors, and sometimes those can be bad behaviors, but the motivation is the same.

You: To take an example, why do most people go to work?

Parent: To get paid, I guess.

You: Right, positive consequences. And why do people avoid speeding in their cars?

Parent: Maybe they don't want to get a ticket?

You: Exactly—negative consequences.

☐ Add to Worksheet	Get examples from the parent about consequences they see as associated with the child's positive and negative behaviors, and write them in the appropriate box on the **Four Factors** worksheet.
☐ **Discuss Conflict Cycles**	Point out how certain patterns are especially common among children who have behavioral difficulties. One example is a child not following through on a request from the parent. Discuss this example and have the parent come up with a real example from his or her experience.

Example script

Let's walk through an example. Suppose a mother asks her daughter to clean her room, and the daughter says no. That might lead the mother to ask again or even scold. That can build into shouting that ends with the mother giving up. In that way, the daughter gets out of the job she was trying to avoid (cleaning up). The mother is rewarded, too, because she probably feels better when the shouting stops, even though her daughter's room isn't clean. So the daughter learned an effective way of getting out of the chore, and because both the mother and daughter got something out of that pattern, it is even more likely to repeat itself the next time a request is made.

Point out how such patterns are even more common when one takes into consideration the child and parent characteristics already discussed (factors 1 and 2). When child and parent characteristics don't match up well, conflict cycles are more likely.

☐ **Connect to Program**	Point out how understanding these patterns of behaviors and consequences will be a major focus of this program, because much of what will be learned is how to break unwanted patterns by changing some of the consequences for both good and bad behavior.
☐ **Describe Factor 4: Life Events**	Point out that all families have events or experiences that can make matters better or worse at any given time. A child might start going to a new school he likes better than his old one. A parent might lose a job. A favorite relative might come to visit. Mom and dad might be fighting.
	Point out that negative or stressful events can get in the way of effective parenting and lead to more of the unwanted patterns and situations discussed so far.

Example script

Try to think of a time when you're under a lot of stress, from work or from family issues or just a build-up of daily hassles. What happens to the way you manage your child's behavior during those times? Do you become more consistent or less consistent? Are you really paying close attention to your child's behavior and following through on what you say during these times, or does it seem like your mind is elsewhere? What do you think happens to your child's success rate at getting out of chores and other things you ask him to do?

☐ Add to Worksheet	Get examples from the parent about life events that are positive and those that are challenging for the child and family, and write them in the appropriate box on the **Four Factors** worksheet.

☐	**Summarize Four Factor Model**	Summarize the factors that contribute to child behavior that you have reviewed thus far. Using the worksheet as a visual guide, explain how these factors can influence each other and can sometimes lead to very difficult challenges for the child and family.

Example script

All of the factors we've discussed so far today can affect each other and interact with each other, sometimes making things even more difficult at home. For example, if you were to become sick, it could create a strain on the family's financial situation, which could lead to fights between you and your spouse about money, which could lead your child to become upset and start misbehaving more. Basically, all of these factors are connected to each other, and an event in one area can affect things in many other areas as well.

☐	**Describe Goals of Treatment Program**	Explain that one goal of this treatment program is to try to identify and change the bad interactions among child, parent, situations, and life events wherever possible in an effort to decrease the behavior problems of the child.

During treatment, you will be showing the parent how to do three things:

- to recognize his or her own "risk" factors, change these factors when possible, or try to prevent these factors from interfering with his or her effective parenting of the child
- to recognize certain "risk" factors in the child, attempt to change these factors when possible, and to accept those factors that cannot be changed and find ways to cope with such factors
- to change the consequences the child experiences for some of his or her behaviors, to make it more rewarding for the child to show good behavior and less rewarding for the child to show negative behavior

☐	**Reinforce Participation**	Remind the parent how critical his or her participation is in the success of this program. Emphasize that no matter how effective these techniques have been shown to be with other parents, they will not help in this case unless the methods are used. Stress to the parent that you cannot do these techniques for him or her. They must be practiced in earnest if they are to change the child's behavior. Also, revisit what a unique and powerful influence the parent has on his or her family. Sometimes, parents can feel helpless and powerless when faced with a chronically oppositional child. It is important to reinforce to such parents, letting them know you intend to empower them and support them in their role as a parent.

☐ 🏠 **PRACTICE ASSIGNMENT** *Childproofing*	Ask the parent to childproof his or her home if he or she has not already done so. Oppositional children are more likely to damage property and valuables and more likely to create accidents for others than are children without behavioral challenges. Encourage the parent to review each room in his or her home for potentially harmful objects or substances (e.g., heavy or sharp items, detergents), for valuable property that could be accidentally damaged, or for items that the parent wishes to protect that are now within easy reach.
☐ **Answer Questions**	Answer any questions at this time and thank the parent for his or her participation.

Leave 'Em Laughing

End the session on a positive note with the parent by perhaps talking about things that are unrelated to his or her child, or discussing an area of interest you have in common with the parent. Also, the parent might be feeling overwhelmed by the challenging tasks he or she is undertaking; it can sometimes be helpful to leave a few minutes at the end of the session for the parent to share concerns or the challenges he or she has faced with the child since the previous session. The end of each session should be used to praise the parent's efforts and to convey support and encouragement.

Share with Child (if possible)

At the end of the session, if the child is available, it can be helpful to brief him or her on the materials covered.

☐ **Review Concepts**	Explain that you spent this session talking about patterns at home and that you will be working with the parent to see how to change some of these patterns to make things go more smoothly. Use this time to answer any questions that the child might have, and to indicate that you will be checking in with him or her each week after meeting with his or her parent.

Helpful Tips

- It is important to balance your emphasis on problems by also highlighting the strengths of the child and family. Talking at length about child and family problems can be difficult or embarrassing; the parent needs to know that you recognize and appreciate his or her positive qualities and those of the child and family.

- In some cases, the person in the parental role may not be the child's biological parent. The caregiver may be an adoptive or foster parent, or a kinship care provider. Whoever the caregiver is, it is important to identify his or her own strengths and challenges in the parenting role.

- A significant risk in this session is that the tone can become too didactic, with the therapist "teaching the parent about the four factors that lead to child problems." Try to avoid this risk. Before even mentioning the four factors, you will seek the *parent's* ideas about what causes are responsible for the child's problem behavior. Throughout the remainder of the session, you will seek to connect the *parent's* ideas to the four factors and to all of the concepts you introduce. The tone of the session should convey that the parent is the true expert on this particular child, that you respect the parent's ideas, and that you are seeking to learn about the child and family from the parent.

How's Your Style?

- Did you praise often?
- Did you review often, by asking questions?
- Did you simplify the steps as needed?
- Did your pace match that of the parent?
- Did you stay on track?

One-on-One Time

Goals

- The parent will understand how the style of his or her interactions with the child greatly affects the child's motivation to work for him or her
- The parent will establish a more positive interaction pattern with the child through regular "one-on-one time"

Materials

- *Fear Thermometer* and *Fear Ladder* (2 unrated copies for anxiety/trauma), *Feelings Thermometer* (for depression), or *Behavior Rating Scale* (for disruptive behavior)
- Blank sheet of paper for the best supervisor-worst supervisor activity
- *One-on-One Time* handout
- *Parent Observation Record*
- Pens, pencils

> ⧗ *If time is tight*: Go over the handout on how to attend to and monitor the child's behavior.

Main Steps	Remember to start by setting an agenda together and reviewing any practice assignments.
☐ **Obtain Weekly Ratings**	If the main focus is traumatic stress or anxiety, use the 0 to 10 scale of the *Fear Thermometer* to obtain *Fear Ladder* ratings from both the child and his or her parent. If the main focus is depressed mood, use the *Feelings Thermometer* to take a rating. If the main focus is disruptive behavior, take a parent rating with the *Behavior Rating Scale*.
☐ **Discuss Attention**	Ask the parent whether he or she believes receiving attention from others can have an impact on someone's behavior. Continue this line of discussion by asking the parent to think about how the quality of the attention we receive from others, even as adults, affects our desire to work with them.

☐	**ACTIVITY** *Best Supervisor/ Worst Supervisor*	Ask the parent to put aside thoughts about his or her child for a moment and instead concentrate on someone really awful for whom he or she has worked in the past. This person could be a supervisor, a team leader, a coach, or a teacher. Ask the parent to describe the characteristics or behavior of that person that led to the parent's negative feelings about him or her.
		Draw a line down the center of a blank page. At the top of the left-hand column, ask the parent to write "Worst Supervisor" (or teacher, coach, etc.) and to then list at least five characteristics of the worst person for whom he or she has worked. Ask the parent to be specific about the feelings he or she had toward this person. Then ask the parent to write "Best Supervisor" (or teacher, coach, etc.) at the top of the right-hand column and list at least five things about that person.
☐	**Debrief after Activity**	At the conclusion of the activity, ask the parent which one of these two people he or she would be more likely to work hard for and why. Discuss how our motivation to work hard for someone can be affected by how we feel about that person.
		Ask the parent which of the two columns is more relevant to the types of interactions that are going on now with his or her child. Ask if the parent can see how increasing the "best supervisor" qualities might help to motivate the child to be more cooperative and to meet parental expectations.
☐	**State Goal One: Improving Attention**	Indicate to the parent that the first goal for this week is to improve the quality of parental attention given to the child. The parent will learn ways to make attention much more powerful and rewarding by following just a few special rules.
		Acknowledge that simply providing positive attention may not be sufficient to change the behavioral difficulties the parent currently has with his or her child, but indicate that this skill can make some of the other parenting skills work better.
☐	**State Goal Two: Build a Positive History**	Explain that the second goal of this module is to improve the interactions occurring between the parent and child through the use of regular periods of positive interaction called "one-on-one time." Building (or rebuilding) a history of these positive interactions is important: the parent can think about "banking" these positive exchanges now to help with the challenging times that may arise later (i.e., "cashing in" on the positive relationship). Building a positive history with the child is like building up a bank account, but instead of money it is a strong parent-child relationship that is building up.
☐	**Cover** *One-on-One Time* **Handout**	Provide the parent with the *One-on-One Time* handout. Explain that the handout reviews the new methods of paying attention to child behaviors that you will be going over together today. Go over each of the points in detail, and make sure you answer questions along the way.

☐	**Discuss How to Start**	If the one-on-one time is set for a standard time each day (e.g., after school, after dinner), the parent should say to the child at that time "This is our one-on-one time. What would you like to do together?" Indicate to the parent that the child should be able to choose the activity, within reason. Suggest that almost any activity is fine, so long as it does not involve watching television or playing video games.
		If the one-on-one time is not scheduled for a particular time each day, the parent should simply approach the child while he or she is playing alone and ask to join in.
☐	**Emphasize How to Narrate**	Point out to the parent that the main way to interact involves narrating what he or she sees the child doing, to demonstrate to the child that the parent finds his or her play interesting. With younger children (under age 10), the parent's commentary should be especially exciting and action-oriented.

> **Example script**
>
> *One way to understand how this works is to imagine that you are a sportscaster describing a game. Your description of the child's behavior should be interesting, detailed, and generally a running, uncritical commentary on what you are watching happen. Use a tone of voice that is interested and excited, as this style of speaking can be highly rewarding to children.*

☐	**Manage Expectations**	Warn the parent that although this technique sounds easy, it usually requires quite a bit of practice. Assure the parent that people often make mistakes during one-on-one time by giving too many instructions, asking too many questions, or not providing enough positive feedback or attention. Some parents find they don't know what to say during one-on-one time. Remind the parent that this is a skill that will improve with practice, and they should not expect instant success.
		Also acknowledge that one-on-one time will not miraculously cure all of the child's problems. However, the parent can expect the child to come to view the parent as a more rewarding person to be around. Many families report at least a slight improvement in their relationship with their child after only one week. Suggest to the parent that the one-on-one time should become a part of their normal household routine for an indefinite period of time.

☐	**Deal with Concerns**	Provide the parent with time to discuss any of their concerns about or reactions to one-on-one time.

If the parent expresses concern that one-on-one time will set up the expectation that the parent will always be unconditionally positive, there are several ways that such concerns can be addressed:

- You can point out that many thousands of families have used these same techniques with their children, and you have not yet heard of this becoming a problem.

- Also remind the parent that most people expect a certain amount of appreciation from their employers, spouse, and children. Explain that the child desires attention in much the same way the parent does.

Example script

Few people like to continue making an effort at something if they feel like their work isn't being appreciated. Think of how many relationships break up because one partner thinks he or she is being "taken for granted." When people provide this reason for the break up of a relationship, they usually mean that they felt their contributions to the relationship were unappreciated.

☐	**Address Time Management**	Some parents will indicate that they are just too busy to spend time playing with their child. Assure the parent that you appreciate that they have many demands on their time, but emphasize that tremendous gains can result from a small investment of 15 minutes each day. Remind them that this 15 minutes might soon result in getting back much more time in a few weeks, as they will be less occupied with responding to their child's negative behavior throughout the day. Also remind the parent that at the beginning of treatment they agreed that addressing their child's concerns was a "high priority" for them. If necessary, discuss with the parent any factors that might have changed since that time and work with the parent to address and problem-solve the limitations on their time. Be careful not to shame or guilt-trip parents here. Problem solve with them in a supportive way.
☐	**ACTIVITY** *Practice One-on-One Time*	After reviewing the steps involved in one-on-one time, engage the parent in a role-play in which you act as the child. Set up a situation in which you are involved in a play activity and the parent joins in for one-on-one time together. Pay close attention to the parent's use of narration, his or her use of comments rather than questions, instructions, or criticism, and his or her use of encouragement and praise. The role-play should last at least 5 minutes to give the parent a sufficient amount of experience with attending to the child in a nondirective manner.

Debrief after Activity	After the role-play has been concluded, discuss the parent's thoughts about his or her performance. Provide the parent with specific feedback about his or her use of narration, avoidance of questions and instructions, and use of praise and encouragement. Make specific suggestions with respect to how the parent can improve his or her attending skills, and remind the parent that most parents find the attending skills much more difficult to use in practice than they thought they would. Practice again until the parent feels comfortable.
☐ ⌂ **PRACTICE ASSIGNMENT** *One-on-One Time*	Explain to the parent that during the coming week he or she is to practice one-on-one time on a daily basis. Discuss with the parent how he or she plans to implement daily one-on-one time at home during the coming week.
	Pick an activity that is likely to go well. You want the parent and child to experience success with this practice, so start with something the child can already do without difficulty or redirection if possible.
	Ask the parent to use the **Parent Observation Record** to indicate what he or she did during each day's one-on-one time and how well it worked. The parent might also wish to note specific problems encountered with one-on-one time so that these concerns can be addressed with you later.

Leave 'Em Laughing

End the session on a positive note with the parent by perhaps talking about things that are unrelated to his or her child, or discussing an area of interest you have in common with the parent. Also, the parent might be feeling overwhelmed by the challenging tasks he or she is undertaking; it can sometimes be helpful to leave a few minutes at the end of the session for the parent to share concerns or the challenges he or she has faced with the child since the previous session. The end of each session should be used to praise the parent's efforts and to convey support and encouragement.

Share with Child (if possible)

At the end of the session, if the child is available, it can be helpful to brief him or her on the materials covered.

☐ **Review Concepts**	Explain to the child that this week his or her parent is going to be spending more time playing or spending time with the child on an activity that the child chooses. Ask the child if he or she has any questions about the new way that his or her parent will be interacting with him or her at home.

☐ **ACTIVITY** *One-on-One Time* *with Child*	Provide the child with an activity or some toys that he or she finds enjoyable and ask him or her to play so that the parent can observe his or her activities. Ask the parent to announce to the child that he or she will play with the child for a while. While the parent and child are playing, pay close attention to the parent's use of narration, use of comments rather than questions or instructions, and use of encouragement and praise. The role-play should last at least 5 minutes to give the parent a sufficient amount of experience with attending to the child in a nondirective manner. After the role-play has been concluded, excuse the child from the room, and discuss the parent's thoughts about his or her performance. Give lots of praise for any success! Provide the parent with specific feedback about his or her use of the narration, avoidance of questions and instructions, and use of praise and encouragement. Make specific suggestions about how the parent can improve his or her attending skills, and provide support and reassurance.

Helpful Tips

- Some parents will indicate that one-on-one time does not seem directed towards any of the problems they originally came to treatment to address. Remind the parent about the job supervisor example at the beginning of the session and reiterate the need for the parent to teach his or her children to respond to and enjoy their attention, which will later be used as a major strategy for behavior change. This is really training for the child that helps him or her begin to enjoy and thus respond more to parental attention.
- When discussing choosing a time to play with the child each day be sure to adapt your instructions to the age of the child. For example, if the child is 9 or older, the parent need not select a standard time each day to spend with the child, but may instead find a convenient time each day to join the child in whatever activity he or she is already enjoying.
- When teaching the parent to narrate his or her child's play, suggest that this running commentary works best with younger children, and the frequency of comments should be reduced for older children. The parent should exercise his or her judgment as to how much narration to employ with the child. The important point to convey to the parent is that he or she should be spending time with his or her child without criticizing, directing, or controlling the child's behavior. The parent should instead watch and appreciate what the child does.
- Remind the parent that during one-on-one time there is virtually nothing that must be taught to the child that cannot be postponed for another time. Even if the child is not playing up to the standards expected by the parent, the parent should avoid taking charge of the child's play and trying to teach the child alternative ways of playing. It might seem like the child is not learning, but if the parent is attending properly, there is lots of really important learning going on.
- If two parents are working on this skill with their child, they can take turns playing with the child. If there are other siblings present in the home, one parent can take the siblings to another room for activities while the second has one-on-one time with the child. After 5 to 10 minutes, the parents can switch roles, giving each partner a chance to practice with the child.
- If the child chooses a competitive game to play during one-on-one time, the parent should allow the child to invent new rules to the game or even "cheat" without reprimanding the child during the playtime. The goal of the playtime is not to learn how to play games properly, but to practice giving attention to the child.

How's Your Style?

- Did you praise often?

- Did you review often, by asking questions?
- Did you simplify the steps as needed?
- Did your pace match that of the parent?
- Did you stay on track?

Praise

Goals

- The parent will understand how to provide appropriate praise for his or her child's positive behavior
- The parent will understand how to reward independent play with appropriate attention

Materials

- *Fear Thermometer* and *Fear Ladder* (2 unrated copies for anxiety/trauma), *Feelings Thermometer* (for depression), or *Behavior Rating Scale* (for disruptive behavior)
- A book or magazine and toys or puzzles for the role-plays
- *Parent Observation Record*
- *Praise* handout

> ⧗ *If time is tight: Teach the parent to "catch his or her child being good" and to respond with attention, appreciation, and labeled praise.*

Main Steps	Remember to start by setting an agenda together and reviewing any practice assignments.
☐ **Obtain Weekly Ratings**	If the main focus is traumatic stress or anxiety, use the 0 to 10 scale of the *Fear Thermometer* to obtain *Fear Ladder* ratings from both the child and his or her parent. If the main focus is depressed mood, use the *Feelings Thermometer* to take a rating. If the main focus is disruptive behavior, take a parent rating with the *Behavior Rating Scale*.
☐ **Introduce Praise**	Introduce the idea that a child's rate of positive behavior can be increased by the type of parental attention that follows that behavior. Point out how praise can be used as a tool to increase behaviors that are most desired by the parent.
☐ **Discuss Attention as a Motivator**	Discuss the specific kinds of disruptive behavior often seen in the child, asking the parent specifically about his or her beliefs about why this type of behavior persists. Many parents will indicate, correctly, that their child engages in these disruptive behaviors in an effort to gain attention from the parent. Highlight that, although the disruptive behavior is a problem, the fact that the child is motivated by parental attention is a very good sign. That means attention can be used as a powerful tool to promote positive behaviors as well.
☐ **Discuss Praise for Follow-Through**	Point out that one type of behavior to praise involves the child's following through on a request or instruction. For children who do not engage in many positive behaviors and do not spontaneously do chores or pitch in, this type of praise will be more common, at least at first. The point is to increase the rate of follow-through in such children by providing positive attention when it happens.

☐	**Cover What Makes Praise Better**	There are several aspects of praise that make it more effective. Review these with the parent.

There are several aspects of praise that make it more effective. Review these with the parent.

- Follow through has to be noticed. Thus, when a parent makes a request, he or she should stay in the area and pay close attention to whether or not the follow through occurs. Parents should not issue instructions and then go on to something else.
- Praise works best when it comes quickly. Thus, the parent should praise at the first sign of follow through.
- Praise works better if it is "labeled," meaning that it names the specific behavior being rewarded.

Example script

I really like it when you pick up your clothes so neatly.

I really appreciate your coming inside so quickly when I called you.

☐ **ACTIVITY**
Praising Follow-Through

Engage the parent in a role-play in which you act as the child. Have the parent think of a simple instruction to issue (e.g., "Please pick up your clothes now") and then praise you for obeying. Observe the parent's behavior during this exercise to make sure he or she watches you perform the behavior, narrates what you are doing, and praises your follow-through. Make sure that the praise is "labeled," or specific to your actions. Provide the parent with feedback on his or her use of praise after the role-play is over.

☐ **Discuss Praise for Good Behavior That Happens by Itself**

Point out that another time to praise is when a child does something positive (e.g., performs a chore, helps a sibling) *without having been told or asked to do so.* This type of praise is especially important if this is a new behavior for the child. Point out that the same aspects of praise are important here: the behavior must be noticed, it must be praised quickly, and the praise should be "labeled."

☐ **Highlight Natural Patterns of Attention**

Ask the parent whether the child gets more attention when he or she is behaving well or behaving poorly. The parent should realize that bad behaviors naturally attract more attention. The idea is to reverse this pattern and to try to start noticing good behaviors when they happen.

Example script

Have you ever had to interrupt your phone conversation to correct, reprimand, or discipline your child for being disruptive? Of course! Most parents have. But have you ever interrupted your phone conversation to praise or attend to your child for <u>not</u> disrupting the call but instead playing quietly nearby?

Few parents will indicate that they have actively taken time out of an activity to praise their child for good behavior. The point is that if children want to receive parental attention, they are often more successful in getting it by being disruptive, particularly if the parent is paying attention to someone else. Suggest to the parent that if the situation were reversed, such that parental attention were given for positive behavior, the child would increase his or her independent play.

☐	**Focus on Independent Play**	Point out how, like follow-through, independent play is an especially important behavior. Suggest to the parent that in order to decrease the extent to which the child disrupts him or her to get attention, the parent first needs to start attending to the child's independent play very frequently. Tell the parent that the frequency of this attention can be gradually reduced as the child spends longer periods of time without disrupting the parent when the parent is engaged in other activities. Praise for independent play has several steps: • The parent should assign the child some desirable activity to perform while the parent is occupied. • Praise should be issued about once every minute at first. Over time, these intervals can be lengthened. The instruction to stay in the desirable activity can be repeated as well. • The parent should think of these as "training periods" during which the main purpose is not for the parent to cook a meal or read a magazine, but to teach the child how to play independently.
☐	**ACTIVITY Praising Independent Play**	Engage in a role-play exercise with the parent. Instruct the parent to issue an instruction to you (the child) to play independently while he or she (the parent) reads a magazine. When role-playing this technique with the parent, pay close attention to the frequency with which the parent provides praise and the type of praise given. Provide the parent with feedback on his or her use of the technique following the role-play.
☐	**Debrief after Activity**	Discuss the parent's reaction to using this technique in the role-play situation. Suggest to the parent that many parents abide by the philosophy of "let sleeping dogs lie." Essentially, many parents think that it is best to not pay attention to their child when he or she is behaving quietly and appropriately, for fear that the parent's attention will only spark new occurrences of undesirable behavior. In fact, the opposite is true: paying attention to, and encouraging the child's independent play from time to time will make independent play more rewarding to the child and more likely to continue.

☐ **Discuss Concerns**	Review common concerns that parents may have. These include:	

- Some parents feel that their attention will trigger new episodes of negative behavior. For one thing, the child likely knows that if he or she continues to play appropriately, he or she will lose the parent's attention because that's what's happened in the past. If the parent can commit to regular praise using the steps above, over time this should no longer be a problem.
- Some parents also complain that they are not able to finish their own activities if they must stop frequently to attend to the child's independent play. Assure the parent that these interruptions will only be a problem at the beginning of the process. Over time, it is quite possible for a child to learn to play independently for increasingly longer periods of time between praise. Eventually, the child will be able to play alone for the entire time that the parent is involved in his or her own task and will no longer require such frequent reinforcement for playing quietly and independently.

☐ ⌂ **PRACTICE ASSIGNMENT**
Praise at Home

Review the practice assignment for the coming week with the parent. Explain to the parent that before you meet again he or she is to choose one or two occasions when the child often disrupts his or her activities and to practice his or her attending and praise skills at those times. Suggest to the parent that it is often useful to concentrate initially on situations at home. Parents may also wish to use talking on the telephone for practicing this method. If the parent chooses this activity for practicing giving praise, suggest that he or she arrange for another caregiver or friend to call daily for the sole purpose of practicing this procedure. This allows the parent to interrupt the call frequently to appropriately attend to and praise the child's independent play without being too disruptive to the other caller. Ask the parent to record what happened on a *Parent Observation Record*. Provide the parent with a copy of the *Praise* handout.

Leave 'Em Laughing

End the session on a positive note with the parent by perhaps talking about things that are unrelated to his or her child, or discussing an area of interest you have in common with the parent. Also, the parent might be feeling overwhelmed by the challenging tasks he or she is undertaking; it can sometimes be helpful to leave a few minutes at the end of the session for the parent to share concerns or the challenges he or she has faced with the child since the previous session. The end of each session should be used to praise the parent's efforts and to convey support and encouragement.

Share with Child (if possible)

At the end of the session, if the child is available, it can be helpful to brief him or her on the materials covered.

☐	**Review Concepts**	If the child has come to the session with the parent, bring the child into the session and explain to the child that there will be some changes in communication in the family that are meant to be helpful for everyone. You can tell the child that for the next week, his or her parent will be paying more attention to the child when he or she is playing quietly and independently and not disrupting the parent. Ask the child if he or she has any questions about the new way that his or her parent will be responding to his or her behavior at home.
☐	**ACTIVITY** *Praising Independent Play*	Provide the parent with a book or magazine to read. Make sure that there is an activity available in which the child can engage independently and that he or she finds enjoyable (e.g., drawing, reading, playing with a game or puzzle). Instruct the parent to issue an instruction to the child to play independently while he or she reads a magazine or book.
		Pay close attention to the frequency with which the parent provides praise and the type of praise given. Make sure that the parent expresses appreciation of the child's play activities and that the praise provided is specific to the child's actions. After the activity, excuse the child briefly, and provide the parent with feedback on his or her use of the technique.

Helpful Tips

- For children who are doing well with independent play, this module can be presented in brief form and combined with another skill (e.g., Active Ignoring) in the same session.
- For parents who may be reluctant to praise children just for doing "normal things," it can be helpful to use the analogy of work for the parents: *Imagine if you received a paycheck only during a workweek in which you did something extraordinary. People receive a paycheck for doing the basic requirements of their job. For children, praise is the currency, so it is important to praise them just for having regular, appropriate behavior (like buckling their seatbelts, or sitting straight at the dinner table) as well as for exceptional behavior.*

How's Your Style?

- Did you praise often?
- Did you review often, by asking questions?
- Did you simplify the steps as needed?
- Did your pace match that of the parent?
- Did you stay on track?

Active Ignoring

Goals

- The parent will be aware of the ways in which unwanted behaviors are sometimes rewarded through attention
- The parent will learn how to remove attention for mild inappropriate behaviors (e.g., complaining, whining, reassurance seeking), while increasing attention for more appropriate alternatives
- The parent will feel comfortable about using the new skill
- The parent will understand the concept of an extinction burst and will know to look for it

Materials

- *Fear Thermometer* and *Fear Ladder* (2 unrated copies for anxiety/trauma), *Feelings Thermometer* (for depression), or *Behavior Rating Scale* (for disruptive behavior)
- *Active Ignoring* handout
- *Parent Observation Record*
- *Magazine or book for role play*

> ⧗ *If time is tight: Illustrate the link between parental attention and child behavior and demonstrate how to decrease the child's display of negative behaviors by removing attention and rewarding alternative behaviors.*

Main Steps	Remember to start by setting an agenda together and reviewing any practice assignments.
☐ **Obtain Weekly Ratings**	If the main focus is traumatic stress or anxiety, use the 0 to 10 scale of the **Fear Thermometer** to obtain **Fear Ladder** ratings from both the child and his or her parent. If the main focus is depressed mood, use the **Feelings Thermometer** to take a rating. If the main focus is disruptive behavior, take a parent rating with the **Behavior Rating Scale**.
☐ **Review the Importance of Consequences**	If you have not already done so, introduce to the parent the idea that behavior is strengthened or weakened by its consequences (that is, what comes after the behavior). Explain that regardless of what a child is learning to do, his or her skills will be strengthened or weakened by the events that follow them.

☐	**Review the Importance of Reinforcement**	If you have not already done so, briefly discuss the idea of *reinforcement*. In order for a behavior to increase in strength, that behavior must be reinforced, or rewarded, after it occurs. Also, the reinforcement cannot come at other times, only when the behavior occurs. Explain that if a child is reinforced regardless of whether he or she has performed the behavior, the reinforcement will have no effect on the future performance of the behavior. However, if a child is reinforced if and only if the behavior is performed, the behavior will be more likely to occur again. Discuss the ways in which behaviors are increased in frequency and intensity by reinforcing them, either with tangible rewards or with attention from others.

Example script

If you cook a new recipe and you like how it tastes, you are likely to cook that meal again, because it is rewarding.

If you do a favor for someone and she thanks you or gives you a gift, you are more likely to do another favor for her later.

☐	**Discuss Removal of Reinforcement**	If you have not already done so, point out to the parent that just as behaviors can be made to occur more often by the consequences that follow them, behaviors can also be lessened in strength or frequency by ignoring them. If a child continues to engage in a behavior, but receives no reinforcement or attention for this behavior, the behavior will begin to happen less often.

☐	**Review Example Problems**	Discuss some examples of what usually happens when whining or complaining occurs. Be sure to point out how such behaviors are often rewarding for the child. Make clear how the behavior is related to the consequences.

Example script

You: What happens when your child complains about cleaning his room?

Parent: We argue. I try to tell him why he has to do it anyway, but he just argues.

You: So does your child end up cleaning up his room?

Parent: Not usually. Usually I just get too fed up and I do it myself and then punish him—you know, take away a toy or something.

You: So in a way, your child kind of gets his way—he does not have to clean up? And on top of that, he gets to see you feeling upset, gets you to come into his room, and even to clean up.

Parent: Uh huh. I guess he's pretty smart that way.

You: So there is kind of a reward in it for him if he keeps arguing.

Parent: There sure is.

☐	**Review Example Solutions**	Point out that the way to change this situation is not to respond. Responding can provide attention in a way that ends up being a reward.

Example

You: What would happen if you just didn't argue? If you just set rules for morning chores and enforced them?

Parent: I guess my child would probably just give up complaining about brushing his teeth eventually. Probably lose some rewards or privileges if he didn't brush his teeth in time for school.

You: But do you think the complaining would stop, if you didn't respond to it?

Parent: Probably after a while.

☐	**Review Important Steps**	Introduce the important features of "successful ignoring", and provide the *Active Ignoring* handout at this time. Remind the parent of the following:

- Do not get drawn into arguing, scolding, or even talking. Many parents feel that they have to continually re-explain to their child why they are ignoring their child during the behavior. The time to explain was before the behavior started.
- Do not express anger or interest, either verbally or in your facial expression or movements.
- Do not make eye contact with your child, and do not even glance at him or her more than briefly.
- It will help to get absorbed in some other activity (e.g., going into another room, reading a book).

☐	**Emphasize Attending to Good Behavior**	Emphasize that paying attention to good behavior is at least as important as ignoring the bad behavior. Attending and ignoring are meant to work together.

Example

You: The "active" part is the most important part of this skill. So tell me, when do we usually notice children, when they are good, or when they are bad?

Parent: It sure is easy to notice when they're bad.

You: Right. What we are going to try to do now is to notice when your child is good. As soon as you notice, you can tell him things like, "that's really nice," or you can answer his question, or smile at him. That's how you can reward the right behaviors. For kids, it can be helpful if the difference in your attention and ignoring is really striking—almost like the difference in turning on and off the light.

☐	**Deal with Concerns: Guilt**	If the parent expresses uncomfortable or guilty feelings about the idea of ignoring, clarify again that he or she is not being asked to ignore the *child*, but simply to ignore the unwanted *behavior*. The parent should provide plenty of praise and attention when the child is doing well and not performing the unwanted behavior. So the child is not really getting less attention, he or she is just getting it at different times and for different reasons.
		Remind the parent that this skill can feel very unnatural at first, because it feels natural to respond to whining and complaining, for example. Assure the parent that this skill is not harmful for his or her child. In fact, failure to use active ignoring could lead to bigger problems later.
☐	**Deal with Concerns: True Distress**	Point out that sometimes the child's behavior will be honest—even though it is reinforced by attention. For example, a complaining child may actually have a mild stomachache on the way to school. Thus, this skill is not about proving the child is "faking." Rather, the purpose is to get the child to develop a better way of coping when feeling bad. The parent will usually know whether the distress is serious enough to warrant real action, or if it is more of a routine concern that could go away on its own.
☐	**Select a Behavior**	Pick a behavior that the parent would like to work on. Make sure the behavior is something mild or attention-seeking. Good examples are whining, complaining, asking too many questions, pouting, or acting grumpy or upset.
☐	**ACTIVITY** *Practice Active Ignoring*	Engage in a role-play activity in which you act as the child. Instruct the parent to read a book or magazine and to use the techniques that you just discussed. Remind the parent that when you are misbehaving he or she should try to ignore you, and when you are good, he or she should praise or pay attention. Alternate (about every minute) between engaging in appropriate (e.g., sitting quietly) versus inappropriate behavior (e.g., complaining or reassurance seeking). If you can pick the behavior identified by the parent in the previous step, that is ideal.
☐	**Explain Extinction Burst**	Inform the parent about the idea of an "extinction burst." Use examples to express the idea that when we are used to getting rewarded and the rewards suddenly stop, we often try harder and feel frustrated before quitting. The parent needs to be aware that active ignoring may be frustrating for his or her child at first, and may cause a temporary increase in the unwanted behavior. Emphasize that a temporary increase *does not mean that the parent should give in.* On the contrary, it is usually a sign that the parent is effective at ignoring—in other words, the strategy is working. It is important to stick firmly to ignoring during extinction bursts and remind oneself that they are always time limited.

Example script

You: Have you ever pushed a button for the elevator, and it didn't come? What do you usually do then?

Parent: Oh I always push it again!

You: Right. In fact, sometimes people push it many times, or jiggle it, or even hit the button or the elevator door. That's because they are expecting a reward (the door to open) and when they don't get it, there is an "extinction burst."

☐ ⟐ PRACTICE ASSIGNMENT *Active Ignoring*	Explain to the parent that during the coming week he or she is to practice active ignoring. Remind the parent to respond to the chosen undesirable behavior with active ignoring each time it occurs, and to praise the opposite or lack of the behavior. Pick something that is likely to go well. You want the parent and child to experience success with this practice, so start with something the child can already do without difficulty or redirection if possible.
	Ask the parent to use the *Parent Observation Record* to indicate what happened during active ignoring and how the child reacted. The parent might also wish to note specific problems encountered with active ignoring so that these concerns can be addressed with you later.

Leave 'Em Laughing

End the session on a positive note with the parent by perhaps talking about things that are unrelated to his or her child, or discussing an area of interest you have in common with the parent. Also, the parent might be feeling overwhelmed by the challenging tasks he or she is undertaking; it can sometimes be helpful to leave a few minutes at the end of the session for the parent to share concerns or the challenges he or she has faced with the child since the previous session. The end of each session should be used to praise the parent's efforts and to convey support and encouragement.

Share with Child (if possible)

At the end of the session, if the child is available, it can be helpful to brief him or her on the materials covered.

☐ Review Concepts	If the child is available, meet with the child and parent together and explain to the child that there will be some changes in communication in the family that are meant to be helpful for everyone. For the time being, his or her parent is not allowed to respond to certain behaviors anymore (use the behavior that the parent has already identified with you). Ask questions to make sure the child understands.
	Note: If the child is not available, make sure the parent explains and introduces this skill to the child *before using it for the first time*. Doing so will minimize the extinction burst that often results.

Example script

Remember, if you complain and whine about going to school in the morning, Mom is not allowed to talk to you about it. Sometimes you might forget and bring it up or try to talk with her, but she is not supposed to pay any attention. These rules are going to help everybody handle things better in the morning.

☐ **ACTIVITY** *Practice Active Ignoring with Child*	Repeat the role play that you performed earlier with the parent, now with the child instead of you. Make sure that the child has an activity that he or she can engage in, such as reading, drawing, or playing with a puzzle or game. Ask the child to switch between appropriate play and mildly inappropriate behavior (i.e., whining, complaining). Remind the parent about when to pay attention and when not to pay attention.
	After the role-play has been concluded, excuse the child from the room, and discuss with the parent his or her thoughts about his or her performance. Give lots of praise for any success! Provide the parent with specific feedback about his or her ability to alternate between ignoring and attending. Make specific suggestions with respect to how the parent can improve his or her active ignoring skills, and provide support and reassurance.

Helpful Tips

- If the four-factor model has been covered, point out how attending to negative behaviors is a good example of the "situations" factor: a pattern that causes problems because the rewards are coming at the wrong time.
- If working with a child with anxiety, active ignoring is best for such behaviors as whining, crying, excessive reassurance seeking, or complaining (especially somatic complaints), coupled with praise for independent or brave behaviors.
- If you have previously covered material related to rewards, you can shorten your review of reinforcement in the beginning of this module.

How's Your Style?

- Did you praise often?
- Did you review often, by asking questions?
- Did you simplify the steps as needed?
- Did your pace match that of the parent?
- Did you stay on track?

MATCH
Protocol

Giving Effective Instructions

Use This:

To teach the parent how to give instructions in a way that will improve the child's follow-through.

For Caregiver

Goals

- The parent will understand *when* to give instructions so that they will be more effective
- The parent will understand *how* to give instructions in terms of both their verbal and nonverbal aspects so that they will be more effective
- The parent will rehearse a "follow-through training" and agree to practice more at home

Materials

- *Fear Thermometer* and *Fear Ladder* (2 unrated copies for anxiety/trauma), *Feelings Thermometer* (for depression), or *Behavior Rating Scale* (for disruptive behavior)
- *Giving Effective Instructions* handout

> ⧗ *If time is tight: Teach the parent the basic steps for giving instructions more effectively and introduce "follow-through training" periods.*

Main Steps	Remember to start by setting an agenda together and reviewing any practice assignments.
☐ **Obtain Weekly Ratings**	If the main focus is traumatic stress or anxiety, use the 0 to 10 scale of the **Fear Thermometer** to obtain **Fear Ladder** ratings from both the child and his or her parent. If the main focus is depressed mood, use the **Feelings Thermometer** to take a rating. If the main focus is disruptive behavior, take a parent rating with the **Behavior Rating Scale**.
☐ **Discuss Effective Instructions**	Explain the importance of giving effective instructions. Build the parent's enthusiasm for this module by letting them know that this is one of the simplest, most efficient, and most effective things a parent can do to improve a child's behavior. Following instructions is one of the most important things a child can learn, and doing well at this generally means a child will improve in lots of other areas.

☐ **Discuss When to Give Instructions**	Explain that one problem common among children who do not follow instructions is that they end up getting more instructions than the average child. They may go around all day with parents and teachers making and repeating all kinds of requests (e.g., stop this, do that). For instructions to be more effective, the parent needs to use them more sparingly and be prepared to enforce those that are given. The parent must first make sure that:
	    • The instruction is for something that is really important
	    • The parent is willing to see the request to completion

☐	**Discuss How to Give Instructions**	Explain that once the above conditions are met, it is important to pay attention to *how* an instruction is given. Two things can make instructions more effective: (1) the words we say, and (2) the way we say them.
☐	**Discuss Less Effective "Words We Say"**	Introduce the *Giving Effective Instructions* handout. Review for the parent several kinds of instructions that are less effective. It might help to write these down. They are (1) "Let's" instructions: those that start with the word "let's", (2) "Vague" instructions, which don't spell out a clear behavior for the child to perform, (3) "Question" instructions, which involve parents asking the child instead of telling, and (4) "List" instructions, in which parents string together a long list of instructions all at once. Review the examples on page 1 of the handout, and see if the parent can come up with another example in each of the four categories.
☐	**Discuss More Effective "Words We Say"**	Then review with the parents how these instructions could be said more effectively. First review the examples on the right side of page 1 of the handout, then come up with more examples together. These could include: • Less effective: Would you please stop teasing your brother? [question] More effective: Stop teasing your brother. • Less effective: Let's clean up some of your toys now. [let's] More effective: Please clean up your toys now. • Less effective: Behave yourself on the way to school. [vague] More effective: Stay in your seat and face forward when you ride the bus this morning. • Less effective: Get ready for dinner. [vague] Less effective: Come on! Get ready for dinner and get in the kitchen right now—it's your turn to set the table. [list] More effective: Please wash your hands (wait for task to be done). Now please put the silverware on the table.
☐	**ACTIVITY** *Labeling Ineffective Instructions*	Once the parent understands the difference between ineffective and effective instructions, engage in a brief game. Issue several ineffective instructions to the parent, and have him or her identify what kind of mistakes they are. For example, call out things to them like, "Why don't you clean your room?" to which they should reply, "a question." Once the parent is doing well at this game, ask him or her to restate your instructions in a more effective way. For example, when you say, "Let's get dressed for school," a parent should say, "That's a 'let's' instruction. The better way to say it is "Please get dressed for school." For a parent doing really well, you can increase the challenge with some doubly ineffective instructions. For example, you can say, "Why won't you behave?" [question AND vague] or "Let's pick up these toys, get dressed for school, brush your teeth, and get your lunch ready." [Let's AND too many]. Remember to have the parent restate these instructions in a more effective way.
☐	**Discuss "How We Say Them"**	Explain to the parent that having now covered the *words we say*, it is time to cover *how we say them*. Review common problems with how instructions are said. Turn to the second page of the handout.

☐	**Discuss Eye Contact**	Point out making how eye contact when issuing instructions can increase the child's follow-through. The parent should be aware that he or she needs to look directly at the child when giving instructions to ensure the child's undivided attention, particularly when children have difficulties with attention. It may also help to kneel or sit, to get down to the child's level. Calling out an instruction from across the room—or from another room—is less likely to be successful.
☐	**Discuss Distractions**	When issuing instructions, the parent should also make every effort to reduce significant distractions. For example, if there is music playing or the TV is on, the first instructions should involve getting the TV or music off before giving instructions for something else.
☐	**Discuss Prompts for Transitions**	Point out that if a request involves stopping one activity to start another, it will work better if the parent first gives a prompt. For example, rather than saying, "Please brush your teeth now" when a child is watching TV, it is more helpful to say, "In 5 minutes, you will need to turn off the TV." The parent should return in 5 minutes, make sure the TV gets turned off, and then issue the next instruction: "Please brush your teeth."
☐	**Discuss Tone**	Point out that instructions are more likely to be met with resistance or a struggle if the child is aware that the parent is angry. The more calmly something is said, the better.
☐	**Discuss Check-Ins**	Let the parent know that when issuing instructions, it is also helpful to have the child repeat the instruction back to the parent to ensure that the child has understood the request.

Example script

Parent: (in calm tone) Brian, please wash your hands. (making eye contact) What do I want you to do right now?
Child: Wash my hands.
Parent: Yes, that's right. Please wash your hands. |
| ☐ | **ACTIVITY Practice Giving Instructions** | *Role-play with the parent how to give simple instructions, followed by praise. First play the role of parent, so that you can model effective instructions for about 2 minutes. Then, inform the parent that you will play the role of his or her child, and he or she will act as the parent, issuing simple instructions. Pay close attention both to what is said, and to how it is said. Provide lots of praise when parent get it right, and support the parent with feedback when needed.* |

☐	**Introduce Follow-Through Training**	Discuss the importance of a child's being able to comply with an instruction—what we will call "follow-through." For the child to become more successful at following through with parental instructions, it will help to create extra learning opportunities for the child. Thus, it will be useful to have the parent actually increase the rate at which they give instructions to their child during a brief follow-through training period, thereby providing the child with more opportunities for learning. These should:
		<ul><li>Last 3 to 5 minutes</li><li>Occur 2 or 3 times each day</li><li>Include a series of very simple tasks (e.g., pass the salt)</li><li>Be followed with praise</li></ul>
		Remind the parent that the increased instructions are to occur only during the training periods for now. The parent should continue to choose carefully when issuing instructions outside of these training periods.
☐	**Pick a Time for Training Periods**	Suggest to the parent that these training periods be tried during times of the day when the child is not already engaged in some really fun activity, but instead when the child appears to be between play activities. Waiting to conduct the training periods during such "down times" is likely to increase the chances of success.
☐ ⌂	**PRACTICE ASSIGNMENT** *Follow-Through Training at Home*	Explain to the parent that before the next session you would like him or her to practice these follow-through training periods described above, as often as twice a day. The parent should be reminded to provide praise to the child when instructions are followed successfully.

Leave 'Em Laughing

End the session on a positive note with the parent. You might do this by talking about things that are unrelated to the child, or discussing an area of interest you have in common with the parent. Also, the parent might be feeling overwhelmed by the challenging tasks he or she is undertaking; it can sometimes be helpful for the parent to have a few minutes at the end of the session to share concerns or the challenges he or she has faced with their child since the previous session. This time at the end of each session should be used to praise the parent's efforts and to convey support and encouragement.

Share with Child (if possible)

At the end of the session, if the child is available, it can be helpful to brief him or her on the ideas that were covered with the parent.

☐	**Review Concepts**	If the child is available, tell the child that for the next week, his or her parent will be asking the child to do things, such as chores and other small tasks. Indicate to the child that his or her parent will also be providing him or her with praise when he or she follows through on these instructions. Ask the child if he or she has any questions about the new way that requests will be handled at home.

☐ **ACTIVITY** *Practice Instructions with Child*	Ask the parent to try a follow-through training with his or her child, similar to what was assigned for practice at home. Ask the parent to give instructions to engage in an easy task, such as bringing an object to the parent or performing a small job for the parent. Make sure that the parent issues one instruction at a time, waits for follow-through from the child, and provides the child with praise for follow-through before issuing another instruction. This exercise should last approximately 2 minutes.
	Pay close attention to both what is said and how it is said. Also note whether the parent persists with the instruction he or she issues (e.g., does the parent repeat the instruction if it was not followed the first time?) and note the strategies the parent uses to address poor follow-through (e.g., does the parent attempt to make eye contact with the child, ask the child to repeat back the instruction?). Finally, note the parent's use of praise following the child's follow-through.
	After the role-play has been concluded, excuse the child from the room, and discuss what the parent thinks about his or her performance. Give lots of praise for any success as well as for the parent's efforts! Provide the parent with specific feedback about his or her ability to issue commands and to follow them with praise. Make specific suggestions about how the parent can improve his or her ability to give instructions, and provide support and reassurance.

Helpful Tips

- The parent can create "chore cards" for extended tasks, such as when asking the child to clean his or her room or do his or her homework. When the parent has created "chore cards" for extended tasks, he or she can write down the steps involved so that the child can carry the card with him or her while performing the job. Using "chore cards" can help to insure that there is no debate from the child over the exact steps of the task assigned. For example, a Chore Card for "Cleaning Up Room" might say, "1. Put toys in closet. 2. Make bed. 3. Put books on the shelf. 4. Pick up dirty clothes and put in basket."
- The parent may also wish to assign time limits for certain instructions. When assigning time limits for completion of tasks (e.g., cleaning up room), the parent should set a specified time on a kitchen timer to let the child know the time limit as well as the consequences that will occur if the time limit is not met.
- Parents should be reminded that even instructions delivered in the most effective way possible may not work when they first try this at home. If that happens, parents should be encouraged to handle the child's noncompliance as they typically have done in the past. Discuss with the parent that in subsequent sessions, you will be discussing alternative ways to handle the child's lack of follow-through.
- If children do not follow instructions given during the follow-through training periods, the parent should simply ignore the noncompliance for the moment and issue another brief instruction, requesting that the child do something else for the parent.
- Some parents can feel that giving direct instructions violates rules of etiquette and lacks the courtesy of favors or requests are typically used when asking others to do things for us. Point out that many parents find this new skill to feel "unnatural" or "awkward" at first, but it is precisely that feeling of things seeming very different that will make the instruction more noticeable to the child and will signal a clear change in the interaction for both parent and child. Also, assure the parent that he or she can always preface instructions with the word "please." The goal is simply to avoid issuing directions that sound like requests for favors, such as "Why don't you pick up your clothes now, all right?"

How's Your Style?

- Did you praise often?
- Did you review often, by asking questions?
- Did you simplify the steps as needed?
- Did your pace match that of the parent?
- Did you stay on track?

Rewards

For Family

Goals

- The parent will understand the concept of reinforcement
- The parent will establish a reward program for the home that encourages positive behavior and follow-through with instructions and requests
- The child will understand and agree to the reward program
- The child will demonstrate increased motivation to participate in positive behaviors and in practice exercises that are part of the therapy program

Materials

- *Fear Thermometer* and *Fear Ladder* (2 unrated copies for anxiety/trauma), *Feelings Thermometer* (for depression), or *Behavior Rating Scale* (for disruptive behavior)
- *Rewards* handout
- *Parent Observation Record*
- Blank paper and a pen

⏳ *If time is tight: Teach the parent how tangible rewards can be used to increased desired behaviors, and work with the parent to set up an organized system of rewards.*

Main Steps	*Remember to start by setting an agenda together and reviewing any practice assignments.*
☐ **Obtain Weekly Ratings**	If the main focus is traumatic stress or anxiety, use the 0 to 10 scale of the *Fear Thermometer* to obtain *Fear Ladder* ratings from both the child and his or her parent. If the main focus is depressed mood, use the *Feelings Thermometer* to take a rating. If the main focus is disruptive behavior, take a parent rating with the *Behavior Rating Scale*.
☐ **Meet with Child**	Meet with the child alone prior to meeting with the parent. Explain to the child that you will be spending some time talking about the different kinds of activities that the child enjoys doing. Discuss the idea of rewards with the child, and elicit several items or activities that the child would find rewarding. Be sure to ask the child for smaller and larger items that would be rewarding, while reminding the child that rewards do not have to be large to make us feel good. Getting the child's input is particularly important given that items or activities that are not valued by the child will not work well as rewards. Excuse the child when you have finished this discussion.

☐ **Introduce Rewards to Parent**	Discuss with the parent that some children require additional incentives, or rewards, to display the behaviors that we would like them to display. Let the parent know that he or she might already employ an informal reward program with the child. Many parents provide positives when their child complies with rules and directives by promising special privileges, activities, allowances, or tangible rewards. In such cases, the only change you will be working on will be to help the parent develop a method of accounting that will allow both the parent and the child to know whether the child really has earned the privilege that was promised. In other cases, the parent may have less of a system in place, in which case you are going to go through all the steps of creating a reward program. Let the parent know that using a formal reward system will allow him or her to have greater influence over the child's behavior.
☐ **Make a List of Rewards**	Work with the parent to add to the list of items and activities that the child finds rewarding. Try to have 10 to 15 items in total. Be careful to ensure that the parent contributes only those things that are truly enjoyable to the child. Encourage rewards that are small, can be given quickly, and do not cost much (if anything at all). For example, it is best to work with such things as praise, playing a game with a parent, going for a drive together, going to the mall together, watching a TV program, getting to stay up an extra half hour, picking a favorite meal for that night's dinner, or renting a movie. Things like getting a bicycle or a new pet should be discouraged, or else saved for the completion of the treatment program altogether. It is much more important to work on a list of things that can be given out day to day. Including some rewards on the list that the child is already receiving will help make sure the program will be sustainable.
☐ **Make a List of Desired Behaviors**	Work with the parent to create a list of desired behaviors. Choose no more than three, and try to include one behavior the child already does pretty well, to set the stage for success. More behaviors can be added later, after these the program is going well. Some of the behaviors on the list might be directly related to elements of the therapy program (e.g., completing practice assignments), whereas others might be related to general conduct, such as following a house rule or obeying a parental request.
☐ **Link Rewards to Behaviors**	Establish the connection between rewards and behavior (sometimes called the "reinforcement schedule"). Select each behavior and decide a reward (or choice among several rewards) that can be paired with it. For younger children, the rewards will need to be especially frequent, so that every time the behavior occurs, a small reward is given.

☐ **Discuss Amount of Rewards**	Explain the importance of the amount of reward given (sometimes called the "richness" of the reward program). Point out that if too few rewards are given, the child will lose interest, and if rewards are too large or are given too often, the child will not work as hard to improve. The idea is to find that point in the middle that keeps the child interested and working.
	The "richness" of the program will also change over time. The child should be rewarded more often in the beginning, to provide the opportunity to experience success. As time progresses, the program should become more challenging, so that more good behavior is expected to obtain the same level of rewards.
☐ **Discuss Timing of Delivering Rewards**	Warn the parent that he or she is to provide the reward only *after* the desired behavior has occurred, never before. Also, rewards not only follow the desired behaviors, but they are "connected," meaning they do not occur at any other times. Inform the parent that he or she should not negotiate with the child or agree to an "advance" in rewards, particularly if the child wishes to participate in some desired activity now that he or she has not yet earned. Remind the parent to follow the rule that if the child has not completed the desired behavior, he or she is not allowed to have access to the reward.
☐ **Discuss Close Approximations**	Tell the parent that children are much more likely to display desired behavior to get rewards if the parents go out of their way to notice and reward the desired behavior very frequently during the first week. Suggest to the parent that he or she should, for now, reward the child even for close approximations to the desired behavior just to show the child how easy it is to earn rewards and to increase the child's desire to work with the parent to earn more rewards. Excessive strictness during the first week can be counterproductive, such that the child will not maintain a high level of motivation for cooperating with the program.
☐ **Discuss Praise**	Remind the parent that the best reward is still going to be praise. Thus, when administering the rewards, the parent should use a pleasant tone of voice, taking care to label for the child exactly what behavior is being rewarded and providing enthusiastic praise and appreciation to the child along with the reward. With enough praise, most children will learn over time to self-praise and to take pride in their own accomplishments. Thus, in the long run, they won't need rewards to keep the new behaviors going.
☐ **Emphasize Patience**	Emphasize to the parent the importance of being patient with this program. Advise the parent that some children might show changes in compliance during the first day of the program, whereas others might take several weeks to show significant gains. Some children might even refuse to engage in the desired behaviors, thinking that if they resist, the parents will give up and provide them with rewards anyway. Tell the parent that in such instances the program should stay in effect and that you will problem-solve together how to get the program working over time.

☐	**Manage Concerns: Bribery**	If the parent expresses concern that the reward system seems like bribing his or her child, discuss with the parent how this program differs in two ways. First, bribes are often given before an expected behavior (e.g., I give you a sum of money and then you let me join the team). Second, "bribery" generally means to offer an incentive for an illicit, immoral, or illegal act by another person. Indicate that this reward system is clearly not for those purposes but rather is similar to parents being paid for working. In a sense, it is simply a fair wage for a fair day's work by the child.
☐	**Manage Concerns: Special Treatment**	Many parents are also concerned that their child is being rewarded for doing things for which other children are not given rewards; in this case, the parent should be reminded that all children are rewarded for behaving well, they are just not rewarded so systematically (i.e., most children are provided with privileges, treats, or other rewards, but the fact that such things are provided for good behavior is often not made explicit and sometimes not even connected to good behavior).
☐	**Manage Concerns: Making Time**	If the parent expresses concern about how time-consuming the reward program might be, assure him or her that although the program will take more time during the initial few weeks, it will eventually become a habit for the parent and should help the parent get back more time in the long run as the child's problems improve.
☐	**Review Program with Child and Parent**	Meet with the child and parent together to discuss the list and schedule of rewards. Work to resolve in advance any disagreements or misunderstandings between the child and parent about how the system of rewards will work. The child should be told that, after meeting a particular task (e.g., doing his or her chores when requested to do so), he or she will get to pick something from the rewards menu. Discuss with the child and parent that these rewards are to be an ongoing part of working together. Suggest that the parent post the reward menu somewhere in the house (e.g., child's bedroom).
		If the child is not available to participate in this part of the module, encourage the parent to schedule a time to sit down with the child and go over these issues before starting the program.
☐ ⬆	**PRACTICE ASSIGNMENT** *Rewards at Home*	Provide the parent with a copy of the *Rewards* handout and a *Parent Observation Record*. The practice assignment requires the parent to review the handout and to record on the *Parent Observation Record* each time the desired behavior occurred and what he or she did when the behavior occurred. The record will be reviewed to see if the rewards are being given quickly and consistently, and to track whether the desired behaviors are occurring with the desired frequency.

Leave 'Em Laughing

If you have been working primarily with the parent up until now, end the session on a positive note with the parent. Perhaps you can talk about things that are unrelated to his or her child or discuss an area of interest you have in common. This time at the end of each session should be used to praise the parent's efforts and to convey support and encouragement.

If you have been working primarily with the child up until now, end the session on a fun note with the child, by starting a game or some other activity that will leave the child feeling really good about the work you have done together today.

Special Cases

Anxiety	When working with the parent to create a list of desired behaviors to target with rewards, the list should include current treatment goals (e.g., practicing coping skills or items on the **Fear Ladder**).
Depression	Rewards may be used to support depression treatment by targeting behaviors needed for the treatment to work. For example, the desired behaviors might include completion of role-plays or activities with the therapist, or completion of practice assignments by the child between sessions.
Younger Children	The reward schedule should be as easy as possible at first, and the more immediate the rewards the better. The program can always be made more challenging later. As a general rule, the child should get rewarded on the first or second day of starting the program. After he or she does well, the behaviors on the list can be changed to be more challenging, or they can be rewarded less frequently.

Helpful Tips

- The key to a successful reward program is to keep the schedule from being too easy or too hard. Each meeting after the program is first established may require consideration of whether to adjust the reward or the points given for each behavior. If the child has not earned any rewards, the program should definitely be made easier (e.g., can the goal be approximated or done halfway at first? Can a simpler task be chosen for now?). If the child is getting rewards very often, it is time to make the program slightly more challenging. When discussing such changes with a child, it is helpful to emphasize the similarity with someone "getting in shape." As you get better and stronger, you lift more weight or run farther each day. This is a sign that you are really making progress.

- With frequent behaviors (for example, saying "please" or "thank you"), it is not always possible to give out rewards each time the behavior occurs. In such cases it can be helpful to provide the child with a point system or sticker chart. Older children can simply earn points that are recorded on a score sheet. Younger children can get tokens (e.g., plastic game chips) or stickers to put up on a calendar or chart. In the latter case, it can be helpful to make this calendar or chart together in the session. Each time the child performs the desired behavior, a point or token or sticker is given. These points can later be cashed in for items on the menu.

- An important consideration with this module is sensitivity to class or economic background of the family. With all families, it is important to emphasize that the best rewards do not cost money, but with economically disadvantaged families, it is especially important to be explicit about this issue. Be sure that at least 10 items on the rewards menu do not cost any money, and be especially reassuring that consistency, frequency, and immediacy of reward delivery are *always* more important than the material value of the reward.

- If both parents live at home with the child, both should be strongly encouraged to be active in administering rewards to their child. Having both parents participate in the reward program increases the consistency of child management procedures between the parents.

- Parents should review the list of rewards with the child every few weeks to see if new rewards should be added, or if others should be removed from the list because they are no longer of value to the child.

- If the parent is worried that he or she might have difficulty remembering to reward the child consistently, it is often helpful for parents to place small reminders to themselves in conspicuous places. For example, the parent might place small stickers or reminder notes in places that they see often, such as on a clock, mirror, telephone, or television.

- If the parent asks how long the reward program will be kept in place, explain that such a program often lasts about 2 months. Most commonly, families will find that the program gradually becomes phased-out without any systematic efforts to do so. If the parent wishes to remove the program formally, suggest that he or she do so for 1 to 2 days to see how well the child behaves without formal rewards. If the child is able to maintain the expected positive behaviors during this time, the parent can continue to extend this trial period indefinitely, and if problems arise, the program can be resumed as needed.

- After the reward program is working well, it is possible to add a rule in the system that allows points or tokens to be taken away from the child, or if points or tokens are not being used, there can be a list of behaviors that are associated with loss of privileges.

How's Your Style?

- Did you praise often?
- Did you review often, by asking questions?
- Did you simplify the steps as needed?
- Did your pace match that of the child or family?
- Did you stay on track?

MATCH
Protocol

Time Out

Goals

- The parent will understand how to use time out as a means of dealing with moderately disruptive behaviors (throwing tantrums, hitting, being mean or disrespectful)
- The parent will implement a time out program at home or adapt an existing one

Materials

- *Fear Thermometer* and *Fear Ladder* (2 unrated copies for anxiety/trauma), *Feelings Thermometer* (for depression), or *Behavior Rating Scale* (for disruptive behavior)
- *Time Out* handout
- *Parent Observation Record*
- Blank paper and a pen

> ⏳ *If time is tight: Teach the parent how to stop moderately bad behavior by quickly placing the child in a boring place and removing all rewards and attention from the child's behavior for a set period of time.*

Main Steps	Remember to start by setting an agenda together and reviewing any practice assignments.
☐ **Obtain Weekly Ratings**	If the main focus is traumatic stress or anxiety, use the 0 to 10 scale of the *Fear Thermometer* to obtain *Fear Ladder* ratings from both the child and his or her parent. If the main focus is depressed mood, use the *Feelings Thermometer* to take a rating. If the main focus is disruptive behavior, take a parent rating with the *Behavior Rating Scale*.
☐ **Introduce Time Out**	Review with the parent that time out is a method of mild discipline that involves a brief interruption of pleasant activities for the child. The child is quickly removed from the situation in which his or her misbehavior occurs and placed in a quiet, boring place. Children do not like being in time out because they lose attention, temporary freedom, and more importantly, the power to upset and manipulate their parents. Thus, putting a child in time out when a particularly undesirable behavior occurs will decrease the chances that the same behavior will occur again in the future. Provide the *Time Out* handout.

☐	**Discuss Benefits**	Inform parent of the short- and long-term benefits that can result from employing time out: • The problem behavior will occur less often • The parent will have a chance to "cool off" • It is milder and safer than other types of discipline sometimes used by families (e.g., screaming, spanking) • Children will learn to consider the consequences of their actions because the consequences are predictable
☐	**Discuss When to Use Time Out**	Refer to page 1 of the *Time Out* handout. Explain that time out should be used for stopping moderate misbehavior (i.e., rude, aggressive, destructive, or nasty acts; behavior that might be dangerous to self or others even if it wasn't intended to be). Advise the parent that *time out is not the preferred technique for dealing with passive or mild misbehavior* (e.g., sulking, whining). Examples of behaviors appropriate for time out appear on the handout.
☐	**Pick Behaviors**	Move to page 2 of the handout. Instruct the parent to select 1 to 3 target behaviors for time out. Explain that other behaviors can be added once the family has had the chance to practice time out for a while. When starting out, try to pick behaviors that occur at least once a day, that are easily defined, and that can be observed at home. The parent should write these on the handout.
☐	**Emphasize Use of Positive Skills**	Point out that time out will work best in the context of frequent use of attention, praise, and rewards. Time out only teaches a child what not to do; it does not teach a child what to do. Thus, the parent must also use incentives like attention, praise, and rewards to teach the child positive behaviors to do instead. These behaviors should be the opposite of the time out behaviors (e.g., being kind instead of being mean to a sibling). The parent should write examples on the handout.
☐	**Pick a Location**	Work together to select a place for time out, and write it on the handout. The location should be: • Dull (i.e., no other people available, away from toys, games, TV, books, pets, windows). • Not be scary or humiliating (e.g., a dark room or facing the corner). • Centrally located (the child should be able to get to the time out place within 10 seconds). • Out of the way so that other family members are not tempted to talk to or interact with the child in time out
☐	**Review the Steps**	Move to page 3 of the *Time Out* handout. Review the specific steps, using one of the behaviors you picked on page 2 of the handout. Don't forget to point out that if the child has not followed through on an instruction, it must be repeated after the time out is over.
☐	**Discuss Immediate Time Outs**	Point out to the parent that some behaviors will be serious enough that they do not require a warning (e.g., aggressive or dangerous behavior). These can also include violations of house rules (e.g., use of foul language, if there is a known rule in the house against it). Ask the parent to list some behaviors that would warrant a time out without warning for his or her child.

☐	**Discuss Follow-Up**	Inform the parent that in all but the rarest cases, the incident should be dropped once the child has served a time out. The parent should resist the temptation to scold or humiliate the child. When the time out is completed, the child should be told that he or she may go play. If the child remains annoyed after the time out, the parent should be encouraged to ignore this behavior. The child has a right to these feelings as long as the misbehavior does not continue.
☐	**Review Common Problems**	Review with the parent the common problems associated with implementing time out, including: • **Arguing**: Arguing can be ignored. If it escalates to shouting and yelling, the parent can reset the timer. • **Refusing to go to or leaving time out**: When the child refuses to go to time out or leaves, the parent can guide him or her gently to the time out area. Another option is for the child to lose a privilege or toy until the time out is performed (e.g., video games). If this loss of privilege does not work, the parent can take away all privileges available to the child. • **Being out of the house**: The parent should plan with you how to implement time out if the child misbehaves in a public place, such as a grocery store. Encourage the parent to bring the timer and to look for an appropriate time out place upon arrival, if behavior problems are expected. Examples include the family car or a nearby park bench.
☐	**Encourage Frequent and Calm Use**	Advise the parent not to wait for problems to become extreme before issuing a time out. If the parent uses time out only when he or she is angry and frustrated, time out is probably being used too infrequently or is not occurring immediately after the target behavior. In such cases, mistakes can happen, like the parent shouting or choosing an excessively long time out period due to his or her feelings of anger.
☐	**ACTIVITY** *Practicing Time Out*	Engage in a role-play with the parent in which you play his or her child. In your role, begin to engage in one of the target behaviors that the parent has agreed to address with his or her child at home. When you begin displaying the target behavior, the parent should then put you (as the child) into time out. Provide praise and supportive feedback when the role-play is over. It is often helpful to the parent if you role-play again, this time exhibiting some of the challenging behaviors (i.e., refusing to go, arguing, leaving time out) discussed earlier. This added challenge gives the parent an opportunity to practice using time out under more realistic conditions.

☐	**Discuss Introducing Time Out**	If the child is not available today to meet with you, discuss with the parent how he or she will explain time out to the child. The parent should choose a time when everyone is relaxed and not upset. Both parents should be present for this discussion with the child if possible; this will help the child understand that both parents have the same expectations for the child's behavior. The parents should tell the child that they love him or her, and that they want to help the child remember good ways to behave (using whatever language fits best for the child). As a part of this, the parents want to help the child remember not to do [identify the target behaviors], because these behaviors are causing some problems for the family. The parent should not ask for the child's agreement with this statement or argue with the child about this. The parents should note that the child will be required to have a time out (spend a certain amount of time in the time out place) when these behaviors happen.
☐	**ACTIVITY** *Practice Introducing Time Out*	If the child is not available today, role-play a discussion with the parent in which you act as the "child" while he or she explains to you the behaviors that will be targeted with time out, how the time out procedure will work, and what this new strategy will mean for the family.
		As the parent explains time out during the role-play, try to ask the parent questions that you imagine his or her child might ask. This activity should help the parent learn how to talk to the child about time out, and it will also help you size up the parent's level of understanding of this strategy. This is a good time to review any misperceptions or misunderstandings, and to work with the parent on the most effective way to explain time out to the child.
☐ ⇧	**PRACTICE ASSIGNMENT** *Time Out at Home*	The parent should be instructed to begin introducing time out in his or her home, focusing for now on one or two behaviors. Using the *Parent Observation Record*, the parent should record every instance in which time out was used, the child's behavior that prompted the time out, and how well the parent felt he or she was able to implement the time out procedure. The parent should also record the length of each time out in the middle column.

Leave 'Em Laughing

End the session on a positive note with the parent. Perhaps you can talk about things that are unrelated to the child or discuss an area of interest you have in common. Also, the parent might be feeling overwhelmed by the challenging tasks he or she is undertaking; it can sometimes be helpful for the parent to have a few minutes at the end of the session to share concerns or the challenges he or she has faced with his or her child since the previous session. This time at the end of each session should be used to praise the parent's efforts and to convey support and encouragement.

Share with Child (if possible)

At the end of the session, if the child is available, it can be helpful to brief him or her on the materials covered.

☐	**Review Concepts**	Bring the child into the session and explain to the child that there will be some changes in the way the parent will handle the child's behavior when the child engages in certain behaviors (inform the child of the specific behaviors that you and the parent have agreed to target in the coming week). Explain that these changes are meant to be helpful for everyone. You can tell the child that for the time being, the parent will respond to these behaviors by having the child go quickly to a quiet place for a set amount of time (indicate the duration that has been chosen). You and the parent should emphasize to the child that he or she is still loved by the parent, but that some of the child's behavior has been causing problems, and the parent will be changing how he or she has been responding to that behavior. Use questions to make sure the child understands how time out will work at home, and invite the child to ask the parent any questions he or she might have.
☐	**ACTIVITY** *Practice Time Out with Child*	Ask the child and parent to engage in a role-play involving time out. Prior to beginning this exercise, you and the parent should agree upon the behavior to be used (you may refer to the handout for examples). Part of the treatment room or area should also be designated in advance as the time out area. After explaining how time out will work to the child, ask the child to perform the behavior (in a "pretend" or "make-believe" manner), with the understanding that the parent will then direct the child to time out. For this practice, the time out should last only about a minute, so as to demonstrate the point of how time out works. Pay close attention to the way in which the parent directs the child to time out, making sure that the he or she uses fewer than 10 words in 10 seconds, labels the child's misbehavior, and issues clear instructions for the child to go to time out. If the child exhibits oppositional behaviors in response to the instruction to go to time out (i.e., talking back, arguing, refusing to go), note how the parent handles these behaviors. Note the parent's response to the child when time out has ended. After the role-play has been concluded, thank the child and excuse him or her from the room. Ask for the parent's thoughts about his or her performance. Give lots of praise for any success! Provide the parent with specific feedback about his or her ability to use time out. Make specific suggestions with respect to how the parent can improve his or her time out skills, and provide support and reassurance.

Helpful Tips

- Some parents might say "Oh—I've tried time out, and it doesn't work." You should acknowledge that time out takes a lot of patience and effort, but assure the parent that much of the success of time out is in the fine tuning. There are dozens of different ways to do time out, and that what you are going to practice today is a procedure that really does work. If it is not successful right away, encourage the parent not to give up. Troubleshooting can often reveal simple changes that will improve the success of using time out.

- If a parent is new to time out, prepare him or her for the possibility that time out will be challenging at first. For example, the child might throw temper tantrums, which can be distressing to parents. Let the parent know that during such tantrums, he or she may feel like giving in to the child so that the tantrum will stop. Advise the parent that giving in to the child in such situations might stop the tantrum, but it will actually increase the chances of the time out behavior happening again in the future. Reassure the parent that a high rate of negative behavior in response to the time out procedures initially can mean that the child is really concerned and hence the technique is actually working as planned.

- Advise the parent that using time out inconsistently greatly weakens the effectiveness of this strategy and makes it much more difficult to implement in the future.

- If the child is unavailable for the session, the parent will need to be prepared to explain time out to the child and answer questions before using it at home.

How's Your Style?

- Did you praise often?
- Did you review often, by asking questions?
- Did you simplify the steps as needed?
- Did your pace match that of the parent?
- Did you stay on track?

Making a Plan

Goals

- The parent will identify high-risk situations for his or her child's misbehavior
- The parent will learn steps to prevent misbehavior in high-risk situations
- The parent will practice these steps at home with his or her child

Materials

- *Fear Thermometer* and *Fear Ladder* (2 unrated copies for anxiety/trauma), *Feelings Thermometer* (for depression), or *Behavior Rating Scale* (for conduct problems)
- *Making a Plan* handout

> ⧖ *If time is tight: Review the handout on how to anticipate behavior problems and manage behavior before it becomes disruptive.*

Main Steps	Remember to start by setting an agenda together and reviewing any practice assignments.
☐ **Obtain Weekly Ratings**	If the main focus is traumatic stress or anxiety, use the 0 to 10 scale of the *Fear Thermometer* to obtain *Fear Ladder* ratings from both the child and his or her parent. If the main focus is depressed mood, use the *Feelings Thermometer* to take a rating. If the main focus is disruptive behavior, take a parent rating with the *Behavior Rating Scale*.
☐ **Identify Routine Challenges**	Ask the parent to identify times or events that make his or her child's behavior especially challenging. Give examples such as grocery shopping together, going to a neighbor's house, or taking a long drive somewhere.
☐ **Discuss Being Caught off Guard**	Point out that most parents are too busy to think ahead about these kinds of situations, or if they do think ahead, they are too busy or tired to get fully prepared for them. For example, some parents will enter public places, such as stores, without fully thinking through how they will manage their child's behavior should it become disruptive. Then they are forced to respond to their child's behavior in the moment, without an advance plan. Under these circumstances, the parent might be frustrated with the child, worried about the reactions of others who are watching the scene, and upset or angry. Note that all of these factors can work together to make it very challenging for a parent to develop a reasonable and effective method of dealing with the problem once it has started.

☐	**Discuss Making a Plan**	Point out how anticipating behavioral problems is a key concept in learning to manage a child's behavior effectively, whether in public situations, across transitions in major daily activities, or in many other more routine situations. "Making a plan" means that a lot of misbehavior can be avoided by thinking ahead about the child's potential misbehavior and by making a plan clear to the child before entering the situation. Even if misbehavior is not avoided completely in such situations, the parent will at least have established a quick and thoughtful reaction to the misbehavior before it goes too far.
☐	**Review *Making a Plan* Handout**	Provide the parent with the **Making a Plan** handout. Review the five steps with the parent.
☐	**ACTIVITY** *Making a Plan*	After reviewing the steps involved in making a plan, engage the parent in a role-play in which you act as the child. If possible, work with the parent's example on page 3 of the handout, and rehearse the time leading up to the situation (you do not need to rehearse the entire situation). For example, if the task involves going out to a public place, you could ask the parent to walk with you as if you were the child and he or she was preparing to enter a public area (perhaps walking up to the door to the treatment room or the outside door to your building).
		Prior to entering the door, the parent should go through steps 1 through 4 from the handout with you. Pay close attention to the way in which the parent sets up the situation (perhaps assigning you a planned activity, or pointing out that you just had a snack), explains the rules to you, offers incentives, and explains the consequences.
		After the role-play, discuss what the parent thinks about his or her performance. Provide the parent with specific feedback about his or her preparation, the rules he or she chose to use, the types of incentives offered, and the manner in which the consequences were explained. Make sure the parent's language and tone corresponded appropriately to his or her child's age. Praise the parent for his or her performance and repeat the role-play, if necessary.
☐	**Manage Concerns: Parenting in Public**	Check in to see if the parent feels that setting rules and administering rewards and consequences would be comfortable in public. If the parent thinks he or she might be embarrassed or uncomfortable, these concerns can often be addressed by explaining that behavior problems are less likely to develop in the first place if the parent follows the steps of prevention you have just reviewed. Suggest that the odds of a problem developing are further reduced by the parent's use of ongoing attention, praise, and rewards for his or her child's good behavior in the public place. Explain that even when misbehavior does develop, it will often be at a much-reduced level of disruption because the parent will respond to it swiftly and with a clear plan before the behavior gets out of hand. Reassure the parent that such steps are more likely to reduce opportunities for the parent to experience embarrassment in public.

☐ ⬆ **PRACTICE ASSIGNMENT** *Practice Runs*	Review the practice assignment for the coming week with the parent. Explain to the parent that during the coming week he or she is to plan at least two "practice runs" of the situation chosen on the last page of the handout. The practice run should look as much like the actual situation as possible—for example, if the activity is shopping, the parent should plan two "fake" shopping trips solely for the purpose of making and practicing the plan (no real shopping needs to get done). Ask the parent to record information about these practices on the *Parent Observation Record* for review at the next session.

Leave 'Em Laughing

End the session on a positive note with the parent. You might do this by talking about things that are unrelated to the child, or discuss an area of interest you have in common with the parent. Also, the parent might be feeling overwhelmed by the challenging tasks he or she is undertaking; it can sometimes be helpful for the parent to have a few minutes at the end of the session to share concerns or the challenges he or she has faced with the child since the previous session. This time at the end of each session should be used to praise the parent's efforts and to convey support and encouragement.

Share with Child (if possible)

At the end of the session, if the child is available, it can be helpful to brief him or her on the materials covered.

☐ **Review Concepts**	Bring the child into the session and explain to the child that this week his or her parent is going to practice a special task with him or her, such as going to the store or getting on the bus together (the situation should be the same one the parent role-played with you). Indicate to the child that there will be certain rules that he or she is expected to follow, and his or her parent will discuss these rules with the child beforehand. Ask the child if he or she has any questions about the new rules that he or she will be asked to follow when practicing together with his or her parent.
☐ **ACTIVITY** *Making a Plan*	If possible, repeat the role-play you performed earlier with the parent, now with the child taking your place. The parent should focus on going through steps 1 through 4 from the handout with the child. Pay close attention to the way in which the parent sets up the situation (perhaps assigning the child a planned activity or occupying him or her with a toy or a book), explains the rules, offers incentives, and explains the consequences.
	After the role-play, thank and excuse the child and discuss with the parent his or her thoughts about his or her performance. Provide the parent with specific feedback about his or her preparation, the rules he or she chose to use, the type of incentives offered, and the manner in which the consequences were explained. Make sure the parent's language and tone corresponded appropriately to his or her child's age.

Helpful Tips

- When discussing incentives for the plan, consider items from the child's formal reward system, if one is already in place.

- Remember that incentives do not have to be large or costly. Examples of small incentives might include stickers, stamps, pencils, choosing the dessert at home that evening, or extra time to play a game with the parent.
- If the consequences in the plan involve removal of the child from a public place, explain to the parent that short intervals of time out (e.g., 2 to 3 minutes) generally work well in public, given that the child is missing out on many interesting activities and is most likely embarrassed about having to spend time in a boring location.

How's Your Style?

- Did you praise often?
- Did you review often, by asking questions?
- Did you simplify the steps as needed?
- Did your pace match that of the parent?
- Did you stay on track?

<table>
<tr><td>MATCH
Protocol</td><td colspan="2"># Daily Report Card</td></tr>
</table>

MATCH Protocol # Daily Report Card

Use This:
To establish a way to monitor behavior at school so it can be linked to an existing home reward program.

For Caregiver

Goals

- The parent will understand how to link behaviors at school to a home reward program
- The parent will make a list of school behaviors to prioritize for the program
- You and the parent will establish communication with the school
- The parent will implement a tool for daily monitoring of school behavior

Materials

- *Fear Thermometer* and *Fear Ladder* (2 unrated copies for anxiety/trauma), *Feelings Thermometer* (for depression), or *Behavior Rating Scale* (for disruptive behavior)
- *Using a Daily School Behavior Report Card* handout
- Blank *Daily Report Cards*

> ⧗ *If time is tight: Teach the parent how to use a system for learning about the child's behavior at school and how to connect that behavior to the home reward program.*

Main Steps	*Remember to start by setting an agenda together and reviewing any practice assignments.*
☐ **Obtain Weekly Ratings**	If the main focus is traumatic stress or anxiety, use the 0 to 10 scale of the *Fear Thermometer* to obtain *Fear Ladder* ratings from both the child and his or her parent. If the main focus is depressed mood, use the *Feelings Thermometer* to take a rating. If the main focus is disruptive behavior, take a parent rating with the *Behavior Rating Scale*.
☐ **Establish Targets**	Review with the parent any behavior problems at school that are occurring with any regularity and that should be the target of this program. Work to develop a list of concerns that the parent feels would be important to address.
☐ **Establish Communication with School**	If you are not already in contact with the child's school, obtain permission from the parent and plan to contact school personnel about possible behavioral goals.
☐ **Encourage Relationship with School Staff**	Encourage the parents to identify at least one teacher or other adult at the school with whom they can communicate and develop trust. Collaboration between parents and school is key. Sometimes this will require some facilitation on your part.

☐	**Introduce Daily Report Card**	Review with the parent the concept of the daily report card. It is a way for school personnel to report to the parent daily on the child's behavior, which can then be tied into the reward program at home. Essentially, good behavior at school can earn rewards at home, whereas poor behavior at school will result in few or no rewards.
☐	**Review Handout**	Review the *Using a Daily School Behavior Report Card* handout and the blank daily report cards, pointing out the advantages of using this system. At this time, answer any questions about how the report card might work.
☐	**Develop List**	Develop the initial list of ideas about four or five priorities that are consistent across parent and school staff reports.
☐	**Design a Daily Report Card**	Finally, go over some examples of daily report cards, and work with the parents to design a program that seems workable for his or her child. fill out a blank daily report card together.
☐	**Exercise** *Mock Report Card*	Once you have devised a report card program with the parent, run through an example of how it will work once the report card comes home. Present the parent with examples of completed report cards and ask him or her to describe how he or she would use that information to provide rewards or consequences. The parent should have a clear understanding of what rewards to give depending on what the card looks like. If you decide to role play, play the part of the child bringing home a daily report card and look for the parent to praise good behavior when giving rewards.
☐	**Encourage Easy Start**	Explain that the daily report card should produce rewards for the child initially. This will be important in building the child's motivation to participate. Thus, it should initially be easy enough for the child to earn rewards and perhaps only certain classes or a portion of the day should be covered at first. As the child gets the hang of it, the report card program can be adjusted to include more challenging classes and behaviors.
☐	**Encourage Consistency**	Remind the parents that the daily report card will only be successful if the parents request to see it each day and act on the results consistently
☐	☝ **PRACTICE ASSIGNMENT Daily Report Card**	The practice assignment for this week involves the parent working with one or more people at school (this can be coordinated by you if needed) to begin using the daily report card in conjunction with a home reward program.

Leave 'Em Laughing

End the session on a positive note with the parent by perhaps talking about things that are unrelated to his or her child, or discussing an area of interest you have in common with the parent. Also, the parent might be feeling overwhelmed by the challenging tasks he or she is undertaking; it can sometimes be helpful to leave a few minutes at the end of the session for the parent to share concerns or the challenges he or she has faced with the child since the previous session. The end of each session should be used to praise the parent's efforts and to convey support and encouragement.

Share with Child (if possible)

At the end of the session, if the child is available, it can be helpful to brief him or her on the materials covered.

☐	**Review Concepts**	Meet with the child and parent together to discuss the list and schedule of rewards. Work to resolve any discrepancies between child and parent about how the daily report card will work. The child should know that after meeting goals at school, he or she will get points or get to pick something off the menu of rewards. Remind the child and parent of the importance of consistent use of the daily report card. If the child does not bring it home, no rewards will be given for that day.

Helpful Tips

- If the school already has a similar program, tool, or behavior checklist as part of a classroom behavior program, do not reinvent the wheel. Work with the school and family to integrate the existing program in with the rewards program at home. The idea is to get the school and home programs working consistently and together.

How's Your Style?

- Did you praise often?
- Did you review often, by asking questions?
- Did you simplify the steps as needed?
- Did your pace match that of the parent?
- Did you stay on track?

Looking Ahead

Use This:

At the conclusion of
treatment for conduct
problems to review and
prepare for termination.

For Caregiver

Goals

- The parent will think about behavior problems that might arise in the future and how his or her existing skills can be used to address them
- The parent will plan how to adjust, maintain, and generalize his or her newly acquired skills
- The parent will consider whether or not to continue a reward system if one is in effect
- The parent will feel prepared for the termination of treatment

Materials

- *Behavior Rating Scale*
- *Looking Ahead* handout
- Paper and pencils for written exercises

> ⧗ *If time is tight:* Review with the parent the new skills he or she has learned during treatment, and assist in thinking of ways to generalize these new skills to other behavioral concerns that might arise in the future.

Main Steps	Remember to start by setting an agenda together and reviewing any practice assignments.
☐ **Obtain Weekly Rating**	Take a parent rating with the *Behavior Rating Scale*.
☐ **Review Program**	Review with the parent the following items: • Which specific skills and strategies covered in treatment the parent is likely to find most useful for handling the child's misbehavior at home • Some of the most challenging behaviors to which the parent will need to apply those skills • The "high risk" situations that the parent will need to watch out for in order to continue to apply these new tools consistently and effectively (e.g., family stressors, the child's move to a new school, the parent's own personal characteristics that influence the way he or she addresses the child's behavior)

☐	**Manage Expectations**	Give the parent a copy of the *Looking Ahead* handout. Tell the parent that it is normal to expect some challenges ahead, both in terms of the parent's attempts to apply these new skills consistently and effectively and also in terms of possible reemergence of the child's challenging behaviors. Remind the parent that it is easy for both child and parent to slip into old habits, especially after things have been good for a while.
		Reassure the parent that this is all very common, and that almost no one can expect to handle his or her child's behavior perfectly all of the time. Instead what are needed are good skills and strategies to use when the parent begins to recognize either misbehavior on the part of the child, or reliance on prior strategies for parenting (i.e., yelling at the child instead of using time out). Remind the parent that by using the tools and skills learned in treatment, he or she can have more control over the child's misbehavior than before, and fix problems more quickly when they arise.
☐	**Discuss Lapse and Relapse**	It might also be helpful to discuss with the parent the distinction between a "lapse" and a "relapse." Explain that lapses are natural and involve minor steps backward, for either parent or child, whereas a "relapse" is having everything go back to square one. Remind the parent that if lapses occur, these can be tackled by reviewing the handouts given by the therapist and practicing the skills again. As suggested by the four factor model, children's lapses will be more common during stressful times, and it is perfectly normal for stressful situations to make it difficult to address the child's behavior in a consistent and effective fashion. Emphasize to the parent that "lapses" are perfectly natural, and if handled carefully are unlikely to become "relapses."

> **Example script**
>
> *If you start to find that some of your child's disruptive behaviors have returned, it's important that you do not jump to the conclusion that you are back at square one. At these times you need to remember that all of the skills you learned during treatment will always be there for you to call on. All you need to do is use them when you start to notice problem behaviors.*

☐	**Discuss Monitoring**	Explain that the handout asks the parent to begin keeping a record of any new misbehavior that arises, noting the circumstances in which the behavior occurs, what the child did, how the parent responded, and whether that response was successful. The parent should review the record after 7 to 10 days to see if it reveals whether the parent has drifted away from applying the new skills and returned to old habits. Once the parent is aware of how he or she is handling the new behavior, he or she can make adjustments accordingly.
☐	**Discuss Making a Program**	If a new behavior problem appears (or an old one reappears), encourage the parent to consider first using the *Making a Plan* worksheet to guide the development of a plan that could prevent the behavior from becoming more frequent. If the misbehavior persists, suggest to the parent that he or she should return to a formal program of both rewards and consequences to address this particular behavior.

☐	**Highlight What Helps**	Remind the parent that if formal use of rewards and consequences is required, then administering them *immediately and consistently* is the key to gaining control over any new problem behavior. Suggest that the parent continue to keep a record of the problem behavior throughout this time. If the misbehavior persists, suggest that he or she schedule another appointment with you, being sure to bring any notes along for you to review.
☐	**ACTIVITY** *Stump the Parent*	Remind the parent that he or she now has all of the skills necessary to cope with the vast majority of behavior problems displayed by most children. The goal now is to begin thinking about how to use these skills in managing any future problem behaviors that might arise.
		Suggest to the parent a game in which you will pose hypothetical behavior problems to the parent and request that he or she think about how to manage these problems using the skills and methods learned during the treatment program. Prompt the parent when necessary, but the parent should do the majority of this problem-solving on his or her own. If the parent does need some guidance, use questions to help lead the parent to suggest the correct use of a procedure.
		During this exercise, be sure to watch out for and correct many parents' natural tendency to drift toward punishment methods as the first means of dealing with new behavior problems that you pose. Continue to stress to the parent the principle of positives before negatives (rewards before consequences) when designing a behavior change strategy to address his or her child's behavior.
☐	**Schedule Booster**	During this session it is also often helpful to schedule a booster session approximately 3 to 6 months in the future for further monitoring of the family's progress with these new techniques. Suggest to the parent that a booster session can be a time for him or her to check in with you about his or her success in applying the tools he or she has learned, ask about any new difficulties that may have arisen, and discuss ways to continue to maintain the gains he or she has made in the long-term.

Leave 'Em Laughing

The final session should involve a feeling of celebration, so leave time to provide genuine praise and positive feedback to the parent and to review his or her many successes with the program.

Share with Child (if possible)

At the end of the session, if the child is available, it can be helpful to brief him or her on the materials covered.

☐	**Review Concepts**	Briefly review the successes of the child in the program. Be sure to emphasize that the child's effort in adapting to the new rules and earning rewards was a major part of that success. Point out some of the positive things that are happening in the family now that could not have happened previously (e.g., better grades at school, a new friend, a happier family with fewer arguments, or other accomplishments).

☐ **Say Thanks and Goodbyes**	Thank the parent and child for their help and support during the program. Let the parent and child know that you have enjoyed getting to know them, and that you are now having them take over all the rules and rewards at home, as formal treatment is ending. Point out that the progress was primarily due to the child and family's efforts, not to your own. It is important that the parent and child take responsibility for their success and attribute gains to their own efforts.

Helpful Tips

- The overall tone of this session should be warm and upbeat. The parent should leave feeling pleased with his or her accomplishments and the gains that he or she has made with the child.
- When discussing how to apply the skills and tools that the parent has acquired during treatment to future behavior problems, emphasize only those skills that you believe are highly likely to work well.
- If this module lasts for more than one session, it is often helpful to assure the parent that he or she can contact you between sessions if problems arise.
- If the family is particularly concerned about ending treatment, you can check in with the parent over the phone approximately once per month following the termination of treatment.

How's Your Style?

- Did you praise often?
- Did you review often, by asking questions?
- Did you simplify the steps as needed?
- Did your pace match that of the parent?
- Did you stay on track?

Booster Session

Goals

- The parent will decide whether or not to continue the reward system, if one is still in effect
- You and the parent will review the **Daily Report Card** (if appropriate) and consider whether or not to continue it
- The parent will review successes and challenges encountered with previously taught skills
- You will make adjustments or additional recommendations as needed

Materials

- *Behavior Rating Scale*
- Child's daily report card (if available)

⧗ **If time is tight**: *Review the child's status with the parent to determine whether additional adjustments or interventions are warranted.*

Main Steps	*Remember to start by setting an agenda together.*
☐ **Obtain Rating**	Obtain the **Behavior Rating Scale** rating from the parent.
☐ **Discuss Reward Program**	If the child is on a reward program, discuss the parent's thoughts on the continuation or termination of the program. Suggest to the parent that he or she might want to try suspending the record-keeping part of the reward system for a few days, allowing the child to continue to earn privileges based on how he or she behaves. If the child continues to behave well without the formal reward program in place, the parent can permit the child to have access to daily privileges. If the child misbehaves during this time, some privileges will be lost that day depending on the nature of the problem behavior. The parent should remind the child that privileges will continue to be linked to good behavior and the performance of chores or tasks at home. Assure the parent that if the child's misbehavior increases without the formal reward system, the full system can be reinstated.

☐	**Review Daily Report Card**	If the daily report card was used and is still in place, the parent should be instructed to reduce the frequency of its use over time. Suggest the following guidelines: • After the child has 2 good weeks in a row, the daily report card can be used only on Wednesdays and Fridays, with each report card referring to the multiple preceding days • After another 2 good weeks, the card can be used on Friday only to refer to the entire week • After another good week, the card can be discontinued altogether Just as with the reward program, the child should understand that if problems resurface the report card can be reinstated.
☐	**Provide Feedback and Support**	Discuss with the parent his or her continued use of other parenting strategies learned, and provide praise for their effective use. Some continued feedback might be needed and can be offered at this point as well.
☐	**Review Progress**	Finally, discuss with the parent his or her satisfaction with the child's progress and whether it appears that goals have been met, or whether additional treatment or other supports are still needed. Work with the parent to review and evaluate progress, define long-term goals, and outline plans for additional supports or services if needed.

Helpful Tips

- During this phase of treatment, some parents ask about their child's need for adjunctive treatment with psychopharmacology. Children with symptoms of attention-deficit/hyperactivity disorder, in particular, may continue to manifest symptoms of inattention and hyperactivity following this treatment program. If the child has not previously been placed on medication for attentional concerns, and the level of symptoms continues to cause significant impairment at home, in school, or in social functioning, you can suggest that the parent consult a physician to discuss medication options.

- When discussing how the skills and tools that the parent has acquired during treatment can be applied to future behavior problems, emphasize only those skills that you believe are highly likely to work well.

- If the family remains concerned about having ended treatment, you can arrange to check in with the parent over the phone periodically following this session.

How's Your Style?

- Did you praise often?
- Did you review often, by asking questions?
- Did you simplify the steps as needed?
- Did your pace match that of the parent?
- Did you stay on track?

Worksheets, Handouts, and Records

MATCH

Fear Thermometer

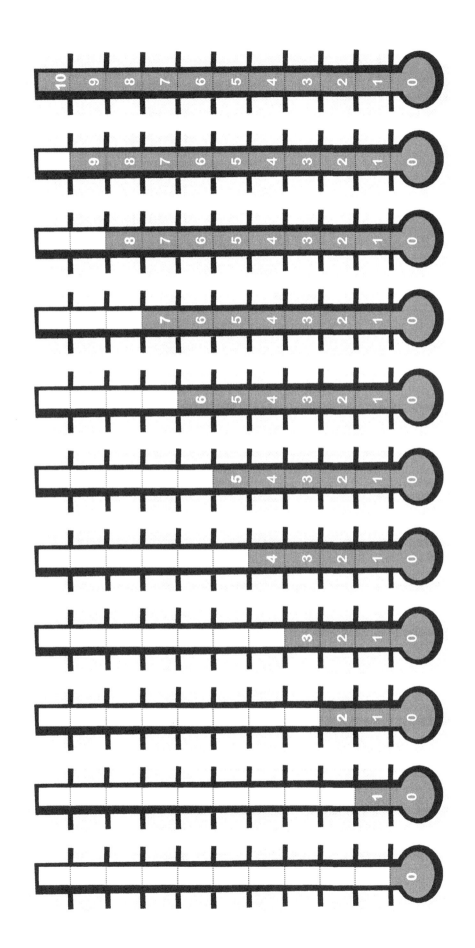

Fear Ladder

Date: _____

Filled out by:

☐ Child

☐ Mother

☐ Father

☐ Other _____

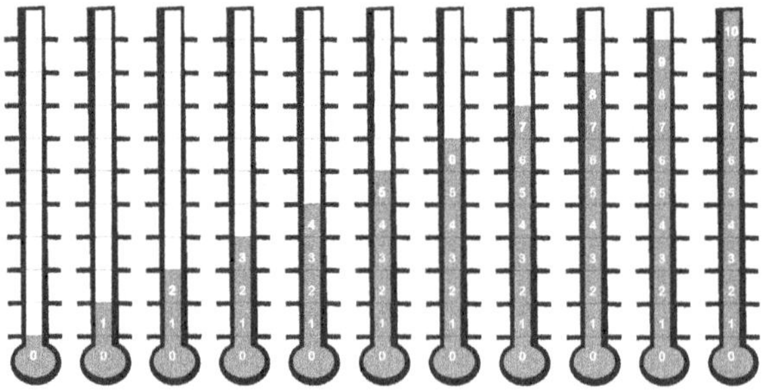

ITEM

How scary is this item today? Please give a rating from 0-10.

_____

_____

_____

_____

_____

_____

_____

_____

_____

_____

_____

Learning Your Anxious Feelings

What does YOUR anxiety feel like?

We want you to practice some different exercises to create different feelings in your body. The exercises will help us learn what your anxiety feels like for you. Later, they can help us know how to practice together to make these feelings less scary or uncomfortable.

I will show you some of these exercises first, and then you can take a turn. After each exercise, I will ask you to give 3 different ratings with the Fear Thermometer:

(1) how **strong** the feelings are

(2) how **anxious** the feelings make you feel

(3) how **similar** the feelings are to what you usually feel when you are panicked or anxious

Go ahead and give it a try!

	How Strong?	How Anxious?	How Similar?
Move your head side to side (30 sec)			
Hold your head low between your legs (30 sec), then lift quickly			
Run in place or do jumping jacks (1 min)			
Hold your breath (45 sec)			
Tense all your muscles or hold a push-up position (1 min)			
Spin in a swivel chair (1 min)			
Hyperventilate (1 min)			
Breathe through a small straw or as slowly as possible (2 min)			

Body Map

Where do you feel anxious feelings?

Worksheet—Anxious Feelings & Thoughts / 1 of 3

Body Map

Where do you feel anxious feelings?

Thought Bubbles

What are your anxious thoughts?

Worksheet—Anxious Feelings & Thoughts / 3 of 3

Learning About Anxiety

You've learned a lot about anxiety this week. The games and activities on this worksheet will help you remember some of the most important things you've learned.

Anxiety Wheel

Use the wheel to find the three parts of anxiety. Starting with the letter F, write down every other letter in the spaces below (that means write a letter, skip a letter, write a letter, skip a letter).

Start here.

1. F __ __ __ __ __ __ __

2. __ __ __ __ __ __ __ __

3. __ __ __ __ __ __ __

Find Your Feelings

People get all sorts of feelings when they get scared. Circle all the ways *you* feel when you get scared.

FAST HEARTBEAT	TINGLY HANDS	BREATHLESS	BLUSHING	HOT
SHORT OF BREATH	BUTTERFLIES	DRY MOUTH	FIDGETY	DIZZY
STOMACHACHE	UPSET TUMMY	HEADACHE	SWEATY	SHAKY

Look at the words you circled above. Can you find them in the word search below?

```
R  S  H  O  R  T  O  F  B  R  E  A  T  H  F  A  G  T  E  A  J
L  T  W  P  S  N  S  U  U  H  Z  W  I  U  K  O  F  H  W  I  U
H  O  T  K  W  W  J  V  T  Y  U  I  N  G  S  D  I  Z  Z  Y  P
Q  M  L  X  E  Q  T  I  T  D  H  B  G  H  P  V  D  N  B  M  S
Y  A  O  E  A  T  B  R  E  A  T  H  L  E  S  S  G  L  D  I  E
X  C  G  V  T  R  E  D  R  X  C  C  Y  V  J  R  E  X  L  C  T
S  H  A  K  Y  A  N  E  F  A  S  T  H  E  A  R  T  B  E  A  T
H  A  M  Z  F  P  O  D  L  R  P  Q  A  U  S  K  Y  D  T  M  U
Z  C  K  B  L  U  S  H  I  N  G  L  N  C  Q  A  Y  B  K  E  M
F  H  G  F  S  N  F  Y  E  M  M  G  D  R  Y  M  O  U  T  H  M
H  E  A  D  A  C  H  E  S  I  B  J  S  C  A  Z  B  O  J  N  Y
```

Thoughts Bubble

When people feel nervous or scared, they often have certain thoughts. List a thought that *you* have when you feel nervous or scared.

Example: When I hear
a dog bark, I think it's going to bite me.

Actions Scramble

When people feel nervous or scared, they act in certain ways. Unscramble the letters to name what these people are doing because they're nervous or scared.

YNRCIG

___ ___ ___ ___ ___ ___

UNNNIGR

___ ___ ___ ___ ___ ___ ___

NILLEGY

___ ___ ___ ___ ___ ___ ___

Circle the Right Answer

1 What do you do when you feel nervous or scared? Circle the things you do.

RUN AWAY   **YELL**   **WORRY**

STAY BY MOM   **GET MAD**

CAN'T MOVE   **CRY**   **STAY AWAY**

Anything else? _____

2 Anxiety is meant to be … (circle one)   **GOOD**   **BAD**

3 Anxiety is … (circle the right answer)

… the body's washing machine

… the body's helicopter

… the body's alarm

Stoplights

Give an example of a "red light":

_____

Give an example of a "yellow light":

_____

False Alarms & True Alarms

Anxiety can cause problems when we feel nervous or afraid even when there is no real danger around us. Match the pictures with the correct words.

False alarm

True alarm

False alarm

True alarm

False alarm

Fixing False Alarms

What's the best way to fix false alarms? Fill in the letters below to find out! (Hint: This is the best way to get over feeling nervous or scared, and it's also the best way to get better at other things, like playing an instrument or playing a sport.)

P ___ ___ ___ ___ ___ ___ ___

By practicing things that make you nervous or scared, you can get rid of your false alarms and become braver. When you practice, you should start with smaller, less scary things and work up to bigger things.

Example: Pretend you have a friend who is afraid to talk to other children on the playground. Here are some things your friend could do to practice. If your friend keeps practicing, eventually he or she will be able to talk to other children on the playground.

#1 Smile at another child	#2 Say "hi" to another child	#3 Ask the other child's name

Now you try! Imagine you have a friend who is afraid of riding the bus. Make up some things your friend could practice to help him or her become brave enough to ride the bus. Remember to start with smaller things and work up to bigger things.

#1

#2

#3

Anxiety Detectives

What do detectives look for? (circle the right answer)

Cupcakes

Baseball gloves

Clues

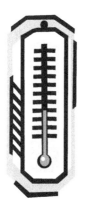 By using the fear thermometer and filling out the fear  ladders, we will collect clues and track your nervous or scared feelings to help you become braver!

 Great job! Now we're ready to get started and collect some clues for you!

Worksheet—Learning About Anxiety / 6 of 6

Helping Your Child Succeed

Encourage at-home practice. Many parents are surprised to learn that what happens at home and school is actually more important than what happens with the therapist. Therapy is similar to music lessons. If a child is taking piano lessons, his or her teacher reviews progress and assigns new things to practice. But if the child doesn't practice at home, he or she will never learn to play the piano. Similarly, a child who does not practice the techniques and activities assigned by the therapist is unlikely to make progress.

Coach your child. Therapists and parents act as coaches to help a child develop new skills. Your child will be most successful if you take on an increasingly larger coaching role as therapy progresses.

Make the program a high priority. The more energy and enthusiasm your family can commit to the program, the higher your child's chance of success. For now, the program may need to come before other things, like school plays, sports events, or family travel.

Be willing to work hard. If you are willing to work hard in the short term, you and your child will have better long-term results. For example, it can be tempting just to let your child have fun and relax by watching TV or hanging out with friends instead of practicing the week's assignments. In the short-term, this may put your child in a good mood, but the long-term anxiety problems won't go away. Working hard now can mean the anxiety problems can be much better for months or years.

	Uninterested child	Enthusiastic child
Uninterested parent	Lowest chance of success	Possible success
Enthusiastic parent	Possible success	Highest chance of success

Remember that practice is safe. Sometimes your child might feel uncomfortable during practice, complaining or even crying. No parent likes to see his or her child feeling distressed, and you might be tempted to stop the practice. However, try to remind yourself that the practice is safe. Your child is not in danger. The best thing you can do for your child is to be supportive and help him or her face the challenge. With practice, what is difficult for your child now will become easier over time.

Stay relaxed. When parents are anxious, treatment can become more difficult. Anxious parents have a particularly hard time watching their children practice things that are difficult for them. This is why the therapist takes on the primary coaching role in the beginning of treatment, deciding what pace is best for your child.

Attend therapy sessions faithfully. You should do everything possible to make sure you and your child attend all therapy sessions and that you are available to speak with the therapist—in person or by telephone—as necessary.

Speak up. Don't be afraid to let your therapist know what isn't working. The practice assignments aren't always easy, especially in the beginning. Parents who communicate about how the program is working for them and their family help their children succeed. The therapist can help you solve some of the problems you might face, even with things like lack of time or doubts about your child's progress

Parent Interview

1. In your earlier interview with [*assessor's name*], you talked about several problems your child has been having. You mentioned [*list the main problems and the symptoms of anxiety*]. When did you first notice that your child was having these problems?

2. What are the most common situations in which your child displays anxiety? What are the most common triggers for your child's anxiety? Are there specific things he or she does when he or she is feeling anxious?

3. What kinds of things does the anxiety prevent your child from doing? What kinds of activities have become difficult for your child because he or she experiences anxiety in these situations?

4. Now, I'd like to ask you about how your child gets along with others. How does he or she get along with family members at home? Is there anyone he or she is particularly close to? Anyone that your child does not get along with? Any particular problems at home that might affect his or her anxiety, or make his/her symptoms of anxiety worse?

5. Does your child have friends? How many? Is there a special friend he or she can share feelings with? Does he or she go to parties or sleepovers? Is he or she able to keep friends? Any problems with peers? Does your child have any close relationships with adults outside of the family? [*You should explore the child's social skills and quality of social network.*]

6. All of us have some qualities or ways of acting that draw others to us and make others want to be with us, and other qualities that others might not respond as well to. What qualities do you think your child has that draw kids his or her age to him or her? How about qualities or ways of acting that kids his or her age might not like as much? Does your child have any special qualities that adults respond really well to? How about qualities that might put adults off or make them respond negatively? [*You should explore the positive and negative ways the child presents him- or herself, in order to get information that might facilitate working with the child in subsequent sessions.*] What are some specific things you think your child should do more to get along with other kids? How about with adults?

7. How is your child doing in school? How are his or her grades? How about achievement test scores? Do the teachers think he or she is performing up to his or her ability?

8. Does your child have any specific skills, like sports or music, that he or she is particularly good at? Are there any skills he or she really wants to be good at, but isn't yet? How about clubs or organizations that he or she is a member of? Any that you think he or she would like to become a member of? [*You may wish to find a club or organization that the child could try out. Explore with the parent the feasibility of the child's joining that club.*]

9. Is there anything else that I should know about your child?

Understanding Anxiety

Is Anxiety Good or Bad?

A little anxiety can be a good thing. It can help an athlete get ready for the big game or a businessperson get ready for a big presentation. It helps all of us get out the door to be on time for work or school. It is only when people become anxious at times when there is no real danger—often called "false alarms"—that anxiety becomes a problem. For example, a student who usually earns good grades but panics during a test would be having a "false alarm."

Anxiety is a problem only when a child becomes anxious in the absence of any real danger or trouble.

How Does Anxiety Work?

The main purpose of anxiety is to help us be alert to danger and therefore be able to avoid it. In the early stages of anxiety, when the threat is not too close, a person feels worried or tense, starts focusing more on the possible threat, and cuts back on activities like running or playing. One researcher refers to this stage of anxiety as "stop, look, and listen." If a threat gets closer, the cautious feelings of "stop, look, and listen" will intensify, and the body will physically prepare to meet the danger. This is a natural response and can be genuinely useful in the face of a real threat. At this point, the body enters a second stage of anxiety, often called fear or panic. You might know this as the "fight or flight" response.

Animals often demonstrate these behaviors. For example, you may have noticed that if you approach a bird, it will freeze and stare at you—stop, look, and listen. If you continue to walk toward it, it will panic, either flying away in a sudden flutter of energy or, if necessary, trying to defend itself. In this case, increased alertness and speed help the bird protect itself.

Similarly, if a child who is walking to school suddenly hears a dog bark, she might pause and think about what to do next—stop, look, and listen. If the dog becomes aggressive and starts running toward her, she will move on to stage two, experiencing increased heartbeat, faster breathing, changes in blood pressure, and a rush of chemicals, designed to help the body increase strength, speed, and alertness. Some of these chemicals, such as adrenaline, can also bring side effects such as shakiness or nausea. This natural response will help her respond to a real threat by fleeing from the dog or, if necessary, even fighting it.

Why Is My Child Anxious?

Anxiety in children and adolescents has many different causes, including biological factors (things in your body), psychological factors (thoughts and feelings), and social factors (like school and friends). Most often, an anxiety disorder results from a combination of a child's "sensitive personality" with other things that add up over time, particularly early feelings of being out of control and specific negative experiences.

Sensitive Personality

"Sensitive personality" means that some children tend to be more easily worried, frightened, upset, or sad than others. They react more strongly to bad situations or to objects and information that seem threatening. A child with a sensitive personality has an increased risk of negative emotions throughout life, which can lead to anxiety disorders and sometimes depression.

Sense of Control

Children who have a sensitive personality and who feel they cannot control the things that happen in their lives are more likely to have a negative response to bad experiences. This sense of things being out of the child's control can be aggravated by situations that limit a child's opportunities to experience the world, to master challenges, and to get help when necessary. A child needs to develop a sense that he or she has some degree of control over bad situations, either by making them go away or by learning skills to cope with them.

Bad Experiences

In a child with a sensitive personality, bad experiences can shape the child's anxiety in particular ways. For example, a sensitive child who is stung by a bee might develop a phobia of bees. If the child is teased by classmates, social anxiety might develop. If the child is treated harshly by a stranger, separation anxiety may result.

Anxious Thoughts

Children with anxiety problems tend to see the world more negatively than other children do. They are very good at imagining what can go wrong. This tendency shows up in three important ways: (1) the things they pay attention to, (2) the way they interpret situations, and (3) the "self-talk" they engage in.

Attention

Anxious children focus more on negative things. For example, when researchers show children pairs of words on a computer screen, anxious children are more likely to look at words that seem threatening, such as "storm" or "crash." So anxious children tend to look for danger signals.

Interpretation

When presented with an unclear situation, anxious children are more likely to interpret it as dangerous. For example, when an anxious child is asked to imagine possible explanations for an unfamiliar noise, the child is more likely to offer negative answers such as, "a burglar."

Self-talk

Anxious children also generate more negative "self-talk" than non-

Anxious thoughts lead to anxious feelings—racing heart, sweaty palms, fast breathing— by creating "false alarms" when there is no real danger.

anxious children. That is, they are more likely to tell themselves things like, "I'll never be able to do this" or "I don't know what I'm doing."

How Cognitive Behavior Therapy Can Help

Cognitive Behavior Therapy is the most successful treatment approach for anxiety. It teaches children to tell the difference between real danger and a false alarm. When anxious children learn to identify which situations are safe, they can reduce or eliminate unnecessary tension, worry, fear, and panic. Children develop these skills primarily through practice exercises that teach them to use reasoning and experience to realize that many situations that may seem dangerous and scary are actually safe. Because anxious children tend to avoid the things they are afraid of, they tend to limit their opportunities for these practice experiences. A therapist or a parent can act as guide who encourages and supports the child to engage in these difficult experiences and to learn to recognize safe situations. Most of Cognitive Behavior Therapy is about practice that will help your child view the world in a new way.

Before-and-After Practice Record

Take ratings before and after each practice. Remember, keep going ____ times, or until your ratings come down to a ____. Good work!

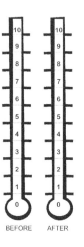 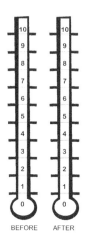 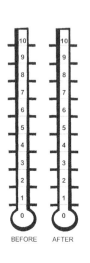 

Date: _____   _____   _____   _____   _____

Item: _____   _____   _____   _____   _____

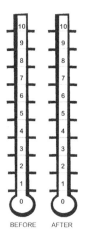 

Date: _____   _____   _____   _____   _____

Item: _____   _____   _____   _____   _____

Start-and-Stop Practice Record

Take ratings as you practice. Remember, keep going until your ratings come down to a _____. Good work!

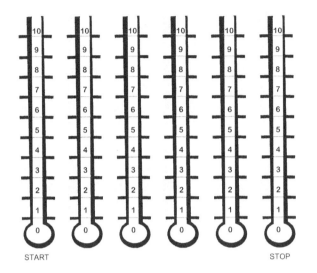

Date: _____

Item: _____

Date: _____

Item: _____

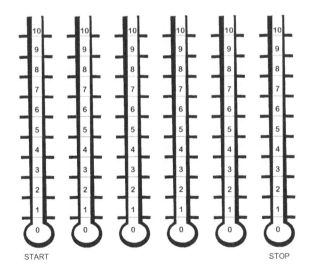

Date: _____

Item: _____

Date: _____

Item: _____

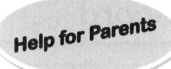

Practice

How Will Practice Help My Child?

Practice is the best possible way to overcome fear because it helps your child get used to doing things that are difficult at first. Through practice, your child will quickly learn to do things that were too hard before.

Practicing to reduce fear and anxiety is a lot like practicing a musical instrument or a sport. A child who practices guitar will get better at playing guitar. A child who practices soccer will get better at playing soccer. And a child who practices doing the things that make him or her nervous will get better—less nervous—at doing those things. For example, with practice, a child who is nervous around dogs can become more comfortable around them.

Practicing things that cause anxiety may not feel good at the time, just as music practice or exercise drills might not always seem fun. Practice is not

Practice can decrease anxiety about:

Animals • High places • Riding the bus • Going to school • Being teased • Being embarrassed • Swimming • Being in the dark • Being away from parents • Talking to other people • Trying to be perfect • Feeling out of breath • Feeling out of control • Getting a shot • Being around adults • Being around other children • Many, many other things

always easy, but you can make things easier by offering help and support to your child.

How Do We Practice?

Practice is similar to physical exercise. Your child will need to start slowly, with small tasks. Then, as your child gets in shape, he or she can take on bigger challenges and practice more often. We will work together with your child to make sure he or she is practicing the right amount.

1 Choose a target fear	Pick a fear you'd like your child to work on (e.g., standing near a dog, sleeping over at a friend's house, or talking to other children). Try to start with something that is not too challenging. You might even want to break things down into steps so your child can work on one smaller, easier thing at a time. Your child can move on to more difficult things as he or she progresses. **A fear I would like to see go away is:** ....
2 Pick a time to practice	Choose a time when everything is calm and no one feels rushed. Sometimes practice can take a while, so remember to leave plenty of time. **An example of a good time to help my child practice is:** ....
3 Take ratings	Take ratings every few minutes. Remember, the ratings range from 0 to 10, and higher numbers mean higher amounts of fear or anxiety. Over time, our goal is for the numbers to go down. Use the Practice Record to keep track of the ratings. This is the best way to see how well the practice is working and to figure out what to practice next.

4	**Be patient**	Sometimes it will take a while for your child to get used to something. Small children might even cry or protest during practice. Wait as long as you need to, stick with the practice, and keep telling your child how well he or she is doing. It may seem to take a long time, but soon your child will get used to whatever he or she is practicing.
5	**Practice, practice, practice**	Once you and your child get the hang of things, you can repeat a practice as much as you want. It's a lot like exercise: the more your child does, the better your child will feel. This is the best way to help your child with anxiety or fears. But don't forget to leave some time for fun things, too!
6	**Move on to something harder**	Once your child gets comfortable with a certain practice, you can try something a little tougher. Again, this is just like exercise. If your child can lift 5 pounds easily, he or she can try moving to 6 or 7. Just be careful not to make things too hard too fast. Otherwise, your child might become frustrated. We can help you figure out what to practice and how quickly to increase the difficulty of practice.
7	**Keep a regular routine**	It's important to help your child "stay in shape." Even after something gets easier, you'll want to have your child practice it again every once in a while, just to make sure it sticks.
8	**Praise & support**	Your child will need plenty of praise and support from as many people as possible. Practice can seem boring sometimes, but it is the very best way to stop feeling nervous or afraid. It will be worth the effort, so try to encourage your child and help him or her stay interested.

Help! Practice Isn't Working!

PROBLEM: **My child's ratings won't go down.**

TRY THIS: *The things you are practicing might be too hard for right now. Try working on something else, or breaking things into smaller steps. Another possibility is that the practices may be too short, not giving your child enough time to get used to things. Eventually your child's fear or anxiety will decrease, and the ratings will come down.*

PROBLEM: **My child's ratings go down, but the next time we practice, the ratings are right back up where they started.**

TRY THIS: *Usually when this happens, it means there has been too much time between practicing. If you've been practicing once or twice a week, try increasing to four or five times a week. Sometimes, you might need to practice every single day to see the ratings go down.*

PROBLEM: **My child is too scared to get started.**

TRY THIS: *This means you may be trying to do too much at once. Try breaking things down into smaller steps. Try to think of ways to make the practice easier without making it shorter. There are other solutions we can try, too, so don't be afraid to ask us for help.*

PROBLEM: **My child's ratings are going up, not down!**

TRY THIS: *This can happen if you stop in the middle of practice or if the practices are too short. Be sure to allow plenty of time in each practice for the ratings to come down. For now, you might try going back to something easier.*

PROBLEM: **My child says he or she doesn't need to practice anymore.**

TRY THIS: *Explain that practice is about building a skill. If you don't use it, you may lose it. Even when things aren't hard anymore, it's important to check back to make sure you can still do them. This is how you can keep the fear or anxiety from coming back.*

What's New?

What I couldn't do because of anxiety:	What I can do now:

Maintaining Success on Your Own

Congratulations!

You and your child have probably put in many hours of practice and have worked hard to make progress. Learning the skills to overcome anxiety isn't easy. Your child and your family deserve a lot of credit.

What Happens Now?

The number of meetings will now gradually decrease. There will probably be some progress checks and question-and-answer sessions every couple of weeks—or maybe even less often—as you and your family take over the work on your own. There may be a few things that still need to be worked on after the program is over. This is normal. In fact, it's part of the plan. Your child and your family will work together to use the new skills you have developed, and as you do so, your child's confidence will increase. With your support, your child will keep facing fears and practicing on his or her own. Children often continue to improve for six months or more after finishing the program.

If you have any questions about how to continue the program on your own, be sure to ask them now. Use the last meeting as a time to celebrate and do something fun together.

Staying in Shape

Like exercise, learning to cope with anxiety can be difficult and tiring at first. With time, it becomes easier and more natural, especially if you make it part of your regular routine. But just as a person who stops exercising can get out of shape again, a person who stops practicing bravery might start to have a hard time dealing with anxiety again.

It's important to help your child continue to practice. The practice

Some ways I can help my child keep practicing:

_____

_____

_____

doesn't need to be as difficult or intense as it was in the beginning, but doing a little bit now and then will help your child stay in shape.

Try to help your child think of ways to challenge him- or herself a few times a week. You might think of this as "mini practice" exercises. And don't forget to keep practicing the new skills you've learned, as well.

Remember to Praise

Praising your child will continue to be a great way to keep things on track. Be sure to tell your child how proud you are of all the work he or she did to get this far. Try to point out how well things are going—even little things—to help nurture your child's enthusiasm and courage.

Things I can look for to praise:

_____

_____

_____

What If the Anxiety Comes Back?

There is a big difference between a "lapse" and a "relapse." Lapses are minor and completely normal. A child with anxiety can expect to have lapses every now and then throughout life, especially during stressful times. It just means a few things need to be practiced again.

If your child has a lapse, remember what you learned at the beginning of the program: a little anxiety is normal and can sometimes even be helpful. Don't immediately assume that your child is having a relapse, or a full return of the original problem. Relapses almost never happen, and if they do, it is usually because the child stopped practicing or because someone panicked during a lapse. Stay calm, and remember that your child already has the skills he or she needs to handle this. Encourage your child to use those skills.

If things get to a point where even the new skills and techniques don't seem to be working, you can always ask for assistance to get things back on track. Sometimes just a few simple suggestions can point you and your child in the right direction.

STOP

STOP will be an important part of getting braver. When we talk about STOP, S stands for *scared*, T stands for *thoughts*, O stands for *other thoughts*, and P stands for *praise*. Let's learn more about STOP.

 S is the first letter in the word *scared*. Let's learn more about feeling scared.

Scared Scramble

Unscramble the letters below to find other words for feeling scared.

ERVOUNS

--- --- --- --- --- --- ---

IERWROD

--- --- --- --- --- --- ---

DAARIF

--- --- --- --- --- ---

Figuring out Feelings

See if you can figure out how the people below are feeling.

This person feels	This person feels	This person feels	This person feels
How do you know?	How do you know?	How do you know?	How do you know?

Feelings Match

Here are some of the feelings you might have when you are scared. Draw a line to match the word with the picture it describes.

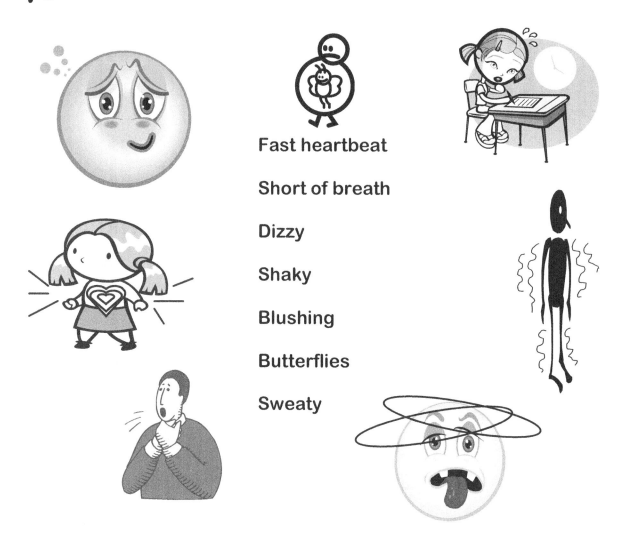

Fast heartbeat

Short of breath

Dizzy

Shaky

Blushing

Butterflies

Sweaty

When Do You Feel Scared?

It is important to know when you feel scared, nervous, or worried, so that you can practice feeling better. What are some times when you feel like this?

Example: When the teacher asks me a question.

1. _____

2. _____

3. _____

T is the first letter of the word *thoughts*. Let's learn more about the way thoughts work.

Good Thoughts/Bad Thoughts

Write something good that will happen.

I get to play with my friend this afternoon!

Write something bad that will happen.

Everyone will laugh at me.

Thoughts & Feelings

The thoughts you have can change how you feel. What thoughts do these people have about the rollercoaster? Who feels better? Write in the thoughts they are having.

Worksheet—STOP / 4 of 7

O stands for *other thoughts*. We can learn to have other thoughts about things so that we don't feel scared or nervous.

Practicing Other Thoughts

Try writing some other thoughts below.

No one at my new school will want to be my friend.

Other thought:

If I can't answer the teacher's question, everyone will laugh.

Other thought:

Your Other Thoughts

Think of some scary or nervous thoughts you have sometimes. Write some down, and see if you can think of OTHER thoughts that are not so scary.

Thought:

Other thought:

Thought:

Other thought:

P stands for *praise*. Don't forget to tell yourself that you are doing a terrific job when you use S-T-O-P to make yourself feel less nervous or scared!

 Stands for "Scared"

 Stands for "Thoughts"

 Stands for "Other thoughts"

 Stands for "Praise"

Feelings Thermometer

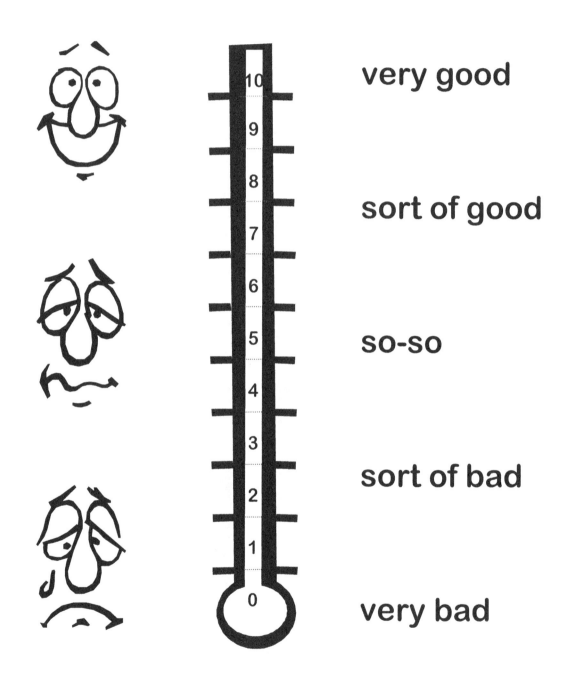

10	very good
9	
8	sort of good
7	
6	
5	so-so
4	
3	sort of bad
2	
1	
0	very bad

Daily Feelings Record

Take a feelings rating every day by circling the number on the thermometer.
Remember to write down what was happening to make you feel that way.

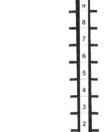

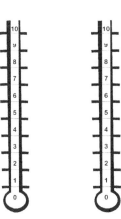

Date: _____ _____ _____ _____ _____

What was
happening: _____ _____ _____ _____ _____

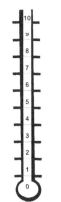
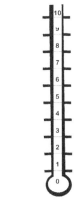

Date: _____ _____ _____ _____ _____

What was
happening: _____ _____ _____ _____ _____

How I Show My Feelings

When I am in a bad mood ...

These are the things I usually do (activities, people I spend time with, etc.):

This is how I look and sound to other people (eye contact or not, slumping or standing up, sad or happy voice):

This is what I think about myself and my world:

This is how my body feels (antsy, sleepy, relaxed, etc.):

This is how I act around others:

When I am in a good mood ...

These are the things I usually do (activities, people I spend time with, etc.):

This is how I look and sound to other people (eye contact or not, slumping or standing up, sad or happy voice):

This is what I think about myself and my world:

This is how my body feels (antsy, sleepy, relaxed, etc.):

This is how I act around others:

Thinking-Feeling-Doing

Everybody feels sad, down, grumpy, or upset sometimes, but getting stuck in these feelings can be a problem. To get unstuck, we can change how we THINK and what we DO, because thinking and doing have a big impact on how we FEEL.

Imagine a Rainy Day

Circle the person below who feels better. What makes that person feel better?

_____

_____

_____

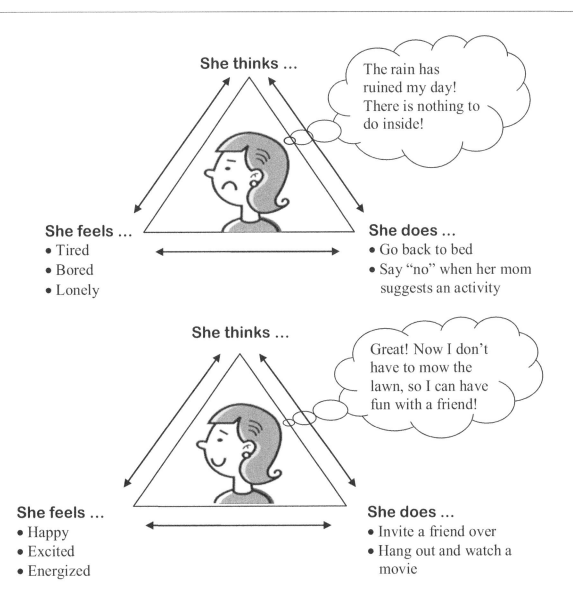

She thinks …

The rain has ruined my day! There is nothing to do inside!

She feels …
- Tired
- Bored
- Lonely

She does …
- Go back to bed
- Say "no" when her mom suggests an activity

She thinks …

Great! Now I don't have to mow the lawn, so I can have fun with a friend!

She feels …
- Happy
- Excited
- Energized

She does …
- Invite a friend over
- Hang out and watch a movie

What Do YOU Think, Feel, and Do?

What about YOU? Think of a time recently when you got stuck in a bad mood. What did you THINK, FEEL, and DO? If you had different thoughts or took different actions, would you have felt differently?

What was happening?

_____

_____

_____

What could you have thought instead?

_____

_____

_____

You thought ...

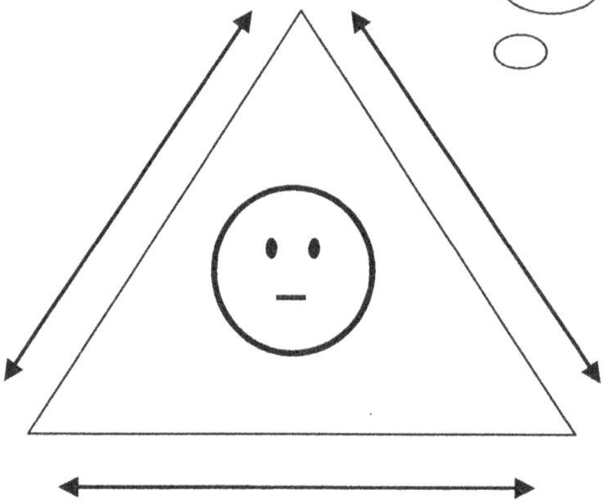

You felt ...

_____

_____

_____

How might you have felt instead?

_____

_____

You did ...

_____

_____

_____

What could you have done instead?

_____

_____

Parent Interview

1. In your earlier interview with [assessor's name], you talked about several problems [child's name] has been having. You mentioned [list the main problems and the depressive symptoms]. Is this list correct, or should it be changed in any way? When did you first notice that [name] was having these problems?

2. What situations seem to trigger [name]'s depressed feelings? Are there particular situations in which [name] has seemed especially upset or distressed recently? Was there a particular life situation or event that might have caused [name] to have these problems (e.g., a divorce, a death in the family)?

3. What are the most common ways [name] shows his/her bad mood? Are there specific things he/she does when he/she is feeling depressed? Are there specific things he/she thinks when he/she is feeling depressed?

4. When he/she is feeling depressed, what kinds of things have you seen him/her do (e.g., ride a bike, talk to a friend)—that usually **improve** his/her mood? [Give the parent plenty of time and encouragement to answer this question. Learning what **improves** the child's mood can be very helpful to you in planning treatment and identifying the most helpful coping skills for the child.]

5. Now, I'd like to ask you about how [name] gets along with others. How does [name] get along with family members at home? Is there anyone [name] is particularly close to? Anyone that [name] does not get along with? Any particular situations at home that might affect [name]'s mood?

6. Does [name] have friends? How many? Is there a special friend he/she can share feelings with? Does he/she go to parties or sleepovers? Is he/she able to keep friends? Any problems with peers? Does [name] have any close relationships with adults outside of the family? [Explore child's social skills and quality of social network]

7. What qualities or characteristics do other kids like about [name]? How about ways of acting that kids his/her age might not like as much? Does [name] have any special qualities that adults respond really well to? How about qualities that might put adults off or make them respond negatively to your child? [Explore the positive and negative ways child presents him-/herself, in order to get information that might facilitate working with the child in subsequent sessions].

8. How is [name] doing in school? How are his/her grades? How about achievement test scores? Do the teachers think he/she is performing up to his/her ability?

9. Does [name] have any specific skills, like sports or music, that he/she is particularly good at? Are there any skills he/she really wants to be good at, but isn't yet? How about clubs or organizations that he/she is a member of? Any that you think he/she would like to become a member of? [You may wish, as a part of your treatment, to find a club or organization the child could try out. Explore with parent(s) logistical feasibility of the child's joining that club.]

10. Is there anything else I should know about [name]?

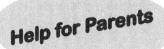
Help for Parents

Understanding Depression

Depression in Children and Adolescents

Depression is relatively common in children and adolescents, and can look very different than it does in adults. For example, children who are depressed may seem cranky rather than sad, or lose interest in doing activities they once enjoyed. They may show changes in their sleeping or eating habits, say negative things about themselves or others, or expect bad things to happen in the future. Some depressed children seem tired and unmotivated, while others may seem restless. Almost all children can feel bad in these ways sometimes—that's normal; but it's a problem when kids get "stuck" feeling sad, down, or upset. The good news is, there are

Depression can make children irritable, or less interested in doing things they once enjoyed.

some effective ways to help children feel better and manage their feelings—so that they don't get "stuck."

What We Think and Do Changes How We Feel

We are all affected by the things we think to ourselves and by the things we do in response to our feelings. If it is raining and you think to yourself, "Oh, no! Now all my plans are ruined!" you might feel pretty bad, and in response you might just get back into bed and sleep all day. If you did that, you might miss out on lots of chances to feel better. On the other hand, if you thought, "I'm glad it's raining; now I can stay inside and finish that great book I've been reading!" you would probably feel happy, and do something you enjoy. Children who have difficulties with sad or cranky mood are more likely to have negative thoughts about events in their lives, and also less likely to choose activities that will help them feel better. In this program, your child will learn ways to improve his or her mood by changing thoughts, changing behaviors, or changing both.

Why Is My Child Depressed?

Depression in children and adolescents has many different causes, including biological factors, psychological factors (such as thoughts and feelings), and social factors (such as school and friends). Depression can often result when a child with a "sensitive personality" loses a sense of control and experiences multiple stressors.

Sensitive Personality

"Sensitive personality" means that some children tend to be more easily irritated, upset, or sad than others. They react more strongly to bad situations or to information that seem threatening. A child with a sensitive personality has an increased risk of negative emotions throughout life, which can lead to mood disorders.

Sense of Control

Children who have a sensitive personality and who feel they cannot control the things that happen in their lives are more likely to have a negative response to bad experiences. This sense of things being out of control can be aggravated by situations that limit a child's opportunities to experience the world, to master challenges, and to get help when necessary. Children need to believe that they have some control over bad situations, either by making the situations go away or by learning skills to cope with them.

Stressful Experiences

Among children who have a sensitive personality, stressful experiences can shape mood, too. For example, sensitive children who experience failure may come to believe that they will never succeed, even if they have been quite successful in the past. A sensitive child who is rejected by peers may withdraw from social experiences. This same child may perceive things to be overwhelmingly negative even when they are not, or give up easily when the going gets tough.

Negative Thoughts

Depressed children tend to see the world more negatively than other children do. They are very good at imagining what might go wrong. This tendency shows up in three important ways: (1) the things they pay attention to, (2) the way they interpret situations, and (3) the "self-talk" they engage in.

Attention

Depressed children focus on the negative more than most children do. For example, they are more likely to pay attention to signs that things are not going well, and more likely to remember unhappy events than happy ones.

Interpretation

Depressed children are more likely than others to think negative thoughts about themselves, others, and the world. For example, when depressed children are asked to think of reasons why they did poorly on an exam, they are more likely to think "because I am not smart" instead of "because the exam was hard."

Self-talk

Depressed children also generate more negative "self-talk" than non-anxious children. That is, they are more likely than other children to tell themselves things like, "I'll never be able to do this" or "Things will never work out."

Negative thoughts can lead to hopeless feelings; helpless feelings can lead children to give up rather than try to solve problems in their lives.

How Cognitive Behavioral Therapy Can Help

Cognitive Behavioral Therapy is the treatment approach for children and adolescents that has been tested most and shown to work. It helps young people develop coping skills to address their specific difficulties. Several skills are taught to children. The therapist will work with your child to identify the skills that will help him or her the most. Children develop these skills primarily through practice exercises. Because most depressed children have developed certain habits of thinking and behavior, it can feel strange or artificial to them, at first, to try new ways of thinking or behaving. A therapist or a parent can act as a guide who encourages and supports the child as the child tries these skills out. Cognitive Behavioral Therapy involves practice—practice that helps children learn new coping skills and view the world in a new way.

Helping Your Child Solve Problems

Five S-T-E-P-S for Problem Solving

Some children have a hard time solving problems that arise in their lives, such as problems with friends, schoolwork, or how to manage a bad mood. They may feel hopeless about solving these problems, or perhaps they will try one solution and then give up when it doesn't work. Because we all have to face problems from time to time, learning a step-by-step approach to solving them can be valuable. When your child has a problem, encourage him or her to try the S-T-E-P-S approach shown below. Offer support, but try to help your child come up with his or her own ideas as much as possible.

S — Say what the problem is.

T — Think of possible solutions. (Try to think of several here. Don't worry yet whether they are "good" or "bad" solutions.)

E — Examine each possible solution, looking at the good and bad aspects of each one.

P — Pick one solution to try out.

S — See if it worked. If it worked, great! If it did not work, then go back to your list of solutions and try another one.

Five S-T-E-P-S to Problem Solving

S Say what the problem is.

_____

_____

T Think of solutions.

1. _____

2. _____

3. _____

4. _____

E Examine each solution you listed above. What good & bad things might happen if you did each one?

GOOD	BAD
1. _____	1. _____
2. _____	2. _____
3. _____	3. _____
4. _____	4. _____

P Pick one and try it out. Which one are you going to try?

_____

S See if it worked. If it worked, great! If it did not work, then go back to your list of solutions and try another one.

Doing Something Fun to Feel Better

Mood rating after I imagine a bad day:

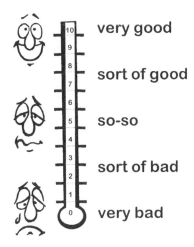

What my therapist and I did for fun:

_____

Mood rating after the fun activity:

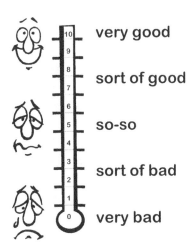

Ten Things I Can Do to Feel Good!

1. _____

2. _____

3. _____

4. _____

5. _____

6. _____

7. _____

8. _____

9. _____

10. _____

Scheduling Time for Fun

Write down one fun activity you can do each day. Write your *Feelings Thermometer* rating before and after each activity.

Day and Plan	How I Felt Before (0-10)	Activity I Did	How I Felt After (0-10)
	very good sort of good so-so sort of bad very bad		very good sort of good so-so sort of bad very bad
EXAMPLE **SATURDAY:** Play soccer with my friend after lunch	5	Played soccer with my friend after lunch	8
SUNDAY:			
MONDAY:			
TUESDAY:			
WEDNESDAY:			
THURSDAY:			
FRIDAY:			
SATURDAY:			

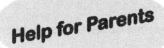

Activity Selection

Activities Can Help Your Child

When children feel sad, down, upset, or cranky, they may withdraw from activities that used to make them feel good. They may feel too tired to do the fun things they once enjoyed, or believe that these activities are now pointless or uninteresting. When this happens, they miss out on opportunities to feel better—just when they need these opportunities most! It will help your child prevent getting stuck in bad moods if he or she will deliberately schedule pleasant activities every single day—making sure that these are activities he or she really enjoys.

What Kinds of Activities Will Help?

Here are four simple, inexpensive kinds of activities that can lead to good feelings:

1. **Doing activities that we have enjoyed in the past.** For nearly all of us, there are some activities that are almost guaranteed to make us feel better.
2. **Doing things with someone we like.** Activities we do with a friend can make us feel really good. Even something simple, like talking on the phone or eating lunch together at school, may help a lot.
3. **Staying busy by getting involved with a group or club.** Joining a group or a club can help us stay really busy. We may get so involved and so busy that we don't have time to worry about how we feel. Also, the activities we do with our group or club may be fun, too.
4. **Helping someone else.** Helping another person gets our minds on other people, and that can be good for all of us. Knowing that we are helping someone can also give us a good feeling inside.

How You Can Help

When you see that your son or daughter is feeling bad, or sad, or grouchy, you can help him or her to get involved in new activities. Maybe your son or daughter could call up a friend and plan an activity together with that friend. Or maybe you can help think of a club or group (maybe at school or church/temple) that your child could join, to stay really busy. And finally, maybe you can help think of something your son or daughter can do to help another person.

Your child has worked with the therapist to write down ten activities that he or she really likes to do—activities that make him or her feel good. Try posting the list in a prominent place in the house, like on the refrigerator door, so that you will easily have good ideas to suggest to your son or daughter.

Learning to Relax

How Do You Feel BEFORE Relaxing?

This is how I feel **BEFORE** relaxing (when I'm thinking about a stressful situation):

This is how I feel physically:

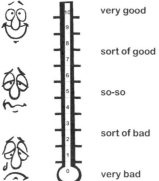

_____

_____

_____

How Do You Feel AFTER Relaxing?

This is how I feel **AFTER** relaxing:

This is how I feel physically:

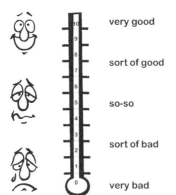

_____

_____

_____

What's Your Favorite Part of Relaxing?

Which part of relaxing do you like the best? Rank them: #1, #2, and #3!

_____ Breathing out Stress & Breathing in Calm

_____ Tensing & Relaxing Muscles

_____ Imagining a Calm, Relaxing Place

Relaxing at Home

Practice relaxing **twice** this week by using your relaxation audio file. Write the situation that made you tense, your *Feelings Thermometer* rating when you were tense, and your *Feelings Thermometer* rating after you did the calming activity.

Situation that Made Me Feel Tense	How I Felt Before Relaxing (0-10)	How I Felt After Relaxing (0-10)
	10 very good 9 8 sort of good 7 6 5 so-so 4 3 sort of bad 2 1 0 very bad	10 very good 9 8 sort of good 7 6 5 so-so 4 3 sort of bad 2 1 0 very bad
Situation 1:		
Situation 2:		

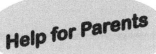

Self-Calming Through Relaxation

How Can Relaxation Help My Child?

When children feel sad, worried, or upset, they may feel tense and agitated in their bodies. One way to help children change the way they feel emotionally is to help them change the way they feel physically. Relaxation training can improve mood because children are more positive and calm when they feel physically relaxed.

What Can My Child Do to Relax?

Alone or guided by instruction on the relaxation audio file provided by the therapist, your child can relax in three ways: 1) by taking deep, slow breaths, 2) by tensing and relaxing various muscles, and 3) by using his or her imagination to think about a peaceful scene. With practice, your child can learn to relax when he or she is feeling bad or after upsetting events have happened. This kind of self-calming through relaxation is a skill that can be used almost anywhere at any time!

1. **Deep, Slow Breathing.** Your child can take deep breaths—"breathing out stress, and breathing in calm."
2. **Deep Muscle Relaxation.** Your child can tense and relax various muscle groups (hands, arms, shoulders, etc.) until most of the muscles in his or her body are relaxed.
3. **Picturing a Peaceful Scene.** Your child can imagine a calm, peaceful scene and hold that picture in mind while relaxing.

How Can I Help?

Learning to relax requires lots of practice! The first thing you can do is try to help your son or daughter find a quiet time and place to practice relaxation at home. If there are siblings, your child might choose to have them join in the practice, or he or she might need to find a private place and/or use headphones to practice relaxing alone with the recording. Second, when you see that your child is feeling bad, worried, or tense, you can encourage him or her to practice using the relaxation skills—with or without the recording. Finally, if you use relaxation skills in your own life, you might talk with your son or daughter about how relaxation skills help you calm down and feel better in certain situations (as a simple example, maybe it helps you to just take 3 deep breaths when you have to wait in long line at the supermarket or you are late for an appointment).

a

My Relaxing Place

My relaxing place is _____

What I *see:*

What I *smell:*

What I *feel/touch:*

What I *hear:*

What I *taste:*

Quick Calming Practice

Learning to make our bodies relax is a good way to keep from feeling too nervous, upset, or tense. **Quick Calming** involves relaxing our tense muscles, taking deep breaths and exhaling slowly, and thinking of a peaceful place. Quick Calming can be used anywhere. It is especially good to use when other people are around, like before a test, or when you've been caught off-guard by a situation that makes you tense.

Practice Instructions

One day this week, practice Quick Calming using the following steps:

1. Find a time when you are in a public place, such as sitting on the bus, in your classroom at school, or in a waiting room.

2. Use the **Feelings Thermometer** to show how you feel <u>before</u> you start using Quick Calming.

3. Do the three steps of Quick Calming (they spell **ReST**):

   - **Relax your muscles**
     - o Relax the muscles, especially those that feel most tense
   - **Slow your breathing**
     - o Take slow, deep breaths and exhale slowly each time
   - **Think of a peaceful place**
     - o Picture a peaceful place and imagine that you're relaxing there

4. Use the Feelings Thermometer to show how you feel <u>after</u> you used Quick Calming.

Day of the week: _____

How I felt <u>before</u> Quick Calming

very good

sort of good

so-so

sort of bad

very bad

How I felt <u>after</u> Quick Calming

very good

sort of good

so-so

sort of bad

very bad

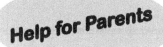

Quick Calming

When children feel sad, worried, or upset, they may feel tense and agitated in their bodies. One way to help children change the way they feel emotionally is to help them change the way they feel physically. Relaxation training can improve mood because children are more positive and calm when they feel physically relaxed.

One kind of relaxation your child can use is called Quick Calming. This is a way to calm down in public when it's hard to find a private spot, when time is short, or when your child is caught off-guard by a stressful situation. With practice, your son or daughter can learn to use Quick Calming to feel more relaxed and calm in a variety of situations. There are three steps in Quick Calming (they spell **ReST**):

Relax your muscles.

Focus especially on the muscles that feel most tense.

Slow your breathing.

Take slow, deep breaths and exhale slowly each time.

Think of a peaceful place.

Picture a peaceful place and imagine that you're relaxing there.

How Can I Help?

When you see that your child is feeling bad, worried, or upset in public or when time is short, encourage him or her to use the Quick Calming skill. Situations when Quick Calming may be useful include (1) waiting for a performance or test to begin, (2) after an argument with a friend at school, and (3) learning at the last minute that weekend plans have been cancelled. Your reminders will help your son or daughter remember that there is a good way to calm down quickly when something bad has happened or when feelings of stress and tension have come up quickly.

My Negative Self and My Positive Self

What are the things you do to show the world that you are in a good or a bad mood? Make a list below of the ways you show your **Negative Self** and your **Positive Self**.

	Negative Self	Positive Self
How I <u>Look</u> (eye contact, posture, dress)	1. 2.	1. 2.
How I <u>Act</u> (how do I behave?)	1. 2.	1. 2.
What I <u>Say</u> (about myself, others, the world)	1. 2.	1. 2.

Practicing My Positive Self

Pick a person, place, and time to try out your positive self!

The person I picked is: _____

The place I picked is: _____

The time I picked is: _____

Before	After
very good / sort of good / so-so / sort of bad / very bad My rating is: _____	very good / sort of good / so-so / sort of bad / very bad My rating is: _____

How My Face and Body Will Look	Did I Do It?		
1.	No	A Little	A Lot
2.	No	A Little	A Lot
How I Will Act and Talk	**Did I Do It?**		
1.	No	A Little	A Lot
2.	No	A Little	A Lot
Things I Will Say	**Did I Do It?**		
1.	No	A Little	A Lot
2.	No	A Little	A Lot

Presenting a Positive Self

How Can Presenting a Positive Self Help My Child?

Presenting ourselves in a positive, optimistic way can improve our mood and improve our social relationships. When children feel sad, down, or worried, they may have a hard time presenting themselves in a positive way. This can cause other people to feel uncomfortable and respond in a way that only makes things worse! Fortunately, presenting a **Positive Self** is a skill that can be learned—just like sports or math.

There is an important connection between self-presentation, mood, and relationships. Specifically:
- If we present a negative, gloomy self to the world it can make us feel bad, and it can also make other people uncomfortable around us and less likely to spend time with us.
- Showing a **Positive Self** to the world can make us feel better, and it can also make other people more comfortable with us, and more likely to spend time with us.

How Can My Child Present a Positive Self?

Showing a **Positive Self** is a skill, like sports, dancing, or math. It involves specific kinds of behavior that people can **practice**, and **get better at when they do practice**.

Your son or daughter is working with the therapist to identify several specific behaviors he or she uses to show a negative self and to show a positive self. These behaviors generally fall into three categories:
- How your child looks (e.g., how his or her face looks, how his or her body looks)
- How your child acts (e.g., toward family, toward other kids)
- What your child says (e.g., about him- or herself and his or her activities, about other people, about the future)

How Can I Help?

When you notice that your son or daughter is showing a **negative** self—being sad or grouchy or gloomy—you can remind him or her to try to show a **Positive Self**. Remind your child that **showing a Positive Self helps us feel good about ourselves, and it can make other people want to spend time with us.** You could also remind your son or daughter about some of the specific things he or she can do to show a **Positive Self**.

Changing B-L-U-E Thoughts

B-L-U-E thoughts are thoughts that are too negative to be true. B-L-U-E thoughts make us feel bad.

B laming myself

L ooking for bad news

U nhappy guessing

E xaggerating

Come up with some B-L-U-E thoughts for the examples below.

That test today was really hard!

Give an example of Blaming Yourself

Oops! I accidentally painted that tree purple!

Give an example of Looking for Bad News

My recital is tomorrow.

Give an example of Unhappy Guessing

On my math test I got 21 right and 4 wrong.

Give an example of Exaggerating

Worksheet—Changing B-L-U-E Thoughts / 1 of 2

Double Bubbles

What we think can change the way we feel. Practice changing unrealistic **B-L-U-E** thoughts to more realistic **TRUE** thoughts. Remember to ask yourself the following questions:

- **What's the evidence?**
- **Is there another way to look at the situation?**
- **What would you tell a friend who had this thought?**
- **What if it _is_ true—would that really be so bad?**

Double Bubbles on My Own

Think of a situation from your own life when you had a **B-L-U-E** thought. Examine the evidence to see if the thought is realistic. Try to come up with a more realistic **TRUE** thought, and see whether it changes your feelings thermometer! Remember to ask yourself the following questions:

- What's the evidence?
- Is there another way to look at the situation?
- What would you tell a friend who had this thought?
- What if it <u>is</u> true—would that really be so bad?

What was the situation? _____

_____

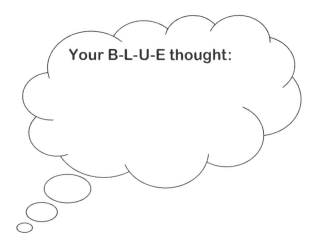

Your B-L-U-E thought:

A more realistic TRUE thought:

This thought made me feel ...

This thought made me feel ...

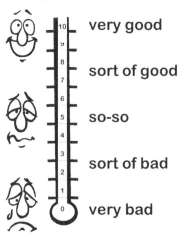

very good

sort of good

so-so

sort of bad

very bad

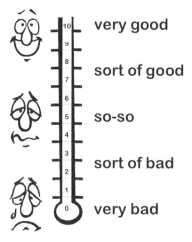

very good

sort of good

so-so

sort of bad

very bad

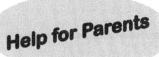

Changing
B-L-U-E Thoughts

Why Are Thoughts Important?

The things that we think about ourselves, others, and the world have a big impact on the way we feel. Some children have a tendency to think negative thoughts in response to situations that may be challenging. For example, these children might think, "I'm not good at math" when they struggle with their homework, or "Nothing ever works out for me" when they don't get invited to a party or make a sports team. These negative thoughts make children feel even worse, and sometimes feel like giving up. It is useful to consider the clues that support or don't support these negative thoughts. Changing overly negative thoughts (BLUE thoughts) into thoughts that are more realistic (TRUE thoughts) can improve your child's mood and help him or her view the world in a different way.

There are four kinds of negative thoughts to look out for, which spell out the word "B-L-U-E":

B laming myself	Assuming that bad things are all your fault
L ooking for the bad news	Ignoring the good things about a situation
U nhappy guessing	Telling yourself bad things will come true
E xaggerating	Imagining a disaster or making something seem worse than it is

How Can I Help My Child Change B-L-U-E Thoughts?

When you notice that he or she is having negative or B-L-U-E thoughts, encourage your child to be like a detective and answer the following questions:

- What's the evidence that this thought is true?
- Is there another way to look at the situation?
- What would I tell a friend?
- What if it is true—would that really be so bad?

Then help your child come up with a more realistic, TRUE thought!

Coping Through TLC

When something bad has happened, TLC strategies can help you cope. T is for "Talk to a friend." It is important to think of friends you can talk to when something has gone wrong, or you are feeling down. That way, you'll know you're not alone. L is for "Look for the silver lining." Sometimes good things can come from bad situations. C is for "Change the channel." That means thinking about things that make you feel good instead of about things that make you feel bad.

T alk to a friend

L ook for the silver lining

C hange the channel

Talk to a Friend

List some people you can talk to when something bad has happened. It could be friends or family members.

1. _____

2. _____

3. _____

4. _____

5. _____

Worksheet—Coping Through TLC / 1 of 4

Look for the Silver Lining

Every dark cloud has a silver lining. Even though it seems strange, a good thing can come from a bad situation. Try thinking of some silver linings for the situations below.

Because of this bad situation: I got this silver lining:

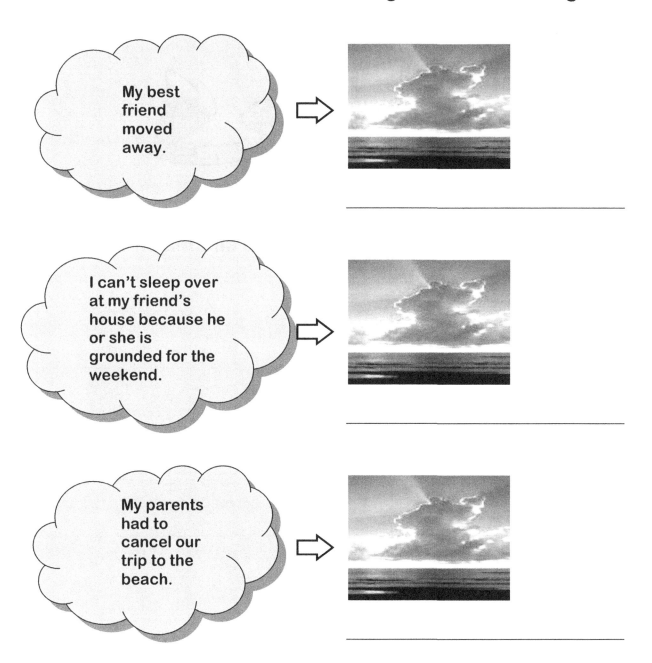

My best friend moved away.

_____

I can't sleep over at my friend's house because he or she is grounded for the weekend.

_____

My parents had to cancel our trip to the beach.

_____

Change the Channel

When something bad happens, you'll feel bad if you just keep replaying it over and over again in your head. To stop thinking about things that make you feel bad, you need to get your mind on something else. In other words, you need to *change channels*. Below, list some ways that you can change channels.

Things I can do to change channels:

1. _____

2. _____

3. _____

4. _____

5. _____

Try TLC on Your Own

Next time something happens that puts you in a bad mood, use TLC!

Situation that made me feel bad: _____

Before	After
very good — 10, 9, 8	**very good** — 10, 9, 8
sort of good — 7, 6	**sort of good** — 7, 6
so-so — 5, 4	**so-so** — 5, 4
sort of bad — 3, 2	**sort of bad** — 3, 2
very bad — 1, 0	**very bad** — 1, 0
My rating is: _____	My rating is: _____

What kind of skill I will try	What I did or thought
Talk to a friend. Thinking things over with someone who could help me feel better.	
Look for the silver lining. Finding a good thing caused by a bad situation.	
Change channels. Doing something to take my mind off the bad stuff.	

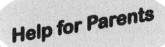

Using T-L-C
When Bad Things Happen

How Can My Child Cope When Something Bad Happens?

Sometimes children face bad situations that they can't change—like when a good friend moves away. Even when a bad situation can't be changed, children may still be able to control how the situation affects them—especially how they feel in response to the situation. There are three good things your son or daughter can do to control his or her feelings when bad things happen. These three things spell out **T-L-C**.

Talk to a Friend

One great approach is to talk to a friend about the situation. A friend may have a different perspective or good advice, or maybe it will help just to have the friend listen and understand.

Look for the Silver Lining

It really is true that most dark clouds have a silver lining. When bad things happen, there is often a good thing that comes out of them. If a good friend moves away, this friend might become a great email pen pal—and someone to visit during vacations. Or maybe this frees up more time to spend with another kid who could become a new friend.

Change the Channel

Finally, when unhappy thoughts keep replaying over and over in your child's mind, it can be useful for him or her to get really involved in doing something completely different. This can help distract your child from thinking about a situation that can't really be changed.

How Can I Help?

When you know that something bad has happened, something that is making your son or daughter feel bad, take a look at the list of **TLC** skills, and encourage your son or daughter to try one of these three things. This may help him or her get better control over emotions and feel more upbeat. It might also be helpful to ask your child to give a *Feelings Thermometer* rating before the activity and after the activity.

My Favorite Skills for Feeling Good

You have learned several new skills to help you feel better when you feel mad, sad, upset or down. Because everyone is different, some skills may help you more than others. Which skills are the most reliable tools in your "toolbox"? When would you use these tools?

My Favorite Skills Are:

1. _____

Example: _____

When I can use this skill _____

2. _____

Example: _____

When I can use this skill _____

3. _____

Example: _____

When I can use this skill _____

Following My Plans

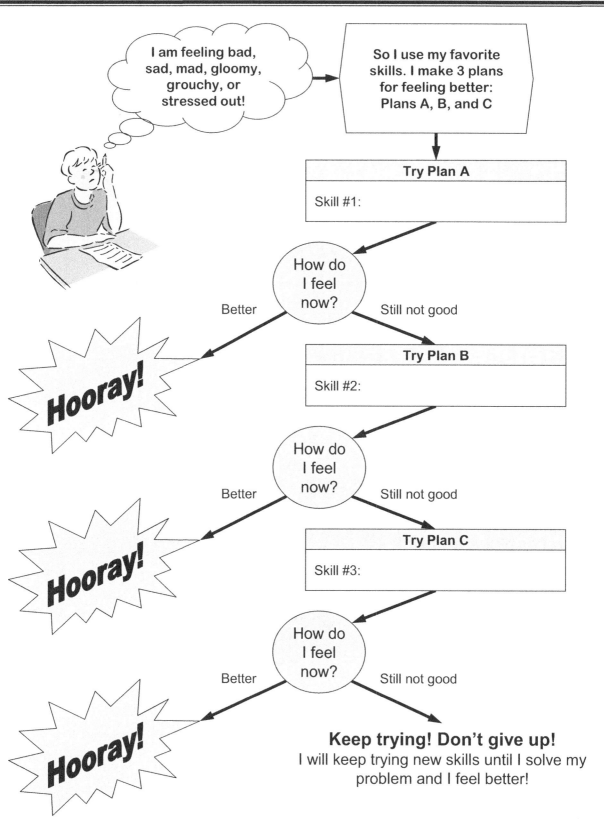

I am feeling bad, sad, mad, gloomy, grouchy, or stressed out!

So I use my favorite skills. I make 3 plans for feeling better: Plans A, B, and C

Try Plan A

Skill #1:

How do I feel now?

Better

Still not good

Hooray!

Try Plan B

Skill #2:

How do I feel now?

Better

Still not good

Hooray!

Try Plan C

Skill #3:

How do I feel now?

Better

Still not good

Hooray!

Keep trying! Don't give up!
I will keep trying new skills until I solve my problem and I feel better!

Practicing My New Skills

When you feel bad, try using the skills you have learned. Write a skill for Plan A, Plan B, and Plan C below. Then write how you think it will help. After you try each one, write down that you did it and give a **Feelings Thermometer** rating. Remember: don't give up—keep trying until you feel better!

What's making me feel bad: _____

My Feelings Thermometer rating right now: _____

very good

sort of good

so-so

sort of bad

very bad

What I would like my rating to be: _____

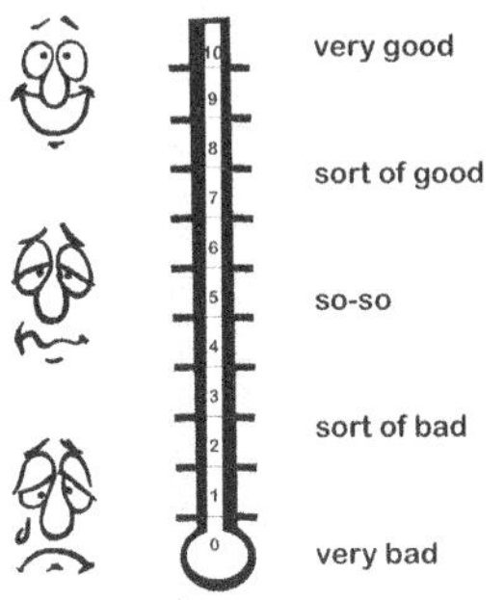

New Skill I Will Try	How It Will Help	How Did It Go?
Plan A:		Did I try **Plan A**? Yes No My rating after **Plan A:**_____ Am I done trying? Yes No
Plan B:		Did I try **Plan B**? Yes No My rating after **Plan B:**_____ Am I done trying? Yes No
Plan C:		Did I try **Plan C**? Yes No My rating after **Plan C:**_____ Am I done trying? Yes No

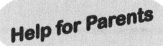

Plans for Coping

Why Children Need a Backup Plan

When kids feel bad or sad, it is easy for them to feel helpless and to believe that the situation is hopeless. Sometimes, when something happens that makes kids feel bad, they may have to try two or three coping strategies—and keep trying—before they feel better. Complicated situations can't be changed right away, and bad moods don't go away in an instant, so it is important for kids to keep trying different solutions until they find the right combination of coping skills to make them feel better.

Your child has been working to identify his or her three favorite coping skills to use when he or she feels bad. Using only one of these skills may not be enough to solve a challenging problem or to turn bad feelings into good feelings. So, it's important for your child to try all three of his or her favorite skills— Plan A, Plan B, and Plan C—whenever he or she is trying to solve a problem and feel better. Your child should keep trying these plans one at a time until the problem is solved and he or she feels better. In other words, if Plan A fails, your child will move to Plan B, and then to Plan C, and keep trying until he or she feels better!

How Can I Help?

For some children who face problems and begin to feel bad, it can be hard to try even one coping plan, and it can be tempting just to give up if the first plan doesn't work. You can help your child by learning what his or her three favorite coping skills are and then making sure that he or she uses those skills, rather than giving up too soon. When your child is feeling bad, encourage him or her to try his or her favorite coping skill—that is, Plan A. Make sure that he or she has really given Plan A a good try. If Plan A doesn't solve the problem and your child still feels bad, then encourage your child to try Plan B, and then Plan C, if necessary. The basic idea is not to give up, but instead to keep trying until some progress has been made and your child feels at least somewhat better.

Challenges and Goals Interview

Thank you for taking the time to meet with me today. In order to be as helpful as I can, I'd like to start off by getting some information about what's going on with your child from your point of view. This will help me better understand the problem and help us set goals together.

1. **Challenges**: Can you tell me what you see as the three biggest challenges going on with your child right now? How are things for your child at school? With friends? At home with family?

2. **Goals**: What would you like to see change with your child? What would let you know that your child is doing better? Are there smaller steps along the way that would be signs of success that we could look for? What would those look like?

Thinking Ahead

What could get in the way of your goals? What could you do about it?

Transportation - How Do I Get There?

Is a car available?   A ride?   Will there be parking?
Do I need a map?   What about weather?   Have I left enough time?
A bus schedule?   Traffic?   Do I have a backup plan?

> **Solutions**

Schedule - Is This a Good Time?

Is this time too early or too   Will I need child care?   Is this too close to
late?   Will we be too   something else?
Is this the best day?   tired/hungry?   Do I have a backup plan?

> **Solutions**

Support - Who Is Helping Me?

Do I have a partner or   Are there others?   Will my family make time
other adult at home?   How do they feel?   for me to practice?
Is that person "on board?"   Are my other kids OK?   Do I have a backup plan?

> **Solutions**

My Routine - How Will This Fit in?

Does this work with my
day to day life?
Is my family prepared?

What might get in the way
at home?
Who shares the parenting?

Is that person involved
enough?
Do I have a backup plan?

> **Solutions**

Finding Time - Can I Make Time for This?

What else needs to get
done?
What might come up?

What are the best and
worst time for me to
practice at home?

What might have to get
dropped for now?
Do I have a backup plan?

> **Solutions**

Other Issues - Did I Miss Anything?

> **Solutions**

What Can Help

Practice at home. Many parents are surprised to learn that what happens at home and school is actually more important than what happens with the therapist. Therapy is similar to music lessons. If someone takes piano lessons, his or her teacher reviews progress and assigns new things to practice. But if that person doesn't practice at home, he or she will never learn to play the piano. Similarly, a parent who is unable to practice new techniques and activities assigned by the therapist is unlikely to get the best results with his or her child.

Rely on your coach. Therapists can act as coaches to help you develop new skills to handle challenges at home. Ask for help when learning new skills, practice them together, and make sure you feel ready to try them on your own.

Make the program a high priority. The more energy and enthusiasm your family can commit to the program, the higher your child's chance of success. For now, the program may need to come before other things, like school plays, sports events, or family travel.

Be willing to work hard. If you are willing to work hard in the short term, you and your child will have better long-term results. For example, it can be tempting just to drop your child off somewhere after school to have fun, leaving him or her in a good mood afterwards, but that won't help with behavior problems in the long run. Working hard now can mean your child's problems can be much better for months or even years.

Attend therapy sessions faithfully. You should do everything possible to make sure you and your child attend all therapy sessions and that you are available to speak with the therapist—in person or by telephone—as necessary.

Speak up. Don't be afraid to let your therapist know what isn't working. The practice assignments aren't always easy, especially in the beginning. Parents who communicate about how the program is working for them and their family help their children succeed. The therapist can help you solve some of the problems you might face, even with things like lack of time or doubts about your child's progress.

Behavior Rating Scale

Please indicate the number which best describes your child's behavior during the past week.

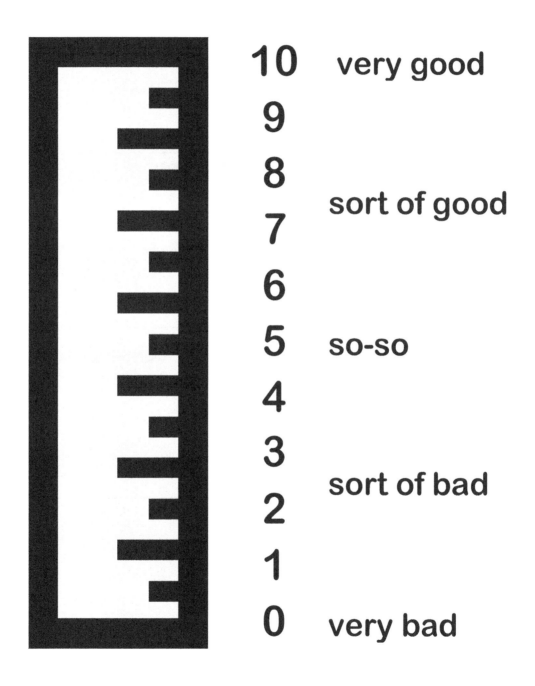

10	very good
9	
8	sort of good
7	
6	
5	so-so
4	
3	sort of bad
2	
1	
0	very bad

Four Factors

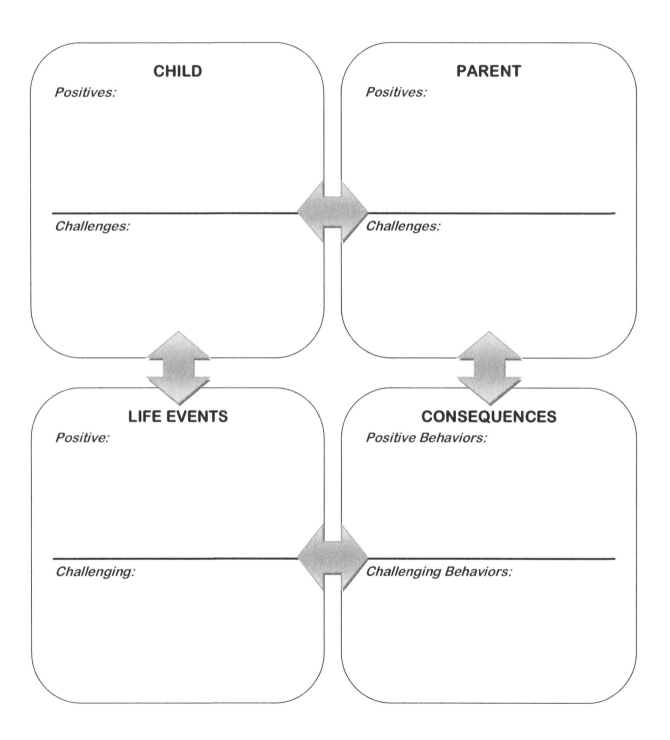

CHILD

Positives:

Challenges:

PARENT

Positives:

Challenges:

LIFE EVENTS

Positive:

Challenging:

CONSEQUENCES

Positive Behaviors:

Challenging Behaviors:

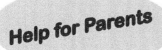

One-on-One Time

Getting Started

1. You can either schedule a regular time together each day, or just try to find a time each day when your child seems to be enjoying a play activity alone. If scheduling one-on-one time, start by asking your child what he or she would like to do together. If one-on-one time is unscheduled, wait until you notice your child playing in a positive way.

2. Next, join in the child's play. Do not try to do one-on-one time when you are upset, busy with something else, or planning to leave the house soon for an errand or trip, as your mind will be preoccupied, and the quality of your attention to your child will be poor.

3. No other children should be involved in one-on-one time. If you have other children in your family, either have another caregiver look after these children while you play with your child or choose a time when the other children are not likely to disturb your one-on-one time with this child.

4. Relax! Casually watch what your child is doing for a few minutes, and then start some positive interactions (see **What to Do**, below) when your child seems to have noticed you and seems open to your attention. The main idea is to have fun with your child.

What to Do

1. After watching your child's play, begin to describe out loud what your child is doing. In other words, narrate your child's play in a way that shows your child that you find his or her play interesting. You can think of yourself almost as a sportscaster describing a baseball or football game over the radio. Try to make your tone of voice exciting and action-oriented, not dull or flat.

2. Now and then, you can also provide your child with positive statements of praise, approval, or positive feedback about what you like about his or her play. Be accurate and honest, not excessively flattering. For instance, you might make comments like "I like it when we play quietly like this," or "I really enjoy our one-on-one time together," or "Look how nicely you've built that!" Try to be very specific about what you like.

3. Try to be as immediate as possible with your approval when you notice something good.

4. If your child begins to misbehave, simply turn away and look elsewhere for a few moments. If the misbehavior continues, then calmly tell your child that one-on-one time is over and leave the room. Tell your child you will play with him or her later when he or she can behave nicely. If the child becomes extremely disruptive, destructive, or abusive during play, use the other skills that you would typically use at those times.

What Not to Do

Don't ask questions. **Don't** give instructions. **Don't** criticize.

One-on-one time is not the time to teach your child anything new, like how to build something higher or draw something better. If you just pay attention and provide lot of description or praise, your child will be learning a lot. It is never a good idea to give backhanded compliments like, "I see that you colored inside the lines. Why couldn't you do that more often?"

Sticking with It

This skill is easy to read about, but it is not always easy to do, especially at first. Many parents make mistakes during the first few playtimes, usually by giving too many instructions, asking too many questions, or not making enough positive comments to the child. Don't worry about making such mistakes. Just try again the next time.

If possible, each parent should spend 15 minutes with the child in one-on-one time. During the first week, try to do this every day or at least 5 times a week. This may sound like a lot, but it will get the best results and be the most rewarding in the long run. After the first week, try to have one-on-one time 3 to 4 times each week. You may want to spend one-on-one time with the other children in your family once you feel things are going well with this child. One-on-one time should become a part of your natural routine— you shouldn't ever have to stop once you start doing this together, and over time, you probably won't want to.

Examples of Ways to Show Approval

NONVERBAL	VERBAL
Hug Pat on the head or shoulder Affectionate rubbing of hair Placing arm around child Smiling Giving a "thumbs-up" sign A wink High five	"I like it when you …" "It's nice when you …" "That was terrific the way you …" "Great job!" "Nice going!" "Terrific!" "Super!" "Fantastic!" "Wow, I never knew you could do that!" "Beautiful!" "Wow!" "What a nice thing to do." "You did that all by yourself. Way to go!" "I am very proud of you when you …" "I always enjoy it when we … like this."

Parent Observation Record

Please write down what your child did. Then write what you did in the next column, and the results in the last column. Use the other side of the page to take notes.

Day	What did your child do?	What did you do?	Did it work? circle one
Monday			yes no unsure
Tuesday			yes no unsure
Wednesday			yes no unsure
Thursday			yes no unsure
Friday			yes no unsure
Saturday			yes no unsure
Sunday			yes no unsure
Monday			yes no unsure
Tuesday			yes no unsure
Wednesday			yes no unsure
Thursday			yes no unsure
Friday			yes no unsure
Saturday			yes no unsure
Sunday			yes no unsure

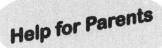

Praise

It is important to provide approval to your child as soon as he or she follows an instruction or request. If you consistently show approval for follow-through, your child will be more likely to follow instructions or requests in the future.

Great Job!

What to Do

1) **Offer immediate praise.** As soon as you give an instruction or request and your child begins to comply, immediately praise the child, using phrases such as:

> *"I like it when you do as I ask."*
> *"It's nice when you do as I say."*
> *"Thanks for doing what Mom asked."*
> *"Look at how nicely (quickly, neatly, etc.) you are doing that."*
> *"Good boy/girl for doing..."*

Feel free to use any other statement that specifically says you appreciate that your child is doing what you asked.

2) **Offer consistent praise.** Begin to use positive attention for virtually every instruction you give your child that he or she follows.

3) **Be alert for especially good behavior.** If you should find your child has done a job or chore or just something nice without specifically being told to do so, this is the time to provide especially positive praise to your child. You may even wish to provide your child with a small privilege for having done this, which will help your child remember and follow household rules without always being told to do so.

4) **Identify instructions that need extra work.** This week you should choose two or three instructions your child follows inconsistently. You should make a special effort to praise and attend to your child whenever he or she begins to comply with these particular instructions.

HINT

After you give an instruction, don't just walk away. Instead, stay and attend to what your child is doing, offering immediate and appropriate praise for follow-through. Once you have praised your child, if you must, you can leave for a few moments, but be sure to return frequently to praise your child's good work.

Active Ignoring

What Is Active Ignoring?

Sometimes kids do things to get attention, to get out of doing things they don't like, or even just to get their parents upset. "Active ignoring" means purposely not paying attention to these kinds of behaviors in order to make them go away. Active ignoring can quickly stop many types of problem behaviors. It does not cause any emotional harm to your child, and it also can help parents feel less angry and upset with their children. It is easy to learn, and with a little practice, it becomes easy to use.

Use active ignoring for:	Don't use active ignoring for:
Fussiness	Hitting, slapping, or pinching
Complaining	Throwing or breaking things
Pouting	Being mean to animals or people
Grumpiness	Disobeying an instruction
Talking back	Cursing or swearing
Making noises	Doing dangerous things
Mild arguing	Threatening others
Whining	Getting a bad grade
Asking the same question over and over	Forgetting to do chores or homework
Repeating things	Being afraid or shy
Doing things to get your attention	Wanting to be alone

Getting Ready

Pick a behavior you'd like to get rid of. Check the lists above to make sure it is the right kind of behavior for active ignoring.

From now on, I will ignore my child when:

Pick some behaviors you'd like to see instead of the problem behavior. These could be things like asking politely, getting along with a sibling, sitting still at the dinner table, or accepting a decision.

From now on, I will try to pay attention and use praise, when my child:

Think of ways to praise your child for demonstrating the behaviors you want to see. There are a lot of things you can do or say to praise your child.

Here is an example of something I could say or do to let my child know I like what he or she is doing:

Pick a time to tell your child and family about active ignoring. Try to choose a time when everything is going well and everybody is calm. Make sure your child understands that you still care about him or her, but that some behaviors will get your attention and others simply will not. Explain that this will be a new rule for living in your family. It is not something the child can argue about, and it is meant to help everyone feel better and have more fun when you are together.

Here is when I plan to explain active ignoring to my family:

What to Do

When the problem behavior happens:

 Ignore it. Look the other way or find some other way not to pay attention—such as reading the newspaper. You might find it helpful just to quietly leave the room.

 Don't explain. Don't argue, scold, or even talk with your child while he or she is misbehaving. You already explained active ignoring before. Now is the time to put it into practice.

 Try not to look upset. Instead, try to keep busy with something like TV, a book, or cooking to help hide your reaction.

 Catch your child being good. This is the "active" part of active ignoring. As soon as the bad behavior stops, pay attention right away. Show that you are interested by looking at your child, talking, and praising. If the problem behavior starts again, go back to ignoring.

 Stick with it. It's important to be consistent, even if things get worse at first. When your child can't get your attention, he or she might not give up right away, but instead might try even harder. This is normal, and it is a sign that active ignoring is working correctly. It means your child understands what you're doing and that it's starting to have an effect. Now is the time to stand your ground.

Help! Active Ignoring Isn't Working!

PROBLEM: Things are getting worse instead of better.

TRY THIS: *Make sure you're ignoring the behavior the <u>whole</u> time. If you ignore a behavior for a little while but eventually give in or get angry, you've accidentally taught your child that the only way to get your attention is to behave even worse than before. So, once you decide to ignore a behavior, stick with it.*

PROBLEM: Active ignoring is frustrating!

TRY THIS: *Sometimes it can be very difficult to keep your cool when your child is whining, pouting, or engaging in other unpleasant behaviors. Try to stay focused on the long term goal. Remember that the more you dislike what your child is doing, the more it's worth getting rid of the behavior. As long as you're sure your child is safe, it might be helpful to leave the room.*

PROBLEM: My child screams and cries.

TRY THIS: *Even though it's difficult, you can ignore this behavior, too. Just make sure your child isn't harming himself or others.*

PROBLEM: My child is becoming aggressive.

TRY THIS: *If your child hits, slaps, throws things, or is going to hurt him- or herself or someone else, it may be time to try other tools, such as "time out." If you don't use "time out"—or even if you just want to double-check that you're using it in the most effective way—be sure to ask for help.*

PROBLEM: Now that I'm using active ignoring, my child is always angry with me.

TRY THIS: *Make sure you are only ignoring the <u>unwanted behavior</u>. If your child is angry, it may be because you've started ignoring him or her <u>all</u> the time, not just when he or she misbehaves. Remember to give your child lots of praise and attention when he or she is good. Ignore only the problem behaviors, not the whole child!*

PROBLEM: Other people in my household aren't helping me.

TRY THIS: *Talk to your family about this at a time when things are calm. Explain that everyone has to work together and follow the same rules or the problem behaviors won't improve. In fact, they might even get worse.*

Help for Parents—Active Ignoring / 4 of 4

Giving Effective Instructions

In our work with many children, we have noticed that if parents simply change the way they give instructions, they can often achieve significant improvements in the child's behavior.

What to Say

	Instead of this:		Try this!

Avoid "Let's" Instructions

"Let's clean up your room." ⟶ "Please clean up your room."

"Let's get out your homework." ⟶ "Please get out your homework."

Don't Ask Questions

"Can you get dressed for school?" ⟶ "Please get dressed for school."

"Could you pick up your dishes?" ⟶ "Please put your dishes in the sink."

Be Specific

"Behave when you're at the table." ⟶ "Please eat quietly at the table."

"Try to be good today." ⟶ "Please listen to your teacher at school today."

Avoid Lists

"Get up and get dressed, brush your teeth, and get your things ready for school." ⟶ "Please get up out of bed now." (*then wait before giving other instructions*)

"Get your homework finished and get all your chores done tonight." ⟶ "Please get out your homework and a pencil." (*then wait before giving other instructions*)

How to Say It

Instead of this: **Try this!**

Get Your Child's Attention First
Giving an instruction from across the room ➔ Going close and getting eye contact

Reduce Distractions
Having lots of people talking or things going on ➔ Making sure there are few distractions

Prepare Your Child for Transitions
Saying, "Turn off the TV and brush your teeth." ➔ Saying, "In 5 minutes, you need to turn off the TV and brush your teeth."

Use the Right Tone
Using an angry or demanding voice ➔ Using a calm and even voice

Be Clear
Giving a complicated instruction ➔ Giving the instruction, then asking for it to be repeated back to you

Rewards

What Are Rewards?

A reward is something you give your child for doing something you want him or her to do. Rewards make your child more likely to show that same behavior in the future. At the same time rewards increase good behaviors, they can also help get rid of bad behaviors. A child who is busy trying to do good things will have less time to do bad things. When things aren't going well, rewards can often quickly increase the good behavior you see from your child. Rewards also help parents and children feel less angry and upset.

Rewards can help your child learn to:

Be on time
Be polite
Share
Do homework
Come home on time
Remember important things
Do chores
Go to bed on time
Do anything else you think is important

A reward doesn't have to cost money. It can be as simple as a smile, a hug, or a special treat like watching TV or playing a game with you. Rewards can be used with children as young as infants, but they can also be used with teenagers and even adults. The type of reward will depend on the age of the child. Choosing a reward that is important to your child will help motivate your child to work hard to earn it.

Getting Ready

Pick a behavior you'd like to see more often. Make sure it's very specific, like "put these dirty clothes in the hamper."

> **Here is a behavior I'd like to see more often:**

Make a list of rewards. Think of as many as you can. They don't have to be big or expensive. Some of the best rewards don't cost anything. For example, maybe your child would like to play a special game with you or to watch an extra TV

> **Here is an example of a small reward my child would like:**

Decide how to keep track of the rewards your child earns. In many cases, you will just give the reward when you see the behavior. However, if the desired behaviors might occur often, you can start a chart with stickers for young children or a point system for older children. Then your child can build up points to be cashed in for a reward.

> **Here is the way I would like to keep track of my contract with my child:**

Use an IF-THEN sentence to come up with a contract for what your child has to do to get the reward. For example, "*If* my child can clear his or her dishes from the table every night when dinner is over, *then* he or she can stay up for an extra 30 minutes on Saturday night" or "*If* my child brushes her teeth at night, *then* she ~~gets~~."

> **Here is an example of an IF-THEN contract I can make with my child**
> **IF:**
>
> **THEN:**

What to Do

 Make a list of rewards. Pick rewards that are inexpensive or free, and can be given quickly and frequently if needed.

 Make a list of behaviors. These should be simple behaviors at first, and remember to spell out how the behaviors will connect with the rewards (either directly or through points or tokens).

 Give the reward (or sticker or point) as soon as the good behavior happens. The more quickly you respond to good behavior, the better the rewards will work. In the beginning, it is also OK to give rewards for behaviors that are only partly successful.

 Little by little, increase the difficulty. As your child gets better at doing the behavior you want, you can increase the demands. Something that used to earn 2 points might now earn 1. Just be careful not to raise the difficulty too quickly so your child doesn't become frustrated and lose interest.

 Praise. It is always a good idea to offer your child praise along with the rewards. Over time, praise will help your child develop a sense of accomplishment and pride in his or her good behavior. Make sure your praise is enthusiastic and labeled—that is, say what it is that you are praising the child for. For example, "Great job putting your clothes away, Rachel!"

Help! Rewards Aren't Working!

PROBLEM: I feel like I'm bribing my child.

TRY THIS: *For now, rewards can provide a boost to help your child learn how to behave. Eventually, your child will learn to behave well and work hard just because it makes him or her feel good. As this happens, the rewards can be made smaller.*

PROBLEM: My child is begging me for the rewards.

TRY THIS: *Don't give in—that just rewards the begging. Remind your child how to earn the reward and then give it if and only if you see the behavior.*

PROBLEM: There's nothing my child wants badly enough to work for.

TRY THIS: *You may already be giving your child everything he or she wants, even when he or she doesn't earn it. Think about all the fun toys or privileges your child has, and choose some to use strictly as rewards that must be earned.*

PROBLEM: My child doesn't follow through.

TRY THIS: *Make sure you give rewards only after your child has actually done what you've asked. Don't reward your child just for promising to do something later. For example, if you say, "You can watch TV now as long as you promise to clean your room when the show is over," your child may not do what he or she promised. When you talk about rewards with your child, you will find it helpful to use IF-THEN sentences.*

PROBLEM: My child is trying really hard, but rewards still aren't working.

TRY THIS: *There are three possible solutions: (1) Make sure you're not asking your child to do something that is just too hard. If necessary, consider breaking things down into smaller steps to help your child succeed. Give a reward for each of the smaller steps. (2) Make sure to give the reward right away, as soon as your child demonstrates the behavior you want. (3) Make sure you're using rewards that your child really likes.*

PROBLEM: Other people in my household aren't helping me.

TRY THIS: *Talk to your family about this at a time when things are calm. Explain that everyone has to work together and that your child will be more successful if all caregivers in the home use the reward program consistently.*

Time Out

What Is Time Out?

"Time out" is the removal of your child from activities, rewards, and attention. Time out is meant to help stop some of your child's behaviors that you find upsetting or harmful, and it can provide quick and lasting results if used properly. It does not cause any harm to your child, and it also can help you feel less angry and upset with your child. It is easy to learn, and with a little practice it becomes easy to use.

Use time out for these kinds of behaviors:	Don't use time out for these kinds of behaviors:
Hitting, slapping, or pinching Throwing or breaking things Being mean to animals or people Disobeying an instruction Breaking a house rule Cursing or swearing Doing dangerous things Threatening others Hostile arguing Damaging property	Fussiness, complaining Talking back Mild arguing Legitimate accidents (e.g., spilling something, dropping something) Whining Asking the same question over and over Repeating things Doing things to get your attention Bad attitude

Getting Ready

Pick two or three behaviors you'd like to get rid of. Check the lists above to make sure these are the right kinds of behavior for time out.

> **From now on, I will give a time out to my child when:**

Pick some behaviors you'd like to see instead of the problem behaviors. These could be things like playing safely and quietly, following through on a task, or being kind to a sibling. They should be the "opposite" of the behaviors chosen for

> **From now on, I will try to praise or reward my child for:**

Pick a dull and boring place for the time out. It should be easy to get to quickly, and it should not have anything interesting nearby.

> **Our time out place will be:**

If you have not done so already, pick a time to tell your child about time out. Choose a time when everything is going well and everybody is calm. Make sure your child understands that you still care about him or her, but that some behaviors will mean that your child must stop what he or she is doing and go to time out. Explain that this will be a new rule for your family. It is not something the child can argue about, and it is meant to help everyone feel better and have

> **Here is when I plan to explain time out to my family:**

What to Do

1. **Give an instruction** (for example, "Please get out of your sister's room," or "Please do not tip back in your chair at the dinner table").

2. **Count to 5** in your head. If your child does not follow through, then...

3. **Give your child a single warning**. Be clear and brief (for example, "If you don't get out of your sister's room, you will have a time out," or "If you don't put your chair flat on the floor, you will have a time out").

4. **Count to 5** in your head. If your child does not follow through, then...

5. **Instruct your child to go to time out.** Do this quickly and calmly. State the specific reason for the time out, but try to use no more than 10 words in 10 seconds.

6. **Don't explain.** Don't argue, scold, or even talk with your child once a time out has been issued. These rules have already been explained before. Now is the time to put time out into practice.

7. **Set a timer.** It can help to use a timer to keep track of how long the time out will be. For most children, 5 minutes is an appropriate length of time. It will help if your child can see the timer, but place it out of your child's reach.

8. **Reset the timer if needed.** If your child is screaming or yelling in time out, you may reset the timer. The time out begins when your child is settled.

9. **Talk calmly afterwards.** After you let your child out of time out, check to see if he or she knows why you gave a time out. If your child says, "I don't know" calmly explain the reason, but don't lecture.

10. **Repeat the instruction** calmly, and go back to step 4.

> **IMMEDIATE TIME OUTS:** Some behaviors are so serious that you can skip the warning. For example, behaviors that involve harm to others or breaking a known rule in your house do not need a warning. If you have questions about when to give a time out without a warning, talk with your therapist.

Help! Time Out Isn't Working!

PROBLEM: My child argues and talks back.

TRY THIS: *Ignore backtalk and arguing. Do not get into a discussion. If the arguing escalates into yelling, simply reset the timer when your child settles down.*

PROBLEM: My child tantrums and makes a mess when I give a time out.

TRY THIS: *Have your child do the time out anyway, and then when it is over, issue an instruction for your child to clean up his or her mess.*

PROBLEM: My child does not believe me when I give a time out.

TRY THIS: *Never give a time out unless you mean it, and never give more than one warning. Once a time out is given, it must be followed through. Over time, your child will learn that you mean it.*

PROBLEM: My child will not go to time out or leaves time out before it is over.

TRY THIS: *You can restate that your child needs to go to time out and gently guide your child back to the time out area. Another option is to take away privileges or toys for failure to follow through on a time out.*

PROBLEM: We are out at a store or a friend's house, so I can't give a time out.

TRY THIS: *When you go out shopping or visit neighbors, it can be helpful to pick a time out place as soon as you arrive and to let your child know about it. You can also bring the timer with you. If you can't find a good time out place, you can have your child sit in a boring place right where you are. Just make sure you can always see your child when giving a time out away from home. If you need help thinking of more ideas, don't be afraid to ask the therapist.*

PROBLEM: Other people in my household aren't helping me.

TRY THIS: *Talk to your family about this at a time when things are calm. Explain that everyone has to work together and follow the same rules or the problem behaviors won't improve. In fact, they might even get worse.*

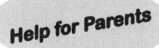

Making a Plan

One of the best ways to deal with behavior problems is to prevent them before they even happen. If you already know what places or times might be especially challenging, it's a good idea to make a plan beforehand so that your child has a chance to do his or her best. Here are the steps:

1. Get Ready

If you know ahead of time that a difficult situation is coming up, try to do whatever you can to be ready. Ask yourself the following:

Will my child have something interesting to do? It often helps to give your child something to do so that he or she does not get bored, because boredom can often lead to trouble. For example, bringing a bag of toys or a few books on a long car ride or shopping trip can help keep your child engaged. Another idea is to give your child a job to do, such as help you check items off of a grocery list—thus giving you the opportunity to interact with your child and to provide lots of praise.

Will my child be too tired? If your child has a harder time when tired, part of the plan should be to allow for enough sleep the night before or even a nap during the day. Otherwise, an event may be moved to a better time. For example, a routinely challenging visit to the doctor's office or a neighbor's house might work better in the morning instead of in the late afternoon.

Will my child be hungry? If you know your child is more difficult when he or she is hungry, plan to bring snacks with you or try scheduling activities right after a meal instead of before. For example, going grocery shopping when your child is hungry might make him or her more likely to demand junk food, and could also make him or her less able to focus on your instructions and requests.

Are there objects or people I can remove? Sometimes you will know of certain things that make situations worse. For example, toys that lead your child to play roughly may need to be put away. Perhaps there is too much noise in the house for the child to hear your instructions. A sibling who does not want to share may cause a fight. Ask yourself what should and should not be in the situation, and who should and should not be there. For especially challenging situations, you should try to set the stage for success as much as you can.

2. Set Rules

If you know ahead of time what is likely to go wrong, make up to three rules for your child to follow. These should be rules that are often violated by your child in that particular place or situation. After you have told your child the rules, ask your child to repeat them back to you. You should avoid starting the event or situation if your child cannot repeat the rules to you.

3. Set up a Reward

Before you go into the challenging situation, tell your child what he or she can earn for following the rules you have just made. For example, you might bring stickers for your young child who accompanies you on errands. Or you could prompt your child that if he or she can play nicely instead of being aggressive on the playground, he or she can stay an extra 15 minutes or have a treat when you get home.

4. Set up Consequences

Before you go into the challenging situation, tell your child what the consequences will be for not following rules or for misbehavior. This should be the loss of privileges for minor rule violations and a removal from the situation for more severe misbehavior. Do not be afraid to remove your child from a situation in a public place, as it is the most effective method for teaching the child to follow rules in such places.

5. Practice if You Can

Some situations are possible to practice beforehand, and if so, it's a good idea to try a "practice run." Situations like going to the dentist or doctor, getting dropped off at school, getting on the bus and quickly finding a seat, coming home and putting away a coat and backpack are all situations that can easily be practiced ahead of time. Walk through some of the steps, and be sure to provide plenty of praise for a good performance.

Getting Started

Pick a situation that is challenging for your child that occurs regularly (like shopping trips, visits to neighbors, school drop-off, or long drives).

My child has extra trouble when:

What are some things you could do to be ready for that situation next time?

Before we try that again, I will make sure that:

What rules does your child need to follow for that situation?

I expect my child to:

What are the rewards and consequences connected to those rules?

If my child obeys the rules:

If my child does not follow the rules:

Will you be able to practice this situation? If so, pick a time when you can practice it together.

Here is when I plan to practice this situation:

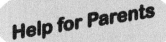

Using a Daily School Behavior Report Card

What Is a Daily School Behavior Report Card?

A daily school behavior report card (or "daily report card") is a way for your child's teacher to give you feedback about your child's behavior in school each day. Once you know how your child has behaved in school, you will be able to give appropriate rewards at home, which will encourage more good behavior in school.

The daily report card is often one of the first interventions you should try if your child is having behavior problems at school. The cards are convenient, they can improve parent-teacher communication by involving both teachers and parents, and they are effective with a wide range of problems.

What Do the Report Cards Look Like?

The report card can be as simple as a note from the teacher each day, but we recommend using a more formal system if possible. Here is an example of a card that could be used for classroom behavior. Note that the behaviors are all worded positively.

DAILY SCHOOL BEHAVIOR REPORT CARD

Child's name: _____ Date: _____

TEACHERS: Please rate this child's behavior today in the areas listed below. Use a separate column for each subject or class period. Please make a check mark (√) if the child demonstrated the behavior or an ✗ if the child did not demonstrate the behavior or demonstrated negative behavior for the specified area. Then initial the box at the bottom of your column. Add any comments about the child's behavior today on the back of this card.

	Class periods/subjects						
Behaviors to be rated	1	2	3	4	5	6	7
Raises hand in class							
Works on assigned classwork							
Follows classroom rules							
Gets along well with other children							
Does well on homework, if any given							
Teacher's initials							

Place comments on back of card

On the left-hand side of the card, list 1 to 5 behaviors to focus on. Be sure to word the behaviors positively on the card—for example, instead of "pushing and shoving" try "Keeps hands to self—does not push or shove." You can gradually add more behaviors as your child improves. Try including one or two positive behaviors that your child already does so that he or she will be able to earn some points at the beginning of the program.

Here is an example of a card that could be used for recess and free time behavior:

DAILY RECESS & FREE TIME BEHAVIOR REPORT CARD

Child's name: _____ Date: _____

TEACHERS: Please rate this child's behavior today in recess or other free time periods in the areas listed below. Use a separate column for each recess/free time period. Please make a check mark (√) if the child demonstrated the behavior or an ✗ if the child did not demonstrate the behavior or demonstrated negative behavior for the specified area. Then initial the box at the bottom of your column. Add any comments about the child's behavior today on the back of this card.

	Class periods/subjects				
Behaviors to be rated	1	2	3	4	5
Keeps hands to self; does not push or shove					
Does not tease others; no taunting/put-downs					
Follows recess/free time rules					
Gets along well with other children					
Plays nicely; no kicking or punching					
Teacher's initials					

Place comments on back of card

On the left-hand side of the card, list 1 to 5 behaviors to focus on for recess/free time. Remember to include one or two behaviors that your child already does well.

How to Use the Reports

At the beginning, the system works best if teachers send the reports home every day. As the child's behavior improves, the reports can be reduced to twice weekly (for example, Wednesdays and Fridays), once weekly, or even monthly until they are phased out altogether.

The child can take a new card to school each day, or you can leave a stack of cards with the teacher. Either way will work, but it is best to choose one arrangement and stick with it.

The target behaviors may include both social conduct (shares, plays well with peers, follows rules, stays in assigned seat) and academic performance (completes math or reading assignments, stays focused on work, follows directions for each assignment, remembers to take homework home, completes homework, remembers to bring homework back to school). You may also choose to target negative behaviors (e.g., aggression, destruction, calling out) that you want to reduce; but remember to list the positive opposite of these behaviors on the card (e.g., instead of "hits others" put "keeps hands to self").

You can adapt the reports to meet your child's needs and to fit the structure of your child's day. For example, in a typical case, a child would be monitored throughout the entire day. However, if a problem behavior occurs very frequently, you may want to have the child initially rated for only a portion of the school day. As the child's behavior improves, the report can be expanded gradually to include more periods/subjects until the child is being monitored for the whole day.

In cases where the child attends several different classes taught by different teachers, the program may involve some or all of the teachers, depending on the need for help in each of the classes. When more than one teacher is included in the program, a single report card may include space for all teachers to rate the child. (The example report cards shown in this handout can be helpful because they have columns that can be used by the same teacher at the end of each subject, or by different teachers.) Alternatively, different report cards may be used for each class and organized in a notebook for the child to carry between classes. For particularly problematic behavior, we encourage teachers to provide a brief explanation to you on the back of the report.

> **TIP:** If getting the correct homework assignment home is a problem for your child, the teacher can require the child to copy the homework for that class right on the back of the report. Then the teacher can check that the assignment was copied correctly before filling out the ratings on the front of the report.

The daily recess and free time behavior reports work essentially the same way as the classroom reports. They should be completed by whichever school staff member is supervising recess or free time.

To get started, you may use the blank report cards at the end of this handout or, with your therapist's assistance, adapt the blank cards to fit your child's situation.

Working with Your Child's Teacher

As you start to decide which behaviors to target, we strongly recommend consulting with your child's teacher (or teachers). The report cards are intended to be as clear and easy to use as possible, and the best way to make this happen is to ask for the teacher's input. You can start by showing the teacher the blank reports at the end of this handout. It might also be helpful to explain that daily feedback is important because the reports will be tied to a specific, predictable set of rewards and consequences at home each day. Frequent feedback will be most effective in shaping your child's behavior.

What Happens When the Reports Come Home?

As soon as your child returns home, you should immediately inspect the card, discuss the positive behaviors (√) first with your child, and then proceed to a neutral, business-like (not angry!) discussion with your child about any negative marks (✗) and the reasons for them. Then ask your child to formulate a plan for avoiding negative marks tomorrow. After the child makes the plan, award your child the usual points or rewards for each check mark on the card. Be sure to remind your child of the plan the next morning before he or she departs for school.

The success of the program depends on a clear, fair, consistent method for translating the teacher's reports into consequences at home. One advantage of daily school behavior report cards is that a wide variety of consequences can be used. At a minimum, you should provide praise and positive attention for your child when the report card shows good behavior. In addition to praise, many children need tangible rewards or token programs. For example, a positive report might lead to television time, a special snack, or a later bedtime. You might also use a token system in which your child earns points for positive behavior reports and loses points for negative reports. Your child can then use the points for a special treat on the weekend (e.g., movie, dinner at a restaurant, special outing). It is fine to use a combination of daily and weekly rewards.

> **SPECIAL TIP FOR RECESS & FREE TIME:** Ask your child's classroom teacher to take a few moments to plan ahead with your child before recess or free time. During this planning time, the teacher (1) reviews the rules for proper recess behavior with the child and notes that the rules are written on the card, (2) reminds the child that he or she is being monitored by the recess monitor on recess duty, and (3) directs the child to give the card immediately to the recess monitor so the monitor can evaluate the child's behavior.

Occasionally, a child may attempt to undercut the system by failing to bring home a report, forging a teacher's signature, or failing to get a particular teacher's signature. To discourage these practices, treat missing reports or signatures as "bad" reports (that is, the child fails to earn rewards or is fined by losing points or privileges).

Daily school behavior report cards help everyone—child, parents, and teachers!

DAILY SCHOOL BEHAVIOR REPORT CARD

Child's name: _____ Date: _____

TEACHERS: Please rate this child's behavior today in the areas listed below. Use a separate column for each subject or class period. Please make a check mark (√) if the child demonstrated the behavior or an ✗ if the child did not demonstrate the behavior or demonstrated negative behavior for the specified area. Then initial the box at the bottom of your column. Add any comments about the child's behavior today on the back of this card.

	Class periods/subjects						
Behaviors to be rated	1	2	3	4	5	6	7
Teacher's initials							

Place comments on back of card

-------------------✂-------------------Cut here after photocopying-------------------✂------------------

DAILY SCHOOL BEHAVIOR REPORT CARD

Child's name: _____ Date: _____

TEACHERS: Please rate this child's behavior today in the areas listed below. Use a separate column for each subject or class period. Please make a check mark (√) if the child demonstrated the behavior or an ✗ if the child did not demonstrate the behavior or demonstrated negative behavior for the specified area. Then initial the box at the bottom of your column. Add any comments about the child's behavior today on the back of this card.

	Class periods/subjects						
Behaviors to be rated	1	2	3	4	5	6	7
Teacher's initials							

Place comments on back of card

DAILY RECESS & FREE TIME BEHAVIOR REPORT CARD

Child's name:
_____

Date:
_____

TEACHERS: Please rate this child's behavior today in recess or other free time periods in the areas listed below. Use a separate column for each recess/free time period. Please make a check mark (√) if the child demonstrated the behavior or an ✗ if the child did not demonstrate the behavior or demonstrated negative behavior for the specified area. Then initial the box at the bottom of your column. Add any comments about the child's behavior today on the back of this card.

Behaviors to be rated	Class periods/subjects				
	1	2	3	4	5
Teacher's initials					

Place comments on back of card

-------------------✂-------------------Cut here after photocopying-------------------✂-------------------

DAILY RECESS & FREE TIME BEHAVIOR REPORT CARD

Child's name:
_____

Date:
_____

TEACHERS: Please rate this child's behavior today in recess or other free time periods in the areas listed below. Use a separate column for each recess/free time period. Please make a check mark (√) if the child demonstrated the behavior or an ✗ if the child did not demonstrate the behavior or demonstrated negative behavior for the specified area. Then initial the box at the bottom of your column. Add any comments about the child's behavior today on the back of this card.

Behaviors to be rated	Class periods/subjects				
	1	2	3	4	5
Teacher's initials					

Place comments on back of card

Looking Ahead

At this point, you have learned a wide variety of methods for changing your child's behavior. Hopefully, you have found these methods to be effective in helping your child do his or her best. However, all children occasionally engage in challenging behaviors, and there is no reason to think that your child will not occasionally show new problem behavior in the future. This is completely normal. Fortunately, you now have some effective ways to deal with these problems. You just need to take the time to think about the problems and plan your strategy.

What to Do

If a new problem develops or an old problem returns, follow these steps:

Write the Problem Down

Take a copy of a **Parent Observation Record**, or you can just use a plain notebook. Write down, at a minimum, what was happening when the behavior occurred (for example, note when and where you were and what was going on), what your child did (be specific), what your response was, and whether or not it was successful.

Check for Old Habits

Keep this record for a few days, studying it to see what clues it may give you about how to deal with the problem. Many parents find they have returned to some of their old, ineffective habits of dealing with the child and that this has caused the problem. Here are some common "old habits" to which parents often return:

- Repeating your commands too often
- Not giving effective commands
- Not providing attention, praise, or a reward to the child for following the rule correctly (that is, stopping the reward program too early)
- Not providing discipline immediately for the rule violation
- Stopping the special one-on-one time with the child

Obviously, if you find yourself slipping back into these old habits, you will want to correct them. Go back and review your handouts from this program to make sure you are using the methods properly.

See if You Can Prevent the Problem

At the first sign of trouble, review the **Making a Plan** worksheet. It is designed to help you prevent misbehavior from happening in the first place by changing the situation, setting clear expectations and rules, and clarifying the rewards and consequences up front. It is possible that making a new plan will be enough to address the behaviors that you have noticed. Also consider whether you have continued to use praise often for good behavior and whether you have continued to give instructions in a clear, effective manner. If those strategies have faded, it can be time to bring them back.

Set up a Program if Necessary

If those strategies do not seem to be working, you should consider returning to a formal program of rewards and consequences for managing the problem:

1) Explain to your child exactly what you expect him or her to be doing in the problem situation.
2) Set up a reward system for following the rules.
3) Use praise to reward appropriate behavior quickly and consistently.
4) Use time out immediately, each time your child doesn't respond to a warning.
4) Keep recording the behavior problem in your notebook so you can notice when it begins to improve.

If You Still Need Help

If these methods aren't helping, call your therapist for an appointment and bring along your notes.

Made in United States
North Haven, CT
18 May 2023

IAN JONES
UNLOCKED

IAN JONES
UNLOCKED

With Bob Howitt
and Margot Butcher

Celebrity Books
Sports & Personality Book Publishers

Acknowledgements

I wish to acknowledge the enormous love and support of my family – Betsy, Wac, Flora, Greg and Bruce – and to extend my sincere thanks to the players and members of the Kamo Rugby Club who gave me my start in rugby; also to the players, coaches and management, too numerous to mention, who have helped shape my career and given me so many 22-carat memories.

Special thanks to Garry Frew, sports editor of the *Northern Advocate,* a long-time supporter; to the Atchison family, Michael in particular, for providing the scrapbooks spanning my career; and to all the photographers whose outstanding work has allowed us to illustrate this book so worthily.

Thanks to Margot Butcher of Perfect Words who helped us meet the publishing deadline by taking responsibility for the Jones family, Northland and WRC chapters.

Finally, a big thank you to author Bob Howitt and publisher Bill Honeybone and the team at Celebrity Books for encouraging me to undertake the project.

New Zealand's northernmost rugby union is sometimes referred to as North Auckland and at other times Northland in this book. That's because in 1994 the name was officially changed from North Auckland to Northland. It is, we assure you, one and the same thing.

©1998 Ian Jones

First published in 1998 by Celebrity Books
46A Taharoto Road, Takapuna
Auckland 10, New Zealand

Layout/design by Benefitz Graphics Ltd, Takapuna, Auckland.
Typeset by Benefitz Graphics Ltd.
Cover art by Dallas Bennett.
Printed in China through Colorcraft Ltd, Hong Kong.
Celebrity Books is the imprint of The Celebrity Book Company Limited
PO Box 331630 Takapuna, Auckland, New Zealand.

ISBN 0-9583729-4-2.

Contents

Dedication

To my wife Janine and my nieces and nephew (Olivia, Grace, Jasmine, Sam, Dayna and Ella) for providing me with hours of fun and laughter and for ensuring that my feet remain firmly on the ground, because to them I'm not an All Black, just plain old Jonesy and Uncle Ian.

Unlocked

Introduction

John Sturgeon, the All Black manager through until the second Rugby World Cup, had a phrase for it, when everything was going supremely well. In his best West Coast drawl, he'd say, "Kamo, she's 22-carat." Coming from a man who'd spent most of his working life in and around mines, you appreciated that nothing could get much better than that.

Well, I've got to say, when I consider what Ian Donald Jones has managed to achieve in less than 10 years, almost entirely thanks to the game I was obviously put on this earth to play, rugby, I can't do better than fall back on Sturge's great line. Life really has been 22 carat.

I'd have settled for a 9-carat career, to be honest; 18-carat would have been a bonus; 22-carat wasn't even a consideration. As a son of a fitter and welder, I didn't start out with any lofty ambitions, although loftiness was what would project me to the top in rugby. Loftiness in a purely physical sense, that is, thanks to a rare blending of genes by my parents, neither of whom is of exceptional stature. Somehow, a father who stands 1.80m and a 1.75m-tall mother managed to produce a son who grew to 1.98m (which is 6ft 6in for those not metrically inclined).

If there was one attribute I developed which paved the way for a 22-carat existence, it was probably my dedication to training, initially with swimming and then with the sport which has consumed my life over the past decade, rugby. I've always possessed a passion for rugby and approached every game – which at first-class level now number in excess of 250 – with enthusiasm and a determination to give of my best.

It's been the love of the game which has motivated me since I first participated at the age of five. Now as a thirty-something veteran, I can swear that nothing has changed. Except that my salary, thanks to rugby becoming professional in 1995, has as many digits in it as my telephone number in Whangarei used to.

I was lucky enough to be a footballer in the right place at the right time. If I'd played when Pinetree Meads, the legendary lock who's inspired us all, did, I would have had to juggle my rugby commitments with a job. Instead, I am now categorised as a professional rugby player. They pay me to play rugby. That's definitely 22-carat.

Fotopacific

John Sturgeon

When I was first selected as an All Black trialist in 1989, and from that, a few months later, chosen to tour Wales and Ireland with the All Blacks, I'd just come out of my apprenticeship as an electrician. I was living at home and working in Whangarei for Ian Bradley, a dedicated rugby man who never quibbled about the amount of time I needed to take off to play rugby.

All Blacks touring in '89 received the IRB approved daily allowance of £20 ($NZ55) which was dutifully handed out in a brown envelope each Monday morning by manager Sturgeon. With meals, laundry and travel paid for, the only expenditure we as players had were toll calls back to New Zealand and any drinks we bought down at the local. With the amount of money I spent on phone calls over the years, I regret I never bought Telecom shares!

The envelopes would get tossed into my suitcase and come out when I was squaring up at the hotel accounts desk. Happiness when I was unpacking back home was to come across a couple of unopened envelopes. The only guaranteed profit for the players was out of the team fund, or the cabbage patch as we referred to it, which accumulated as we went along through ticket sales. I actually bought my first car, a Falcon Ute, from my share of the carve-up out of that first tour.

Because of my commitments to rugby, I was never the most employable individual. After chucking in my job as an electrician – I had to, I simply wasn't there often enough – I helped Dad and my brothers build a couple of home units. For a while I didn't have a regular job. I was a rugby bum, doing odd jobs and surviving because I lived at home rent-free.

If someone had suggested then that within 10 years rugby would be fully professional, I for one would have scoffed. None of us even dreamt of such a development, to be honest. I played for New Zealand for the honour of doing so and I can honestly say that the advent of professionalism has not changed that. It's why the All Blacks are so successful. Certainly the rewards have increased, unbelievably so, but it's the black jersey and New Zealand's rugby traditions that matter most, not the pay cheque, when you're on the countdown to an international.

In 1991, Kevin Roberts, the then operations manager with Lion Nathan whose contribution to the All Blacks would be immense, helped create a job for me as a Lion Breweries representative in the north. The bonus was the company car. They were an excellent company to work for, totally flexible when it came to rugby commitments. That job gave me a good insight into the corporate world. Lion was pro-active with its workers, training them well and involving them in appropriate courses.

When I took the important decision in 1994 to move to Auckland... North Harbour, strictly speaking... for the betterment of my rugby, Lion was most accommodating, continuing to employ me, offering me a trade marketing role in Newmarket where I came under the significant influence of Peter Scott, the company's sponsorship manager.

It was around this time the All Blacks Club was being developed through the initiative of the national coach Laurie Mains and that man again, Kevin Roberts. They installed Iain Abercrombie, a more than useful footballer in his day who'd narrowly conceded the test hooking spot to Sean Fitzpatrick in 1986, as the manager with John Kirwan as marketing manager. When JK decided he'd run his course in rugby and threw in his lot with the Warriors, I was invited to replace him, a role I jumped at.

Rugby in New Zealand (and Australia and South Africa) is effectively funded now by the multi-million dollar deal struck in 1995 with Rupert Murdoch's News Corp but before then the rugby bosses were fighting a desperate battle to stop leading players crossing over to the rival (professional) league code. Which is where the All Blacks Club played a vitally important role in the lead-up to the World Cup, finding jobs – which ensured financial security – for a considerable number of high profile players, among them Zinzan Brooke. Zinny was on the brink of signing a lucrative deal with a Japanese club when the All Blacks Club intervened and secured him an excellent position with Sky Television. As a result of that Zinny graced All Black teams for three further years.

There were five major sponsors and 50 corporates backing the All Blacks Club in 1995 who in return for their financial input were guaranteed a certain accessibility to the players. It was my job to see the players met their obligations.

One of the major sponsors I dealt with was Philips, which remains heavily involved with rugby, these days sponsoring the Tri-nations championship. The managing director in '95 was Alistair Sutherland with whom I struck up an excellent relationship, eventually leading to me being offered a position with the company, one I willingly accepted.

That allowed me to establish a good work ethic with a major company, with an eye to the future. Once my rugby's over, I'm hoping to move into the field of human resources and man-management within the company which would involve me effectively becoming a mediator, a role I'm sure I would enjoy. I've had the best tutor around in John Hart, the All Black coach. He was a human resources person with Fletcher's for many years. Touring under John is like being involved in one long corporate seminar.

Things began to happen in rugby in New Zealand at an almost bewildering pace in 1995, thanks to the initiative of the NZRFU which took it upon itself to start formalising contract payments to players (many months before the IRB finally declared the game professional). It was the end of the brown envelope era.

The first tangible benefit for the players was the black Ford Futura cars, allocated to the World Cup squad members and most of the management. If we thought that was luxury, before the year was out we would have the NZRFU and the WRC falling over each other to contract us for amounts which I'd previously only considered possible by taking up tennis and reaching the finals at Wimbledon. Rugby, "the great amateur game", was about to become rugby, "the great professional game". And I, Ian Jones, had the good fortune to be part of it all.

Just prior to touring Australia and South Africa in 1992, I met Janine Graham, an accountant with Westpac Bank and sister of Garth, who was my tradesman when I was working through my electrical apprenticeship. Peter, Janine's other brother, is a staunch Kamo player and supporter. He earned the nickname of Sturge when he became the senior team's manager.

Janine and I didn't have long to develop our relationship before I was off on the 10-week tour of Australia and South Africa. It was a sample of what life can be like when your partner is an international rugby player. Surprisingly, it didn't frighten off Janine. She took me on as a would-be electrician, largely unemployed bloke whose greatest skill in life was the ability to play rugby.

She's shared the ups and down of life with me. We can spend up to five months apart in the course of a year because of my commitments to rugby and Philips. People say that's not normal, but it's normal for us. The holiday home we have up north is pretty special and compensates for a lot. It's where we indulge ourselves in swimming, diving, boating and relaxing.

When we decided to marry in November 1996, we wanted it to be special,

Ian Jones Collection

There's no better way to prepare for a wedding than by staging the honeymoon first. That's how we did it in Fiji in 1996.

a fitting ceremony away from the public gaze. We chose Fiji which we both love. Although we both come from large families, only 20 close family members and friends were in attendance at the Sheraton Hotel, Nadi, when Janine and I took our vows. The uniqueness of our wedding was that we celebrated the honeymoon before the ceremony. There was method in this, because the day after the celebrations I had to fly off to London to play for the UK Barbarians. So we had 12 idyllic days in Fiji, in which the corks of more than a few bottles of Moet and Chandon were popped, prior to the wedding ceremony. It was the best holiday I ever had, especially good because I was sharing it with family and friends.

When Steinlager was the only sponsor of the All Blacks, that was where the workload stopped; indeed, until Laurie Mains came on board in 1992, we weren't fulfilling our commitments there too impressively. It was a hangover from the amateurism days, I'm sure. You know the attitude: no one's paying us to play, so no one's going to make us do anything we don't want.

That mindset altered pretty dramatically in '92, first after Kevin Roberts addressed us and threatened to pull the Steinlager plug if we didn't give them our wholehearted support and then as more sponsors came aboard. Laurie and Kevin had the All Blacks functioning as a professional concern for some time before rugby officially abandoned amateurism.

As rugby became more professional, so did our commitments off the field. We were no longer merely locks or halfbacks or midfield backs in the public gaze for a few hours each test day before returning to the anonymity of our personal lives. We became role models. Unbelievable as it seems now but for a variety of reasons (the Springbok tour, spinal injuries, a reluctance to embrace television), rugby actually slipped behind soccer in the early 80s as a high profile sport, then yielded to league when the Warriors, hyped to Mars and back, burst on the scene five years ago. That would change dramatically in the 90s through intelligent marketing backed up by quality performances on the field. The All Blacks became a hot product.

As rugby's sponsorship pie was cut into many pieces, more corporates wanted a share of the action, as a consequence of which our responsibilities became greater. This included making television ads, some of which can take up to 12 hours . A classic example of this was the ad promoting the Super 12 competition in 1998. The backs had to do their thing while we forwards were required to hit a scrum machine. Nothing wrong with that, except that the footage had to be shot at night, under lights at the North Harbour Stadium at Albany. Filming started at 6pm and finished, can you believe it, at 5.30 the next morning! Packing down in endless scrums in the wee hours of the morning isn't a great way to spend a night. Not when you've got to drive to Taupo next day to join the Chiefs for a training session.

The All Blacks are involved in a lot of promotional work these days with individual sponsors (and in my case, with Philips). It's more fun now, with sponsors and players having learnt to interact with the public.

When I first entered the international scene, players survived as personalities on their natural ability. Some, like John Kirwan, had entrepreneurial skills and thrived in front of television cameras. Others, like some of the country boys, gave monosyllabic answers at best. All that's changed. We are expected to handle ourselves in public with a degree of aplomb and receive media training from the likes of Jane Dent to ensure that happens. It's all part of being the best. For several seasons now – and let's hope it continues, notwithstanding the hiccups at Melbourne, Wellington and Christchurch as this book was about to go to the printers – the All Blacks have been the best team in the world. Our off the field image is expected to match that.

New Zealand rugby has been blessed in my time with many outstanding personalities. John Kirwan was one of the most flamboyant, a dynamic footballer and athlete who projected himself powerfully; Inga Tuigamala became a huge personality who was being developed by the NZRFU as the image of rugby when he defected to league; Buck Shelford epitomised the game's passion and commitment, being seen as a Maori warrior; Marc Ellis, a natural entertainer, was lost but has come back to rugby; Jonah Lomu made an unbelievable impact worldwide – and not just among the rugby fraternity

– for his achievements at the World Cup in 1995; Sean Fitzpatrick and Zinzan Brooke became icons through their often heroic on-field achievements and their great leadership skills.

There have been others, too: Richard Loe, notwithstanding his notoriety tag, Michael Jones, Carlos Spencer, Norman Berryman, Eric Rush and Goldie (Jeff Wilson).

It's an exciting time to be involved in rugby, with great challenges (the Super 12, the Tri-nations and Bledisloe Cup, the NPC)leading up to rugby's holy grail, the Rugby World Cup. Look what winning soccer's World Cup did for France. Hopefully, New Zealand will experience that ecstasy in November, 1999.

But that's the future. This book is about the events of the past decade or so, a marvellous time to have been involved in rugby for it has not only seen the introduction of World Cups and law changes that have produced a thrilling, crowd-pleasing modern game but a full revolution, the transformation of the game from an amateur to a fully professional sport, from the brown envelope era to massive player contracts.

All of that was a long way from Kamo where this story starts.

Niels Schipper

The Kamo Kid

You know the nice thing about being selected to represent Northland (or North Auckland as it was then) for the first time back in 1988, apart from the obvious buzz of knowing I'd broken into the big time? It was the gentleness of it all.

The *Northern Advocate* rugby writer Garry Frew quietly recorded the fact that Ian Jones from Kamo would make his debut against Counties in the national championship match against Counties at Pukekohe Stadium, locking the scrum with veteran Mike Budd. No screaming headlines. No suggestion that Northland coach Danny O'Shea had uncovered New Zealand's latest teenage whizz-kid, which more often than not, in my time, is how newcomers to the Auckland squad have been announced. My selection didn't even make a headline in the *Advocate,* just a mention in passing in the thick of the story. Somebody called Jones was being given a run. Nothing to get excited about.

I guess it's the rural influence, but Northlanders prefer to let their actions do the shouting for them. The brashness of the city-slickers isn't the way of the people in the far north of New Zealand. They'll support their own, they'll back them financially and spiritedly, they'll follow them around the globe. But don't ever expect bold headlines proclaiming tomorrow's new stars. That's not the way it is.

That gentle introduction was just what I needed back in '88. It allowed me to ease into representative rugby as a youngster; indeed, to get through my first eight games for Northland – all of them NPC fixtures – without any unrealistic expectations upon me and without alerting opponents to the fact that I might be a lineout jumper of some potential. I was, after all, only 21.

And there are some pretty mean individuals operating at NPC level who are only too eager to deal to young whippersnappers who have been commanding an unreasonable share of the headlines.

Two weeks before my debut I'd occupied a seat among the reserves for the Bay of Plenty NPC game, which isn't as impressive as it might sound. I'd played the curtainraiser for the Northland Colts and coach O'Shea used to top up his reserves bench with under-21 players.

Northern Advocate

Danny O'Shea

Anyway, although Northland won that Bay of Plenty encounter comfortably enough, I watched the forwards struggling to compete at the lineouts because they lacked genuine height. I felt I could make a difference. I wanted to be there. It wasn't a cockiness or an arrogance. I just knew I could make a difference given the opportunity. I certainly didn't proffer this opinion to anyone. It was just something I felt.

That winning team, predictably, was unchanged but when Northland then crashed to defeat against Otago, struggling to win its share of lineout ball again, changes were made. I know Danny O'Shea had grave reservations about introducing a lanky teenager to his pack. I weighed 98kg and in Danny's book that was too light. He's a great guy, Danny, a man who's made a massive contribution to rugby in the Far North, but as a selector and coach he was a traditionalist who believed locks were the grunt men, ideally carved from granite. He was more concerned with power than fitness and finesse.

But in mid-1988 Danny found himself between a rock and a hard place. He'd criticised the New Zealand selectors for not inviting me along to the national colts trials in Wellington – he appreciated my potential, he just didn't think I had the stature to operate at NPC level – and they in turn had fired a salvo at him. "If you don't think enough of Ian Jones to play him in your Northland team, why should we consider him for the New Zealand Colts team?" they asked.

So for the Counties game, Danny took the plunge. I was in, locking the scrum with Mike Budd who was 10 years and 5 months my senior. And he weighed 10kg more! Mike's a champion fellow – someone who remains a close friend – and I was grateful to have him alongside me that afternoon at Pukekohe. It wasn't that I needed protection, just a case of him giving me confidence.

A lot of people, rugby writers prominent among them, questioned from those early days my ability to compete at the highest levels of rugby. They saw my "stringbean" physique as vulnerable against opponents they considered to be of classic New Zealand build. Fitness and athletic ability didn't come into it. I was slim and weighed under 100kg. The text books said you couldn't be an All Black lock, or probably even compete at first division level in the NPC, without extensive bulking up, and that was that. The same people probably argued that rugby would always remain amateur too!

While my physique obviously troubled other people, it was never a concern to me. I never once thought I could not compete against bigger opponents, which is how it was that afternoon at Pukekohe Stadium in 1988. I got on with the job of jumping in the lineouts and securing the balls directed at me. Twenty and stringbean I may have been, but I don't believe I lost any of my throws that day.

There was a time, once, when I actually had to lose weight to play. Can you believe that? I was a winger at the time, an overweight winger! Not quite of Jonah Lomu proportions, I must concede, but as a member of the Whangarei Grizzlies under-15 team I was teetering on the allowable weight limit of 52kg for the tournament for intermediate school pupils at Kaikohe. You were weighed on the morning the tournament opened and if you pushed the scales to 53kg or higher, you were not allowed to participate.

Several of us, including Errol Brain, were borderline cases, so on the journey north our coach made the bus driver stop at the bottom of Snake Hill, on the outskirts of Moerewa. With three jerseys on, we had to run to the top of the hill. The next stop was Ngawha Springs, famous for its mud pools, where the weighty ones were forced to soak in the hot pools for an hour. Drained of energy but several kilograms lighter, and feeling I imagine like jockeys do after desperate sessions in the sauna, we were then presented for "weighing in" – in our underpants.

Miraculously, we all checked in under 52kg, some admittedly with only ounces to spare. Then it was across the road to the dairy and a huge feed of meat pies. I'm sure by the time the first game kicked off, we were all well over the allowable weight limit. I think I was over 55kg by the end of the week!

One of the reasons I never felt threatened when I entered the first-class scene was because of the magnificent grounding in the basics I'd received from two of Northland's favourite rugby sons, Tuck Waaka and Frank Colthurst, while in the first XV at Kamo High School.

News Media

Frank Colthurst

Northern Advocate

Tuck Waaka

They'd both been through the rough and tumble of representative rugby – Frank for more than a decade as a hooker with Auckland, Thames Valley and Northland, Tuck as a tearaway loose forward with North Auckland, Auckland, Bay of Plenty and New Zealand Maori – and they recognised the importance of instilling the basics into young players.

Schoolboy rugby is where those basics need to be underlined. If you have coaches of the calibre of Frank and Tuck, with mana, and the ability to explain the rudiments of the game in simple terms, it will have a prolonged effect.

Tuck instilled in the boys at Kamo High the need to pass both ways, to kick with both feet and to run with the ball in hand. Sounds obvious, but it became apparent as we progressed along the rugby chain that Kamo boys were among the privileged few in terms of learning the fundamentals.

Tuck, having mastered the art of loose forward play, also taught us how to read a game, how to anticipate happenings and elementary matters like where to go to from a lineout. You run straight lines, not in arcs. The average kid wouldn't have a clue about that. But it's as elementary in a rugby context as learning your times table is to mathematics.

Frank Colthurst's influence came from his years of commitment as a tight forward. He's never been a bragger but a doer. His advice was invaluable, especially for an aspiring lock like myself.

He emphasised that I had three jobs to do: I had to claim the ball from kick-offs, win the lineout throws that were directed at me and push in the scrums. They were, and still are, a lock's main duties. You can't get away from that, even today, and the game has loosened up an enormous amount from when I first broke into representative play.

The spectacular stuff, running with the ball, lending assistance to the backs and scoring tries – adventures which often bring you generous mentions in the media – is really bonus material after you've tended to the basics.

In 1984 I was selected in the Northland secondary schools team for the Northern Region tournament in Auckland where my locking partner was a bushy-haired fellow from Mahurangi College called Robin Brooke. The No 8 sticking his head between us was a kid from Tikipunga High School, Errol Brain, who was the captain. Errol always had leadership qualities. With his calm demeanour, he was captaining teams from the age of 14, perhaps even earlier.

I had never encountered Robin Brooke until that tournament because Mahurangi didn't play in the Northland-wide competition. It's amazing to think that eight years later we would be locking the All Black test scrum and would establish a partnership that would create a world record for tests together.

I don't know whether anyone watching our performances back in '84 saw us as future internationals. They would probably have dismissed me as too skinny to become an All Black. And Robin probably looked too hairy. He was a lot bigger than me, a robust farm boy. What impressed me was that he was so skilful. He could kick like a back, which distinguished him from most tight forwards. Like us Kamo kids, he could do all the basics well. Someone had tutored him well also, I remember thinking.

The following year we were involved together at the Northern under-18 tournament, Robin with Auckland, myself with Northland. I was selected for the North Island under-18 team from there, along with Errol Brain and a solidly-built prop from Auckland named Olo Brown. Robin missed out. Remarkably, I would encounter Robin only once more during the next six years – in a Ranfurly Shield challenge at Eden Park – before we were selected to lock the All Black scrum together against Ireland at Athletic Park in 1992.

That was largely because Robin forsook Northland to seek fame and fortune in Auckland, a trail blazed by his older brothers Marty and Zinzan. Their contribution to Auckland and, in Zinzan and Robin's case, New Zealand rugby would be massive.

There was never any question that I would not play my club rugby for Kamo after leaving school, but as luck would have it, my emergence in the club coincided with Tuck Waaka and Frank Colthurst's decision to switch their allegiance, too, from Kamo High to the Kamo club.

Kamo maintained an excellent policy of not hastening young players into senior ranks, allowing them instead to gain confidence in the under-21 grade. Which brings its own rewards. Too many clubs have been left to lament decisions to promote teenage stars to bolster the sagging fortunes of their senior team. I'm not saying youngsters can't survive at top senior club level, but, with rare exceptions, it's only in powerful teams where older, experienced individuals can protect them. Otherwise, the batterings young players take can break their bodies and their hearts and seriously undermine burgeoning careers.

A classic example of what can eventuate involved an inexperienced young footballer early in the 1987 season. The "victim" was a fresh-faced young fellow called Ian Jones. The occasion was the Kamo-Old Boys senior clash at the Kamo Recreation Ground. Now Kamo versus Old Boys is no ordinary encounter, much more than a local derby: it's one of the annual grudge matches. No matter how humble either club's standing on the ladder might be, when they clash only one thing matters – victory. And in 1987 success was especially desirable because the Old Boys encounter was the showpiece of the Kamo club's centennial celebrations.

It happened that Kamo was hanging on grimly to a narrow advantage with about 25 minutes to play, but because of Mike Budd's domination of the lineout, Old Boys appeared to be gaining the ascendancy.

That's when Frank Colthurst decided I was needed, which was a pretty big call by Frank. And a huge challenge for me, because my experience at senior level had involved only a couple of low-key, nothing-on-'em matches late the previous season. This was Kamo's biggest game of the year, almost the equivalent of the Gallaher Shield final at Eden Park. I was being asked to stop Mike Budd from controlling the lineouts. He was 30, I was 20!

Getting me on the park involved a level of deceit because in those days

Stephen Baker, Northern Advocate

Nothing delights a Kamo fan more than winning against the old rival Old Boys. To achieve it in 1987, the club's centenary season, was just about the ultimate.

strategic substitutions weren't permitted. But suddenly there was a Kamo forward lying on the ground writhing in agony. He was plainly too seriously injured to continue (although miraculously the damage subsided the instant he arrived on the sideline). Some skinny bloke called Jones was going on as his replacement.

"Get us some lineout ball, for God's sake," was Frank Colthurst's instruction as he squeezed my shoulder and shoved me towards the action.

I probably should have been awe-struck because spectators were packed four deep around the Kamo Rec that afternoon and nothing mattered but that Kamo should defeat Old Boys. But I didn't allow their presence to distract me. I was totally focused, I recall, and determined to do the job requested of me by Frank. He'd trained me well for this moment. I wasn't about to let him down.

The one thing I knew I could do better than most players at that stage of my career was jump high. I was tall to start with and I seemed to have a greater natural spring than most of those around me. It was the quality I utilised that afternoon. If it was our throw, I made certain I secured the ball two-handed and delivered it back to our halfback. If the throw was Old Boys', I did my darndest to disrupt Mike Budd.

Obviously, I unsettled him. Unable to effect two-handed catches himself because of my influence, he resorted to one-handed tapdowns, which allowed our forwards to surge through on to his halfback. The game was beginning to swing Kamo's way.

I am pleased to call Mike a dear friend these days, but about 10 minutes from the conclusion of that local derby 11 years ago, I wasn't so sure. Not after he'd decked me. I didn't see the punch coming, but I sure felt it. The crowd obviously saw it because the booing that ensued could have been heard, I'm sure, five kilometres away in Whangarei. And the referee obviously didn't see it, because Mike Budd played on.

Mike threw the punch in sheer frustration but it backfired on him and his team. My team-mates were incensed at seeing their 20-year-old knocked to the ground. It was all the motivation they needed. Old Boys never got back into the game.

Mike came and apologised at the after-match function. I didn't really care by then because the centenary celebrations were in full swing and I'd discovered that a couple of glasses of beer acted as a mean anaesthetic to someone with a swollen jaw.

I'm proud to note my name on the Life Members' board at the Kamo clubrooms. I think the first nomination might have followed the team's famous win in the centennial encounter that afternoon in 1987!

Frank decided I was an asset he needed permanently in his pack after that. I adjusted comfortably to the higher level and my jaw didn't take any more punches that season.

A month or so after the centennial match, I was in action for Kamo in a home game one Saturday morning. The game was early so the players and supporters could get along to Okara Park to watch the final All Black trial, leading up to the selection (in Whangarei that evening) of the World Cup squad.

Now the truth is I wasn't feeling great that particular Saturday. In fact, I was feeling downright hungover because one of my mates had celebrated his 21st birthday the night before. A three o'clock kick-off would have been a challenge; the 11am start didn't bear thinking about.

Anyway, the show had to go on and there I was going through the motions. It was probably the only occasion in my entire senior rugby career when I would probably have turned the crystals in a breathalyser green! Fortunately, Kamo's opponent that morning wasn't one of the competition's giants and we were managing a few tries.

My hangover notwithstanding, I happened to be in the right place from one of our breakaways and trotted across the goal line to score. Having forced the ball, I looked up at the cluster of spectators standing behind the deadball line and to my surprise saw that John Hart and Alex Wyllie, Brian Lochore's assistants as All Black selectors, were among them. I wondered what would bring them to the Kamo Recreation Ground. I presumed they'd come out for some fresh air and to get away from the hurly-burly of their hotel. They obviously hadn't come to see Ian Jones.

It was a full 10 years later that the truth was revealed to me: having a free morning, they did venture out to Kamo to check out the form of one Ian Jones whom they'd been told possessed a degree of potential. How did they score me? Apparently, a couple of Ss – springheeled and stringbean. And short on power. Oh well, I was only 20 at the time… and hungover!

I had a charmed run in 1987 and 1988 because no one knew anything about me. And let me assure you, that's a huge advantage because once you're in the spotlight, video analysis means opponents are ready to ambush you. That's why I feel sorry for young players whose arrival at senior club or representative level is preceded by extensive media hype. While it might massage their egos, I can assure young footballers everywhere the best possible way to embark on a sporting career is unannounced. Your first year is your easiest, as long as your cover isn't blown. The rugby world is cluttered with would-be stars who have struggled to fulfil the potential shown in their first season at the top. No, it's not that their talent has diminished (unless they've suffered serious injury); it's that opponents, now aware of them, will have studied video tapes of their play and pinpointed strengths and weaknesses.

Suddenly the explosive threequarter who left opponents gasping with his left-footed sidestep one season will find defenders waiting for him the first time he executes it the next.

That's why I so enjoyed my debut season with Northland in '88. Hell, I couldn't even make a headline in the *Northern Advocate*. No one was going to know about me anywhere else.

I suppose I could have been apprehensive about making my first-class debut at Pukekohe Stadium, because the previous season, while playing there for Northland B, I'd broken my jaw. It was all terribly innocent – I simply collided with another player's elbow while bringing the ball down at a lineout. While the jaw felt numb, I didn't regard it as anything serious and played out the full 80 minutes.

That night on the bus journey back home, we stopped at Warkworth for a pub meal. The steak I ordered was thick and juicy and appetising, but I couldn't do anything with it. My jaw wouldn't function. It was difficult enough to swallow liquid, without trying to chew steak. An x-ray at Whangarei Hospital the next morning confirmed a broken jaw, which unfortunately put me out of the Northland Colts' tour around the middle of the North Island.

Northland teams back in the 1980s had a novel way of determining who would room with whom – it was all done by numbers. Number one roomed with number two. Number three roomed with number four. Because I was number five for the Pukekohe game, I got to room with number six, Frank Lamborn, an experienced loose forward who was coming up to 50 games for Northland.

Frank was an ideal rooming partner for a newcomer like myself – hard-nosed and intense but calm and laidback. He treated me like an equal, which I appreciated. I was really confident because I knew I could help the team. Probably there was an element of youthful innocence about it, but I never once thought I couldn't compete against bigger, and obviously much older, opponents.

And nothing has ever changed. From that day at Pukekohe to now, I have never taken the field at representative or international level bearing an inferiority complex. While plenty of others have had concerns about my lack of bulk and weight, it's never bothered me. I knew what I could achieve and I set about making it happen. It would be nice to record that I celebrated my representative debut with a victory, but Counties edged us out 14-12. We competed well though and the team had the confidence to use me regularly in the lineouts.

I remember the surge of pride as I pulled on the North Auckland jersey in the dressing room. I was in the presence of All Blacks – Fred and Kawhena Woodman and Ian Dunn – and others who'd played more than 100 games for Northland (Charles Going and Neil Ruddell) but I felt comfortable. I was happy to be there. I wasn't nervous.

From that day, Charles Going became a great personal friend and valuable training partner. He taught me so many little things. He used to remind me that if you didn't get the little things right, they'd become major issues.

Nerves didn't encroach in my second outing either for Northland but I think I might have been slightly overawed by the galaxy of talent that surrounded me as Northland intrepidly challenged mighty Auckland for the Ranfurly Shield on Eden Park, my first experience of the famous stadium.

My opposite was Marty Brooke while Mike Budd opposed Gary Whetton. It was disconcerting to realise I was playing against the same superstars who'd been my heroes when they won the World Cup the previous year. Someone cruelly suggested the first things our boys had packed for the trip were their autograph books! It wasn't quite that bad, but obviously our coach Danny O'Shea had a difficult job getting his players focused. Any team featuring Michael Jones, Sean Fitzpatrick, Steve McDowell, a couple of Whettons, Zinzan Brooke, Grant Fox, Joe Stanley and Terry Wright – mostly all at the peak of their careers – had a huge psychological advantage going into any encounter on Eden Park.

Considering the manner in which the Awesome Auks demolished international and provincial teams alike during the late 1980s, we did tolerably well to restrict them to 43-15.

I have two vivid recollections of the occasion. One was the immaculate grooming of Eden Park which was like a bowling green. The second was when I sneaked through a lineout to see if I could cause any strife on Auckland's side and came face to face with Steve McDowell, protector of blue-and-white territory. Very deliberately, but not too maliciously, he introduced me to his trademark, a short, sharp jab to the jaw, a gentle reminder of where I belonged!

While I respected my illustrious opponents that day, I competed determinedly. Our scrum was dealt to embarrassingly, but we won our share of lineout possession.

After the Eden Park humbling, Northland's record was three defeats from four NPC outings, not an auspicious start to the competition. The previous year the team had struggled to get clear of the relegation zone. It would be depressing to be down there again.

Far from that, Northland prospered. In succession, we defeated Canterbury (29-3 at Whangarei), Manawatu and Taranaki on the road and finished off with another crushing home win against North Harbour. We finished fifth in the NPC, behind unbeaten Auckland, Wellington, Otago and North Harbour, and scored 31 tries. It was one of Northland's better seasons. The team was never going to win the NPC but it was great to be so competitive.

Canterbury was my first home game, for which the Northland squad members were required to assemble late morning at the Grand Hotel in Whangarei, the Grand being something of an institution in the town. The building was seriously old and our team room arguably the dingiest, most uninviting room in the place. I unwisely asked Chris Hull what standard of dress was required. "Just casual," he assured me. I've never believed anything he's told me since. There was the new boy Jones in his smart v-neck pullover, everyone else resplendent in jackets and ties. There was just time for me to sprint upstairs and change before the coach began addressing us.

John Stone, Northern Advocate

You can tell from this photo why some guys play lock and others prefer halfback. Sharing a moment of delight with me is Chris Hull.

While Northland was a mighty team to play for, you'd have to say that certain aspects of the match preparation and the general arrangements were less than ideal. The Grand Hotel always turned on a sumptuous lunch which many of the players couldn't resist. Huge platefuls of food are not recommended three hours before a rugby game, but some of the boys weren't prepared to miss a feasting opportunity like this. Some would eat so much, they'd fall asleep!

Amateurism ruled in the 1980s and unions never parted with a dollar more than they had to. The Northland union never flew its representative players anywhere a bus could take them and expenses were apportioned by a method which surely came straight from the Scottish Rugby Union. For driving to midweek training sessions you received a petrol allowance (remembering that some of the guys faced more than three hours' driving for the round trip). But there was no compensation for driving the same distance for the game itself. Why? Because you were expected to turn up to represent Northland. Hard to argue against that kind of logic!

One of the more bizarre dressing room rituals indulged in by Northland teams in the countdown to representative matches in the late 80s was to get each player to run the gauntlet (in boots, on a concrete floor) between two lines of his team-mates who would punch and pummel him every inch of the way. It supposedly prepared you for battle!

Not all of the personnel associated with the team were always as professional as they might have been. One day Mike Barry, who was recovering from a torn rib cartilage, required a cortisone injection but about 20 minutes after receiving it began to hyperventilate. The "injector" checked his medical kit and said, "Oops, I've given you the wrong drug – that was meant for Con [Barrell]."

Con was a chronic asthmatic who needed an injection to get him through a game. While our medical person raced off to the hospital for a replacement dosage, Con, tensing up as the game approached, began to go blue around the lips. Asthma was heavily upon him by the time he received his injection.

Women were discriminated against when I first entered the Northland rugby scene. After-match functions were for men only, and that was that. However, things changed following Auckland's visit to Okara Park in 1989 when Grant Fox and Gary Whetton took exception to having their wives excluded from the reception. They kicked up a big stink and the following season the after-match shows were declared open.

I managed to pick up four tries in my first season of NPC play, getting my first one against Canterbury at Okara Park and scoring two against Wellington at Athletic Park. In that Wellington game I opposed Murray Pierce, the celebrated All Black, and was delighted when he approached me after the game. To that point, being so new to top-level rugby, I'd not had a lot of involvement with opponents. He made the effort, congratulated me on my game and happily engaged me in conversation, something I truly appreciated. He didn't need to do that. I found him a neat guy.

Fate would determine that we would travel together as All Blacks to Wales and Ireland the next year and in 1990 I would fill the test locking position he left vacant when he unexpectedly took off to try his luck with Natal in South Africa

Although I missed out on the New Zealand Colts experience in 1988, the year finished on a high when I travelled to Scotland with the privately-arranged New Zealand Youth team, coached by the great Fred Allen and the man who was Northland's junior coaching co-ordinator, Sid Going.

The Scottish Rugby Union, in an unprecedented move, allocated us the curtainraiser to the Wallabies test at Murrayfield, which was an amazing experience. We were up against the best under-21 players in Scotland, including two future stars Craig Chalmers and Tony Stanger, while our team was drawn from clubs throughout New Zealand and included a lot of players who had never operated above colts level. We did have a cagey captain in Pat Lam, however, a dynamic front rower who even then was shaving most of his hair off, Bull Allen, and a slick halfback in Stu Forster.

Our game was telecast live throughout Scotland and, fairly predictably, we were billed as the New Zealand Juniors. Fortunately, we lived up to the star status, scoring a length-of-the-field try two minutes from time for a dramatic victory. After the game the Scottish coach approached Fred Allen and asked him how many of his team would qualify for the New Zealand Colts team if it was being chosen the next day.

"Probably about four," said Allen, honestly. "Aaah, Jesus!" replied the Scot, "we'll never be able to beat you bastards."

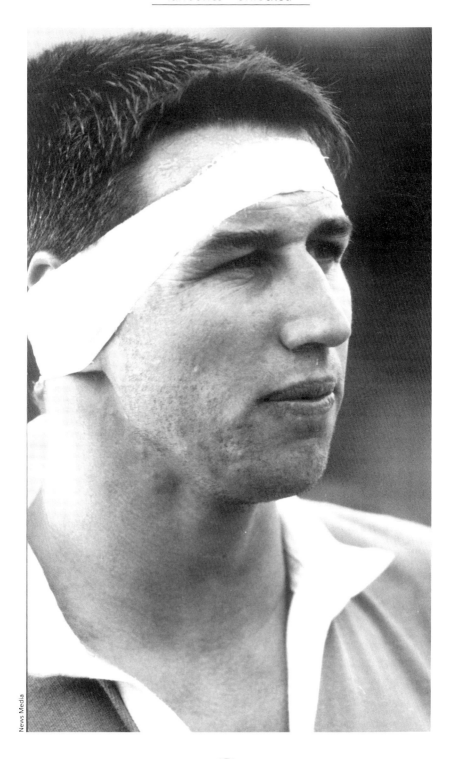

News Media

2

The Fisher Terrace Gang

There's not a lot to Kamo. Once a small, semirural settlement on the outskirts of Whangarei, as the town expanded it became a suburb like any other. But we've always had a strong, independent community spirit and a certain claim to fame as the last set of traffic lights in the north.

Fisher Terrace, Kamo, was the setting for an idyllic childhood. It was a new street in a fairly new subdivision when my parents first moved there, with a broad view over the city. All Kamo homes are built on mines; there's 30 miles of underground roads beneath them. By the time we left Fisher Terrace when I was 14 it had developed into a typical suburban Whangarei street, but in my memory I can still see the wide, green expanses that were the remnants of the farmland and mines it had sprung from and the homeland upon which we played as kids.

Being a new subdivision, quite a lot of young parents had moved into Fisher Terrace around the same time to raise their kids. That meant there was a whole lot of us kids who'd always hang out together, the "Fisher Street Gang". We were quite varied in age (I was the baby), but that never seemed to matter. We were just one big, close bunch.

The Fisher Street Gang included myself and my two older brothers, Bruce and Greg; Blyth Tait and his two sisters (they were our next-door neighbours); the Ackers' three kids and two Brackenbridges. The amazing thing about this one little street, this gang of friends, is that so many of us went on to represent New Zealand in sport: myself in rugby, Angela Brackenbridge in table tennis and Blyth in equestrian eventing. Richard Ackers represented New Zealand

Bryan Young

Blyth Tait

Combined Services. Brian Maunsell, the Olympic hockey player, also lived in the same street, while test cricketer Bryan Young lived about 100 yards up the hill in another street and used to play cricket and rugby with us on the Taits' front lawn. Bryan was a couple of years ahead of me at school and close mates with my brother Greg. Another real good mate of ours was Robbie Nasemith, one of the America's Cup boys.

Blyth, of course, became an Olympic medallist and number-one ranked rider in the world. For a few years there he and I used to duel it out for the Northland Sportsman of the Year award. If one of us didn't get it, it would be Bryan Young. Those three names just kept cropping up!

My mother, being a nurse, actually delivered Blyth Tait when he was born in 1961. His father, Bob, was a Northland rugby rep, but Blyth was never a great rugby player and played soccer in winter. But we'd still all spend hours together just kicking a ball around up at the school or in someone's backyard. All of our parents treated us as their own kids and looked out for us all as we moved from one house to another.

We got into a bit of trouble one day when I was seven. The whole gang was swinging from the crossbar of the goalposts at school; I rocked too far back, the goalposts came crashing down on us and I split my cheek. I was rushed up to hospital, but I was fine. Another time my brothers locked themselves in a Mini and wouldn't let me in – so I put the hose through the car window to flush them out!

People say there must have been something in the water at Fisher Terrace but I think we were just very lucky to have all that parental support and each other to play against and spur each other on. Whenever one of us had a big game, the whole street would go and watch. Or we'd all go out and watch Blyth ride.

Ian Jones Collection

The Jones boys of Kamo – from left, Greg at seven, Bruce at nine and a yet-to-sprout-up Ian at five.

The gang's still pretty close even today. My parents have travelled down to Puhinui in South Auckland to watch Blyth compete, while Blyth's parents have followed the All Blacks overseas and supported us at the 1995 World Cup. The Fisher Street families have remained great friends.

Most of the Fisher Street gang went to Whau Valley Primary School, Blyth Tait and myself included, then on to Kamo Intermediate, which was just up the hill, and Kamo High. Sport was my thing at school.

I was never great shakes academically. I certainly wouldn't put myself down as a scholar, although I really enjoyed my time at school and the teachers and friendships that were forged there and got through School Cert and UE all right. For a long time my aim was to join the police, but in my sixth-form year our first XV coach, Frank Colthurst, offered me the opportunity to start as a cadet for Wrightson's, the big stock and station agency for which he worked. I worked for Wrightson's that summer, but while I was there an opportunity came up for an electrical apprenticeship. I thought great, a trade will make it easier for me to travel, do my big OE! I completed the apprenticeship and became an electrician. All these years later I still haven't done my OE, though I did manage to get around and see the world a bit in the end!

Of course, growing up in the north means growing up with water. We used to practically live in the sea over summer, holidaying at our bach on the Whangarei Heads. Looking out across the harbour, we'd often see heaps of orca coming in to chase the stingrays. They're stunning animals to watch – my family are right behind Greenpeace, me included.

Water sports were always a huge part of our life. Dad taught us to sail P Class yachts at the bach when we were young and I still love boating today. Dad and my uncle Nook are brilliant yachtsmen, a love they inherited from their father. Both were champions in Northland, representing the Whangarei Cruising Club. Nook sailed nationally as well, racing seven-footers in the Tanner Cup.

I should explain that "Nook" isn't my uncle's real name. It's Alistair, but he's always been known as Nook, while my dad, Warren, has always been "Wac" (pronounced "wok"). I've never in my life called Nook "Uncle Alistair" and I don't think he'd know who I was talking to if I did.

There's several stories about how they came to be known as Wac and Nook. One is that Nook couldn't pronounce Warren when he was a toddler, so he just called his brother Wac and it stuck. Meanwhile, the babysitter's nickname for little Alistair was "Snooky Pookums", which became shortened to "Snook" and then "Nook". Who would have thought that a two-year-old's nickname would still be going strong 60 years later! I'm sure that many people around Whangarei today have no idea Wac and Nook have "real" names; they probably just think the family's a bit different!

The great thing about Northland is that it's such a wonderful playground for leisure and sports. We had a ball growing up there. We did a lot of waterskiing and diving – I got my dive certificate when I was 15. All three of us brothers dived round Whangarei Harbour, while I was also an avid lifeguard. I used to compete in surf lifesaving for Waipu Cove.

But my number-one interest in summer was always swimming. It was my first great love in sport, my first passion. Dad was president of the Whangarei Swimming Club for a while. He was real keen on swimming; he got all three of us brothers into it. Mum used to take us down to the Whangarei Olympic 50 metre pool and ferry us around to swim camps or to compete in carnivals every Saturday all through the summer – along with Con Barrell and his brothers. If we were at the bach, we'd do some distance training by swimming around an island in the bay – a good half hour's swim. Mum usually walked around the island to make sure we didn't take a shortcut.

These were the days before Whangarei had a heated pool so we really only had four months of the year that we could train. Freestyle and backstroke were my specialties, backstroke mainly. I had a few Northland age-group records in backstroke, while my best time for 100m freestyle was 59 seconds. Not too many swimmers from Northland had broken the minute barrier.

As I got older, I started going to the Auckland championships and then competed in the nationals for the first time when I was 14. As a teenager I was nationally ranked and finished third in the 100m backstroke at the national championships one year behind Paul Kingsman, who went on to medal at the Olympics.

Paul was the gun swimmer in my age group. Anthony Mosse was a couple of years older and an even bigger star in our eyes back then. Locally, Northland had a good swimmer by the name of Murray Parker. He ended up moving down to Auckland and swam at the Commonwealth Games in Brisbane in 1982. Another top guy was Michael Davidson; he also moved down the line. It seemed clear to me that the good swimmers had to move from the north to take up their training in Auckland.

I'd have loved to have represented New Zealand in any sport and I used to wonder how far I'd go in swimming, but moving away from my friends and family in Kamo didn't hold much appeal, particularly at that age.

Representing New Zealand was the goal, no matter what sport it was. I just wanted to achieve. As it turned out, rugby was where I got my breaks. I was making rep teams for rugby towards the end of my school days, and when I started working at 17, swimming started drifting into the past. My parents offered to help me go to Auckland and board if I wanted to take my swimming career further and train year-round, but swimming's a harsh sport. It takes so much dedication, and when I left school and started working the motivation started to drift.

We had to get up early to be at the pool for our 5.30am training session, then return after school for our afternoon session. I didn't mind the training, even though the hours meant giving up a few other things. At times I quite enjoyed it. Mum says I was a bit more disciplined than my brothers, but then I probably took it a bit more seriously. If I've ever wanted to do something, I've put my heart and soul into it.

I have huge respect for swimmers who keep it up. The discipline and dedication they must put into their sport is phenomenal. I know swimming taught me self-discipline, taught me how to train. We probably would have only swum 10 to 12 kilometres a week, certainly not as much as Danyon Loader, but it was enough to give me a good base, both fitness-wise and in terms of teaching me a work ethic, a good training ethic.

Also, swimming's such an individual sport that you've got to learn to motivate yourself to go out there and do it yourself, learn to train by yourself. In some respects it's a lot tougher than rugby, which, being a team environment, means you always have people around you to drag you with them and pull you up to speed. Swimming gave me a sense of focus that I used in my rugby training. Even today, when training's hard, I still draw on the thoughts I learned back then. It stood me in good stead. I still love the sport.

It was partly because of swimming that I never had too many sporting heroes when I was young, even though sports was everything when I was growing up and supreme in our household. Like every young swimmer in the world, I looked up to Mark Spitz, the American who had won seven golds at the Munich Olympics. But I didn't have posters of idols plastered all over my bedroom wall.

But I was certainly interested in rugby. When I was growing up in the 1970s, North Auckland had the Ranfurly Shield (in 1972 and 1978) and we had some pretty famous All Blacks right in our own province. Guys like Sid Going and Joe Morgan. I didn't really have to look beyond Northland to find my heroes. They were probably the first people I noticed and looked up to as "achievers", though I'd never in a million years have run out with an autograph book.

I remember the 1978 Ranfurly Shield season really well. North Auckland versus Manawatu down in Palmerston North that year was quite a famous game for Northlanders. We listened to it on the radio at home, me, Dad, my brothers. A guy called Chippie Semenoff kicked four penalty goals to win the Ranfurly Shield 12-10, after it had been 10-9 to Manawatu with time up on the clock.

The Ranfurly Shield was such a source of pride in Whangarei that it generated a real rugby passion in people, especially in impressionable youngsters like me. There was a big parade in town when the victorious team got back from Palmerston North. For every defence of the shield after that, North Auckland would have a street parade the morning of the match. We'd always go down and watch, and from there go along to the game. It was a real neat time.

I'm sure I got my love of sport from Dad. He has a huge knowledge of sport. No matter whether it was rugby, basketball or volleyball, I remember as long as it was played well, he'd follow it. Dad played rugby for Hora Hora in the 1950s, back when the Kamo club was still pulling itself back together after the war, before playing for Kamo itself.

Dad was always a bit smaller than the rest of us in the family. He played first-five. He was also a ballboy during the 1950 British Lions tour – a framed photo of the occasion used to hang on the wall of his study when we were growing up. My brother Greg was also a ballboy for North Auckland games, though I never was.

Dad probably didn't get to play as much rugby as he would have liked because of the time involved in running the family business. He had the Shell service station in Kensington, which was his father's before him. Uncle Nook was also involved in it, while from the age of 12 we'd work there, too. Christmas morning it was always just us three boys manning the station.

Back in the old days, if for some reason the power was down, you could hand-wind the pumps. Whenever there was a blackout, my brothers and I would be the ones called up to get on the crankshaft pumping the gas through! It was hard work and you could bet your bottom dollar the power cuts would always happen on a rotten, cold, wet day. You'd dream of returning to that lovely warm lounge. With modern pumps that's a thing of the past.

Living up in Whangarei, it always seemed quite a long way to go to see a test match in Auckland, so with that and the service station, we always used to watch the All Blacks on TV, like very many other people around the country I expect. We'd always get up at three or four in the morning to watch a game overseas, too. You'd never miss a test.

The only time I've ever watched a test match live was in 1989. A group of my friends and I went down to see the Bledisloe Cup game. That's the only time I've "been" to an All Black test match as a paying member of the public!

It was a perfect day. Northland had virtually block-booked a section of the old North Stand and we drove down in a minibus, driving home that night. The All Blacks won. I remember John Gallagher's try, and it was Timmy Horan and Phil Kearns' debut game. Before the year was out I'd be an All Black myself.

Unless you lived in the main centres, in those days you didn't see an All Black unless there was one playing for your province. I can't remember an All Black ever coming to our school. We go to schools quite often these days and I enjoy being able to do that for the kids, knowing how I might have felt if it had been me. The kids are just over the moon.

Rugby was always my sport in winter and I've played it for as long as I can remember. As much as I love the game, I'm also very grateful that I had the chance to try all different sorts of sports when I was growing up – Mum and Dad never pushed us one way or the other. All three of us Jones boys took up tennis and table tennis, while I also really enjoyed cross-country and athletics. I belonged to the harriers for a while. It's often been reported that I played basketball at school, too, but actually that was one of the few sports I didn't get into. Volleyball, on the other hand, was an absolute passion – it was the "cool" sport at Kamo High when I was there; we won quite a few competitions. I still like playing beach volleyball in summer.

Swimming and rugby were the ones that took up most of our time, however. I started playing organised rugby when I was five, in the Kamo midgets – the "barefoot brigade". We played barefoot right up until I was 12. For a long time I can't actually remember having a position, not until I reached the under-13s and played centre. Later I played on the wing. I was always basically in the backs. It wasn't until I started to grow like Jack's beanstalk in my teenage years that anyone thought of putting me at lock. Tony Bennett, the coach of the "Grizzlies" (the team I used to play for in the Athletic Attic tournament), was the one who changed me from a winger to a lock. That was at under-13s level and I've been there ever since.

I played all my JMB (Junior Management Board) rugby in the black and white Kamo colours; there was no other club as far as I was concerned. We used to play at Kensington Park, a fantastic venue that's still the focus today for a whole range of sports – netball, hockey, rugby, soccer, cricket, you name it. It had been an old racecourse when I was at primary school and when we were young it seemed absolutely huge.

Every Saturday morning hundreds of kids would swarm around Kensington Park. It was alive with noise and excitement. We'd meet at a rotunda in the middle and find out who would be our captain for the day – we'd all take turns. Then after the game we'd go back to the rotunda where we'd all get a free ice-block – yum!

After getting our ice-blocks, generally my friends and I would go and watch Bruce and Greg play. Then you'd end up watching the seniors if they were playing at Kamo. That was your day. You'd stay in your jersey all day, muddy knees, bare feet and all, happy as Larry.

I have very warm memories of Kensington Park and the lifelong friends I made on those weekend afternoons. It's a neat place, I'm very fond of it. I drive past from time to time and see all the kids out there like I used to be. Nothing's changed and that's just great.

It was through the Kamo Rugby Football Club that I made my first overseas rugby trip – two weeks in Rarotonga with the Kamo under-15s in 1982, when I was 14. We raised all the money ourselves, about $23,000. It was around this time I really started to shoot up and my mother reckons it's because I spent so much time standing in chicken manure, shovelling away to raise money!

The team to Rarotonga included Errol Brain, who later went to Counties, and Geoff Crawford, who went on to play lock for North Auckland. The memories include being ordered by the locals to stop training on a Sunday there, because it was a sacred day. Also, at the same time we were in Rarotonga, David Bowie was there filming a movie. We sneaked into the Rarotongan Hotel to watch and got his autograph.

Not long after that, when I was 15, I made the Kamo High first XV for the first time, pulling on Kamo High's red and green jersey with a great deal of pride. The school's phys-ed teacher, Tuck Waaka, and long-serving North Auckland hooker Frank Colthurst were the coaches and we were very well served. I ended up making the Northland under-18 team, but never made it to the national secondary schools system. Probably I was deemed too skinny to be any good.

Throughout this time I was growing like crazy. Both of my brothers are about 6ft 2in and I thought I'd end up about the same – but I just kept stretching! There's quite a bit of debate about where the height comes from, because there's tall people on both sides of the family. Mum's reasonably tall, even though she's one of the shorter ones in her family. My mother's grandfather was a huge man, about 6ft 5in. Dad's of average height, but his mother was tall and her father (my great-grandfather) exceptionally tall. Some people swear I get my height from Dad when they see photos of my great-grandfather, "Long Jim" – his build was quite similar to mine.

Some people think that because I'm a Jones and I'm from Northland, I must be related to the Jones and Hilton-Jones rugby families up this way (the ones that produced Peter Jones). I'm not – Dad's father was Australian. But I am connected to another famous rugby name of the north: the Finlaysons.

We grew up with stories of the famous Finlayson brothers, "Bunny" and "Tote". It gets pretty complicated, but to cut a long story short, my grandmother Flora's grandfather Alex and Bunny's grandfather John were brothers. Therefore Kamo's only two test caps are related by blood.

It doesn't stop there, either: Bunny's brother Tote married my grandmother's sister! I'd hate to work out exactly how I'm actually related to some of my extended family; we're all just "cousins" or "uncles" as far as I'm concerned. It's much easier that way! It's such a big, interconnected clan that relationships that seem distant or tenuous on paper have always seemed closer than they actually are, in any case. I grew up kicking around with the Finlayson boys and the McKays and all our various mates. We're also related to the McLeods, which means I'm distantly related to Grant and Neil McLeod, New Zealand hockey representatives.

One of Bunny Finlayson's All Black caps used to hang on the wall at home when we

Bunny Finlayson

Tote Finlayson

were growing up. His 1928 All Black blazer also hung in the Kamo rugby clubrooms. He was the shining star of Northland's first eminent rugby families.

His parents, Norman and Annie Finlayson, began their family of one girl and eight boys late last century on their farm at Maungaturoto. Incredibly, all eight of their sons grew up to play rugby for Northland, five at first-class level. Among the boys, the eldest were the twins, Jack (who became the first Northlander to be elected president of the NZRFU in 1950) and Bain. Then there was Owen, known as "Tote". The story goes that it was because he was as solid as a totara stump. Then there was Stuart; then Innes (Bunny), who was born in 1899 and passed away in 1980. While everyone in the family was tall, he was especially tall, seemingly higher than his 6ft 2in. Then came another set of twins, Angus (who went on to represent Auckland) and Callum (who went on to represent Otago); and Danny.

Bunny and Tote both played senior rugby for Kamo when they moved down from Maungaturoto in 1920. Bunny was centre, Tote a forward. They played alongside a winger by the name of Cyril Going – father of All Blacks Sid and Ken Going.

In 1920, Cyril's cousin Cecil and the Finlayson brothers were Kamo's representatives in North Auckland's very first match when North Auckland beat South Island Country at Kensington Park. Bunny had the honour of scoring North Auckland's very first representative try, a feat for which he was awarded a gold medal. He was a hard runner with a long stride, crashing through tackles and galloping up the field like an early version of Jonah Lomu. Apparently people would holler and scream, "Give it to Bunny!" from the sidelines.

When Ken, Sid and Brian Going played together for North Auckland in 1967, it wasn't a record. In 1923, Bunny, Bain, Tote and Angus all played in the same side for North Auckland against both Auckland and King Country.

Bunny went on to play 36 games for New Zealand – a heck of a lot for the era he lived in. Included in his six tests were all four on the All Blacks' 1928 tour of South Africa. In the All Blacks, Bunny was a loose forward. At almost 99kg, he was the heaviest All Black on the field when they played Great Britain in the first test in 1930. I was almost exactly the same weight (98kg) when I broke into test rugby in 1990, but I was the third lightest in the pack!

The Finlaysons were of Nova Scotian descent, like our relatives, the McKays and the McLeods. Originally from Scotland, the Nova Scotians were a flock of 1500 pioneers who followed the Reverend Norman McLeod to Nova Scotia in Canada, then to Australia and finally New Zealand. Mostly farmers, they settled in Waipu in 1853 and spread out across the land towards Whangarei.

My grandmother on my Dad's side stills lives in Whangarei. Her maiden name was Flora McKay – her parents, Sally and "Long Jim", changed the spelling of the family name to avoid confusion with other MacKays in the area. Sally's brother ("Uncle Danny") owned the land that became the Northland Golf Course, while Long Jim farmed at Purua, about 20km northwest of Whangarei, after he left Waipu.

Long Jim and Sally owned one of the most distinctive houses in Kamo, the "tower house" in Three Mile Bush Road just out of town. The big, stately home with its distinctive turret was called "Kinross" after the county in Scotland and was the place where my grandmother Flora grew up. The Scottish heritage was still quite strong in those days – my grandmother's bridesmaids wore kilts at her wedding. Back in those days Kinross was set on 30 hectares of land; so big that they used to host rodeos there. It was sold out of the family in 1941 and though the house still stands and is a local landmark, these days the land is all subdivided.

Flora met my Dad's father when he was a merchant sailor in port in Whangarei. Clinton Jones was from Sydney and the water was his life. Mad on yachting, he sailed 18-foot yachts in Sydney Harbour before he came out to New Zealand to live in the 1930s. He loved rugby as well and it's said he was a good player.

Mum's side of the family, meanwhile, comes from the opposite end of the country. Her family can trace their roots in New Zealand back to 1840 in Banks Peninsula. Mum moved up north to Herekino, just outside Kaitaia, when she was nine. Then the family moved again and she went to school in Whangarei. And ever since she's been a Northlander.

Mum's side is the academic side of the family. Both of her parents and her sister were teachers and there's also a doctor and a lawyer among my cousins on that side. Didn't rub off on me, though I guess I still wound up as a "professional"!

My mother's mother, Marjorie Shaw, was an amazing lady. She's probably had the most profound impact on me of all my family. Marjorie had a very difficult time of life in her later years when she was suffering from a number of painful illnesses and diseases, including rheumatoid arthritis and lung disorders. She had to take a lot of heavy medication and was quite a sick lady in her last years – but you'd never hear her complain. Nothing was an issue. She was an incredible lady, amazingly strong-willed and tough.

Her strength and resilience always impressed me something wicked. More than anyone she taught me how to be tough to the end. She died when I was 18. I try to remember her in the work I do for the arthritis foundation.

I think Marjorie's strong will came through in all of the boys while physically our parents say we were all always naturals when it came to sport. We certainly loved playing and I remember my older brothers being good at

Northern Advocate

Building flats in Whangarei. It wasn't my fault if I was the only one working when a photographer from the local newspaper called in!

just about anything they tried.

In rugby, Bruce, the eldest, was a prop, then a flanker. But he did a cartilage in his knee at first XV level and needed an operation. It's quite a simple operation these days, but back then it was quite a big procedure and he had to hobble around with a big cast on his leg for ages. Unfortunately it spelled the end of his playing days, but Bruce became the number-one supporter. He'll watch all my rugby and always has. In this way he became a different kind of role model for me through his good advice. My other brother, Greg, is two years older than I am. He's an outstanding sportsperson and was a brilliant rugby player, a skilful No 8/flanker. But he won't mind me saying his training ethics were never great. He had more of a "have a go" sort of attitude, getting into sport on the day with a fully committed, boots'n'all attitude rather than expending energy in practice! He probably could have done a lot better, but he loves life and that's the way it always was.

When I left school, I played a couple of club games at under-21 level with Greg which was really cool. He's had an influence on the way I play. As far as being gutsy and having a go, I drew inspiration from Greg.

Both of my brothers have been the best supporters a guy could ask for, but they do still rib me about one occasion. The three of us were going to work together as subcontractors to build some flats in Whangarei one year, but really it was my brothers who did all the work because it turned out that I had other commitments with my rugby. The local paper found out I was involved and rang me up for a story – All Black at work. The next day there was a photo in the *Northern Advocate* of "builder Ian Jones" with my toolbelt and spade digging in at these flats – there was no mention of my brothers. To this day our family calls them "The Flats That Ian Built"!

The immediate family have always been tremendously supportive, and that's been a real help to me over the years. Regardless of what I'm trying to achieve, in swimming or rugby or whatever, regardless of where I am in the world, they're there for me. Mum was the legendary washer of clothes, the taxi service and definitely filled our stomachs, and you don't get anywhere in sport without that. My cousins, aunties and uncles, the wider family, have been fantastic as well. I still get faxes and phone calls from them every time I make a test team. I can't appreciate it enough. Now my wife Janine's family has joined the support brigade as well. I guess we're a typical, big, close Northland clan and I've been very lucky to have this tight family network. I wouldn't be without it.

News Media

3

Northland Made Me

We have real pride in our community up north and I think it's this deep-set pride that surfaces when we play sport or any form of competition. Never was this stronger than in the days of the old *Top Town* series on television, the zany competition that used to pit town against town all around New Zealand. I actually represented Whangarei in *Top Town* in 1986. We used to have to compete in all sorts of obstacle courses and races to sort out which town had the strongest and fittest locals and our Whangarei team made it all the way to the grand final.

Kamo is the absolute epitome of Northland pride. To many dyed-in-the-wool Kamoites, Kamo is the greatest place on Earth and it's got a special community spirit. That's why the support for its local rugby club has always been outstanding. There was certainly never any question I would play my club rugby anywhere else after I left school. In any case, the club, boasting some of the best facilities in Northland, was just a five-minute walk from home!

Kamo's usually been strong in the local club competition. No wonder when you look at some of the luminaries that have represented the club over the decades: homegrown All Blacks Bunny Finlayson and Bevan Holmes (who played 31 times for New Zealand in the early 1970s, though never got to play a test), Otago All Black Lindsay Townsend (whose arrival led Kamo to its postwar resurgence in the late 1950s), test cricketer Brian Dunning, All Blacks Geoff Valli, Nick Allen and Richie Guy (who later became NZRFU chairman) and New Zealand amateur heavyweight boxing champion Charlie Dunn.

Kamo was originally a coal mining town so its biggest rival has always

Rugby News

Kamo, a great little town… famous for breeding outstanding sports people and for having the most northern set of traffic lights in New Zealand.

been Hikurangi – the other mining town. You still have to push your way through the crowd on the sidelines if you want to see a club match between these two. Hikurangi were the rough, tough, bruising marauders from the north, with strong forwards who would smash you over and walk their sprigs over your back. Kamo, meanwhile, always had the smooth moves in the backs. Great ingredients for a rivalry.

These days the miners have all gone and Kamo represents a good cross-section of Whangarei. Being on the outskirts of town, the townies are blended with a bit of country spirit and farming stock. It's a family club, always strict on rules – I remember getting told off in no uncertain terms one day for wearing my rugby socks in the squash court.

Apparently it was always well known around Northland that drugs would never be tolerated at the Kamo club, whereas this wasn't always the case in some places around Northland. In Frank Colthurst's day the Kamo players were even nicknamed the "Raro boys" – because they drank only orange juice before a game. Another unwritten rule was that if you didn't train, don't expect to play.

There's a whole tradition of dedication to the game inside Kamo's walls and I don't think players have ever had a problem motivating themselves to play for the black and white jersey.

Apart from Hikurangi, our other big rival has always been Old Boys. We play them for the McMahon-Norton Trophy, named after two promising 23-year-old players, one from Kamo and one from Old Boys. Tragically, they died the same week in 1975.

Then there's City. It was always interesting playing City at Fishbone Park, their home in Whangarei. The ground was notoriously tidal because there was a creek that ran the length of one side of the ground – to get onto the park, you have to go over a little bridge. If it had been raining and it also happened to be high tide, the ground would be absolutely full of water and muck. You knew it would be horribly boggy. But if it was a nice day and the tide was out, it was fine. The only certainty was that whatever the weather or tide, we'd always play.

There's another place called Pipiwai, our near neighbours, about half an hour up the same road as Kamo. At Pipiwai they didn't have any hot showers. They, too, had a creek running along one side of the field, so after the game everyone used to strip off, dive into the cold creek, wade across to the other side and stand on a rock ledge to dry off like shags! I believe they've since built a marae with hot showers, but the locals may still prefer the creek.

The more I played rugby around Northland, especially in interdistrict competition, the more I came to appreciate the special character of rugby in the region. People have gone to extraordinary lengths to keep the game alive and flourishing against the odds over what's really a sparsely-populated, but huge, terrain.

Northland sport was built from hardworking farming stock, gumdiggers and miners, people with a hard, knuckle-down attitude. One of the reasons Northland rugby has been so strong is the famous all-round strength of its farmers. They just didn't get injured the way gym-built bodies do – people from rural communities all round the country will tell you that. The Goings are a great example of the impact farming families had on rugby in the North. The Joneses/Hilton-Joneses were another powerful rugby farming family from up Kaitaia way. It's not so strong nowadays, but it's still true that if the farming community's rugby is strong, then Whangarei rugby is strong. It was a two-way street, too. Rugby was always important to rural districts because the supporters would bring new economies into the area.

Some of the toughest people – and best competitors – in Northland come from the tiniest communities. A great example is Danny O'Shea, who was my North Auckland coach from my debut in 1987 to 1989. He was also a good player, playing for the Northland Colts in the curtainraiser to a Springboks tour match in 1956.

Danny's from Maungakaramea, a small place 12 miles out of Whangarei. The town basically is just a dot on the map and consists of a school, a retirement home, a butcher's shop and the Maungakaramea Garage, where locals not only get their petrol, but their mail and groceries as well. It's also got a sports complex – the sole recreational focus of the region.

Despite its tiny population, Maungakaramea has produced not only Danny O'Shea, but test cricketer (and later, New Zealand cricket coach) Bob Cunis, Northern Districts cricketer Murray Child, New Zealand hockey rep Sandra Snell and the Bints and Morriseys, two names quite well known around Northland in sport generally. The local butcher, meanwhile, is "Bear" Morgan, a Northland rep golfer.

You'd be hard pressed to find a couple of streets in Auckland, Wellington or Christchurch with that much sporting talent packed into a small area, yet you find it in this tiny place out in the wops of Northland. Why? I reckon it's because of the people themselves. When you've got people like Bob Cunis and Danny O'Shea, you've got someone to watch and mould the young sportspeople growing up under their wing.

Then there's the great rivalry between country areas. People want desperately to beat their neighbouring areas, as well as the "town teams", of course. It's a great focus for them and fires up their sport. And in such small places people are fiercely proud. Everyone knows each other and wants to beat each other: if one family's competitive, the next will pick up on it.

Every little pocket of population in Northland has its own distinct character. Maungakaramea is known as a stronghold of hockey, cricket and dog trials. Springfield, a little further along, produced a different crop of sportspeople and it seems to keep going with every generation. Go anywhere in Northland and you'll find familiar families, names that have achieved such-and-such in sport over the years. The Goings and the Morgans in Hikurangi. The Cunises and O'Sheas in Maungakaramea. There's a long list, right through the north.

Outlying settlements like Maungakaramea and even Kamo have been blessed with very good facilities for rugby. The reason is that the rugby club was the heart of the community: if there was a wedding reception or a meeting out in the country, it was always held at the rugby club. It was also the place for youth. That's why money was invested in the clubrooms and grounds.

Living in the north I guess you get used to the scenery, but it's not a bad place to hit the road in the team bus. The only bugbear is the huge distances teams have to travel to play each other. It's a big island past Whangarei. A big island past Kaitaia even, still another couple of hours to drive to the top.

From schooldays onwards I can remember some great rugby trips around Northland. You can get a real bond going on those long trips, a real closeness. That was the best thing about them. We spent such a lot of time on the bus together that you had to develop a good spirit.

At school we'd play throughout the Whangarei subunion. Later, when I played interdistricts rugby, Northland would travel to play Hokianga, which is Rawene and around that area; Mangonui, which is Kaitaia and north; Bay of Islands, which is Paihia and Kerikeri; Northern Wairoa, which is Dargaville; and Otamatea, which is Maungaturoto and south. You're talking a lot of travelling in this subunion competition, two and a half hours to drive all the way up to a place like Rawene. People have to be pretty keen to do that.

What's so special about the north is that people are keen. When I played for North Auckland, a good percentage of our trainings were at Okara Park in Whangarei. That was ideal for me; I lived just 10 minutes away. I was a local. But we had guys in our team from Dargaville and Kerikeri, which is an hour and a half's drive from Whangarei; and guys from Kaitaia, which is more than two hours away. Week after week these guys would drive all the way down to Whangarei for two hours' training on a Wednesday evening, then they'd have to drive all the way back home because they had to get up and work the next day.

I've always admired the commitment of people like that. Some players wouldn't pull into their driveway until after midnight and quite often in winter the roads weren't much chop for driving.

North Auckland has done so well in spite of guys having to drive down to NPC games on the Saturday morning – in my time, probably only 50 per cent of the team were "local". The other thing is, we hardly ever flew anywhere. If we had a game in Auckland, we'd bus down: the planes that came to Whangarei were never big enough for us all anyway. On the way home, some of the guys would have to get off the bus in Whangarei and then have to drive again for another hour or two. It was a real mission. But they did it, and never with any fuss – that was how much guys wanted to play for North Auckland. It was pretty special that they did that for the team, I think. It certainly wasn't easy. From time to time someone would write off their car because they'd hit a couple of cows on the road or something like that.

You couldn't ask players to come down and train more than once a week in the circumstances, but North Auckland rugby had a brilliant incentive for getting us all together on the Wednesday. Every Wednesday, after we'd trained and showered, North Auckland would put on a dinner. A lady called Audrey Thoms would cook us a real nice meal – it might be blade steak, mashed potatoes and peas, heaps of gravy. There was generally dessert, too – a home-made apple pie or rhubarb pie.

Audrey used to give us all marks out of 10 according to how polite we were at this dinner. Then, at the end of every year, the Audrey Thoms Trophy was presented to "the nicest player" in the team. Mike Barry won it five times, but one year there was a mix-up and the winner was Ian Jones!

As you got used to touring around the north, you realised that all the rugby centres have their own special character. I really enjoyed Hokianga – Rawene and Punguru. That was Dame Whina Cooper's turf, the west coast of Northland. It's a rugged, isolated part of the country and the hospitality there is just out of this world. Whenever we went up to Rawene as the North Auckland team, it was as big a deal as when the All Blacks come to Whangarei. The locals seldom came to Whangarei to watch rugby because it was quite a distance, so whenever we played there it seemed everyone and his dog would come out to watch and support their team. They loved it. It's a real shame it's such a mission for them to get to Auckland because they're as passionate supporters of All Black rugby as anyone else in New Zealand.

Kaitaia was always tough. It was a long journey up there, a good couple of hours by bus and when you got there you were met by some real hard rugby. Whangarei, I guess, was always a bit of a glamour side – we were the "townies" with a good swag of the North Auckland players in our team, so teams like Mangonui really gave it to you. And we didn't always dominate.

There's one particular game that will always stick in my mind. It was a Vikings game against a Hokianga Selection XV organised to open the new ground at Punguru. To get to Punguru, you had to get the ferry from Rawene. As we were warming up, this Vikings side containing a lot of the flashy city boys and North Auckland players, we noticed the Hokianga side looked a bit short – it didn't look like there were 15 men. Then out of the bush bursts this horseman with his rugby boots slung around his shoulders. He hurtled right down to the edge of the field, hitched up his horse, put on his boots and started warming up with the rest of the players! That's Northland for you.

Northland abounds with hard, dogged characters and unsurprisingly a fair few of them have turned up in rugby. People like Ted Griffin, who coached Northland for 22 years. I met him only once – he was just stepping back from the scene when I was coming through. It was when I first made North Auckland and he congratulated me on making the team. I certainly knew of him though, knew his reputation. He was the Godfather of rugby in the north, a legend when it came to motivating great players like Peter Jones.

One character I'd like to mention is a man named Dave Jurlina. Dave was a farmer from a beautiful place called Taipa, which is just up from Cooper's Beach in Mangonui in the Far North. A hooker, he was a bit older than the rest of us in the North Auckland team and had the misfortune to play in an era when we had a number of good hookers like Mike Barry and Willie Phillips.

After Dave played his first few games for North Auckland in 1982, he was to make way for another hooker and would have played most of the next decade for North Auckland B. Finally, around 1991, North Auckland was short on hookers again and he was called back to the reserves bench for the A side.

After that, Dave was in and out of the representative team – as soon as he got off the reserves bench it seemed he'd be back there warming the timber again. He reserved a hell of a lot for North Auckland, went on a lot of our trips without really being "a player". That can get pretty boring after a while, I'm sure – let alone disheartening.

It would have taken Dave a good two hours every weekend and training night to travel down from his farm – and he would have had to get people in or his wife to do his work on the farm in his absence. But he never once moaned or complained. His passion was for the game and he had his heart set on gaining his North Auckland blazer, which was awarded when you'd started in 12 representative games. As far as Dave was concerned, the travel and hassle was a small sacrifice for playing – and earning that North Auckland blazer.

I was captain of North Auckland by the time Dave Jurlina finally played his blazer game in 1993. It had taken him almost 12 years to get there and the day he got it, everyone was absolutely rapt for him. His wife came down to watch and he himself was proud as punch. That summed up for me the special spirit of rugby in the north: there was always total commitment to the cause. Mind you, once he got his blazer, I think he retired on the spot!

Another Northland legend I'd like to mention is Garry Frew. Garry's been

Dave Jurlina, in possession, a very special footballer who took 12 seasons to earn his North Auckland blazer.

Graeme Blown

Garry Frew

a sports journalist and editor at the *Northern Advocate* for as long as most people can remember and has received an MBE for his work. He also played a mean game of table tennis, at which he represented New Zealand from 1954 to 1968. He's a real hard, feisty competitor around the table-tennis table, which belies his warm personality. What's more, he's a Kamo man. He captained the Kamo senior cricket team in his day, played rugby for Kamo at junior level and was also a leading squash and tennis player for Northland. Garry's done an enormous amount of work for sport in Northland both on and off the field and has an amazing knowledge of local sport which he's shared with the entire community.

4

Jumping to Conclusions

Play Rugby and See the World became my catch phrase in 1989. First, it was a none-too-demanding trip to Surfers Paradise with Kamo, followed by matches in Canada and the United States with Northland and, before the year was out, action in Vancouver, Wales, Ireland and England with the All Blacks. The All Blacks! Can you believe that? The skinny kid from Kamo, unwanted at the Colts trials the year before, reluctantly taken on board by the Northland coach and boasting only eight games at first-class level, was about to become an international.

Well, that would happen in October. Such sensational developments weren't even contemplated when the Kamo seniors headed off for a pre-season romp to Queensland where, it must be conceded, the sun and surf and bikini-clad locals had greater appeal than the rugby.

At Surfers the team was accommodated in luxurious apartments, three to a room. I finished up sharing with Chris Hull, a halfback, and Con Barrell, a hulking prop. Chris, a veteran of almost 70 games for Northland (and an always amusing character) exercised his seniority by claiming the double bed. I pounced on the single bed, leaving Con, very much the new chum, to occupy the camp stretcher. It wasn't the ideal situation for a front rower. The first time he dropped his 110kg frame onto the stretcher, three of the bands holding it together snapped!

It has nothing to do with our rugby careers, which developed along largely parallel lines – we both played for Kamo and Northland before becoming All Blacks – but it's worth mentioning anyway that Con and I were born two days apart in the same hospital in April, 1967. Indeed, our mothers shared

Ian Jones Collection

Chris Hull, comfy on his double bed during a Kamo club trip to Surfers Paradise. Young Con Barrell, in the background, had to make do with a camp stretcher!

the same room. It's not true that as a baby I threw a rattle at Con, and that he dropped it!

The Surfers Paradise venture was possible because of the phenomenal fundraising achievements of the Kamo guys, brilliantly co-ordinated by club stalwart Eric Weston. Working truly as a team over the summer, we distributed thousands of telephone books throughout the Whangarei region, went scrub cutting, planted kikuyu grass and painted the clubrooms. In addition to which, yours truly, along with another good Northland representative Mike Gunson, installed the floodlighting for the training ground. I was, after all, an electrician!

We had great working bees which helped build team spirit mightily. It's one of the sadnesses of the professional age that so few top-flight players have time to spend with their clubs. Some of the 1998 All Blacks have had virtually no club involvement at all, which is a huge shame. They've missed something.

Early in the '89 season, Mike Barry, Northland's hooker, and I received invitations to represent New Zealand Barbarians against mighty Auckland at Ericsson Stadium (Mt Smart as it was known then). We were chuffed to be involved and excited about having a weekend in the big city of Auckland. We were accommodated in a luxurious city hotel and had John Hart as our coach.

Having played only eight representative matches, I hadn't qualified for a Northland blazer, but was pressured into borrowing Bill le Clerc's. It was a cardinal sin to wear a blazer you hadn't earned, but my mates felt that for such an important occasion, turning up in a v-necked sweater was infra dig.

Mike and I planned a big night on the town following the Saturday game. But everything turned to custard. Mike suffered a broken rib and was taken to hospital. So much for the revelling. I finished up watching television in my hotel room!

Super 12 hadn't been dreamed up back in 1989, but Super 6 (or the South Pacific championship as it was tagged then) had; unfortunately, it was restricted to a pretty exclusive club. Only Auckland, Wellington and Canterbury were involved from New Zealand, along with New South Wales, Queensland and Fiji.

On the initiative of the Otago Rugby Union, frustrated at being continually shut out of the Super 6, the rival Canz series was born. North Auckland was invited to participate, along with Waikato and Otago, against Canada and two Argentinian clubs, Banco Nacionale (the great Hugo Porta's team) and San Isidro. It provided an exciting opportunity for players in the north, only a handful of whom had made it into national sides, to experience overseas travel.

That first year, Northland journeyed to Vancouver to play Canada. To make the trip worthwhile, matches were also arranged against a USA Eagles selection at Monterey and a Crimson Tide side at Victoria. For the fellows from Kaikohe and Moerewa, even those from Whangarei, taking in the sights of San Francisco was a mind-boggling experience. So was the visit to Alcatraz. The island, with its high-security prison, made such a deep impression on Chris Hull that he based his entire captain's team talk, for the game at Monterey, on the Birdman who'd defied the odds in escaping from the island. With the Birdman's commitment, thundered Chris, there was no way Northland could lose. I don't know that we'll ever hear John Hart using that theme, but full marks for originality.

After the Eagles game, which we were lucky enough to win, we found the Americans had set up a rugby market, selling merchandise from stalls near the field. This proved too much for Mike Barry who rushed back to his room and gathered a selection of his (second-hand) gear, including a couple of New Zealand club jerseys . The lure of New Zealand rugby souvenirs proved too much for the locals – Mike sold the lot.

The outing at Victoria was a romp against a team of extremely modest ability. As the score soared past 80, I felt irked that I was one of the few Northland players who hadn't contributed a try. So I loitered with intent out among the backs until I finally got on the scoresheet. I also scored in the

Canz game against Canada but a late penalty goal by their fullback Mark Wyatt tipped the game Canada's way 21-20. I found Vancouver a delightful city, little suspecting that five months later I would be returning as a member of Alex Wyllie's All Blacks.

After the Canadian game I was introduced to Gareth Rees, Canada's talented flyhalf. It was to be the start of a long-standing friendship. We've kept in touch ever since and run across each other in various rugby cities around the world.

We arrived home from Canada in mid-May and I expected my main focus over the ensuing weeks would be with Kamo in the senior club competition, because Northland's NPC campaign wasn't kicking off for a couple of months. So you can imagine I was blown away when I learned the names of the four locks selected for the All Black trial in Hamilton in May – Gary Whetton, Murray Pierce, Albert Anderson… and me. The announcement took some digesting. After all, Pierce was 31 and had played 80 games for Wellington, Whetton was 29 and a veteran of 112 games for Auckland and Anderson at 28 had featured in 117 games for Canterbury, while I had just turned 21 and could claim eight outings for Northland. I was very definitely the odd one out, in a position where traditionally only players who'd served lengthy careers at provincial level were involved.

Being pitched in amongst the cream of New Zealand rugby talent – remembering that the All Blacks were indisputably the greatest team in the world at the time, having not lost a game since 1986 – could have been intimidating. I was very much the new kid on the block, but I went to Hamilton confident I could be competitive. In fact, there's never been a game in my entire career, which by mid-1998 involved more than 250 first-class encounters, when I took the field concerned I might not measure up. Slim-lined I might have been, but I was naturally tall, athletic and able to jump high. I always considered it was the other opposition's job to match me, not vice versa.

What I did find a little unsettling in Hamilton was the fact that I was the solitary representative from Northland. After a mere handful of games at representative level – I couldn't even wear a Northland blazer to the trials because I hadn't qualified for one – I knew personally almost none of my fellow trialists. Oh, I knew *of* them, because they comprised most of the individuals who had won the first World Cup for New Zealand in 1987. They were my heroes then. Now I was right in amongst them.

They weren't Kipper, Bullet, Foxy, Buck, Gee-Dub, Zinny and Fitzy at that first encounter. I think I almost called the All Black captain Mr Shelford! I was the quiet, shy kid from up north who kept his mouth shut, did what he was told and engaged almost no one in conversation the whole time I was in

Hamilton.

I was locking with Albert Anderson in what was effectively The Rest of New Zealand against the shadow test line-up. Our coach was Earle Kirton and our captain Mike Brewer. We had Zinzan Brooke at No 8, Inga Tuigamala on the wing and Frano Botica at first-five but we were very much the underdogs against the best team in the world.

Naturally, my main concern was winning any lineout throw directed at me. I was in the trial because of my leaping ability, so it was absolutely imperative I achieved an immediate rapport with the hooker who would be throwing the ball in. That thrower turned out to be Waikato's Warren Gatland, these days making a name for himself as coach of Ireland. In 1989, we were roommates.

Things would have been far less complicated for me if Mike Brewer hadn't insisted on formulating the lineout calls. We liked to keep matters simple back in Northland. No matter how complex the number "called" before each lineout, if the first digit coincided with the number on your back, it was your ball. Not exactly Einstein inspired, but at least the boys in blue knew where the ball was going. But Mike Brewer was a bloody mathematician, wasn't he! When he barked out a code, say 22 35 46 8, you added the first two numbers and if that matched the number on your back, it was your ball coming. A breeze for anyone doing mental arithmetic in a classroom but damned complicated for a nervous 21-year-old trying to combat a couple of the world's best lineout opponents in the heat of battle!

Rooming with Warren Gatland, or Gats as he preferred to be known, was a bonus. He's a real thinker, an intelligent student of the game and he had a major influence on my career at that stage. He talked about accuracy at lineout time and he cleverly determined we would speed the game up to unsettle the test players, tactics which worked mightily.

He was dead right. Had we operated in an orthodox manner, there would have developed, I'm sure, a shit fight between Pierce and myself. But on several occasions Gatland, having alerted me to his intentions, fired in quick throws, which I won effortlessly because each time Pierce was unprepared.

It was a cracking contest and we stretched the test fifteen to the limit. With three tries from Inga the Winger, we held them to 25-31, which was an exceptional achievement against a team which had swept aside virtually every major rugby nation in the world in the preceding two seasons. In the statistics published the next day, it was gratifying to note that our team had won the lineouts, for which Gats could take much of the credit.

Earle Kirton was a delight to have as a coach. I'd never struck anyone quite like him. Flamboyant and extrovert, he imbued all his players with confidence and a determination to have a go. He encouraged the individuals to demonstrate their skills, which is precisely what happened. We were all inspired by his total zest for the game. And he, in turn, was over the moon with our performance. What Earle was able to convey was that rugby is about more than just training and playing. I found the whole occasion most stimulating.

With my flimsy credentials, it was almost preposterous to think I would be considered for the domestic internationals in 1989 against France and Argentina. The selectors (Alex Wyllie, John Hart and Lane Penn) retained the status quo, which was entirely predictable considering the All Blacks' great winning sequence at the time, but I have to confess to a tinge of disappointment that I wasn't named in the test squad. I was nothing if not enthusiastic and optimistic. Once I'd been summoned to the trials, my goal was to make the test fifteen. Oh well, if the selectors didn't want me just yet, the next goal was the end-of- year tour of Wales and Ireland when 30 players would be selected.

My second season at representative level was, as I have explained, far more challenging. I now had a reputation and opponents were targeting me, making it that much more difficult to secure lineout possession. Life had been far more enjoyable when I was anonymous.

The All Black touring party for the UK was to be named the day after Northland's NPC game against Otago at Carisbrook, a match which ended in a draw, a satisfying result for us at the infamous House of Pain. Most of the critics had been including me in their selections, so in anticipation Chris Hull bought a bottle of champagne, to be cracked if and when my name was read out.

Travelling home from matches in the South Island is a prolonged affair for Northlanders. On that occasion we flew from Dunedin to Auckland through Christchurch, then journeyed north to Whangarei by coach. It was a long, wearying day. Having checked out of our Dunedin hotel shortly after 9am, we eventually pulled into Whangarei around 5pm, by which point the All Blacks had still not been named. It had been established, however, that Russ Thomas, the chairman of the NZRFU, would read the names out live on television during the six o'clock news.

Several families had gathered at my parents' home, obviously in expectation of a memorable announcement. Suddenly, I freaked out. I'd been cool and calculating in marking Murray Pierce at the All Black trial and nonchalantly faced up to every challenge confronting me as a Northland representative. But now that the All Black touring team was about to be announced, I was a nervous wreck. There was no way I was going to take in the news with all those people around. I sought solitude downstairs in my own bedroom. If Ian Jones *wasn't* going to be in that blessed touring party, he would need at least a few moments to compose himself.

It's amazing the mileage you can cover in a bedroom that measures no more than 20 square metres! Finally, Russ Thomas worked his way through to the locks and I was there. I don't know which emotion dominated at that moment, relief or joy. But I couldn't contain my smile as I joined the friends and relatives upstairs. The scene of the celebrations would soon move on.

There's not normally much action at the Kamo clubrooms on a Sunday evening, but that night the place was suddenly abuzz. Having a third homegrown All Black named (after Bunny Finlayson and Bevan Holmes) made it a pretty special occasion .

Chris Hull turned up with his rechilled bottle of bubbly and most of the Northland boys put in an appearance. It was a very special occasion, a marvellous reminder of how close the rugby community is in the Far North. The celebrations finally died down at the Kamo clubrooms, only to be rekindled back home. It was a very, very late night, but one I shall always cherish.

I was eminently distinguishable upon arrival at the Poenamo Hotel at Takapuna where the All Blacks were assembling prior to departure. I was the one with two large suitcases crammed with clothing and personal effects.

Toast to selection

My Kamo clubmates help me celebrate my All Black selection back in 1989.

I'm not sure what I expected from the NZRFU but I'd covered all eventualities. I remember the strange look my roommate gave me after I'd struggled up the stairs with my gear. Northlanders were a little unworldly in the ways of All Black touring teams, and it was showing!

By the time Canterbury International and the NZRFU had dished out all their apparel – about $6000 worth per player, beginning with suitcases – I realised I'd seriously over-prepared. I arranged for my bags to be picked up, but not before I'd sneaked a couple of pairs of underpants out. You can never be too careful!

It was all an unbelievable experience, being part of the All Blacks for the first time. I knew several of the players from the trial, but because I'd missed out on the Colts, a lot of the younger guys were new to me. There were nine new internationals and having that in common meant we naturally gravitated towards each other, as a consequence of which I developed close friendships with players like Steve Gordon, Craig Innes, Walter Little and Matthew Ridge. I had never spoken with the coach Alex Wyllie, the manager John Sturgeon or the captain Buck Shelford.

My first roommate turned out to be one of the best, the North Harbour prop Ron Williams. He had a great attitude to touring – go hard on and off the field. Ron's philosophy was that you shouldn't let rugby dominate you 24 hours a day, seven days a week. For those of us who were Dirty Dirties in Vancouver, Ron was our unofficial tour guide. He led us to some memorable bars and nightclubs, then insisted we scoffed pizza before crashing for the night.

He also reminded us that after a night on the town it was important to put 200 per cent into training the next day. I'm not sure the Ron Williams philosophy would go down a treat with John Hart and Mike Banks in these days of professionalism, but Ron's attitude helped those of us new to the international scene then achieve a good balance between rugby and relaxation. Don't get me wrong – we didn't go crazy on the socialising but nor did we focus on rugby to the exclusion of everything else.

The senior members of the team of '89 made a huge effort to involve the new guys, which reflected well on the management. I was fearfully shy that first week, giving monosyllabic answers to questions about my family, my home town and my rugby background. It took me a full week to relax and feel comfortable before I began to initiate conversation myself. It was a big step for someone from Northland, trying to engage in small talk with many of the best rugby players in the world, scarcely any of whom I knew before assembly in Auckland. It's all so different now, thanks to the Super 12. It would be rare for a new international these days not to be on first-name terms with three-quarters of the All Black team, perhaps even more.

You're not a genuine All Black until you take the field wearing that sacred silver fern, so having watched the tour opener in Vancouver from the grandstand, I was eager for action when we arrived in Cardiff.

A weird aspect of the selections for the opening two encounters was that at Vancouver they paired the two front-of-the-lineout jumpers together, Gary Whetton and Steve Gordon, while for the Cardiff game, Murray Pierce and I, both middle-of-the-lineout specialists, were selected.

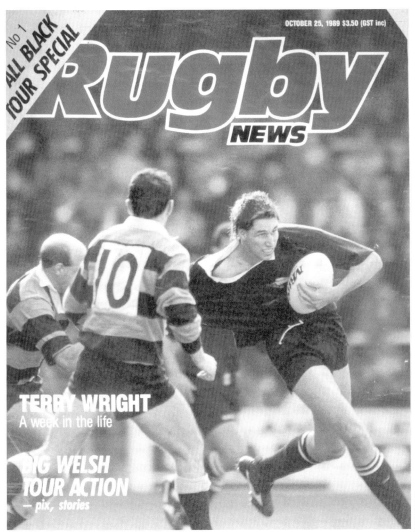

OCTOBER 25, 1989 $3.50 (GST inc)

No 1 ALL BLACK TOUR SPECIAL

RUGBY NEWS

TERRY WRIGHT
A week in the life

BIG WELSH TOUR ACTION
— pix, stories

Rugby News

I made enough impact in my All Black debut against Cardiff at the famous Arms Park to qualify for the cover of *Rugby News'* special tour booklet.

Murray being vastly senior to me – he'd played 24 tests by the time we arrived in the UK – naturally insisted on jumping in his specialist zone, leaving me on debut to operate at the front of the lineout, a position I'd not occupied previously and in which I have hardly ever been used in the near decade since. It would be the only occasion Murray and I locked the scrum together.

Murray also claimed the No 4 jersey, which didn't have any great significance at the time, but it remains the only occasion in my 100 games for the All Blacks that I have taken the field wearing No 5. The selectors got their pairings sorted out after Cardiff and for the remainder of the tour I locked with Gary Whetton while Steve Gordon was paired off with Murray Pierce.

Murray had taken me under his wing after Northland's game in Wellington in 1987 and he continued to offer advice throughout the tour, which I greatly appreciated. He could have identified me as a threat to his position but he was more concerned about the benefit to the team. A true All Black. In the early stages of an international career you usually receive heaps of faxes which understandably dwindle as your test appearances mount up. It speaks volumes for Murray that in 1997, nine years after my debut, he sent a message wishing me well for the Argentinian test at Athletic Park.

Naturally, you want to launch your international career on a winning note, so there were a few of us – Matthew Ridge, Craig Innes and myself – who were sweating when Cardiff trailed just 15-18 with seven minutes to play, but a late try by Mike Brewer got us home. I managed to steal a few of Cardiff's lineout throws and an overall lineout count of 22-7 in our favour was a source of satisfaction, although nothing surpassed just being out there in the black jersey. A great sensation.

In the grandstand at Cardiff was my father. He and Mum were on a European coach holiday in France, but upon learning that my debut would be at Cardiff he interrupted his travel plans to come and watch me, which made it a pretty special occasion for me.

When you're on tour, all you want to do is play, so I was chuffed to be selected for the next match, against Pontypool, in a more natural pairing with Gary Whetton. I donned the No 4 jersey which would remain mine for the next 99 outings! That Pontypool game remains vividly in my memory – for two reasons, one happy, one agonisingly painful. The good bit was that I scored a try, my first as an All Black, the sadness that John Kirwan snapped his Achilles tendon and was invalided out of the tour.

About an hour after the game, while we were still in the dressing room, copies of the local newspaper were delivered, featuring a comprehensive, illustrated coverage of the match. It was quite an experience, sitting there reading about the game we'd just played in!

A week later the All Blacks ventured into the heartland of Welsh rugby to take on the champion club Neath, a side which in winning 43 of its 47 matches before we arrived had scored 345 tries. Their normal strip is black but for the clash with us they produced a white jersey with a black band featuring a silver fern!

I've struck a few partisan crowds back home but nothing that would even begin to compare with the mob – and there were 10,000 of them – at The Gnoll that afternoon. You had to experience it to believe it. It was a cauldron. They kept calling John Gallagher a Pommy wanker, they constantly hurled abuse at the experienced English referee Fred Howard who needed a police escort at the finish and the fervour they generated was almost frightening.

After the game, the *Daily Express* correspondent Terry Godwin was telephoning copy through to his office and made the claim that, "John Gallagher was the man of the match."

"No he wasn't," intruded a furious Neath fan. "Phil Pugh [the Neath flanker] was." Whereupon the fan grabbed Godwin around the throat.

"It took not a little effort to disentangle myself from this fellow and ask him to go away before I could continue," Godwin told us later.

The Neath supporters were unaccustomed to their team losing and you could understand their disappointment, but the manner in which they reacted was, in my opinion, most unhealthy for rugby.

If they thought they were going to unsettle the All Blacks with their insults and their fanatical support for the home team, they were seriously astray. It's what All Blacks thrive on. We draw strength from situations like that. We know when we run out, it's us against them. A lesser team could have been intimated that day but we absorbed everything Neath could throw at us and won going away.

My opponent in the lineout was Gareth Llewellyn, who has gone on to become a stalwart of the Welsh test pack. He was a real handful; in fact, it would be one of the few occasions in my All Black career when I've been outjumped.

There was a hilarious prelude to the afternoon, courtesy of coach Grizz Wyllie. Unamused to find our dressing-room door locked when we arrived at the ground, Grizz, in a controlled display of fury, smashed the door off its hinges. As it crashed to the floor, a little man, obviously a local official, came rushing around the corner with the key. He was observing the wreckage with considerable dismay when Grizz came out, grabbed him by the arm and said, in fierce Grizz-speak, "You're our sentry. Stay there. Don't you dare go away!" Remarkably, he remained on duty for the rest of the afternoon.

While I was ever optimistic that the tour selectors would require my leaping skills for the test matches, I was resigned to the fact that the world's most efficient rugby machine, which by late 1989 had cruised through more than

40 matches without defeat, would effect changes only in extreme circumstances. John Kirwan's tragic injury – he remained with us, on crutches – allowed Postie Innes to make his test debut against Wales. He celebrated in the nicest possible way with the All Blacks' first try, getting another before we wrapped up the game 34-9. The other test debutant, halfback Graeme Bachop – and this was a big call by Grizz Wyllie who'd dropped his Canterbury man Bruce Deans – also scored a try.

Back in those days – not now, thank God – the All Blacks pooled their ticket allocation, selling them off at whatever was the going rate to boost the players' team fund, or cabbage patch as it came to be known. It provided a huge source of revenue at test time. Somehow, I finished up on the ticket committee on that tour, along with Murray Pierce and Ron Williams.

In the run-up to the internationals, Ron and I, two of the Dirty Dirties, were involved almost exclusively in quitting the ticket allocation. The going rate was established by the Back Seat Boys, Gary Whetton, Grant Fox and Murray Pierce, and it was the responsibility of Ron and I – Murray, of course, being required to focus on his test duties – to effect the best sale possible.

Our modus operandi was for Ron and I to set up in a hotel room. We didn't actually announce ALL BLACK TEST TICKET SALES on the door, but everyone knew what was going on. Eager purchasers would phone in, we'd advise them the going rate and when they arrived, Ron would escort them up to the room. I'd check off their names in a book I'd drawn up, hand them their tickets and put the cash in a drawer. Because tickets for that Welsh test were at an absolute premium, we had no difficulty selling the lot. Which presented only one problem – what to do with all the cash? And we're talking close to £30,000. It was so much, I was reluctant to hand it in at reception for safekeeping. I didn't want the hotel management knowing the extent of our operation. So I went off to Cardiff Arms Park that Saturday afternoon with £30,000 in a laundry bag stuffed into my breast pocket. Ron Williams was my minder. I have to confess I was more worried about the cash than who was winning the international! It wasn't the wisest thing I've ever done. After that experience, we used the hotel safe.

Before we pulled out of Wales – and I must say Ireland was so delightfully serene by comparison – Grizz, who'd toured 17 years previously, took us on a nostalgic visit to the Angel Hotel, the scene of Keith Murdoch's fateful clash with a security guard. Murdoch remains the only All Black ever to have been sent home from an overseas tour. Grizz bought us a beer and told a quick story, perpetuating the legend of the Angel.

Not being required for the last three matches in Wales, I was eager for action when we hit Ireland and was delighted to be named for the midweeker against Leinster at Lansdowne Road. Although my appearances were few on that first tour, I did have the satisfaction of playing at two of the great rugby stadiums of the world, in Cardiff and Dublin.

Lansdowne Road is but five minutes from the centre of Dublin. When we as a team arrived there about an hour before kick-off, the place was almost deserted. What's going on, we thought! Don't Dubliners turn up to midweek rugby matches? What we didn't appreciate was that because of the stadium's proximity to the city, most of the fans would still be in the pubs and restaurants. By kick-off, some 20,000 were packed into the ground.

Steve McDowell was the star as we overwhelmed Leinster in the second half. He was at his best, bumping guys off all over the place. After one dynamic surge, he was grounded inches short of the goal line. He placed the ball – and I scored. Steve had done all the work and I got the try.

Murray Pierce

I was in the grandstand for the game in Cork against Munster, famous for being the only team to defeat Graham Mourie's Grand Slam side of 1978. To attend a game at Musgrave Park (or at Thomond Park in Limerick) is to experience something quite unique in rugby, for there is a deathly quiet when goalkicks are being taken. In France and Italy, goalkickers have to endure shrill whistling, down in Carisbrook the kids used to pound the tin fence while kickers were lining up the ball and all over the globe home-town fans do their best to distract visiting kickers. But in Munster territory, an absolute hush descends over the crowd. It's eerie. Grant Fox reckons it was far more unsettling than having thousands booing him.

Murray Pierce scored a try against Munster, his first in five years for the All Blacks, which was pretty special.

My final tour outing was against Connacht at Galway, a city I haven't seen yet since it was shrouded in fog for our entire stay. Frano Botica, who would become a goalkicking machine for the Wigan league team, must look back on that afternoon as his worst kicking performance ever. Unable to control the Mitre ball used that day, he missed 10 of his 13 attempts, but we still managed to score 40 points.

The Irish have a delightful attitude to life. Unlike the Welsh, for whom a rugby contest, particularly one they've lost, is never over, the Irish give a 100% on the field and another 100% to their socialising afterwards. There are no postmortems with the Irish. If they win, they're off to celebrate. If they lose, they're still off to celebrate… usually the fact it was a bloody good game! I do hope the Irish spirit isn't sacrificed in the modern game. They've got it right I believe, perhaps not always on the field but certainly in their after-match approach. It's the camaraderie that makes rugby such a great game and I'd hate to think professionalism would ever diminish that.

The social delights of the country almost brought about my undoing in Belfast, the All Blacks' last port of call in Ireland. When I wasn't selected to play against Ulster, it was obvious my tour was effectively completed as a player because the test pack would obviously be used for the finale against the Barbarians at Twickenham.

So when an old Northland cobber of mine who was living in Belfast, Alistair Sands – we called him Bobby after the prisoner who starved himself to death – invited me out for a drink on match day, I was more than happy to accept. Kick-off wasn't till 7.30pm. Trouble was the hospitality was so overwhelming, I lost track of the time. I also seriously misjudged the distance from my accommodation to the pub where we were indulging ourselves. I thought we were 10 minutes away. In fact, it was a solid 40-minute drive, complicated by the fact it was now peak traffic time. Suddenly, I was in panic mode. What if I missed the team bus?

Assuring my friend I'd pay for any speeding fines incurred, I encouraged him to perform like Ayreton Senna in the interests of my All Black career. As we screeched to a halt in front of our hotel, I could see that most of the Dirty Dirties were already on the bus. The players were obviously due out of their team meeting any minute. I sprinted up the stairs to my room and found a note from Steve McDowell saying that if I couldn't make it, he'd tell Grizz I had the flu. Good old Steve. That wouldn't be necessary though – I'd be there, with a bit of luck.

As I re-emerged in the lobby, now attired in the appropriate gear, I could see the players were boarding the bus. Oh, hell. I was reeking of alcohol and I couldn't risk Grizz or Sturge (John Sturgeon, the manager) copping a whiff of it. As luck would have it, there was a rear door to the bus. I scrambled aboard just in time for the number off, parking myself sheepishly in a remote corner! Normally the Dirty Dirties would position themselves close to the reserves and the team management. At Ravenhill that night, I took myself up the back of the grandstand and watched the encounter in splendid solitude. I owed Steve one for his kind offer. To this day, I don't think Grizz knew what I'd got up to in Belfast. Just as well, or my international career could have been seriously curtailed.

It was a bit of traditional nonsense in those days of amateur touring for a cluster of newcomers to have a go at overthrowing the Back Seat Boys on one of the bus trips. It was easier said than done, because the BSBs in Wales and Ireland (Grant Fox, Gary Whetton and Murray Pierce) had a couple of tough old sentinels guarding them, Steve McDowell and Andy Earl. And getting past them wasn't easy. Anyway, Walter (Little), Postie (Innes) and myself were encouraged to have a go, which we did. It was all good, boisterous fun, with us trying to unseat them. I'm afraid Walter, Postie and I came away rather the worse for wear, with shirts ripped, ties cut and sporting not a few bruises. We made an impression though!

The tour finished on a high note with a thrilling win over the Barbarians, Walter Little getting to play when Joe Stanley cried off. Postie scored another try, so a couple of the newcomers had broken into the top line-up and made their mark. I felt I could have performed worthily if I'd been given the chance but obviously I was along for grooming. My opportunities at test level were still to come.

The tour completed, the guys relaxed at their London hotel on the Sunday morning when the tour fund – the "cabbage patch" – was brought out. The understanding was it would be shared equitably but Mike Brewer had a revolutionary thought. He suggested we buy a Porsche or a Ferrari and raffle it among the players. One individual would go home feeling like a king. It was an interesting concept, but Bruiser was seriously outvoted. For someone like myself, a share of the kitty represented an important pay day. I'd chucked in my job as a sparkie to dedicate myself to rugby and I didn't have a current income. The chances of me drawing the Porsche or the Ferrari were slim. I wanted the bird in the hand – hard, cold cash.

News Media

5

Put to the Test

A lot of funny things happened in the early months of the 1990 rugby season. Funny peculiar, that is, not funny ha-ha. The first, which was to have a profound influence upon my career, was Murray Pierce's decision at the age of 32 to quit New Zealand and try something completely different – a season of Currie Cup action with Natal. Considering he'd played 26 tests and provided a major part of the backbone of the All Black scrum since the mid-80s, his departure was a major jolt to the New Zealand selectors.

The shocks kept coming. Defections to league had been so minimal over the years as to be almost inconsequential to the NZRFU which stoically defended the amateur principles of the game. Those principles received a fair old buffeting, however, when in rapid succession Matthew Ridge, John Gallagher, John Schuster and Frano Botica defected to the professional code. Disappointingly for the national selectors, they didn't announce their league intentions until after the All Black trials in Palmerston North.

League scouts seemed to be lurking behind every pillar, prepared to offer huge amounts for All Blacks who fitted their criteria. No one came near me. There's not a lot of demand for lineout jumpers in league!

The New Zealand selectors were lucky they'd had the tour to Wales and Ireland, because it developed a strong second tier of players who suddenly were required to step straight into the test squad. Walter Little plugged the gap left in midfield by Schuster's exit and I was introduced to fill Pierce's big boots, while Steve Gordon, Craig Innes and Graham Purvis were among the reserves.

I learnt of my test selection in unusual circumstances. The Northland players this time had returned from an NPC game against Southland in Invercargill in early June, pulling out of that southernmost city at the ungodly hour of 7am and arriving in Whangarei in mid-afternoon, in time to check out the feature senior club game at Okara Park. I was sitting on the terraces alongside a good friend Tony Hickling who had a Walkman on. He brought me to attention when he said the test team was about to be announced. He didn't pass the Walkman across but painstakingly repeated the names, one by one, stopping at Ian Jones. Wow, that's me – I'm in!

I was half expecting the news because I'd had slightly the better of Marty Brooke at the trial in Palmerston North. I was lucky, being nicely cocooned in the lineouts between Richard Loe and Steve McDowell, with Buck Shelford in behind. Nobody messed with those guys, which left me free to do what I do best – go high to claim the throw-ins.

My introduction to test rugby would be against Scotland at Carisbrook. Although technically international teams weren't permitted in those days to assemble until Wednesday, the NZRFU always brought the players together on the Tuesday evening, ostensibly for outfitting purposes.

I linked up with the Auckland and North Harbour guys at Auckland Airport and south we flew. But there was a hiccup – a two-hour delay in Christchurch. "Oh well," declared one of the senior pros, who might have been Alan Whetton, "you new guys can honour your initiation while we're here."

Walter, Postie and I looked confused. "It's traditional for the new guys to shout the established members of the side," we were assured. We were dubious about this supposed ritual but decided to play along with it. It would help fill in the time, so we adjourned to the bar.

When we finally arrived at our Dunedin hotel around 8pm, we all had a lovely glow on! Grizz Wyllie greeted us but then we realised, to our dismay, that he was a man with a purpose. After despatching the backs in the direction of the outfitting room, he told the forwards just what we didn't want to hear – there was a scrummaging session lined up. Oh no! We couldn't confess we'd had three pints of beer each, so it was off to Carisbrook to pack down against the Otago forwards. They must have wondered about the beer fumes in the depths of the scrums during the 45-minute session.

When we trained at the Southern club's headquarters at Bathgate Park the next morning, it snowed. That was a shock to the system for a kid from the tropical north, but the weather Gods were on our side because it was a sparkling day for the test itself.

I roomed with Gary Whetton, or Gee Dub as everyone called him. He offered plenty of sage advice, assuring me it was important to get involved early because I would be surprised at how quickly the 80 minutes would pass. He wanted me to believe it was "just another game". Just another game for him, maybe, for this was his 42nd test. But for an exuberant 23-year-old from little old Kamo, it was pretty hard to accept that this was "just another game".

Opposing me was Damian Cronin who'd been around the international rugby scene for some time. As in the trial, I had the good fortune to have Richard Loe and skipper Buck Shelford protecting me at the lineouts, which was enormously reassuring. With accurate throwing from Sean Fitzpatrick, Gary and I completely dominated the lineouts. In fact, I was amazed at how uncompetitive the Scots were. I'd had tougher afternoons in the lineout playing for Kamo.

A dream test debut was completed when I scored a try. It probably should have been Walter Little's try, but I'd thrust my long arm out and beaten him to the touchdown. One test, one try. The man I'd replaced, Murray Pierce, had played 26 tests and not scored any tries.

While being part of the All Black scene was a huge thrill, that first week wasn't quite what I imagined it might be. The coach and captain, for example, scarcely spoke to me. I presumed that Grizz instructed Buck and Richard to look after me in the lineouts, but he issued precious few instructions to me. Almost none, in fact. The attitude with lineouts then was hugely different to now when three people are directly involved on each throw, the jumper and the two lifters. Back in 1989, you were essentially left to your own devices and expected to perform by the simple process of jumping high and securing the ball. The blocks didn't come in contact with you. Their role was to stop the enemy getting through to disrupt you.

Buck Shelford, I quickly appreciated, was a doer more than a sayer, seldom uttering comment throughout the week. Gary Whetton probably spoke more. But Buck generated this incredible strength by his mere presence and he was enormously respected by the opposition. He trained hard and he urged those around him to do likewise.

Walter Little and I were of like mind as we celebrated our first test victory in Dunedin that evening. Our first objective had been to become All Blacks. Having achieved that (the previous year), we focused on playing a test. With that behind us, we now resolved to become regulars in the test side. I realised that my first test was probably going to be my easiest because the Scots knew nothing about me. Eden Park would be a far greater challenge.

Having world-class matchwinners like Grant Fox and John Kirwan, now fully recovered from the leg injury that cut short his UK tour, in your team was like a security blanket for a freshman like myself. I'd seen them pull off so many heroics for Auckland and the All Blacks that, deep down, I regarded them as miracle men. As long as they were on board, we would never lose. I was convinced of that. And at Eden Park in the rematch, the incomparable Foxy salvaged another victory for his team.

The Scots had never defeated New Zealand in 85 years of trying but, by God, they came close in Auckland that afternoon. They'd done their homework since Dunedin and closed us down most effectively. We were jolted by two massive penalty goals, both from inside his own half, by Gavin Hastings and at halftime we trailed 18-12.

But we had Foxy. While Superboot was there, you just knew the All Blacks couldn't lose. That theory would be shattered into a million pieces over the next 18 months, but in June 1990, Foxy reigned supreme. He kicked five penalty goals and a conversion that afternoon at Eden Park and broke the Scotsmen's hearts. We won 21-18, managing just one try against their two.

Another individual who added to our invincibility as a team, I felt, even though his achievements weren't as spectacular as Foxy's or JK's, was the captain Buck Shelford. He possessed dynamic leadership skills. You knew no matter how desperate the situation, Buck would get you through. In his inimitable follow-me style, he'd fuel the furnaces of everyone around him or, if that failed, he'd take on all 15 members of the opposition himself.

It never occurred to me, or any of the other All Blacks, except possibly one or two of the Aucklanders, that Buck was on borrowed time at Eden Park. In one of the most sensational axings in the entire history of New Zealand rugby, the All Black captain would be dropped for the Bledisloe Cup series.

Until I got into conversation with Shelford at the aftermatch function at Whangarei, 10 days before the first Australian test, I was blissfully unaware of the drama surrounding the Northland- North Harbour NPC clash. Peter Thorburn, one of the New Zealand selectors, was in the crowd observing. Apparently, the performance of only one individual mattered – that of North Harbour's No 8, Buck Shelford.

Although I personally felt Buck played well, that which Thorburn reported back to Alex Wyllie and John Hart plainly didn't convince them he should be retained. By the time I got into conversation with Buck in the grandstand, he'd been given the message and was plainly cheesed off. "They're going to shaft me," he said. "They reckon I'm carrying an injury, which I'm not. Then he said to me, "Make sure you enjoy every game you play for the All Blacks, because it could be your last."

Shelford's dismissal – he was replaced at No 8 by Zinzan Brooke with Gary Whetton taking over the captaincy – would cause uproar throughout the land and further undermine the foundations of the all-powerful All Black team which were already starting to creak, although I doubt any of us recognised the problems at that time.

News Media

Wayne Shelford

There was a discernible difference in the All Blacks from the time of assembly in Christchurch for the first of the Bledisloe Cup contests. Buck's dropping had rocked a lot of players' confidence and there was now a strong Auckland bias. Gary Whetton, Foxy, Steve McDowell, JK and perhaps to a lesser extent Alan Whetton were obviously wielding a major influence on the side. Whilst everyone was supportive of Gee Dub as the new skipper, those of us not from Auckland perhaps felt sorry for Buck. And deep down there was a feeling that if this could happen to him, the great Buck Shelford, then, hell, no one was secure.

I wouldn't say there was a division within the team, not initially anyway, but the strong Auckland influence certainly resulted in cliques forming. The Aucklanders plainly didn't have an empathy with Buck. Where they misread the situation, I believe, is that players from everywhere else did. But Auckland had been all-powerful in New Zealand rugby for most of the 1980s and, with help from John Hart, they were determined to transfer that power base into the All Blacks. In theory, it would ensure both Auckland and New Zealand remained supreme. And that might have happened if John Hart had been put in control. But the All Black coaching duties remained firmly with Alex Wyllie of Canterbury. Grizz was a beer drinker being asked to serve an Auckland cocktail. It was never going to work.

Regardless of that, the All Blacks stretched their unbeaten sequence to 50 with victories in Christchurch and Auckland against an Australian team that was developing promisingly under coach Bob Dwyer. We whipped them at Lancaster Park by moving the ball wide to our talented threequarters but at Eden Park there was little in it. George Gregan would cause a sensation by denying Jeff Wilson a match-winning try in Sydney in 1994. Well, I managed virtually the same thing in Auckland that year. John Flett, the Wallaby winger, had weaved through our defence and was about to dive for the try that would put his team in a winning situation. I knew a tackle wouldn't stop him, so I dived under him and knocked the ball from his grasp. It was a one-in-a-hundred situation, but it worked. I believe it caused Bob Dwyer to almost burst into tears!

Wellington can be a depressing place for a sportsman when one of those old man southerlies hits in, as it did the third week of August in 1990. It was shitty all week. The dingy, cold changing rooms at Athletic Park do nothing to inspire you as you prepare for the international ahead. And 10 minutes before kick-off in the final test of that series the solitary light in our dressing room blew out. We hoped it wasn't an omen.

We never fired a shot in that test. We turned to play into the southerly gale 9-6 ahead which was never going to be enough, and when Phil Kearns "did a Fitzy" and scored in the corner, that was it. It took some believing that we'd actually lost because I still had this implicit faith in Foxy and JK to salvage any contest regardless of the circumstances. I didn't think about it at the time, but it's possible the X Factor that had ensured the team's continuing invincibility wasn't Foxy or JK but Buck Shelford.

No one had changed the light bulb, so the dressing room was still in darkness when we returned, which seemed rather appropriate in the circumstances. But there was still plenty to celebrate – we'd already secured the Bledisloe Cup and 50 outings without defeat represented a phenomenal achievement. The sequence had to end sometime.

There were some ominous signs beginning to show that obviously weren't identified by those close to the team. The players were becoming aloof and not a little arrogant, something which would worsen in 1991. We were drifting away from the public, becoming inaccessible. Maybe the older players, who were probably the Aucklanders, dare I say it, were resentful of outside involvement. Those of us not part of the Auckland power base were largely being left to our own devices. We were never encouraged to speak out, to say anything really. John Sturgeon, the manager, was a hell of a nice guy but probably allowed these elements to drift for too long.

Rugby can be full of surprises and a pleasant one that dropped my way was an invitation to represent the British Barbarians for their two centennial matches against England and Wales. The games fell neatly between the conclusion of the NPC and the opening match of the All Black tour of France.

Joe Stanley, Richard Loe, Eric Rush (who was a flanker then) and myself were involved, along with Nick Farr-Jones, David Campese and Michael Lynagh from Australia, a couple of Frenchmen and a cluster of players from the Home Unions. We had a ding-dong battle with England, going down by only two points. I was marking Paul Ackford who was persistently holding me down. So I said to Richard, "Shit's happening – sort it out." Richard, being Richard, did, but unfortunately he identified the wrong Englishman as my opponent and as we ran on to the next play a bemused Wade Dooley was left holding his jaw. "You got the wrong guy," I told Richard. "Never mind," said Richard, "that's for next time!"

We had the satisfaction of defeating Wales at Cardiff Arms Park. Joe and Eric contributed tries and I squared the ledger with Gareth Llewellyn in the lineouts.

After the French tour, I joined the Barbarians for one further outing, against Argentina, again in Cardiff. I've derived great enjoyment from my association with the Barbarians over the years. Their hospitality is legendary, their attitude refreshingly different from what we're accustomed to in New Zealand where we tend to take the game a little too seriously at times. The Barbarians assemble on the Thursday for a Saturday game and always go out to dinner and take in a show on the Thursday evening. Mickey Steele-Bodger has been the driving force behind the club over the past couple of decades and has always had a soft spot for me. I've played six times for the UK Barbarians, more than any other New Zealander. And I can claim to be the only player who's scored tries for and against the club in international fixtures.

Whenever I represented the Barbarians, accommodation was arranged for me at the East India Club, an amazing, exclusive, men-only establishment in Piccadilly. Mickey Steele-Bodger was the chairman. Terribly formal, it's the place where until recently all England rugby and cricket teams were announced and where the International Rugby Board delegates annually met (in the days when the game was amateur). It's compulsory to wear a collar and tie all day and jackets are required after 5pm. Which puts it a long way from the Kamo club in Northland where ties are optional even on so-called formal occasions.

Barbarians rugby is an excellent concept which may perhaps be lost now that we're in the professional era. It's a great vehicle for building friendships among international players.

It was probably symptomatic of the All Blacks' deteriorating image with the media and the public that we received so much negative publicity during our tour of France. It was fuelled obviously by losses in the midweek games at Toulon and Bayonne, but we answered the critics with two crushing test victories, at Nantes and Paris. It was one of the rare times when the All Blacks have gone into a series as the underdog. The French were on a roll and extremely confident of beating us but the quality of our forward play combined with Foxy's boot produced two extremely satisfying victories.

The French can react violently when things aren't going their way and at Nantes in the first test their prop Laurent Seigne was causing mayhem and plainly needed sorting out. By the time the umpteenth scrum had collapsed, we'd had enough. Steve McDowell delivered the shortest, sharpest punch – out of sight of the referee – you'd ever witness, which brought an abrupt end to Seigne's nonsense. He was in fairyland when they carted him off!

I'll never forget the frenzied looks on the French when they ran onto the field at Nantes. The front row all had blood noses. God knows what they'd been up to. For the only time in my entire career I questioned my own size when I focused on their lock Abdel Benazzi. He looked absolutely massive, but what I didn't immediate appreciate was that he was wearing substantial

A souvenir French jersey around my shoulders, I celebrate a decisive victory at Paris in 1990 with fellow forwards Alan Whetton and Richard Loe.

shoulder pads. The guy I marked, Olivier Roumat, was a towering individual as well.

My parents were at Nantes and remarkably, as the national anthems were playing and amidst a crowd of 42,000, I saw my mother in the grandstand. Being my first test overseas, it was a pretty special occasion and great to have Mum and Dad there. It was, of course, the stadium where the All Blacks of '86 took such a hiding, so we didn't lack for motivation that day.

Normally, all clearing kicks when we were in defensive situations were handled by Foxy. But in the first test when Graeme Bachop delivered a pass from a short lineout inside our 22, the receiver was not Grant Fox but Richard Loe. Cool as a cucumber, Loey banged away an immaculate touchfinder.

Between tests we were quartered at La Rochelle, a delightful port on the Atlantic seaboard. It was picture perfect while we were there, and if you're a seafood enthusiast, as I am, it's a destination to die for. We were in buoyant mood when we took on one of France's most famous seafood restaurants and ordered giant platters of what, I'm sure, was that afternoon's catch. Seaweed, cats eyes and calamari were delicacies unfamiliar to me until that evening.

I love touring France and would have appreciated the stay in Paris even more if I hadn't been involved in test match duty, because the Dirty Dirties were the guests of the Moet Chandon champagne producers at Epernay. I was envious of their good fortune but they brought back vast quantities of the famous wine for the rest of the team to share.

The drive from our hotel to the Parc des Princes was a hair-raising experience. The French like to do everything with a flourish and our police escorts who performed as if we were 30 minutes late. There was a shattering of glass as our driver took one corner too tightly but the team made it to the stadium intact.

Foxy's deadly accurate boot and attacking magic from John Kirwan and Michael Jones, both of whom had sustained career-threatening injuries in 1989, saw us whip France 30-12 in Paris to complete a pretty satisfactory mission. Grizz's status as coach appeared secure less than a year out from the World Cup.

I'll never understand why the New Zealand Rugby Union arranged a nine-match tour of Argentina in the year of the World Cup, 1991. Four matches maybe. Six at a pinch. But nine? Ridiculous in a country where language is a burden, where toll calls back to your family can just about bankrupt you and where, against opponents whose approach against world-class opposition is entirely negative, constructive rugby is almost impossible.

We came through undefeated but it was a hard grind, with everyone eager to get home after the first couple of weeks. I've since read of the near coup against Grizz on the tour but I have to confess total ignorance of any such mutinous schemes. If there was any plotting, I certainly wasn't part of it. Not being from Auckland probably excluded me automatically. I basically kept my head down and played footie. I was still inexperienced as an international player and I was set on establishing myself in the test pack. The Auckland influence which had manifested itself in 1990 had plainly escalated in Argentina.

A month after our return from Buenos Aires we were in action against the Wallabies at the Sydney Football Stadium. The playing personnel remained intact but there was one dramatic change – Alex Wyllie was no longer a sole coach. The NZRFU had dramatically appointed John Hart as a co-coach through to the World Cup. It was a huge gamble by the NZRFU council which obviously had received a report on events in Argentina that was unfavourable to Wyllie. But why appoint co-coaches, especially when their animosity towards each other was well documented?

Hart and Wyllie's incompatibility wasn't immediately obvious, because the run-in to the two Bledisloe Cup games, at Sydney and Auckland, was brief, although Grizz was obviously hurting. Hart had plainly been brought in because, in the NZRFU's eyes, he was doing the job asked of him. Grizz obviously interpreted it as Hart taking over his team.

At Sydney, notwithstanding an early try, we were decisively defeated but at Eden Park, thanks to Michael Lynagh having an off day with his boot, we escaped with a 6-3 win, allowing us to retain the Bledisloe Cup. When Lynagh lined up his final kick, I couldn't bear to watch because I was the player who'd been penalised.

In Sydney I'd come up against John Eales for the first time. I didn't know anything about him, which was to his benefit, and he took advantage of it. Of a similar build to me – in an era when lineout specialists were getting larger by the minute – he competed in the air, like me. It was such a pleasant change competing with an opponent in the air instead of on the ground.

So off we went to the World Cup carrying the hopes of a rugby nation confident we could retain the Webb Ellis Trophy. And they had every right to their optimism because since the inaugural World Cup in New Zealand our record in tests was a magnificent 28 wins, one draw and two losses (both against the Aussies).

We scrummaged outstandingly well to defeat England in the tournament's opening encounter, and although our performances against the United States and Italy were somewhat scratchy, we produced some quality rugby in extremely trying conditions against Canada at Lille to qualify for a semi-final showdown with Bob Dwyer's Wallabies in Dublin. We would be judged on the semi-finals and final, not on what went before.

A lot of people forget that we were almost playing Ireland in the semi. It needed a desperate try a couple of minutes from time by Michael Lynagh to get the Aussies through their quarter-final at Lansdowne Road. I wonder how history would be regarding us now had the Irish clung to their lead for another three minutes!

Hart and Wyllie were both passionate coaches and, in essence, bore similar philosophies as regards team tactics. But as individuals they were, as the saying goes, as different as chalk and cheese. For example, on the Wednesday preceding the semi-final, we trained under Grizz on the bottom field at Blackrock with only a smattering of supporters around. On the Thursday when Hart was in charge we were on the top field, watched by probably a thousand Kiwis. There was the difference – one was the grafter who shunned the limelight, the other the entrepreneur who craved it.

Although the record books show we lost to the Wallabies 16-6 in Dublin, we actually played some of our best rugby of the year, particularly in the second spell as we sought to repair the damage done in the first half.

In hindsight, I can say we were too predictable. Having been so dominant for so long, we – and I say we because I guess we're all liable – didn't see any reason to adjust tactically, even though we'd been twice upended by the Wallabies in the previous 15 months. The Aussies read us impeccably. Simon Poidevin, one of the game's most accomplished loose forwards, ran off Grant Fox and Bernie McCahill all afternoon and made a beeline for Craig Innes and John Kirwan. JK received a torrent of ball in the second half but he was overwhelmed by the Australian defence.

The Wallabies were popular winners because they'd been virtually adopted by the Irish. They'd been based in Dublin for a couple of weeks which was to their advantage but they had set a new standard in public relations, an area in which we were seriously deficient. I'm embarrassed now to think back on how we dealt with the public and the media. The Aussies were doing it so well and us so poorly. We congregated in groups and if someone approached us for an autograph, we barely made the effort to sign. If a player made a rude comment, we'd all laugh. Until it was all over, no one suggested to us that others were doing the PR thing better. In the Aussies' case, about a thousand times better.

Our loss in Dublin had a devastating effect upon the team, especially when the reality of it dawned on us the next morning. We arrived simultaneously at Dublin Airport with the Australians, only they were flying to London to prepare for the final at Twickenham while we were taking a plane to Cardiff for a Thursday play-off with Scotland.

It was interesting how the various individuals reacted to the defeat. The younger guys, and into this category I would put Walter Little, Graeme Bachop,

Michael Jones, Craig Innes, Inga Tuigamala and myself, rebounded quickly. Our feeling was that a defeat like this shouldn't happen, that we could do better, and Thursday against Scotland was the place to start, whereas the oldies essentially regarded their year as over and really wanted to go their own ways. I don't think too many of them wanted to know about the Cardiff play-off. Very definitely into this category fell the skipper Gary Whetton and Steve McDowell.

Fortunately, the selectors made several changes for Cardiff, introducing Walter, Inga, Jon Preston and Michael (who hadn't played in Dublin because the game was on a Sunday), and the exuberance of the younger guys inevitably led to a successful performance. We'd come in search of gold for sure, but a bronze medal was better than nothing.

The long flight back to New Zealand would have been a gloomy experience, I'm sure, but only a handful of All Blacks undertook it. Most of the World Cup party headed for Italy and John Kirwan's wedding. I linked up with Craig Innes (Postie) and John Timu for a hugely entertaining jaunt around Europe.

After the pressures of the World Cup it was great to be anonymous as we checked out Geneva, Rome, Florence and Pisa before lobbing into Venice in time for the wedding. Odd thing about that wedding, a 90-minute Catholic service in Italian – they gave you the gift. We each received a piece of Venezuelan glass. Traditionally, you don't give presents to the bride and groom in Italy; you give them money.

Postie, JT and I had some hilarious adventures. None of us could speak Italian, which presented some interesting challenges. On one occasion after we'd remained stationary for 30 minutes in a carriage that we understood was journeying through to Rome, we got out and checked, to find three carriages, including ours, had been uncoupled on a siding. The rest of the train was obviously rocketing along to Rome!

In Pisa, we took so many wrong turnings we finally came across the Leaning Tower… from behind! Not easily done, that. It was a fun-filled few weeks with rugby a particularly low priority. We drank a good amount of vino, laughed a lot, didn't get arrested and made it home safely for Christmas.

6

Plugging into the Mains

Gary Whetton's record for the All Blacks is phenomenal – 101 appearances including 58 internationals, three more than the great Pinetree Meads managed. Two seasons as captain. It should have made him an icon. But the circumstances under which he assumed the leadership, the team's demise at the 1991 World Cup and the subsequent condemnation of the players for their indifferent public relations performance all tended to rebound on Gee Dub.

Gary Whetton typified all that was good and bad about Auckland. As a player, he was a magnificent athlete, a forerunner of the modern lock. He'd be a sensation under today's laws because he was so swift around the field. As a captain, however, he was too aloof, too locked into the Auckland scene. He'd been around for almost 10 years and his career was tapering off when they appointed him captain. I'm sure he would have been a greater asset if they'd used his experience to support another leader.

He was almost in a no-win situation because the public sympathy for Buck Shelford was so intense. You only had to see the Bring Back Buck signs everywhere to understand that. Buck had enormous charisma and when he was so ruthlessly stripped of the captaincy there was an intense anti-Auckland feeling around the country.

In the two and half years in which Whetton and I were All Blacks together, I can't say I really got to know him, because he seldom talked to me, or any of the other younger members of the team for that matter. Fortunately, in 1989 and 1990 I had Murray Pierce as a mentor. He was brilliant, open, friendly… a great communicator. He taught me so much.

But Whetton wasn't like that. I was from Northland and didn't know the Auckland guys personally. On a lot of occasions, and this is after he became captain, he wouldn't say "Good morning" to the likes of Walter Little, Craig Innes or myself. I felt bad for them. At least I had Murray Pierce encouraging me but here was our captain virtually ignoring these guys. I'd look at Whetton at breakfast and wonder why he wouldn't even acknowledge his own players. It was a worry but I didn't consider it was my place to open my mouth. It's funny, but I have a better relationship with Gee Dub now.

The relationship among coach, captain and players in the All Blacks is open and honest now, infinitely superior to what it was back then when a them-and-us scenario had been allowed to develop. The players sensed the tension between the coaches while the Auckland influence was ever apparent. We did things we would not dream of now. Instead of adopting Australia's positive approach, we took a negative one.

It wasn't surprising that in the wake of such a disappointing campaign the New Zealand Rugby Union should decide a complete clean-out was necessary, as a consequence of which John Hart, who was logically next in line to succeed Wyllie, was overlooked. Laurie Mains, Peter Thorburn and Earle Kirton constituted the new selection panel and we soon found the revolution hadn't finished yet. Neither Gary Whetton nor his brother Alan were even invited to the All Black trials in Napier.

That we were under entirely new management was rammed home at a couple of heart-to-heart meetings in Christchurch before the first international of the year. First, Laurie Mains, who had been horrified to discover how Aucklanders had effectively hijacked the World Cup team, warned us that the formation of any cliques would be dealt with summarily. Laurie had already given us the message, loud and clear, on the need for greater fitness. Then we were addressed by Kevin Roberts from Lion Nathan who obviously represented the team's major sponsor Steinlager.

I don't think any of us had ever met Kevin previously and we certainly weren't anticipating anything out of the ordinary. Obviously he was going to deliver the usual sponsor's spiel, after which we'd get on with the business of preparing for a test match. What eventuated represented one of the great wake-up calls any of us had ever experienced.

Kevin Roberts, we all now appreciate, is one of the most dynamic individuals you'd ever encounter, a make-it-happen member of the corporate world whose capabilities were recognised when in 1997 he was appointed worldwide boss of the Saatchi & Saatchi Advertising Agency, based in New York. He's also now an important member of the NZRFU board.

He handed out a Steinlager gift pack to each player, then proceeded, in blokes' terms, to outline some home truths – what the public thought of the

All Blacks, the players' commitment to their major sponsor and the extent of that sponsorship. Steinlager was making a huge commitment to the All Blacks, Roberts assured us, and he expected our support in return. If that wasn't forthcoming, he would "pull the pin". Steinlager didn't want to be associated with a team of losers, a team with a feeble public image.

Everyone was taken aback by Kevin's bluntness but we appreciated being told what was expected of us because until then no one had given us any direction. We gave Kevin the assurance he wanted. Then we turned our attention to making it happen.

Kevin Roberts

Saatchi & Saatchi

As a coach, Laurie Mains was startlingly different from Grizz Wyllie and, from what we'd seen of him at that stage, John Hart. It would take me three years to relate to Laurie, but it was exciting back in 1992 to have a fresh approach. Laurie didn't owe anyone any favours and energetically set about reconstructing the All Blacks his way. We certainly trained a lot harder. Laurie had dispensed with the Jim Blair theory of a maximum amount of gym work and a minimum of road running, adopting a more basic, traditional, gutsy approach. We were expected to carve out the kilometres pre-season, then endure Laurie's masochistic 150s and Down-and-Ups and answer to the beep test.

We didn't give Laurie's international career the kick-start he was looking for, going down pretty decisively to the World XV at Lancaster Park, although I felt I did my bit for the cause that afternoon. In fact, of the 90-odd games I've played in the black jersey, I'd rank that one among my top handful. Unfortunately, the lineout count in our favour of 28-9 almost exactly equalled the final score, in reverse!

I probably should have watched the second half from the sanctity of the grandstand after dislocating both my shoulder and a finger. But because Jamie Joseph had withdrawn on the morning of the game with tonsillitis and Arran Pene had already come on for Michael Jones, we were desperately short of forward reserves. So I battled out the 80 minutes. Although things weren't going our way, I personally found it a stimulating occasion, operating as we were under a new captain (Sean Fitzpatrick) and a new coach. And it was exciting to be sharing in New Zealand rugby's centenary celebrations. Quite frankly, I didn't want to miss out by walking off. I made our doctor, John Mayhew, work overtime. I think he had to click my finger back in about four times! Anyway, I got through but spent a fair portion of the evening in the emergency department of Christchurch Hospital being put back together.

During that first week in Christchurch we were introduced to Laurie's ingenious ruck machine. It was his own invention and he'd broken it in with the Southern club in Dunedin and then used it with Otago. It's not easily described, but if you imagine three tackle bags standing vertically alongside each other, you'll get the picture. It was like a scrum machine on steroids. The guys found it amusing, until Laurie got them driving into it time after time. It was all part of an exciting new era in New Zealand rugby and the guys were responding to the fresh approach.

We put the Christchurch setback behind us, running rampant in Wellington, although I was in the wars again, splitting the tendon that runs down through the finger. Doc Mayhew came to my rescue again, taping the finger. Determined not to suffer a recurrence of that injury, which can be such a distraction for a lineout jumper, I had the finger bound for every training and game for the next five years. It wasn't until one day in 1997 that I wondered what would happen if I played without the security of the tape. I was fine, and I haven't put anything on the hand since.

Not the least satisfactory aspect of the Wellington victory was my outjumping John Eales, who so seriously damaged the AC joint in his shoulder in a second-half tackle that he was out of rugby for the remainder of the season. Another casualty that day, in an entirely different context, was Eales' locking partner, Frenchman Olivier Roumat, who was ordered off for kicking Sean Fitzpatrick.

Largely because of the trouble Eales had given me in Sydney the previous year, I had adjusted my jumping technique for the 1992 season. We both competed for the ball in the air but he'd caught me and the All Blacks by surprise by exploding off the ground, getting into the air before me. Knowing your opponent and his strengths is half the battle, so in '92 I was ready for him. The nice thing about opposing Eales was that ours was a pure contest for the ball in the air.

Often in centenary matches the invitation fifteen finishes up as a weird mix of bits and pieces, but our opposition in that series featured many of the giants of the international rugby scene. Besides Eales and Roumat, the team we disposed of so comprehensively at Athletic Park included Andre Joubert, Jeremy Guscott, Naas Botha, Nick Farr-Jones (who was the captain), Marc Cecillon, Apollo Perelini, Ewen McKenzie, Uli Schmidt and Federico Mendez. The team we engaged in the decider at Eden Park was even stronger, with Gavin Hastings, Tim Horan, Willie Ofahengaue, Phil Kearns and, unexpectedly, Gary Whetton added. Gee Dub was recruited when Eales and Roumat pulled out, which caused Laurie Mains to choke on his corn flakes. His presence didn't prevent us winning again to secure the series.

It was a great time to be involved, the centenary bringing out the best in everyone. The series of dinners staged in the test centres afforded a rare opportunity to meet and speak with some of the legendary All Blacks. Laurie had the team playing attractively and you sensed people were starting to feel good about their national rugby team again.

The selectors stuck with the same combination for the first test against the Irish at Carisbrook, a game we were expected to win effortlessly after Auckland had put 62 points on them the previous Saturday. But when we almost stumbled to defeat, out came the axe. It was to be a most significant selection, ushering in Olo Brown at prop, Robin Brooke at lock and Matthew Cooper at fullback. Brooke thus became my fourth partner in six tests, the others being Gary Whetton, Mark Cooksley and Blair Larsen.

For Robin and I it was the rekindling of a partnership forged seven years earlier in the Northland secondary schools team. And what a partnership it would be. By 1997, we would establish a world record of 43 tests together.

I don't think the pundits anticipated a big future for Robin at the highest level. He'd had trouble securing a regular position in the Auckland team and he wasn't particularly tall for a lock. Which made us an unlikely combination because I wasn't exactly the most robust second rower around. However, the strength of a locking combination is that the two individuals complement each other. If you have two players with identical strengths, something's missing. Robin in those days was a strong grafter, particularly effective in rucks and mauls, whereas I was better equipped for lineout duties and probably more mobile around the field. That's how we started out. Robin now uses his ball skills and athleticism in the open as much as, if not more than, me. He still does the hard graft but he's expanded his game.

People talk about how halfbacks and first-fives, hookers and props, number eights and halfbacks must understanding each other's requirements. Well, the same applies to locks – it's important for us to develop as a pair too. You become very much a partnership and need to look after each other.

If we thought Laurie's training sessions for the domestic tests were a step up from what we'd been accustomed to, we were in for a traumatic time once the new All Black coach had us to himself in Australia and later South Africa. Laurie was convinced that one of the reasons the All Blacks failed at the World Cup was because the Auckland players, who formed the heart of the team, had been taking the "soft option" by doing most of their training in the gymnasium. Laurie was about to sort that out. He believed the only path to true rugby fitness was through running.

We were to be enormously grateful to the Otago guys for wising us up about Laurie's mindset during training sessions. Essentially, the word was "keep your mouth shut" and get on with it. Laurie used to love asking, "Are you buggered?" If you said no, he took great umbrage and set you extra exercises. If you said yes, he'd conclude you weren't fit and therefore needed extra work. It was a no-win situation. So the wise ones trained diligently and said nothing to provoke him.

Martin Toomey, who'd taken over from Jim Blair as the fitness adviser, accompanied us throughout the tour and became to Laurie what Goering had been to Hitler. He'd introduced Laurie to 150s, Down-and-Ups and other agony exercises designed to make the All Blacks the fittest team on earth.

You couldn't shirk the work because you had both Laurie and Marty overseeing you, and the penalties were severe for anyone not giving a hundred.

After most team training sessions, and on match days for the Dirty Dirties, we would be required to do the dreaded 150s which involved a 150 metre sprint after which you'd turn round, walk to the 22 and jog back to the starting point for a repeat. No brains were needed but it was important to achieve a rhythm and not to antagonise Laurie. Or he'd throw in extras for punishment. The most 150s we did in a single session was about 25. For match-related fitness, they were the greatest. They were an agony for a start, but we came to appreciate that nothing built your endurance better.

Only the Otago guys knew about Down-and-Ups before the tour. Laurie varied them by introducing a game-related exercise between the goal line and the deadball line. You'd run 10 metres, dive and twist, do a push-up, then run back. That equalled one. At times, Laurie had us doing close to 60! And that was after the 150s.

There was one classic session the Dirty Dirties endured in Brisbane. Laurie had put them through hell. They'd rucked, done their 150s and now were on Down-and-Ups. Finally, Rigger (Mark Cooksley) started spewing while down on his knees. "Get up, Rigger," barked out Mains, "and spew like a man!"

I'd never encountered Down-and-Ups. While they developed fitness, they also promoted gutsiness, and as the tour progressed you knew you had plenty in the tank to keep going. I didn't mind the 150s because I'd always been a runner but for some of the guys they were a real battle.

With the Down-and-Ups, I benefited again from the Otago guys. Technique was important and I learnt to slide in and execute the push-up. Track suit pants were easier to slide in than shorts. It wasn't a case of cheating, just being smart.

The first test in Sydney became a challenge for me because the IRB had just introduced a law stopping lineout jumpers from tapping with the outside arm and that was something I'd done almost instinctively from my earliest days as a lock. You think you've trained yourself to function correctly but in the intensity of the battle, when you're trying to decipher their calls or ensure your own timing is correct, instinct can easily take over. And it did, three or four times at the Sydney Football Stadium. Considering our losing margin was only one point, I felt pretty guilty about the number of penalties I'd conceded.

The total number of penalties we as a team gave away were 12, which was pertinent at the next training session down in Melbourne. For every penalty, Laurie made us do 10 rucks. He'd set up three tackle bags 15 metres apart and we just kept driving into them until we'd hit 120. It was a shitty day, raining and cold, and we went flat out all the way. Then Laurie ordered 20 150s which were a real challenge on this occasion because most of the guys were fatigued. But that wasn't the end. Before we could go (crawl) back to the hotel, Laurie made us do 60 Down-and-Ups. All you could do was grit your teeth and keep going. Laurie kept reminding us there was only one point between the teams and that superior fitness would put us in front. You had to believe it!

Despite our coach's best efforts to have us fitter than the Wallabies, we also dropped the second test, at Ballymore, this one by two points after Grant Fox had put a drop-kick millimetres outside the upright in the dying moments.

Although only three points separated the teams after 160 minutes of action, we were two tests down, the Bledisloe Cup already conceded. The fact we were playing the world champions wouldn't matter much back home where the fans are notoriously intolerant of losing All Black teams. Opportunities to redeem ourselves were running out.

Before we got a third crack at Bob Dwyer's world champion Wallabies there came a midweek game at Penrith, a league stronghold in the mountains to the west of Sydney. It was always going to be an awkward challenge from the moment it was scheduled for the Wednesday evening. Laurie understandably ruled that none of the test squad would be involved which presented major problems because of the number of players who were injured.

To get a reasonable fifteen together, three loose forwards, Pat Lam, Dallas Seymour and Glenn Taylor, were flown in. The midweek selection was prepared for the game by Earle Kirton while Laurie concentrated exclusively on the test side. The midweekers never got into the game, suffering an embarrassing 40-17 loss. If I could change one thing, it would be that the test players would give greater support. Usually when there's a test the Dirty Dirties are totally supportive. But on this occasion, we didn't reciprocate.

I couldn't believe what was happening out in the middle. I sat in the stand shocked, helpless to do anything, waiting for the comeback that never eventuated. Laurie described it as "a blight on our record".

When you've played 70 test matches, a lot fade into near oblivion, some you recall aspects of, while others remain vividly in the mind as if they happened yesterday. The final test of that remarkable '92 series, at the Sydney Football Stadium, was like that. I have so many amazing memories of the game.

Sam Scott-Young, the Wallaby No 8, had been mouthing off during the week about the worthiness of the haka. His comments weren't appreciated by the All Blacks. But Fitzy putting him out of the game most certainly was. Fitzy was operating one off the ruck, as he did so effectively, and Scott-Young was waiting for him. It culminated in an almighty collision from which Scott-Young never recovered.

Although the Bledisloe Cup was gone, there was so much at stake in this encounter – so much pride on both sides. We were desperate to rectify the two previous losses and the Penrith humiliation, while the Aussies knew a whitewash would confirm them not only as the greatest team in the world but one of the mightiest of all time.

Notwithstanding a couple of rough decisions by French referee Patrick Robin and his touch judges, we won 26-23 after being up 26-10 with 10 minutes to play. Incredibly, at the conclusion of the three-test series, both teams had scored exactly the same number of tries and points.

John Eales and I had another ding-dong battle, a great rivalry that would continue through until now. I'm pleased to record that I've been on the winning side more than he has, but we've had some great personal tussles. After my initial adjustment – once I knew what he was about – we've never changed our styles. We go high and compete for the ball in the air.

When we'd flown out of New Zealand six weeks earlier an extended itinerary to incorporate games in South Africa was only a suggestion. Now it was a reality, the resumption of sporting contacts with the republic having been officially sanctioned. For the first time in 16 years the All Blacks would be tackling the Springboks on South African soil. It was a neat feeling. We were lucky to be in the right place at the right time.

Only Grant Fox and Steve McDowell, who were Cavaliers in 1986, and our coaches Laurie Mains and Earle Kirton, who'd toured in the 1970s, knew anything about the place. For the rest of us, it was an exciting journey into the unknown.

Being quartered in business class for the 13-hour flight through from Sydney to Johannesburg took the agony out of the travel. When it was announced that we would be arriving at close to 1am local time, we naturally didn't expect many people would be there to greet us. How wrong we were.

As we were being whisked through customs we could hear this commotion

News Media

Well, there have got to be a few perks in being an All Black. That's Elle Macpherson delivering a peck on the cheek. The occasion was a celebrity tennis event in Auckland as part of a Bendon promotion.

which had us bemused. What was going on? What was going on was almost indescribable. The terminal was packed to the rafters with locals – black, white and coloured – there to welcome us. It seemed as if half of Johannesburg had turned out and it obviously mattered not that it was the middle of the night.

We were the first All Black touring team since 1976 and we swiftly appreciated what our presence meant to them. It was a very special occasion, something for which we were quite unprepared. It wasn't enough to cheer us at the airport – hundreds followed us all the way into our hotel. I remember thinking, if this is what it's like, what hope do we have against the Springboks!

A much-needed sleep behind us, we adjourned to the Police College the next afternoon for what we anticipated would be a "light" training session, essential to run the travel weariness out of our bodies. We'd been warned that in Johannesburg, which is 6500ft above sea level, we could possibly experience nose bleeds or dizziness, or both.

I'm not sure what got into our coach that day but instead of the stretch, walk and game of touch most guys expected, Laurie decided to crank things up. Maybe it was because a few passes had gone down. Anyway, we finished up doing 15 150s and a series of Down-and-Ups. My nose started bleeding, as did a few others, and I was so short of breath I felt as though I had asthma. We were gulping vast quantities of water but within seconds our throats were parched again. Laurie might feel he was justified in putting us through purgatory that afternoon, but shit…!

The altitude factor was a major concern in 1992, and seeing the All Blacks hadn't won a test at Ellis Park since 1928 this was understandable. Unfortunately, it meant the players saw desperately little of Durban, which with its tropical climate and magnificent beaches is one of the superior rugby destinations, because the intention was to have us stationed on the high veldt for as long as possible. The Australian Rugby Union had insisted on playing its international (a week after us) at sea level in Cape Town which is how come the All Blacks were allocated Ellis Park.

So we lobbed into Durban on the Friday and scampered back up to 6000ft on the Sunday. The wisdom of it all escaped the players at the time and events since have proved that it's not necessary to go to such extreme lengths to perform competently at high altitude.

Durban's King's Park is one of the great rugby venues. Boasting a fabulous climate – even if the World Cup semi-final there in 1995 was played in torrential rain – the people of Natal have a culture all of their own. The fields surrounding the main stadium hold swarms of people, many of them in shorts and T-shirts, enjoying bries (barbecues) before and after the game.

In the Natal game I found myself marking a giant of a man who was a legend in South Africa, Rudi Visagie. As I'd never seen him before, I didn't know what he was capable of. That basically applied to the whole Natal team. They had a substantial height and weight advantage over us, but how good was their rugby?

There were 43,000 spectators packed into the stadium, including not more than a handful of New Zealanders. Because the visit had been arranged so late there were almost no supporters groups along. Having no fans didn't bother us. That's when the All Blacks are at their best – when it's fifteen against the world.

We played sensationally well that afternoon and showed South Africa a style of rugby of which they were unaware. Restricted to Currie Cup action, it was obvious they hadn't caught up with the faster pace of the game as it applied in New Zealand and Australia. The South Africans being the passionate, dedicated rugby nation they were would soon catch up, but it was encouraging to recognise that we had a definite advantage in terms of mobility. The one concerning factor was their lifting in the lineouts. While we knew a neutral referee would prevent lifting in the test, in the provincial games we would have to learn to combat it.

After the match, the All Blacks went into the outfield and circulated among the crowd. The reception was great. They were so delighted to have us in their country.

The one sour note on an otherwise perfect day occurred just as we were getting ready to board our team bus and head back to the hotel. A little black boy who had stolen some meat from one of the barbecues was set upon by police who clubbed him quite nastily right in front of us. No one seemed to care and it certainly never rated a mention in the papers. It was a callous reminder of days gone by in South Africa.

The midweek Free State game at Bloemfontein turned out to be the Ian Jones Show. For the first, and only, time in my international career I captained the All Blacks. I also managed to score a try, pull down my share of lineout possession and prevent a major brawl breaking out. All in an afternoon's work! I was nothing if not diligent in the role. As we warmed up out the back of Bloemfontein Stadium, Laurie Mains came over and suggested I quieten things down a bit. The adrenalin was rushing a bit early!

When Andre Markgraaff was obliged to resign as Springbok coach in 1997 for making racist comments, it wasn't altogether surprising to learn that the individual who had dragged him down – by secretly recording a supposedly private conversation – was Andre Bester, because he caused mayhem that day at Bloemfontein, he and his brother, fellow front rower Piet. They were hell bent on unsettling our players but we kept our discipline throughout. Just!

Deon Viljoen, writing in the *Johannesburg Star* the next day, said that the All Blacks had "overcome a shameful display of foul play to win". He described it as "a game Free State would sooner forget. Their short tempers, ill-discipline and blatant dirty play overshadowed a fine first-half showing."

In the wake of the Penrith disaster, it was critical for us to win at Bloemfontein. The satisfaction of doing so rejuvenated a number of careers. When the midweekers lose, it creates the impression the whole team is weak. Which is why it was hellishly important to remain focused against Free State and complete a good win, which we did.

Peter Scott of Lion Breweries kindly sent me a magnum of Moet and Chandon to mark the occasion of my captaincy. I've still got it, looking for the right occasion to break it open. Perhaps when the All Blacks win the next World Cup…!

It might be presumed that with the South Africans having come in from the cold after more than a decade of purely domestic rugby, they had nothing to teach us. But Robin Brooke and I learnt plenty about the technique of lifting. It was illegal in 1992, of course, but that hadn't prevented the South Africans from perfecting the art. The most blatant example of it came in the

Junior Springboks game at Pretoria where Kobus Wiese and Drikus Hattingh were hoisted skyward with the obvious approval of the referee. We didn't protest at the time, just adopted a "When in Rome" attitude. New Zealanders learn to ruck from the age of five while South Africans learn to lift. The technique I observed then and which still applies, now that supporting (as distinct from lifting) of lineout jumpers has the IRB's blessing, is that the all-important factor is an explosive jump. You're not going to be competitive if you rely on your supports to achieve altitude. Their role is to hold you there – the catcher is responsible for getting himself up there in the first place.

Identifying the lineout as a particular strength of the Springboks – with or without lifting – we scorned orthodoxy in the test at Ellis Park. We weren't prepared to take them on head first, so on our throw we consistently used two-man lineouts. The fact we won the count 20-14 suggests our tactics were pretty successful. I marked a guy I'd encountered at the '91 World Cup and introduced myself to, Adolf Malan.

Rugby News

Robin Brooke and I resplendent in Springbok jerseys after our memorable victory at Ellis Park in 1992. Robin and I would go on to play 46 internationals together.

For us, the test was over after 50 minutes. We'd been on tour for 10 weeks, achieved a lot, certainly in comparison with 1991, and swept all before us in South Africa. We had desperately wanted to succeed in Johannesburg, where no New Zealand team had won a test since 1928. At 27-10, we knew one more score – a try, a penalty goal, a pot, anything – would be the nail in their coffin. But we hit the wall. Exhaustion set in like I've never experienced before or since. Thank goodness we had that 17-point buffer because the Springboks, full of running, claimed two late converted tries.

It was an incredible experience just being there, with 72,000 fans roaring away in this vast stadium, hearing them lustily singing Die Stem (the national anthem of the apartheid days, which Louis Luyt suddenly slipped in). There on the sideline while we stood to attention was a good mate of mine from New Zealand, living in London, Jamie Richards. He had a none too professional looking camera around his neck, having somehow got himself accredited as a photographer. "G'day, Jamie, what are you doing there?" I inquired of him before settling down to the serious business of beating the Boks.

There was a marvellous feeling of achievement as we relaxed in the dressing room afterwards. After 64 years, we'd beaten the bogey of Ellis Park, altitude and all.

When I first started playing at senior level the All Blacks' greatest rivals were the Wallabies and the greatest challenge winning the World Cup or the Bledisloe Cup. I grew up wanting New Zealand to beat Australia because my memories of contests with South Africa were almost insignificant. I could vaguely remember Northland's Joe Morgan scoring a try to win a test in 1976 when I was nine, but apart from the protest-ravaged visit by the Springboks in '81 there'd been almost no contact since. Our parents obviously had greater memories than us. The first New Zealand-South Africa test I'd ever been to was this one I'd just played in. Now I was starting to appreciate the great tradition that existed between the two countries.

The tour of '92, which rates among my favourite rugby memories, put me in close contact with some of the great achievers of the game, some who had earned legendary status while still playing.

I had known nothing of John Kirwan until I found myself a team-mate of his on the 1989 tour of the UK. I was within metres of him when he snapped his Achilles tendon at Pontypool, an incident which taught me that you can never take anything for granted.

JK possessed an amazing zest for life which he even managed to inject into training. He was so much fun. He knew that being an All Black gave him awesome opportunities not available to the average person and he took full advantage of these. His playing ability was awesome.

As a Northlander, I'd followed his amazing exploits for Auckland and the All Blacks through the 80s. I'd also heard stories about him which I suspected fell into the Tall Poppy zone. I suspected that a lot of the people who spread these rumours had never had a one-on-one relationship with John Kirwan in their lives. I decided I'd make up my own mind about JK, and I concluded all the rumours were unfounded.

JK was a rugby player supreme, a star, a surfie. The fact he remained on tour even with the burden of crutches in 1989 said it all. JK didn't make that decision – the team wanted him there. When he finally cracked 50 tests, the players presented him with a surf board, which was neat.

Grant Fox could have disappeared from sight after the unsuccessful World Cup campaign but he came back to play Laurie Mains' game. It illustrated the calibre of the player that, at the age of 30, he could adjust his play to meet the team's requirements and perform outstandingly.

Foxy was an intense individual. Goodness knows how many games he won for Auckland and the All Blacks. He gave you incredible confidence. You knew if Foxy was there, you could win any game from any situation. Just get down the other end and Foxy would fix it! The more pressure that was placed on him, the better he responded.

He taught me how to play golf. Not as well as him, that's for sure, because Foxy's on a low handicap. But under his expert tuition I graduated from the duffer class into a player of modest skill. He had a lot of theories about goalkicking which he transferred into his (our) golf swing.

One of my favourite memories of Foxy is in Argentina in 1991 when he was in charge of the team funds. He had close to $NZ60,000 in a portable steel safe when we flew from Buenos Aires to Mendoza. Transport to the airport in BA had been in a less than luxurious bus. When we reached our destination and began unloading the luggage, Foxy suddenly went ashen. The cash box was still in the back of the bus. Not only was all our money there, so were our passports. Oh, hell!

In a country where Spanish is the predominant language, conveying our concerns from our hotel in Mendoza back to the bus company in Buenos Aires wasn't easy, but incredibly the cash box was recovered intact. In fact, it was still sitting untouched in the back of the bus.

Alan Whetton managed to find a chain with which we tied Foxy to a pillar outside our hotel. The players were allowed to throw stones and mud at him.

The most remarkable aspect of my involvement in the All Blacks in the seven years from 1990 – and seven years in international rugby is a hell of a long time – is that on every single occasion I took the field in a test Sean Fitzpatrick was in the No 2 jersey. The only time he was missing, at Bloemfontein for the massacre of Japan in the 1995 World Cup, we sat alongside each other in the grandstand.

His development as a captain was fascinating. Bruiser (Mike Brewer) had been Laurie Mains' first choice but Sean was the logical successor because of his seniority as a player and because of his excellent relationship with all the players.

The first message Laurie broadcast to the team at the beginning of '92 was that cliques would not be tolerated. Sean, who'd been part of the Auckland gang effectively running the All Blacks the previous few years, took that on board.

Apart from a brief spell as leader of Brian Lochore's New Zealand Colts team in 1984, Sean had never been a captain, so it was a huge learning curve for him, and he had the disappointment of losing his first test as skipper against the World team in Christchurch. But he developed mightily on the tour in '92 and obviously related strongly to Laurie.

Fitzy set the style off the field, creating a closeness within the team. He wasn't tactically a great leader on the field, with Laurie and the other decision-makers deciding on the style of play. Front row is not a good position from which to captain an All Black team. So Sean was lucky to have Foxy and Zinny on that tour. In later seasons when they were missing Fitzy lacked the tactician who could be his eyes, and his own form and the team's performances suffered accordingly.

It didn't assist Fitzy's development as a captain that during 1993 and 1994 the selectors, in striving to establish the best cluster of test players in New Zealand, kept chopping and changing their selections. It was seriously unsettling on the players who were afraid to have a crack for fear of making a mistake and being dropped. There was no feeling of security. Zinny was one player who was in one minute, out the next. Fitzy's own form suffered in this time when he was probably trying to do too much.

Laurie Mains was having his problems with the media and also, unfortunately, with his manager Neil Gray. Sean tried to appease both parties, whereas he probably should have taken a stronger stand.

The All Blacks, and Fitzy, turned a corner in 1995. Publicly, he did everything a captain should. With the advent of professionalism he became a classic pro. He might have retired a couple of times, but the second-half performance by the All Blacks in Sydney in 1994 gave him an insight into what was possible at the World Cup. Like the rest of us, he sensed this was the making of a pretty special team and the arrival of Brian Lochore as campaign manager in 1995 was important, for it allowed Fitzy to focus on training and playing. He was no longer distracted by internal politics.

A footballer with immense strength, skill and resoluteness, Fitzy was never an onfield tactician. He needed that general, that Zinny at No 8, to give him confidence as a leader. But he was an incredible doer, an inspiring leader by example, a player you were always hugely grateful to have on your side.

When I returned from South Africa in late August 1992, it was to the realisation that Whangarei Airport had landing lights installed. I would finally be able to fly back to my home town instead of risking falling asleep driving north over the Brynderwyns.

The lights were supposed to be operative in 1991 and when I came home from Sydney I had looked forward to flying into Whangarei. But after bad weather initially delayed the flight, we were informed the lights were faulty and that we would be transported north by bus. I eventually hit Whangarei at 10pm, four hours later than if I'd taken a rental car and driven!

In '92 the lights were in full working order and my flight landed right on time and my partner Janine was there to welcome me. I was wearied after two and a half months on the rugby trail, but was resplendent in my All Black blazer as I came into the terminal building. A group of friends we knew were there meeting someone off the flight and acknowledged me. "What have you been up to?" they asked. "Oh, I've been overseas," I said. As they wandered away, I asked Janine if television was still being beamed into Northland!

7

Calling on all Reserves

A new competition was introduced in 1993 called the Super 10, involving the elite provincial teams of New Zealand, Australia and South Africa. The New Zealand representatives, who'd earned their positions by top-four placings in the NPC the previous season, were Auckland, Otago, Waikato and North Harbour.

It produced thrilling contests throughout April and May, culminating in a classic grand final between Auckland and Transvaal at Ellis Park, a game telecast live back in New Zealand and which the home team won. It represented an exciting new era in rugby. The only problem was I wasn't involved.

A veteran of 25 consecutive test appearances I might have been, but because of not being in the right place at the right time, I was a mere observer of this enthralling new competition. The only rugby I got to play before mid-May was at club level for Kamo. Not that I didn't enjoy giving one hundred for my club, but outings at Hikurangi, Maungakaramea and Waipu were a few light years away from performing in front of 60,000 fans at Ellis Park.

Now it so happened that as a Northlander I was the only member of the All Black team who had shared in the historic win over the Springboks the previous August *not* featuring in Super 10. At the time I didn't experience more than a level of envy. The frustration was that Northland had got itself relegated to second division in 1992, so there wasn't any chance of it qualifying for involvement in Super 10 in the immediate future. Also, the Canz series which had provided Northlanders with stimulating international action in April the previous year had fallen over because of a lack of finance.

I took all this philosophically at the time but my attitude would alter pretty dramatically a couple of months later when the All Black selectors dropped me, ostensibly because I was "off the pace". It was an experience I didn't enjoy one little bit and it would force me to make a serious reassessment of my future.

When I ventured south to Rotorua for the All Black trials in May, I considered myself adequately fit, having faithfully followed the training schedule sent out to each member of the All Black squad by fitness trainer Martin Toomey. I would come to appreciate that being fundamentally fit and being conditioned for action at the highest level are seriously different. I would probably have been in the top bracket if all the trialists had been set beep tests the day before the trial. But I was mentally off tune and the speed of the game found me out, not surprisingly really for there is a quantum leap from club footie to All Black trial level and beyond.

I might have been exposed to a greater extent in Rotorua but the conditions were so atrocious, with the game being played in a violent rain storm, that I suspect the afternoon was an exercise in futility for the selectors who stuck with their proven performers for the first test against the British Lions, a game we won 20-18 thanks to Grant Fox's precision goalkicking.

I was sitting at home with Janine and Tony Hickling watching the Auckland-Lions match on television the following Saturday when the All Black team for the second test in Wellington was released. The big news was that I had been dropped and replaced by Mark Cooksley. It came as a hell of a shock because there'd been no pre-warning. I hadn't performed outstandingly at Lancaster Park but nor had anyone else, except perhaps Foxy as a goalkicker. One explanation was the first test syndrome.

Not only didn't anyone telephone me in advance to warn me, no one, except my mother, phoned me afterwards! I was a rugby outcast.

At least I'd been retained in the reserves, and after assembly in the capital I was summoned by Laurie Mains and Peter Thorburn who said they were sorry about dropping me but felt I didn't do enough at Lancaster Park, that I was off the pace. At that moment I considered the selectors terribly fickle. I'd played 26 tests in a row and given a hundred every time. Maybe I was taking my selection for granted. That might have been a bad thing but at least it gave you the confidence to perform.

My being dropped fired a warning to the other players: there would be no second chances. It created a sense of unease within the team at a time when coach Mains had developed a paranoia about Aucklanders and particularly the Auckland media.

I was devastated at being ousted from the test line-up. I had always treasured being part of the All Black machine, now even more so when it was

Peter Bush

It's not hard to win lineout ball when no one bothers to jump against you. I'm lonely against the Springboks at Christchurch in 1996.

Niels Schipper

I made my test debut in a white jersey in 1990 and have worn it several times in my international career (always against Scotland).

An Elle of a souvenir. When someone as special as Elle Macpherson gives you a t-shirt, the least you can do is wear it.

Kenji Ito

The name's changed, from North Auckland to Northland. But the colour's stayed the same - Cambridge blue.

Derek Morrison

A pretty special occasion – the Waikato Chiefs match against New South Wales in Hamilton in 1996. I scored three tries!

Ian Jones Collection

Four generations are represented in this photo. On the seat in front is my grandmother Flora with her great grandchildren.

It's what we call "fast ball off the top". Fellow lock Robin Brooke looks on as I deflect the ball towards halfback Justin Marshall. The occasion was the Tri-nations match against the Springboks at Lancaster Park in 1996.

This was a test we had to win - at Pretoria in 1996. It clinched our first series win on South African soil. This try by Zinzan Brooke helped set up the victory.

John Selkirk

being taken away from me. There were two ways to react: I could say "stuff it, that's enough" and bail out or I could take my chances and prove I was worthy of a test spot.

In Wellington, I was totally supportive of Cooksley. That's the way it had to be. As something completely different, I valued the experience on the reserves bench, having only ever been a test player or a Dirty Dirty. The build-up is completely different for a reserve. Suddenly you're *holding* the tackle bags instead of crunching into them!

The experience was good for me. It taught me never to take anything for granted. It also enlightened me on the important role reserves fulfil. They can make or break a team. In reality, I hated being a reserve but a lot of good came out of it. If there was to be a hiccup in my career, then at least I benefited from the experience.

The All Black performance in that second test was a shocker. Sean Fitzpatrick had his worst game at international level and the team was comprehensively outplayed by the Lions, as the 20-7 scoreline would suggest.

Ian McGeechan, the Lions coach, made a prediction that I would be on the field by halftime. Well predicted, Ian. I took the field, if not *by* halftime certainly *at* halftime when Cooksley came off, ostensibly injured, which he wasn't. I heard Laurie advising "Doc" Mayhew to "bring Cooksley off with a leg injury".

While I was delighted to get back into the action, I made no big difference. The two Martins, Bayfield and Johnson, and Ben Clarke were functioning sweetly in the lineouts and our team simply wasn't playing well enough. At the finish, it was a record loss against the Lions, a performance to file away under Forgettable.

I was reinstated for the decider at Eden Park, a game for filing under Thoroughly Memorable. After a classic build-up, we blew the Lions away in the final hour after they'd burst out to a 10-nil lead.

One of Laurie Mains' weaknesses was his desire for the All Blacks to not only win but win in style. He was such a proud All Black, he became utterly intense and this rolled over into his players and restricted their flair. But that week in Auckland he got the best out of us. The training was precise, the mental preparation just about perfect. On the Friday during our journey to Eden Park, to get a "feel" for the test venue, Laurie, so often so deadly serious, suddenly moved down the bus smiling and cracking jokes. "Come on, guys," he said, "we're not going to a funeral. Loosen up." It was a timely gesture and broke the ice, helping the guys to relax. He knew we'd trained well and he encouraged the guys to express themselves on the field. He had made a huge effort that week and was rewarded with a magnificent victory. We probably didn't see that human side of Laurie again until 1995.

By the end of the domestic international programme, which included victories over Australia at Carisbrook and Western Samoa at Eden Park, I made an assessment of my own situation. I'd been dropped (and recalled) and I was not overly happy with my form. My focus obviously was on the 1995 World Cup and to qualify for that I would have to be playing test rugby in 1994. As things stood at the moment, there was no guarantee of that. I concluded the only way to assure myself of selection at the highest level was to get involved in better quality early-season rugby. With Northland not in the Super 10 – in fact, not even in the NPC first division – I was plainly being disadvantaged remaining in the north. Physically I was ready for anything, but jumping from club play straight into international rugby I was mentally way off the mark.

I discussed my predicament with Sid Going, the Northland coach, and others in the north. Northland was *my* territory. Kamo was *my* club. Sentimentally I wanted to stay and play in my home territory. But realistically it would jeopardise my career as an All Black. I needed to play Super 10 to equip myself for international rugby. Once the decision was made, it was simply a case of choosing a new union to play for. I didn't hawk myself around. I selected the union closest to my own, North Harbour, so I would be only a couple of hours' drive from my family. I telephoned North Harbour's chief executive officer, Peter Goldsmith, and coach, Brad Meurant, and let them know of my availability. They said I was most welcome and Brad said he could pretty much guarantee me a place in his team. There was no contract, no formalities. From 1994 I would play my rugby with North Harbour. I just had to trust Brad's team would be good enough to finish in the top four of the NPC to qualify for the next Super 10 series, which it did.

Before then came a tour of England and Scotland, a venture featuring some remarkable highs and lows but for which the supreme academy award had to go to Robin Brooke, or Foodbill as he came to be known.

Although carrying a calf-muscle injury, he was cleared to tour. The medical boys were confident he would soon come right. Huh – after 13 matches he was still on tour without progressing beyond a few training sessions. By that stage he was driving a Mercedes Benz limousine around, chauffeuring the players' wives and partners. It was a classic performance.

His incapacity meant I played the first three games and four of the first five, till Blair Larsen, Foodbill's "temporary" replacement, gave us a full complement of tight forwards. Every week throughout the tour, Foodbill was "going to come right". At Glasgow, the decision was finally made that he would return home, but, wised up, Robin slipped his suitcases in with the team gear and convinced manager Neil Gray that through a "misunderstanding" he would need to stay on for the next few days to reclaim them. Somehow, approval was obtained from the host unions for an extension of his stay. The Scottish Rugby Union invited him to be its guest at the test and then, because of the scheduled visit to Buckingham Palace, it was deemed appropriate for him to be involved. After seven weeks and 13 matches, Foodbill was still there.

Sean Fitzpatrick and I were the accused after South West centre Phil de Glanville was trampled in the third match of the tour at Redruth. He'd taken the ball in and the All Black forwards blew over the top of him. Obviously, a sprig connected with his face, causing an ugly wound. The tabloids made a meal of it and de Glanville uttered inciteful comments, prompting letters to the editor condemning us and leading to a summit conference on rucking.

It's all part of touring England, unfortunately. The Poms have short memories, because only a few months previously their very own Dean Richards had crudely trampled Frank Bunce when the Lions took on North Harbour. There was no malice involved on our part; it was the ugly side of contact sport that can occur. Accidents can happen. Whether it's a whack or a sprig, most rugby players in New Zealand (and I'd suggest South Africa and Australia) would take it on the chin and discuss it over a beer afterwards. I've looked at the video replay of the incident and to this day I wouldn't know whose boot came into contact with de Glanville's face. It was completely accidental, which is why we were upset that the player involved went to the extent he did. The Rugby Football Union issued a statement claiming it was dangerous play beyond the acceptable level and de Glanville called for the culprit to be banned. The All Black management, thoroughly bemused by the whole affair, eventually extended an apology to de Glanville.

We meandered through a lot of the tour. It's not easy to play expansive rugby consistently in the UK because of the weather and the softer grounds. It's a challenge to get the ball wide at times. Also, we were still striving to achieve an understanding of Laurie Mains as a coach.

Playing at the famous stadiums of the world is always a special experience, but Murrayfield was a little deflating in 1993 because a new grandstand was under construction which meant there were effectively only three sides to the ground. Much of the atmosphere seemed to drain through the construction area. I was looking forward to the experience but found it an anticlimax, which is not a term you would use to describe our performance. We blitzed the Scots 51-15, with Jeff Wilson the star, scoring three tries (and adding a sideline conversion) on test debut. There were glimpses of the style that would be adopted in 1995. It was probably our most complete performance of '93, although admittedly against an opponent of modest quality.

With Foodbill still swanning around, my new test locking partner was Steve Gordon. Although we'd been on four tours together – to Ireland and

Wales, France, Argentina and the World Cup – amazingly we had only ever locked the All Black scrum together once, at Cordoba in 1991. Steve and I went back many years, to age-grade tournaments where we'd opposed each other, and to 1985 when we'd operated together in the North Island under-18 side. It was great that on his fifth tour he was finally getting to play a test.

For the England international at Twickenham the All Blacks were accommodated at a country estate, an hour's drive from Twickenham, which didn't have a lot going for it. All our hotels were luxurious, but when you're on tour for six weeks, the last thing you want is to be bottled up in your hotel. Being an hour from central London meant the week dragged. Then on match day road works resulted in traffic chaos, with the result we arrived at the ground less than 40 minutes before kick-off. In normal circumstances we'd have been there with 80 minutes to spare.

The late arrival put everyone under pressure. We couldn't stroll out to check the ground – that had to be rushed. Without using it as an excuse, it was an unsatisfactory preparation and our whole performance that afternoon lacked spark. Neither side managed a try but England kicked a couple more goals than us to win 15-9.

Maybe our robotic style caught up with us, for we were certainly out-thought. The All Blacks were different then from now. It was still a development phase for Fitzy as captain and he didn't have the ability to change tactics in midstream. We were given a game plan which we followed to the letter. You didn't have to be a genius to see that that particular game plan was going nowhere. We were beaten in the lineouts and beaten in the loose. Maybe if someone had suggested to Fitzy that we employ short lineouts, there could have been a different outcome, but we clung doggedly to the original plan. One reason we failed, I believe, is because the senior players didn't have the confidence to speak out.

That loss was one of the hardest to take. It was heartwrenching. We set out to use the same tactics we'd employed against Scotland but were neutralised by England who'd obviously studied our play. I had a terribly frustrating afternoon in the lineouts against Nigel Redman because the South African referee Frik Burger allowed the Poms to obstruct outrageously. Against Doddie Weir at Murrayfield I'd been allowed to jump unobstructed and win quality ball "off the top" to help ignite our backs. At Twickenham, Burger didn't allow an adequate gap down the middle, as a consequence of which Redman and his colleagues were all over me. Sean and I complained to Burger who turned a blind eye to England's antics. "You're getting ball, play on," he said. He'd obviously never been a lineout jumper.

We couldn't retaliate, which we might have done a year earlier. A push-prod-don't-do-that-again-or-else reaction from us would have probably resolved the problem, but after the outcry over the de Glanville incident we didn't dare retaliate or indulge in any kind of crudities. It wasn't worth the risk. So we laboured on. The ball we secured wasn't quality ball, which hampered our attacking opportunities.

Having said all that, we still secured enough possession to win the game. But we had three backs who couldn't kick and our play was too structured. Ben Clarke, Dean Richards and Tim Rodber, three great tacklers, were there waiting for us. Our inflexibility played into their hands.

If Mains as the coach incurred criticism for such a dismal performance, he came in for outright condemnation for including Mike Brewer, who was in the UK as Canterbury International's representative, as a loose forward replacement ahead of Liam Barry. Laurie's defence was that Brewer had the necessary experience to deal with players like Ben Clarke if required to come on, while Barry didn't.

I wasn't privy to the selection policies of the team and I did have a close friendship with Liam. I felt sorry for him. I'd played previously with Mike who was a gifted footballer with infinitely more experience than Liam at that level. But Mike wasn't part of the team and his selection denied an opportunity to someone who was. I could see where Mike was coming from – if you're invited to be an All Black, you'd be a mug to say no. But in involving him, Laurie, I believe, transgressed the very principles he had spelt out so emphatically to us upon his arrival in 1992. Laurie had threatened to eradicate cliques from the All Blacks, but here he was falling back on the old boy network, looking after one of his mates. I didn't express an opinion at the time but I was quite taken aback to find Brewer involved.

The tour finale was an enjoyable experience for me, an opportunity to finally play *against* the UK Barbarians (at Cardiff). I'd three times worn their jersey against international opponents while not being considered senior enough to play against them on my first tour back in 1989. It was great to catch up with Mickey Steele-Bodger again. He and the Barbarians have done so much for the promotion of the game in the UK.

We won the game, not without some anxious moments in the second half, and I had the satisfaction of scoring the final try, becoming the first individual to score tries for and against the Barbarians in international fixtures.

In February 1994 I quit Kamo for Milford on Auckland's north shore, not without some heartburning. But the purpose of taking up residency within the North Harbour union was to achieve top-quality early season competition which I couldn't get in Northland. Boy, I sure got it with North Harbour.

In early April I found myself on a flight to South Africa for a warm-up game at Cradock and a Super 10 contest at Port Elizabeth. Then it was back home for more Super 10 action against Otago and Transvaal. All of these games we won; indeed, we were only a Warren Burton penalty goal (from point-blank range) away from qualifying for the final against Natal at Durban. As it turned out, Queensland advanced courtesy of its 13-10 victory over us, although the Bananalanders probably wished Burton *had* landed that goal because they returned from the final with their star midfielders Tim Horan and Jason Little both in plaster and on crutches.

By the time of the All Black trial in Napier in mid-June, I'd played eight high-quality matches in three countries, including a historic North Harbour victory over the French at Eden Park. If I'd stayed with Northland I would have gone to Napier with only two outings, against the Coronation Shield Districts and King Country, to prepare me. The move had been worthwhile. This time I went into an All Black trial full of confidence after two months of intense competition against many of the best lineout exponents in the world.

Another benefit, which I hadn't foreseen, was the opportunity to train alongside All Blacks who had the same objectives as myself. Previously, back in Whangarei I'd undertaken basic training by myself or with one or two mates around me. In Auckland, there was a core of international players with similar goals I trained alongside. Oh, and one other benefit about living at Milford… whenever I returned to Auckland International Airport from a rugby assignment, I was home in 30 minutes instead of two or three hours.

Although we took out a series against the Springboks, you wouldn't describe 1994 as a vintage season for All Black rugby. We finished up winning two tests, drawing one and losing three, not exactly a record suggesting we were on target to tear opponents apart at the third World Cup the following year.

I was still struggling to come to grips with Laurie Mains' approach. His continuing paranoia about all things Auckland continued to place unreasonable pressures on his players while he and his selectors spread insecurity by repeatedly changing their test fifteen.

When the All Blacks ran out against France in the first test of '94 at Lancaster Park, there were eight changes from the side which had stumbled against England. Injuries and defections had forced the selectors' hand to a degree, but they seemed hell bent on trying out every conceivable combination, particularly in the backline. The shock of two defeats against France caused them to veer off on another tangent. It was all very bewildering.

John Timu gave way to Shane Howarth at fullback and became a winger; Jeff Wilson was supplanted by the now veteran John Kirwan on the right wing; Inga Tuigamala, who'd chosen a career in league, was replaced; Eroni Clarke, Matthew Cooper and Alama Ieremia all had a go at second-five; Marc Ellis passed the No 10 jersey on to Simon Mannix who handed it over to

Stephen Bachop; Stu Forster hung in for a while at halfback, then stepped aside for Graeme Bachop; Zinzan Brooke was an openside flanker against England, a reserve against France and at No 8 against South Africa; I locked with Steve Gordon and Mark Cooksley; Jamie Joseph and Blair Larsen shared the No 6 jersey; Craig Dowd was replaced at loosehead prop by Richard Loe.

You'll find that Frank Bunce, Olo Brown, Sean Fitzpatrick and myself were, incredibly, the only players to make the four consecutive appearances from Twickenham in November to Carisbrook (against the Springboks) in July. If there was method in the selectors' seeming madness, it was not immediately apparent to me.

In my time in the All Blacks, the French have consistently proven the hardest opponents, beating us twice in '94 and again at Toulouse the following year. They demolished us at Christchurch where I had a good contest with Olivier Roumat in the middle of the lineout. At the front, Olivier Merle cleaned us out that day, as a consequence of which I was moved forward to combat him at Eden Park. Merle was an absolute giant, probably the biggest lineout jumper I ever marked. His programme weight was 126kg and he was all of that. His immense bulk didn't lend itself to great elevation and so I was able to outjump him and secure a wealth of quality ball for the All Blacks. Unfortunately, our possession wasn't converted into points and we had the traumatic experience of the French sweeping the length of the field in the last few moments to pull off a fairytale victory. It was the first time since 1970-71 the All Blacks had lost three tests in a row.

It was Andy Dalton, the outstanding test captain of the 1980s, who said that because of the unpredictability of French teams, he never felt confident against them unless his team was at least two converted tries ahead. Well, we were less than one converted try in front at Eden Park after dominating much of the second half when Stephen Bachop missed touch and 90 metres downfield Jean-Luc Sadourny scored a sensational try.

We should have snuffed out the French counterattack but we didn't have the enthusiasm of All Black sides of the past to swarm up in defence. As at Twickenham, we were still too precise and robotic. We didn't counter their flair. We weren't playing like All Black teams could or should. When I reflected on the game from home later, it was with a sense of frustration, knowing we had the potential to play so much better. The French deserved their win but there was so much more we could have done. No one was playing out of his skin.

Lancaster Park marked the entry onto the international scene of Jonah Lomu, then 19. His arrival was trumpeted so loudly, he was a marked man from the moment he pulled on the jersey. He didn't have the advantage I had of easing gently into test rugby. Jonah, of course, is something of a freak but you have to feel sorry for a kid who in his first series was targeted. I'd first seen the sensation that was Lomu in a schools game that was a curtainraiser to a Northland match. He was operating from No 8 then – a real powerhouse. It was exciting to have such a youngster coming through to the All Blacks. His enthusiasm certainly rubbed off on the team. He was a hell of a nice young kid.

In my four and a half years as an All Black, injuries had never been a concern, so it was a rare experience when in the ninth minute of the first Springbok test at Carisbrook I collected someone's elbow or knee in the face after taking the ball at a lineout and went down with what turned out to be a cracked cheekbone. I watched the greater part of the game from the emergency ward of Dunedin Hospital.

The injury kept me out of the second test in Wellington a fortnight later, but I was flown down and watched from the grandstand. It was only the second rugby test in New Zealand that I had attended as a spectator, the first being the 1989 Bledisloe Cup encounter at Eden Park when Phil Kearns, Tim Horan and Tony Daly made their international debuts. Like most Northlanders, I had tended to watch test matches on television from the comfort of my lounge. The '89 expedition south had been in the company of a group of mates from the Kamo club. We travelled down and back in a mini-van in the one day, watching the game from the No 4 stand.

While I was thrilled for the All Blacks winning the series over the South Africans, I didn't feel I deserved to be part of the celebrations, having not directly contributed. I'd been present at the training sessions but I'd had no direct input. Ironically, my absence coincided with Foodbill's return – his first All Black outing in 12 months – meaning the All Black team featured two Bachops (Stephen and Graeme) and two Brookes (Zinzan and Robin).

I was back in at Cooksley's expense for the third test at Eden Park, marking Steve Atherton, my first real experience since 1992 of the Springboks' lineout ability. Obviously, they had to curb their lifting to meet IRB requirements but there was plenty to learn from them in terms of blocking and assisting the jumper. The Boks were the catalysts for the lineout techniques that exist today. To combat them – for they definitely had the superior technique – we used many variations including quickening up the throw (which Warren Gatland had taught me way back in 1989) and shortening the lineouts.

When you look at the consistency of selection that has been achieved in the All Blacks in the past couple of seasons, it's amazing to reflect on the comings and goings back in 1994. For the Sydney Football Stadium night test against the Wallabies, Jeff Wilson came in for John Kirwan, Walter Little replaced Alama Ieremia and Michael Jones took over from Blair Larsen. It was the sixth test of the year but the selectors were still ringing the changes.

New Zealand had never played a test match under lights, so it was a whole new experience. In readiness, we trained at night and left the changing room 10 minutes before kick-off to adjust to the lights. You wouldn't have known that we'd undertaken any special preparation because within 20 seconds of the start we'd conceded a try to Jason Little. We failed to secure Australia's initial kick, and when David Knox placed a perfectly judged bomb towards our goal line, Little, as he has done so often, came racing through to pluck the ball out of the air.

After half an hour we were on the ropes, 17-3 down. To all intents and purposes we were out of the game. The Aussies had played well, but we'd never got into the game. Shell-shocked, we remained out in the middle during the halftime break. To a man, we felt we'd already lost the Bledisloe Cup and therefore the only thing to do was to throw everything at them, to run them into the ground. Let's at least go out with some pride, we vowed.

Well, we did more than that. That second 40 minutes became the inspiration for what would become the All Black trade mark over the next several seasons. Taking quick ball off the top of the lineout, we ran everything at the Aussies, moving the ball wide and producing rugby of thrilling quality. We were encouraged all the way by Laurie Mains. We were genuinely disappointed not to win in the finish – we were only a Jeff Wilson lost ball away from an epic victory – but as we unwound in the dressing room, there was a feeling of, "That's it! That's the formula for the future." It had taken a couple of seasons, but we had finally hit upon the style that would make the All Blacks great again.

That was effectively the end of the All Blacks for 1994 – and it was almost the end of Laurie Mains, for he only just survived a challenge to his coaching post from John Hart – but there was a critically important event still to come… a World Cup training camp in Queenstown in November.

It was a watershed not only in the development of All Black rugby but also in the career of Laurie Mains. It was where the tactics which would revolutionise the game worldwide were formulated. And it was where a lot of us finally realised where Laurie Mains was coming from. I can see now that coaching a high-profile rugby team is rather like a businessman taking over a company. If the company is struggling when he inherits it – as was the situation when Mains took over the All Blacks in '92 – he will take two or three years to implant his style.

Laurie always wanted his team to implement an expansive style but he didn't want to reveal too much to the world in advance of the World Cup campaign. I can understand that, although I have more difficulty accepting the endless selection changes as Mains and his cohorts sought to establish the best possible line-up to make New Zealand great in 1995.

Laurie was such a different character to what most of us had been used to. The fitness levels he introduced us to in 1992 were a revelation. Coming to terms with his style and mannerisms hadn't been easy. But at that camp in late '94 there was an overwhelming consensus among every member of the World Cup squad – every single player was committed to the style we'd displayed in the second half of the Sydney Bledisloe Cup contest.

During the Queenstown camp we split off into groups – well mixed they were too, not too many forwards or backs together – and dissected the season just gone. Every group reached the same conclusion, that we hadn't been fit enough, that we'd been too slack at training. Some groups felt the need for greater guidance on issues like nutrition.

Laurie didn't involve himself directly in the groups. He stood back and listened. The big message coming through was the need for super fitness. Laurie nodded many times that weekend. He knew superior fitness was the key to success at the World Cup. And, boy, was he ever going to ensure it!

8

The Whirled Cup

Thursday night before a major game, particularly when you're overseas, is an important one. It's when you seek deep, relaxing sleep. It doesn't matter if an element of nervous tension causes you to thrash about on the Friday night. The Thursday sleep is the one that counts.

There was no more important occasion in 1995, probably not in my entire sporting career, than the World Cup final at Ellis Park. This was the event the All Blacks had been building towards for four years, and the sensational manner in which we had disposed of England in the semi-final the previous weekend suggested we'd timed our preparation to perfection for the final which, to the rather unexpected delight of the host nation, would be against the Springboks. With such a chequered test record since their return to the international scene in 1992, few had expected the South Africans to go all the way, even with the home advantage.

Robin Brooke was my roommate at the Holiday Inn Crowne Plaza at Sandton. By 10.30pm, two nights out from the final, he'd crashed and was snoring contentedly. It was time for me to turn the light out and do likewise.

The moment I placed my head on the pillow, the room started to spin. I was beginning to sweat also. Strange, I thought. I hoped I wasn't coming down with the flu. I switched the television on and watched a local programme disinterestedly. After an hour or so, I risked putting my head back on the pillow. The room spun even more violently. Oh, hell!

I realised I was going to throw up and took myself to the toilet, closing the door so as not to disturb Robin. Whatever was affecting me was biting in viciously now. I checked my watch. Midnight. Not a good time to annoy the team doctor, Mike Bowen. Hopefully, the worst would soon pass and I'd get something from him in the morning.

The worst didn't pass. While Robin slept on blissfully, I was throwing up repeatedly. How many times can you vomit? There was surely nothing left to bring up. I was variously sweating and shivering. Two nights out from the World Cup, I was one hell of a mess. I kept hoping it was a nightmare I'd wake from. But I knew it wasn't. Around two o'clock, there was nothing for it but to call on the doctor. I'd just have to wake him and get something to control the vomiting. I felt as if I was going to die.

To my surprise, Doc Bowen's door was open and his "surgery" seemed to be in full swing. Instead of me having to wake him, he seemed to be waiting for me. As I started to explain what I'd been enduring, he said very matter-of-factly, "You're number 22."

Because Robin had been sleeping so soundly and was obviously unaffected, I'd assumed I was the only player suffering. How wrong I was. Almost the entire team was afflicted. All were vomiting and many also had diarrhoea. We would establish later that the reason Robin and brother Zinzan (plus Sean Fitzpatrick) escaped was because they hadn't made it back to the hotel for lunch after training. Those of us who had participated in the Crowne Plaza buffet luncheon, which included our manager Colin Meads and coach Laurie Mains, were now paying the penalty.

Doc Bowen gave me an injection which brought the vomiting under control, stopped the dizziness in my head and allowed me to finally get some sleep.

The white board had notified everyone that the first commitment on the Friday was a 10am gathering in the team room, from where we would journey to Ellis Park for a "walk in the park". It should have added "for survivors" because the motley crew that gathered the next morning would have found a game of backgammon exhausting. Some, including Pinetree the manager, were so crook they were still horizontal in their rooms. With about three or four exceptions – notably the Brooke brothers and Sean Fitzpatrick, the lucky ones who'd missed lunch – it was the palest, sickest-looking collection of individuals you would ever see in one room.

All Blacks are disciplined to a fault and no one is ever late for a team meeting. The management are always similarly punctual and ready to roll at the appointed hour. On the Friday, one day before the World Cup final for which the All Blacks were overwhelming favourites, we were the most disorganised rabble you've ever seen. The manager was still in bed, the coach seemed to be having trouble focusing, guys were lying around instead of sitting up to attention. There was a sickly smell in the air. Whatever had struck us had been exceedingly potent and it had swept through almost the entire side.

Those of us who were sufficiently recovered – which represented about four-fifths of the team – undertook the ritual stroll around Ellis Park, although it was disconcerting to have team-mates, superbly prepared athletes at peak fitness, throwing up beside the bus.

Like most of the team, I slept all afternoon, stirring myself for the lineout session in the car park. That was no fun, I can tell you. I tried desperately to be energetic and positive, but my body was lethargic. We tried to pick each other up with comments like, "Come on, we'll do 12 good lineouts to finish." I don't think we managed 12 good lineouts in the entire session! However, the workout was good for me. It jolted me back to life. Obviously, in my case, the illness – which had to have been food poisoning; nothing else could have flattened 23 players simultaneously like that – was passing. I even managed an evening meal and a night's sleep, but in this I was the exception. Some of the guys, like Andrew Mehrtens – who is notoriously susceptible to any bug going – and Jeff Wilson were still vomiting on the Saturday morning.

It was just so frustrating because our training had gone so promisingly. After the massive effort against England on the Sunday in Cape Town, we'd been given Monday and Tuesday off, apart from light gym work. On the Wednesday we'd put a lot of effort into lineouts where I rated my chances against Hannes Strydom. It was our intention to gain quick ball off the top of the lineout and to spin it wide, tactics which had exposed all our other opponents. We would still employ these tactics against the Springboks but unfortunately the diminished energy levels of the players meant the support play, which had overwhelmed every other opponent, would be lacking at Ellis Park.

If the food poisoning wasn't handicap enough for our team, on the Friday evening came the car alarms, piercing the stillness of the night till well into the small hours. They'd never been a distraction previously. But on the eve of the World Cup, the alarms just kept on going off. It was surely orchestrated, but who, what or why we'll never know. It meant disturbed sleep for everyone. In normal circumstances it wouldn't have mattered. But with virtually the entire All Black squad having vomited through the previous night, it was terribly unsettling.

As I lay there in my bed at the Crowne Plaza, the car alarms wailing on, I thought back to the World Cup camps where our campaign had been launched. I particularly recalled Taupo and Laurie Mains' immortal words to me, my body in the throes of exhaustion: "Do you think John Eales is doing this? Do you think any Springbok forward is training like this?" No, Laurie, no bloody way!

What an incredible experience that Taupo camp had been. During the summer we'd diligently worked away on the training schedules individually prepared for us by Martin Toomey and I think most of us suspected Taupo would provide an opportunity for the management of the team to monitor the players' progress. We were to seriously underestimate Laurie Mains' fanatical desire to have the All Blacks significantly fitter than any other team at the World Cup.

Taupo started pleasantly enough for the squad which had increased in size from 1994. Now on board were exciting young players like Andrew Mehrtens and Josh Kronfeld. The Friday was quite mellowish – fitness testing, backs and forwards working separately on technical aspects of their game and some 150s to finish. Nothing exceptional. Apart from one or two players carrying injuries, like Walter Little, everyone came through satisfactorily. We had a couple of quiet beers and retired early, knowing we'd be up early the next morning. Saturday, Laurie assured us, would be a challenging day. That has to rate as one of the great understatements of all time.

We were in the pool at seven o'clock the next morning, a pleasant interlude for a swimmer like myself. That was followed by more fitness testing, this time with weights. Then came the three-kilometre run at Owen Delany Park, an agony at any time. Jon Preston, who has amazing stamina, was first across the finish line, as he always is, while I headed the forwards home in a satisfactory time. Everyone was under the 15-minute qualifying time, although in the case of Waisake Sotutu and Jonah Lomu, they had only seconds to spare.

By now a large crowd had gathered at the stadium to watch as we moved on to the ruck and scrum machines. It was a pretty intense session. There is no finer technical coach of forward play than Laurie Mains and he was insisting we get everything right.

It had been an exhausting morning's work but when we adjourned for lunch in the grandstand, Laurie came out with one of his famous quotes. "Eat at your peril," he warned us. After the demands of the morning, I think we expected the afternoon would be reasonably gentle. It was only February, for God's sake! But you could sense Laurie was a man on a mission. He was determined to identify any players in his squad whose fitness levels were suspect. Wary of what lay ahead, for most of us that lunch comprised a quick snack.

We resumed with sprint testing, Toomey having a sophisticated radar set-up that timed us over 10 metres and 40 metres, from where the forwards moved on to a gruelling two-hour scrummaging session while the backs worked on their moves. Because the test fifteen wasn't established at that stage, there was earnest competition among the various individuals, so the live scrums were anything but gentlemanly. Some of the unsung front rowers, in particular, were out to impress.

Just when I felt I couldn't manage one more scrum, Laurie ordered the balls to be put away. Ah, blessed relief. Please say we can retreat to our hotel rooms now and relax, Laurie. It's been a huge day. What? Now the 150s. Oh, Christ!

We'd been going since 7am and it was now 3.30 when we launched into the 150s. Laurie ordered 22 of them which would become 25 when Jonah annoyed him by dropping off the pace. And there would be a series of Down-and-Ups after that. The temperature was in the high 20s. It was rapidly becoming the day from hell.

With 150s you basically put your brain into neutral, establish a rhythm and keep going. Of course, Laurie and Martin were there to drive you on. Around the 20th 150, when every single part of my body was hurting, Laurie startled me by shouting, "Do you think John Eales is doing this, Kamo? Do you think he's driving himself like this?" If I'd been capable of an answer, which I wasn't, I think I might have suggested that this being the first week of February, John Eales was probably soaking up the sunshine somewhere on the Gold Coast of Queensland, contenting himself with a gentle run before breakfast each morning. He certainly wouldn't be on his 21st Goddamn 150 in sweltering heat. Right at that moment I'd have given anything to swap places with John Eales. I'd have even been prepared to take lessons in goalkicking.

If you were seeking evidence to prove that Laurie didn't intend the Taupo camp to be as gruelling as it became, consider that a visit to the hydro-dam at Turangi was arranged for the Saturday evening. Unbelievable as it may seem, we honoured the invitation. Most of the guys were nearly asleep following the hour-long bus journey from Taupo and found traipsing up stairs and ladders, to view the various facilities, an absolute agony. In different circumstances, the outing would have been a pleasant interlude. That particular night it was like a visit to the dentist.

The relief as we finally tumbled into our beds that night was extreme. Beneath the aching muscles and exhaustion was a sense of deep satisfaction. What we'd achieved was unbelievable and fulfilling. It had been interesting to observe Laurie's expression as the day went on. He'd been hugely encouraged by the players' fight.

Incredibly, Laurie ensured that the intensity was maintained on the Sunday. This was a day when he took centre stage as a master technical coach. Even the best players need reminding of the basics at times and that's what Laurie focused on. As we progressed through 1995, we would be grateful for the repetitious work thrust upon us that day, particularly as it related to body positioning. Laurie masterminded events as if he were drilling a school first fifteen, ramming home the fundamentals. Much of the session concentrated upon rucking, Laurie being convinced that quick ball from rucks was the passport to success at the World Cup. His theory would be borne out months later at Ellis Park, Loftus Versfeld, Bloemfontein Stadium and Newlands.

One of the reassuring aspects of the Taupo camp was that Colin Meads, who would be our manager in South Africa, and Brian Lochore, the newly appointed World Cup campaign manager, were there observing. These men were legends in New Zealand rugby, two of the greatest players the game has seen. While their direct input was minimal, there was an omnipresence about them. You knew you couldn't let them down.

I drove the North Harbour guys back home. On the journey down to Taupo the conversation had been along the lines of, "I wonder what we'll do?" On the return, it was more a case of, "Holy hell, can you believe what we achieved!" combined with much shaking of heads.

The Taupo camp developed a tightness within the All Black squad, a camaraderie that had been missing since before the previous World Cup campaign in 1991. It would be reinforced at the final camp at Christchurch where we knuckled down to serious gut-busting stuff. We'd covered the technicalities at Taupo, now we were into making it happen, in live rehearsals. After all we'd come through, the guys were into helping each other in a big way. There was no one-upmanship.

The series of matches organised prior to the selection of the World Cup squad were cleverly mapped out and stimulating for those involved. I particularly enjoyed playing in the North-South game at Carisbrook, the first such inter-island fixture in nine years, Frank Bunce being the only survivor of the 1986 game. Graham Henry was our coach and it was interesting to learn another person's philosophy. It was a refreshing change from trials and All Black matches and put you together with different team-mates.

Personally, I'd like to see the inter-island fixture reintroduced. I realise the programme for top-flight players is crammed now, but a North-South contest could be used as an alternative to the All Black trial, if not every year, then perhaps every second year. The inter-island game was dropped, as I understand it, because North had become too dominant. Well, based on NPC and Super 12 results in 1997 and 1998, it would be a brave person who would invest heavily on the North Island.

Perhaps one reason I have a soft spot for North-South rivalry is because in that 1995 game I scored two tries. So, too, did Jonah Lomu, the teenage sensation who had come back into the calculations after a spectacular series of performances at the Hong Kong sevens tournament. The first time a lot of us really noticed Jonah was in training in Hamilton prior to the match between the Harlequins (effectively the All Blacks) and Waikato.

We were working out at Rugby Park, taking turns holding the whack bags. Richard Loe, no lightweight at 110kg, was on duty when Jonah slammed into his bag. Richard went about six feet in the air and six feet backwards! It was such an astonishing hit, the whole session came to a halt. We all gawked, wondering if Richard would recover. He did, but it was illustration for a lot of us as to how we might use Jonah the Giant.

Jonah's dynamism wasn't the only eye-opener that week. The hard graft, fine tuning and planning we'd put in at Taupo and Christchurch was now being realised. Waikato was an extremely competitive first division team which had never in its 74-year history conceded more than 64 points, but we blew them away by 96 points to 25. The level of confidence in the team was amazing.

Between Hamilton and the final trial in Whangarei came a team-building sojourn in Waitomo. Instead of rucks and lineouts, the accent was on abseiling, white-water rafting, golf and a couple of sessions in the pub. We trained at Te Kuiti and went along to watch the Otorohanga club's centennial match in which the outstanding performer was Ant Strachan. It was a display which, against the odds, would secure him the second World Cup halfback berth.

I was chuffed when the shadow All Black team trained for the final trial at my club ground, Kamo Rec. Fifteen hundred turned up to watch, indicative of the enthusiasm for rugby in the town. If they were wanting to see their representative working out in the starting line-up, they were disappointed because Andrew Mehrtens, Graeme Bachop, Craig Dowd and myself were named as reserves. The general understanding was that we were certainties for selection, although you can never take anything for granted when it comes to the naming of an All Black team.

I did get involved in the action, about 20 minutes into the second half at Lowe Walker Stadium, by which time my team was about 50 points ahead, another graphic example of the explosive potential of this team. We were, after all, against a selection that was tantamount to the next best team in New Zealand. Everyone who was part of the winning team that night was named in the World Cup squad.

We remained in camp for three days, being quartered at Wellsford and training at Robin and Zinzan Brooke's old school, Mahurangi College. It was here that Laurie Mains mapped out our World Cup programme in specific detail, including the opening sequence against England. Considering that England had to beat Australia to get through to meet us in the semi-finals, it represented remarkable foresight – and confidence – by our coach.

The English, he insisted, were so robotic they would never anticipate anything unorthodox. So we would give them unorthodoxy. If they won the toss, they would automatically choose the end they wanted to defend, giving us the kick-off. If we won the toss, we would take the kick-off regardless. Which meant Andrew Mehrtens would start the World Cup semi-final in Cape Town. And he would start it, Mains told us, by kicking away from the forwards… to Jonah Lomu who, primed, would catch the English unawares by sprinting after the ball.

It wasn't by chance that the All Blacks were seven points ahead of England inside 90 seconds at the World Cup. We practised the start, with the forwards to the right and Mehrts kicking to the left, 10 or 12 times, till we were thoroughly proficient at it. It was Laurie at his meticulous best. The move was then filed away for Cape Town. It wasn't the sort of thing you could practise 48 hours out from the game.

Another ploy we worked on at Mahurangi College would bring handsome rewards in the only domestic international we'd play before the World Cup, against Canada at Eden Park. We introduced a lot of lineout variations, one of which involved Robin peeling around the back in a Willie Away movement, drawing the defence. Everything pointed towards us going wide. Against Canada, as Robin roared around the back, I palmed the ball to halfback Graeme Bachop who flipped a pass to Olo Brown on the short side. Sean Fitzpatrick took the Canadian hooker's line, allowing Olo to rumble clean through to the goal line. Olo doesn't get a lot of tries, so he thought this one was a fantastic move! Any time a member of the tight five scores a try, the occasion is cherished by the rest of us.

It was a move that brought us huge satisfaction. We pulled it again during the World Cup and although it didn't yield a try on that occasion, it plainly fooled the opposition and took us threateningly close to the goal line.

All a backline is looking for is good, swift ball, and that's what we worked on during those days at Mahurangi College – getting the ball from the top of the lineout into Bachop's hands and away to the backline in the quickest possible time. That approach, involving several variations including short lineouts and speeded-up throws, at which Fitzpatrick was the master, would lead to buckets of sensational tries at the World Cup.

We blitzed the Canadians, who were recognised as one of the better emerging rugby nations, by 73-7, with all the new guys, Andrew Mehrtens, Josh Kronfeld and Glen Osborne, excelling. It was hugely satisfying putting into effect the tactics we'd worked on so painstakingly at Taupo, Christchurch, Te Kuiti and Mahurangi College.

Everything was rosy as we approached the World Cup, with one solitary exception – our champion No 8 Zinzan Brooke was fighting a desperate race against the clock to repair a serious Achilles tendon injury sustained in the Harlequins match in Hamilton. No one is indispensable, but Zinny was the best. And we would have been losing a great mate. He couldn't have done more to get himself right. He sat in a decompression chamber at the Devonport Naval Base to hasten the healing process and he underwent acupuncture, a huge ask for a guy with a fear of needles.

We had Mike Brewer and Kevin Schuler as back-ups, so we wouldn't have been doomed, but Zinny is a footballer of rare talent, as he would demonstrate with his 40 metre dropped goal against England. There was general delight when he was declared ready, if not fully fit, to travel to South Africa with the team. Zinny gave Sean Fitzpatrick that important extra pair of eyes on the field.

Fitzy had greater confidence in himself as captain by 1995. Previously, he'd been reluctant to ever change the game plan unless Zinny had prompted it. A major factor in this was that as players we lacked the confidence to speak up, to suggest switching to short lineouts or long kick-offs, or whatever. The All Blacks were a more democratic combination by 1995 and Fitzy had the confidence to alter the tactical approach to suit the mood of the players.

It must have been bloody hard for Sean earlier when we weren't helping him out. Outside influences, such as the spat between the manager and the coach on the 1993 tour of England and Scotland, meant he was being drawn into managerial roles when he should have been spending more time practising. His throwing-in wasn't up to its usual high standard on that tour and it's hard to focus on the captaincy when you're struggling to get your own game in order.

Suffering so many test losses in 1993 and 1994 was traumatic at the time but those reversals worked in our favour at the World Cup because almost no one rated us, allowing us to slip into South Africa almost unnoticed. The bookies had us as fourth favourites behind Australia, England and France – all of whom had beaten us in the two previous years – while some of the local writers rated us only fifth best, slipping the Springboks in ahead of us as well. It was patently obvious no one had been spying on our World Cup camps or seen us demolish Canada. Laurie Mains couldn't have orchestrated it better if he'd tried. As I've always said, your best opportunities come when you're unannounced.

Laurie was more than a rugby coach. He was also a most resourceful builder, which paid a dividend when we discovered that in Johannesburg, where we were quartered for the World Cup campaign, there was no suitable scrum machine. The South Africans are big into the hydraulic machines, but the All Blacks much prefer the basic sled version where spectators are used for ballast. The difference is that one moves, the other is stationery.

Not prepared to compromise, Laurie declared we'd build our own. He had plans faxed through from New Zealand and despatched the builders in the team, Craig Dowd, Simon Culhane and Robin Brooke, to the local warehouse to buy the necessary equipment and one Sunday afternoon, in what could have passed for an episode of *Home Improvement*, the guys constructed this magnificent machine. It was painted black, naturally, pads attached (they were also black), a Steinlager sticker slapped on the side and it was ready for action. It was a marvellous contraption. We'd get the locals to stand on it for our scrummaging practice and it would squeak and groan, but it served its purpose famously. We took it everywhere. It was ours, which made it very special. At the conclusion of the tournament, we donated it to the school at Sandton where we had trained on many occasions.

Being based in Johannesburg meant we were well acclimatised for our pool matches, all of which were staged at altitude, although altitude had ceased to be a concern for New Zealanders by 1995. Through the Super 10, our players had come to appreciate that operating at 6500ft above sea level was more psychological than anything if you were fit and properly prepared, which we certainly were as the World Cup prepared to kick off.

Having the world media focused on other nations allowed us to ease quietly into the tournament, which was unusual in South Africa where New Zealand always generates interest in matters rugby. There was no hype our way whatsoever, with South African interest focused almost exclusively on the tournament opener between the Springboks and the Wallabies in Cape Town. If the press and the South Africans didn't see us coming, the Irish certainly did. They gave us a fire and brimstone welcome at Ellis Park. God knows what we'd done to fire 'em up, but they almost had steam shooting out of their ears in the opening stages. Prop Gary Halpin gave us the fingers after scoring in the opening moments. Whatever motivational technique their coach used had them fired up like no other team I've ever encountered. If he could bottle it, he'd make a fortune!

The Irish game ushered Jonah Lomu onto the world stage. In swatting green-jerseyed opponents aside contemptuously as he set up and scored tries, he captured the world rugby audience and the media's imagination. Thanks to Jonah, the All Blacks wouldn't want for publicity for the remainder of the tournament, although it would be another week or so before many of the critics, particularly those in England, would acknowledge that there were 14 other players besides Jonah wearing black jerseys.

Unlike the Irish, who'd caught us by surprise, the Welsh ensured we were on full alert because their coach, Australian Alex Evans, couldn't stop blabbing to the media. Despite the fact Wales hadn't beaten New Zealand since 1953, he forecast a glorious victory, somehow concluding that, man for man, his side was superior to ours. An interesting theory which we took great delight in dismantling under lights at Ellis Park. Evans certainly had his team pumped up and they pursued a rugged, spoiling game. I found myself up against my namesake, a Jones called Derwyn, who at 6ft 10in was the tallest player I'd ever marked. It can't be fun being a Jones in Wales. When I checked out the phone book on one visit to Cardiff, I found the Joneses occupied about four pages.

Although the Welsh encounter was probably the least spectacular of our performances leading up to the grand final, it was enormously satisfying for the forwards. We kind of hijacked the occasion. I know Laurie was annoyed later that we'd compromised the all-out attacking game which we'd committed ourselves to, but in a weird way we were probably reacting more to the Welsh coach's utterances than to our own that night.

What we quantified was our ability to change tactics to meet the demands of the situation. Inflexibility had been substituted with inventiveness and an overall confidence to try something different. Against the Welsh, that meant replacing standard procedures with four and five man lineouts and speeding everything up. Blair Larsen, my locking partner in those early games while Robin Brooke (still acting out the part of Foodbill) was struggling to get his leg right, was in outstanding form. We scored a couple of our tries from quick, shortened lineouts.

The Japanese game at Bloemfontein was the first test Sean Fitzpatrick had missed since 1986, breaking an amazing sequence of 63 internationals, which, not surprisingly, was the world record. It would be the only gap in Frank Bunce's celebrated test career also. And it was the first occasion I'd been a Dirty Dirty since 1989.

We anticipated a good victory, but 145 points to 17 – bloody hell! Marc Ellis grabbed six tries and as the goalkicker in his test debut Simon Culhane couldn't miss, converting 20 of the 21 tries. The guys had 84 points up by halftime.

After the game, while the players unwound in the dressing room, the Dirty Dirties undertook a strenuous workout under Marty Toomey's guidance. The spectators couldn't have been satisfied with the afternoon's one-sided encounter because a huge crowd stayed behind to watch. I'm sure they'd never seen anything like it as Marty put us through a session of aerobic grids and 15 or so 150s. A good blowout!

Whenever New Zealand plays Scotland, the home team has to wear an alternative strip to avoid a clash of jersey colours. Indeed, my All Black test debut back in 1990 was in a white strip at Carisbrook. As we approached the World Cup quarter-final at Pretoria, neutral territory, the question of which team would change jerseys would be determined by the toss of a coin. Pinetree Meads, our manager, called wrong, so it was white for the All Blacks. We accepted that but we were dirty on the Springboks a fortnight later when they claimed the home team's dressing room at Ellis Park. There is no "home" team in a World Cup and the custom is that the two competing sides on any occasion toss for the home dressing room. There was no toss-up when it came to the final. The Springboks claimed the room with which they were familiar... and that was that!

Once the qualifying action at a World Cup is completed, you have a week between matches, which is a long time in the circumstances, quite different from a tour situation where there are midweek fixtures to focus upon. Because of the intensity of our approach prior to and during the tournament, we adopted a relaxed approach in the week preceding the quarter-final. The hard graft had been done and I guess we needed to conserve energy for the important matches ahead.

We eliminated Scotland 48-30, a game which marked the exit from the international scene of Gavin Hastings, one of rugby's outstanding achievers and personalities. Most teams would be thrilled to head off Scotland by 18 points but we were frankly rather disappointed in our performance at Pretoria. It gave Laurie plenty to work on in the lead-up to the semi-final.

The English were cock-a-hoop after their victory over the Australians, having avenged the result in the final of the 1991 World Cup. When you lose a quarter-final, you're out, so the hapless Aussies were winging their way back home as we launched into an intensive week of training. Laurie produced his How-To-Combat-The-Poms master plan, which he'd had filed away for a couple of months, and we swung into action. I'm not sure what tactical plan Laurie had prepared in the event Bob Dwyer's Wallabies had beaten England. Obviously, he just knew…!

We really stepped up the intensity in our preparation. If we were a 6.5 on the scale previously, we were now at about 9.8. These next two matches were what we had been building towards for four years. Now was when we needed to peak – for 80 minutes against England at Newlands which, hopefully, would carry us through to the final at Ellis Park. Our opponent, we knew having watched the first (soggy) semi-final in Durban, would be South Africa.

It's rarely that everything you plan for comes to fruition in the heat of battle. Human frailties and luck being what they are, inevitability something, or someone, will stuff up. Or the enemy will thwart your best-laid plans. Usually, if you achieve 70% of what you've plotted, you're doing well. At Newlands, on a gloriously sunny June afternoon in the semi-final of rugby's greatest show on earth, the World Cup, for the opening hour we managed 100% of what we'd planned.

Make that 150%, because not one of the All Blacks, nor coach Laurie Mains, I'm sure, ever dreamed that going into the final quarter of this critical encounter we would be ahead by 35 points to three!

Everything we'd trained for came off. Everything. The kickoff to the left worked a treat, with Will Carling, pressured by Jonah, knocking on and yielding a scrum from which, after an initial backline thrust to the right, Jonah scored (taking the direct route over the top of Mike Catt to do so). Within two minutes we were across again, after Josh Kronfeld capitalised on

Ross Setford, Fotopacific

Mike Catt's head-on tackle would have stopped most wingers, but not Jonah the Giant who was in awesome form in the World Cup semi-final against England in 1995.

an electrifying break from inside his own 22 by Walter Little.

Often when points come so effortlessly at the start, a team can lose momentum as the opposition sets out determined to retrieve the situation. Not that day. Against bigger opponents, we controlled the lineouts and moved the ball wide and at speed, bewildering them with the tempo of our play. Jonah the Giant added the finishing touches in spectacular fashion. And if all that didn't thoroughly disillusion them, Zinny's long-range dropped goal most certainly must have. You could see the dismay in their faces. They'd already been blown over by our intensity and now here was a forward drop-kicking a goal. What else can these guys do?

People afterwards asked if revenge – for the loss at Twickenham in 1993 – had been a motivating factor in our preparation and seemed genuinely surprised when I said no. If you think revenge, you cease to focus on the game at hand. Performing well and outsmarting the opposition brings its own satisfaction. Revenge takes care of itself.

The icing on the cake was Graeme Bachop's try which took us out to 35-3. It's damned hard to score from a set piece at that level, but we managed it that time. Zinny had called a move which Bruiser (Mike Brewer) countermanded. Bruiser was confident his move would expose the shortcomings in pace of England's giant loosies, which is precisely what happened.

It didn't pass our attention that the English players and officials gloated at the dinner that followed their Twickenham victory in '93. We absorbed it at the time, confident our turn would come. We couldn't have planned the retribution better if we'd tried. If a 45-29 scoreline wasn't satisfaction enough, South African Airways provided the ultimate bonus. They allocated the winning team seats in business class, while the vanquished had to make do with economy class. Not only that, but we were invited to board the plane first and the hapless Englishmen had to walk past us. A double blow for the losers. I remember thinking, "I must wipe the smile from my face," after the fourth player had gone past!

Laurie Mains had a premonition, or maybe it was just a deep-rooted fear, that someone might try and nobble us in the run-in to the final. It wasn't obtuse thinking, because vast amounts of money had been wagered on the World Cup and apparently the UK bookies stood to lose a small fortune if New Zealand won. Taking nothing for granted, Laurie asked the management of the Crowne Plaza Hotel if we could fly in our own chef from Cape Town. Probably not surprisingly, the request was declined.

Until the fateful lunch on the Thursday, the test preparations had gone swimmingly. We'd needed a couple of days to rebound from our monumental performance in Cape Town, a display which had plainly captivated the rugby world. Jonah Lomu had already stamped himself the commanding personality of the tournament. Now his four tries against England had correspondents worldwide searching for fresh superlatives.

It was important for us to put the English performance behind us. The World Cup wasn't won yet and a proud Springbok team stood between us and the fulfilment of our objectives. Because no one, not even Laurie, had anticipated the South Africans making it through to the final, we didn't have a How-To-Beat-The-Boks plan filed away, as for England at Cape Town. Under Kitch Christie's guidance, the South Africans' game plan appeared basic but it was obvious they were being swept along on an emotional high with, seemingly, the support of the entire Rainbow Nation. That had to be worth half a dozen points at least in a grand final at Ellis Park.

A lot of the All Blacks were fans of the Irish band The Commitments, so when Andrew Strong, their lead singer, turned out to be staying in our hotel in Johannesburg, it was cause for a level of excitement. He was in South Africa, he told some of the boys, doing promotional work for the group's next recording, due for release later in 1995.

We adopted him for a few days. A carton of Steinlager was delivered to his room, we loaned him an All Black leisure jacket, we gave him tickets to the Welsh game and arranged transport to Ellis Park aboard our security van. And we welcomed him into the changing room after our fine victory. He was encouraged to give us a rendition of "Mustang Sally" but he declined, saying he had a sore throat.

He was thriving on the star treatment which may have continued had not Mike Brewer telephoned his wife Bev in Dublin later that night. Bev's parents were close friends of Andrew Strong, and Mike, in magnanimous mood, insisted "Andrew" have a word to his wife. She soon identified him as an imposter.

He turned out to be a classic con artist who'd pulled the same trick with the Irish players a few days earlier. He was an Andrew Strong look-a-like who couldn't sing at all! We claimed our jacket back and sent him on his way.

The dilemma the All Black management faced on the Friday was whether to announce to the world that almost their entire squad was knocked flat with an illness, believed to be food poisoning. What would it achieve? It would alert the Springboks to the fact that their opponents in the final were weakened, that's for sure. Because the world's sporting communication networks were to be focused on Johannesburg on the Saturday afternoon – with a combined audience of hundreds of millions – there surely was no prospect of postponing the kickoff. We weren't going to default. So the show had to go on.

Ellis Park, one of the great rugby stadiums of the world, provided a perfect setting for the final. To be involved there in a World Cup final against the Springboks was surely the ultimate for a New Zealand rugby player. The disasters of Thursday evening and Friday morning behind us, we'd condensed our focus onto what we anticipated would be 80 minutes of desperate endeavour. In the event, it became 100 minutes.

We saw no reason to vary the tactics which had overwhelmed all five of our opponents. Like most of our major rivals, the Springboks had bigger forwards. We knew they would prefer a confrontational game and it was our intention to move them rapidly around Ellis Park and exhaust them. Thanks to the gutbusting efforts demanded by Laurie at the camps back at Taupo and Christchurch, and subsequent to team selection, we knew our stamina levels would survive anything. Anything except, perhaps, debilitating food poisoning.

The early signs were encouraging. Our scrum was strong, our lineout was working a treat and we were piecing together sweeping attacks which had the Springbok defence on full alert and we had our noses in front.

As the game developed and we strove to increase the pace, we found we were struggling to get wide in numbers. Whereas against England we'd consistently hit the breakdowns en masse, now only individuals were reporting for duty. Guys were finding themselves two or three metres short of where they wanted to be.

The South African defence was amazing, it must be conceded, but it shouldn't have prevented us from creating try-scoring opportunities. There was an unfamiliar lethargy apparent and I guess you wouldn't have to be a genius to relate that to the poisoning and the fact we hadn't slept well for two nights.

Parts of our game functioned incredibly well, such as the lineout. I'd managed to shrug off the effects of the illness almost completely, while Robin Brooke and Fitzy, our thrower, had been unaffected. We not only secured all our own possession, we managed to smuggle across several of the South African throws as well. So we weren't short of ball. It was in speed and effectiveness around the field where we were lacking.

The surest sign we were battling came when the talking ceased. It's one of the first indications that players are struggling. In fact, we were more than struggling… we were buggered. All Blacks are always talking among themselves, planning, encouraging each other. Not that day. Silence set in. The frustration was that we knew we had the ability to get to the breakdowns and make things happen, but we were depowered. The Springbok defence played a part in all of this but if we'd had the legs we had at Newlands, we would have overcome that.

In the circumstances, you'd think with the scoreboard reading 9-all, we'd be depressed at the prospect of having to play 20 minutes extra time. But the mood was positive. Notwithstanding the agonies of the previous few days, we'd prepared for this. We knew we were fitter than any opponent. When we were close to exhaustion at Taupo and Laurie was taunting us with questions like, "Do you think the Springboks are training this hard?" we knew they weren't.

Some of us felt we were coming right as we gulped down Powerade at the 80-minute mark. I felt I was getting my second wind. Some guys, like Goldie (Jeff Wilson) and Craig Dowd, had succumbed to the poisoning and been replaced, but for the 15 of us still on the field, there was a grim determination to pull this off. Let's get down the Springboks' end of the field and win. Let's make it happen.

It wasn't to be. Although Mehrts gave us the early advantage with a penalty goal, Joel Stransky soon levelled the scores and then ensured himself of immortality by drop-kicking the winning goal a minute or so before the final whistle. The Boks had won 15-12 and the crowd went wild, as did the whole of South Africa. At their first crack at a World Cup, they were the champions, leaving us to ponder the might-have-beens.

Nothing can adequately describe my feelings – and I know that covers all my team-mates – in those minutes after Ed Morrison blew his whistle to signal the conclusion of the 1995 World Cup. The accolades after our sensational performance against England and the claims we'd lifted the game to a new stratum of excellence mattered not at this moment. We had lost the World Cup final.

I'm sure I speak for the entire All Black squad when I say I wish the Springboks had put 30 points on us. Then as we stood by as Francois Pienaar and his mighty men of South Africa went forward to receive their gold medals from Nelson Mandela, we wouldn't have felt quite so wretched. We would have known the better team had won. But to this day I don't accept the better team won the 1995 championship of the world. Oh, the better team on that afternoon at Ellis Park won, for sure. We had 100 minutes each to make an impact on the scoreboard and South Africa finished up with 15 points to our 12. Finish and klar, as the Afrikaaners say. But had our food not been doctored on the Thursday, how different things might have been.

If the presentation ceremony was hard to bear, so were aspects of the World Cup dinner, staged that evening at a function centre north of Johannesburg. The preliminaries went well enough and we fraternised with the English players who were at the table next to us. Video screens were featuring highlights of the tournament, except that nearly all of them seemed to feature a certain team captained by Francois Pienaar. Wasn't there anyone else in this tournament?

Then came Louis Luyt's extraordinary speech in which he suggested that New Zealand in 1987 and Australia in 1991 were not true world champions because the Springboks had not been present and that the current event was the first true world championship. It was amazing that anyone could even think that, let alone utter it in front of such a distinguished audience.

If that wasn't bad enough, he then requested Welsh referee Derek Bevan, who'd handled South Africa's critical games against Australia and France, to step forward, and presented him with a gold watch. Ed Morrison, who'd controlled the final, didn't get one and nor did any other referee. Bevan was the chosen one because, in Louis' eyes, he'd done the right thing by South Africa. "This man is my referee of the tournament," declared Big Louis. Goodness knows what the other referees were thinking. If Louis Luyt knows humility, he certainly didn't demonstrate any of it that evening.

There were reports that immediately after Louis' outburst the All Blacks and players from several other nations walked out. That's not true. We were appalled at the South African rugby president's comments and some individuals, Mike Brewer and Paul Henderson among them, let Louis know

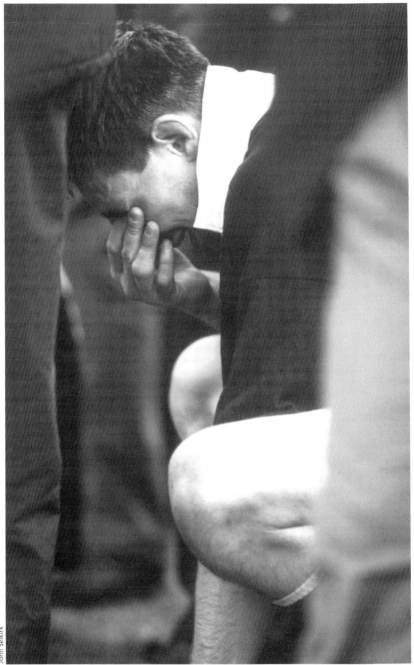

John Selkirk

All Blacks don't cry. Except perhaps when a World Cup you'd prepared for so painstakingly eludes you in the most agonising circumstances, as at Ellis Park in 1995.

what they thought of him. But we didn't depart until the dessert was being served. It was South Africa's night and, notwithstanding the unbelievable arrogance of their leading administrator, we stayed on to honour their victory. Besides, Colin Meads and Louis Luyt were old friends, and I doubt Pinetree would have sanctioned a walkout by his team.

While there was satisfaction in knowing we'd set new standards in the game during the World Cup, we were left holding silver medals while the Springboks had the gold. After retreating to our hotel, there was only one thing for it – to drown our sorrows.

Kevin Roberts, representing our generous sponsor Steinlager, wouldn't allow the guys to think negatively. "You've got to come back and beat these bastards on their own soil next year," he declared, "and prove you are the best team in the world." In a performance worthy of its own gold medal, Kevin confronted endless individuals that night with the same message, sealing each pact by downing a bottle of Guinness. Kevin didn't make it out of bed the next day, but he'd fired the troops with determination to gain revenge in 1996.

News Media

9

The Professionals

I look back to the beginning of that 1995 World Cup campaign as the last age of innocence. We entered that season thinking that our chance to create All Black history, to create rugby history that year, centred on winning the World Cup in South Africa. Little did we know that we were about to become players in another kind of campaign – one that would make something like the World Cup seem as straightforward as a game of knucklebones in the playground.

It was the Tuesday before the World Cup final that we first learned that rugby, the last great bastion of amateurism, was going to turn professional. The news came out of the blue: we were simply told that the chairmen of the New Zealand, Australian and South African rugby unions (Richie Guy, Leo Williams and Dr Louis Luyt respectively) had put together a $555 million, 10-year deal with business billionaire Rupert Murdoch for a three-way professional competition – later to emerge as the Tri-nations and the Super 12 series. Details were sketchy, and we all knew our focus at that time had to remain squarely on the upcoming final. But we all hit the sack that night feeling elated. At long last we were going to be professional!

But two days later came developments even further out of the blue. A group of the "DDs" – including Eric Rush and Mike Brewer – were approached by an Australian named Michael Hill about a rival professional competition supposedly being backed by Kerry Packer, Murdoch's arch enemy. They were invited out to lunch at Harry Viljoen's place in Johannesburg. Viljoen, a rugby man from way back and a successful businessman, was on board with these people in South Africa where they would listen to an even more amazing plan to professionalise rugby. The key difference was that this one – put forward by some Australian business people calling themselves The World Rugby Corporation – was going to create a *global* professional competition.

That evening, all the players gathered together in a room as Eric and Mike reported the details of their meeting with the WRC representatives. We could hardly believe the situation we suddenly found ourselves in. Not only were we about to turn professional, but here were people bidding for our services!

We were all impressed by the WRC concept, it sounded really good and fair. What's more, it was quite detailed and the money was, frankly, seductive. The payment structure had already been worked out. It would be tiered into five levels. The top bracket was "the Jonah Lomu tier" – he had made such an impact at the World Cup that he was now world famous, in a class of his own. He would receive $US1.5 million over three years. After Jonah, the next best 15 to 20 international players (in the WRC's opinion, based on World Cup performances) would receive $US725,000 over three years. The rest of the players would get between $US200,000 and $US300,000.

There really wasn't a lot of fuss about it from our point of view: this was great!

There was certainly no shortage of things to talk about on the long flight home to New Zealand. Back home, we'd been invited to a parliamentary reception with Jim Bolger in Wellington. Downtown Wellington also being the home of the NZRFU's headquarters, it was arranged by the NZRFU that we'd head straight from Parliament to a meeting with Richie Guy where he would outline the SANZAR deal, as it had become known, with Murdoch, and what would be in it for us.

By this stage, all the players had a good knowledge of what the WRC had been offering. The WRC had impressed the black socks off us, quite frankly. They'd thought of everything and were offering a thoroughly professional contract. But we were prepared to listen to both sides, both offers.

Now, with all respect to Richie, his address at the NZRFU seemed very *unprofessional* by comparison to the WRC. We sat in a darkened room as Richie pointed to a whiteboard trying to explain that if we played every test match in 1996, we had the potential to make $150,000. Having played for nothing more than honour and glory himself, Richie must have been quite mystified as we sat there decidedly unimpressed by our sudden opportunity to earn such a handsome salary. We certainly weren't kneeling in gratitude or jumping for joy.

But Richie didn't have any inkling at this stage that he had a competitor. The NZRFU was completely in the dark. Unfortunately, what he was offering on behalf of the NZRFU just didn't stack up. It wasn't even in the same ball park – between one-third and one-fifth of the money the WRC was offering.

It wasn't just the amount of money, but the fact that none of it was guaranteed and there was no insurance backing, which were key concerns for us players. If you weren't selected or you were injured, it seemed you'd be left high and dry under the NZRFU's proposal. Some of us were also a bit miffed that the deal had been signed with Murdoch without so much as consulting a player's representative about what we thought of the proposed competition.

None of us mentioned a bean about the WRC proposal, but, armed with the knowledge of the WRC offer and the kinds of issues Richie should really have been addressing in a meeting like this, we started raining questions. What if you were injured? Where was the insurance? Was any of this money guaranteed? Richie seemed unprepared, unsure of his ground and nervous about answering. We left the meeting agreeing that the NZRFU's proposal didn't seem very "professional" at all.

Richie would have keeled over if he'd known what we did next. Unbeknown to him, when we left the NZRFU building we headed straight to the Airport Motor Inn for a secret meeting with Geoff Levy (the Sydney lawyer who'd dreamed up the WRC idea), Andy Haden (the WRC's agent in New Zealand) and Derek Dallow, a rugby man (he's a North Harbour board representative) and lawyer from Davenports in Takapuna, the firm which also employs Eric Rush. Davenports were to represent the WRC in New Zealand. In a briefcase they had contracts ready for us to sign.

This was more like it. The WRC had all the details worked out and sewn up into glossy printed pamphlets. They were able to answer all of our questions, and then some. They went over everything we'd learned in Johannesburg in detail: the concept, the payment structure, the player guarantees. In return we had to sign a confidentiality contract there and then, which we all did.

The 26 players in the All Black squad left that meeting with plenty to think about and discuss amongst ourselves. The WRC proposal hinged on their ability to sign up enough players around the world by November 22, 1995. That was the deadline they set to obtain financial backing, the day they would know whether their competition would be a runner or not. If they didn't have either funds in excess of $US100 million or contracts for sufficient television rights etc by that date, the whole exercise would be written off.

The WRC were confident they were going to get all the players, but they couldn't get the money to pay them and fund the competition until they had enough players signed up to satisfy a backer – which we understood would be Kerry Packer's empire. The NZRFU, meanwhile, already had a backer – Rupert Murdoch. All they had to do was get the players. This was the fundamental difference between the two camps.

The WRC promised us that if, by November 22, their competition was a goner, they would rip up our contracts, no problem. Most of us were pretty happy with that. But one thing stuck in our throats: we *weren't* happy with the possibility of losing the All Black jersey.

Even though the WRC's stated intention was to "get the unions on board" once they had signed up all their players, there was every chance the unions wouldn't have a bar of some "rebel circus". In fact, knowing some of the administrators involved and the traditionalist stance of the unions, you could bet on it. So there was a real threat that if we signed with the WRC, we weren't going to play for the All Blacks, the official rugby team of New Zealand, anymore. We'd be signing away the symbol of the tradition we upheld, the symbol of New Zealand rugby itself: the All Black jersey. For everyone, that was the most important factor of all. We didn't want to lose the power of the All Black jersey. It was our number-one driving force, and always had been.

Following that year's World Cup, we had a home-and-away Bledisloe Cup test series to contest, one match each in Sydney and Auckland. By now the NZRFU had found out they had a rival for our attention, but they were also conscious of our need to prepare for the Bledisloe Cup. The NZRFU decided it would be inappropriate to distract us with contract negotiations until after the Bledisloe Cup series and gave us our space during the week leading up to the Auckland test. That was very generous of them – but it was also naive. It gave the WRC the opportunity to "get in there first", to beat them to us.

We used the leeway to our advantage, spending much of that week undisturbed in Derek Dallow's office negotiating our WRC contracts (we'd been advised to take them away and consider them independently). By now we were getting right down to the nitty-gritty, talking about which category we should each fall under. Whether you were, in their opinion, a "superstar", a "World XV" player or a "test player".

The NZRFU, meanwhile, honoured their commitment to us and made no contact that week.

The Auckland Bledisloe Cup test behind us, we flew to Sydney. This was to be an emotional match for us, touted by the media as perhaps the last time we'd play together as All Blacks. Perhaps even the end of rugby as we knew it.

At the conclusion of the game, B.J. Lochore handed each of us a letter on behalf of the NZRFU outlining the essence of the contracts that they were going to hand out now that the test series was over. The top players would be paid between $200,000 and $250,000 for our services, 75 per cent of which would be paid in advance, and there'd be a car in it for each of us from Ford whilst we were All Blacks. But still no guarantee or insurance – we had about eight grievances in all. The NZRFU were starting to come up to speed, but they still weren't in the same ball park as the WRC.

A formal reception had been arranged for both teams after the test, but on the way there we convinced the bus driver to detour and drive us to Botany Bay, a swanky part of town where we had secretly arranged to meet with WRC representatives at the house of Brian Powers, Kerry Packer's chief lieutenant. The location was designed to encourage us to believe that the Packer millions were standing behind the WRC dream, but most of us recognised that the WRC still had no guaranteed backer at this point.

Everything was contingent. For the WRC concept to work, a certain number of players had to be signed to their books in each rugby nation, including the cream of the international squads. In New Zealand this number was set at 150. As time went on, the WRC told us they had signed up the required number of top players in most of the other countries around the world. But while we all took the WRC proposal seriously, most of us still hadn't signed any contracts (other than the confidentiality agreement) at this stage. In fact, New Zealand was one of the last countries to sign. We were the hardest ones to convince, partly because of doubts about the financial backing and mainly because of the singular power of the All Black jersey (although once we were committed, we were the WRC's strongest supporters, in many a sense).

As a consequence, the WRC now offered each of the 26 players in the All Black World Cup squad a substantial inducement payment to sign. This payment was nonrefundable even if WRC did not proceed. It was our guarantee, a token of good faith. After all, the stakes for us were high and we were being asked to make a commitment which would mean giving up much of what was certain to us about our careers and rugby.

I don't think players from any other country were offered a similar inducement, just us. Clearly, without the All Blacks, their proposed global competition was going to be like a crown without jewels, so the inducement payment was designed as an incentive for us to commit to the WRC. Described as a nonrefundable payment, it was put in Davenports' trust account where it was to be held on our behalf, pending our signatures on the WRC contracts.

The Botany Bay meeting was the WRC's big chance to sway those players who still hadn't signed with them. When the inducement payment was thrown in, it did the trick. I believe all the remaining All Black players signed that night. I'd actually signed prior to that night. Then we left and went to the post-match dinner. Officially it had been organised to celebrate the occasion of 100 tests between Australia and New Zealand. In the event, we were quietly celebrating something quite different. All around us, meanwhile, tension was brewing. Rugby had been split into two distinct camps.

When we got back to New Zealand, Jock Hobbs, B.J. Lochore and Rob Fisher swung onto the offensive. They toured the country, drumming up support and trying to sign as many provincial players as they could to the

NZRFU. They were zeroing in on the second tier of New Zealand players, the likes of Errol Brain and Stephen Bachop – players who might become All Blacks very quickly if the WRC went ahead and skimmed New Zealand of its World Cup squad. Here something finally went right for the NZRFU. Naturally enough, all players want to be as well looked after as possible and the NZRFU were in a position to offer provincial players a better deal than the WRC. For one thing, under the WRC concept these guys would have had to do a heck of a lot of travelling, perhaps even be based in another country, with very little say in the matter.

The Auckland/North Harbour-based players met up with this NZRFU roadshow at the Auckland Centra. It was here that I was handed my NZRFU contract, which I noted was coming a wee bit more up to speed. But again, having now received a guarantee from the WRC, all of us in the All Blacks were able to compare documents and understand that a guarantee should have been forthcoming in the NZRFU contract. It wasn't.

And so negotiations continued. At this stage, the All Blacks were very strong on the WRC. We had their guarantee, they had our commitment and, with all the other rugby countries falling into line, it seemed that come November 22 we'd pioneer a brave new, global rugby world. The WRC were confident they had the upper hand. Almost everything was in place, now they were just tweaking the screws. And then....

And then we had the video conference. The WRC set up a link between Australia, New Zealand and South Africa. It was a chance for the players from each of these key nations to confirm they were on board and reassure each other.

First Australia came on screen. There sat Phil Kearns, together with Geoff Levy and Ross Turnbull, the Australian masterminds of the whole WRC concept, and a few of the other Wallabies. Phil told the conference that Australia was committed to it, that they'd signed the required number of players there. "We're really excited about it," he said. "It's going to be a goer."

Then it was our turn. The New Zealand conference team was Sean Fitzpatrick, Eric Rush, Mike Brewer, Derek Dallow and myself. Sean spoke for us and said pretty much the same thing as Phil Kearns. We'd got 150 players signed to the cause, we were tight, we thought it was going well.

That left South Africa. We crossed to Johannesburg, expecting to see Springbok captain Francois Pienaar on screen. But instead it was Hennie Le Roux who spoke his name and started to speak. We could see that James Small was sitting beside him, but there was no Francois Pienaar. In fact, we couldn't see anyone from Transvaal at all. Immediately the alarm bells rang. Transvaal was not only home to the bulk of the Springbok World Cup squad (including Pienaar, their inspirational and influential captain, the man who'd held the World Cup above his shoulders), but it was Louis Luyt's stronghold. Had Luyt got to them? What was going on? Hell, where were they?

Sean said, "Where's Francois?"

Le Roux replied they were having some problems with the Transvaal contingent. The Natal and Western Province players and "the guys from sea level" were strong, they were tight. But up in Transvaal there was a hitch.

Right from the moment we first got wind of the WRC proposal, the All Black squad had always been agreed and very strong on the point that the only way the WRC was ever going to be a winner was that if every rugby player in the world bought into the concept. There was no use the All Blacks and Wallabies going if South Africa was staying. It would be the demise of international rugby, because we would no longer be playing against the top Springboks, while the Springboks wouldn't be playing against the top All Black side. When Francois didn't appear on screen that night, we knew inside that it was all over.

The story we eventually heard was that Louis Luyt, at his most ropable, had turned up to a Transvaal training run that day, herded the players into the training shed and sacked the lot of them on the spot. Then he had physically written out their first year's cheques in front of them, offering them the chance of reinstatement. He said, "Either stay for this, or go and you'll never be back." That was why Francois Pienaar never showed up for the video conference: he'd already signed with the South African Rugby Union, as had another 14 Transvaal players.

Back in New Zealand, our WRC contracts had essentially been the basis of our negotiations with the NZRFU. They were our bargaining chip, and a pretty powerful one at that. Now, privately, most of us thought our WRC contracts were worthless. The NZRFU contracts assumed more importance as we all went back to consult our lawyers.

A week or two passed by until it was mid-August and we were all counting down to kickoff for that year's NPC. I headed down to Wellington for a North Harbour game; at the same time the Otago team was winging its way north for another fixture. Otago had stopped off at Wellington Airport, whereupon the players had met with Jock Hobbs. That night, August 10, I watched the news to discover that Josh Kronfeld and Jeff Wilson had signed with the NZRFU.

I still hadn't done anything about my NZRFU contract at this stage. Now I knew for sure that there would be no alternative but to sign. Not only had Josh and Jeff gone, but a big swag of provincial players had signed, including most of Otago and, I understand, the entire Auckland backline. That Sunday, after we'd touched down back in Auckland, Geoff Levy rang Sean Fitzpatrick to set up a phone conference. "It's all over," he told us pragmatically. "Patch up your relationship with the NZRFU; you guys are free to do as you like."

That same morning the NZRFU rang around the remaining 24 World Cup players (Jeff and Josh excepted) to set up a meeting the following day at the Airport Motor Inn back down in Wellington. Previously, Jock Hobbs had looked like a man with the weight of the world on his shoulders. Now he strode into the room beaming, full of confidence. There was no choice anymore. We had to settle our differences with the NZRFU, and he knew it.

After Jock underlined to the squad that the only option available to us now was to sign with the NZRFU, we went up one at a time to one of the motel rooms, where Jock and a couple of lawyers from Kensington Swan sat holding our contracts – the same ones that had been given to us during the NZRFU roadshow.

Once again, we were advised to take them away and make sure we got an independent legal opinion before signing, which I duly did. Jock even recommended a lawyer to me, David Jones (no relation), someone who was always referred to as "DOJ", pronounced Dodge. Before I left, though, I had to list all my existing contracts in a schedule, outlining the expiry details on each – sponsorship contracts and the like. Provided I did that there and then at this meeting with Jock, Jock said the NZRFU would then honour my right to see out these contracts. In particular I had a sponsorship/endorsement contract with Nike. I wrote it down in the schedule, Jock as my witness. I still wasn't happy with my NZRFU contract in part, but I took it away and, when I got to Auckland, rang David Jones.

Even though the WRC was washed up, I believe the entire 1995 WRC episode was very important to us in All Black history. The reason is that it taught us, as amateur players, about the nature of contracts and how to deal with negotiations before we came to negotiate professional contracts with the NZRFU for the first time. When we sat down to discuss a contract with the NZRFU, we'd already been through the process before; we weren't completely green. I've no doubt it saved us from making costly mistakes. We'd also learned the value of lawyers and how to seek and use professional advice – things most of us knew little about before the 1995 "rugby war".

A case in point was the financial aftermath of the WRC proposal. When I sought legal advice from DOJ Jones, he quickly pointed out that even though the WRC wasn't able to kick off as planned on November 22, legally we were entitled to the inducement payment which had been paid into Davenports' trust account on our behalf.

But it appeared the WRC were now reneging on this deal. When they realised they were history, they'd started ringing around players and saying, "Look, if you waive your right to the inducement payment, we'll let you enter into contract negotiations with the NZRFU without a fight."

The fact of the matter is the WRC couldn't stop us from signing with the NZRFU – the contract we had signed with the WRC was entirely conditional on their competition going ahead, and by now it was clear that it wasn't. Secondly, the inducement payment was a contractual guarantee: it was to be paid whether or not the competition went ahead. Legally, there was no way we weren't entitled to that money.

Incredibly, the majority of players nevertheless signed away their entitlement to that guaranteed payment. Some of them were young players, players on the rise who simply didn't want to rock the boat or get into a public scrap with the WRC. But others were simply ignorant of their rights. In the end, just five of us actually stood up for our rights to that money, on legal advice.

Those few who stood up for themselves eventually reached a settlement with the WRC. The terms of that settlement are confidential, but it's fair to say that both sides were happy. It was a big lesson for the rest of the players: it came down to who was smart enough to get legal advice. The thing is, none of the players had ever been in a situation like this before, so they didn't know what they could do. What's more, they weren't accustomed to dealing with professional advisers – and some were scared of them; they probably thought they'd lose the shirts off their backs in the process of hiring them.

At least we weren't so green when Jock Hobbs handed out the NZRFU contracts in Wellington. In fact, after our dealings with the WRC and with the legal professionals we'd met in the process, I think players actually had a better understanding than the rugby union as to what should really be in a player contract. The big problem was that we no longer had any negotiating power. After checking the fine print with our lawyers, most of us ended up signing without much fuss.

Finally (phew!) we could pop the champagne and celebrate the dawn of rugby's professional age. But I was to discover that turning professional had a tendency to create almost as many problems as it solved…

Early in the following year, the phone rang. It was DOJ: " Ian, you'd better pop in and see me. They're trying to change your contract."

Now, that particular week a life-size cardboard advertisement I'd done for Philips had gone on display at appliance stores round the country. In the ad I wore Nike boots, since I had a sponsorship and endorsement contract with Nike. No sooner had this ad gone on display than Tony Ward, the NZRFU's contract manager, was on the phone to me. He was spitting tacks: "Kamo, what the hell do you think you're doing? You know full well that we've just signed Mizuno as the All Black footwear sponsor. This is a slap in the face to Mizuno, it's not on, you can't do this."

I replied, "But Tony, I can do this. If you go and have a look at the contract that you guys signed, you'll verify it."

Of course, when Tony checked the contract he discovered that, yes indeed, the NZRFU had legally agreed to honour any player's pre-existing sponsorship and endorsement contracts so long as they listed them in the schedule, which I had done as required. What's more, the man who had told me to do this, and witnessed it, was Jock Hobbs. Now, Jock was not only a lawyer and NZRFU councillor and official negotiator of the NZRFU at the time we signed that contract, but, by a curious coincidence, Mizuno's agent, the man who represented Mizuno in New Zealand. Hobbs already knew full well that I was legally entitled to endorse Nike apparel and footwear. How on earth could Hobbs and the NZRFU suddenly have a problem with it?

I wasn't the only player in this situation. Jeff Wilson and Josh Kronfeld also had pre-existing contracts with Nike and therefore were entitled to endorse Nike's boots instead of Mizuno's. Having checked the contract and realised I was fully within my rights, Tony Ward rang back to apologise. But a letter to my lawyer revealed that the NZRFU wasn't satisfied. They returned my signed contract to DOJ with a note asking him to have me initial a change they'd made. The change basically said that the NZRFU would approve endorsements for my own sponsors on condition that I did not carry out any promotion or endorsement of products in my capacity as an All Black or as a member of a Super 12 or NPC team!

DOJ hit the roof. I mean, this was totally contrary to the agreement we'd already signed, which stated that "the contractor shall be entitled to carry out promotions, undertake promotional services and endorse products and services pursuant to any contract in existence as at the date the contractor is signing this contract." That was the deal, in black and white. And now here they were trying to renege!

My guess is that they simply got cold feet when they saw my Philips ad. They suddenly realised that they could have a real problem here with their own sponsor. But the time to think about such things is before you sign the dotted line, not afterwards. DOJ wrote back and told the NZRFU that the deal as signed and accepted was the deal and not up for renegotiation. The NZRFU couldn't now turn around and change that deal just because it didn't suit any more.

The stakes were raised. The NZRFU replied, through its lawyers, that it had decided that players who chose to undertake promotions or endorse products or services which were in competition with the NZRFU's sponsors would not be selected as All Blacks. They added, "It is therefore academic whether or not the legal position as set out in your letter is correct."

In other words, they didn't care that I was legally in the right!

Suddenly relations became quite tense. A string of correspondence ensued between my lawyer, Jeff and Josh's lawyers and the NZRFU. This culminated some time later in a meeting in Wellington with a number of NZRFU representatives. Richie Guy started reading the riot act, insisting that we honour the official All Black sponsorship deals. We insisted the NZRFU honour the contract it had signed allowing us to continue work for our own sponsors whether or not they were in conflict with the NZRFU's interests. Incredibly (in view of all the legal correspondence), Richie retaliated, "You haven't got contracts which say that!"

So DOJ pulled out my contract and said, "Let me read it to you."

Richie listened. Then he said, "Aw, that's all legal gobbledygook! That's not what it means."

"Well, that's not the position we're taking."

Stalemate.

As the first test of the 1996 season drew ever closer, the matter assumed more and more importance. Nevertheless, during the weeklong build-up to the first test Jeff, Josh and I trained without problem. No one from All Black management pressured us to wear Mizuno boots, the rest of the players understood and were supportive and as far as we were concerned it was no big deal: the lawyers would continue arguing about it, in the meantime we were wearing our Nikes. However, behind the scenes the All Black management were apparently under pressure to have us wear Mizunos. In fact, the night before the test and unbeknown to us, Harty and Mike Banks had spoken to DOJ and Jeff and Josh's lawyers about our contractual rights to wear Nike boots.

Then came the bombshell. The morning of the test (it was a night game at McLean Park), we got wind that an NZRFU meeting had been held in Wellington where it had been decided that if we weren't prepared to wear Mizuno boots that day, we would be dropped from the All Blacks.

With kickoff only hours away, it was beyond belief. On the morning of a test match, that's the last thing any coach is going to do – and the last thing any player wants to hear. Our mental build-up for the match was affected as a result. We were confused instead of concentrated. But John Hart and Mike Banks came through supporting us to the hilt, saying there was no way they'd allow us to be dropped.

During that morning, Harty had been in further contact with DOJ and the NZRFU, trying to get to the bottom of the issue (the NZRFU had told Harty that we were all to wear Mizunos, end of story). On behalf of the NZRFU, Kevin Roberts was even trying to contact the head honcho at Nike headquarters in Portland, Oregon to see if we could wear Nikes with the swoosh blackened). Harty meanwhile inquired whether we could wear Mizunos with the brand names blackened, but Nike New Zealand wouldn't wear it. DOJ, meanwhile, had been flat out trying to resolve the issue, even threatening a High Court injunction if that's what it took to stop the NZRFU dropping us and to force them to honour our perfectly valid contracts.

Later that afternoon, Josh, Jeff and I were told to meet John Hart in Mike Banks' room. I was worried. Had the NZRFU put their foot down, told Harty we weren't to play? Nervous, I rang DOJ and asked him to advise Harty of my final position before I went along for this meeting. No problem. In fact, DOJ had been in contact with the other lawyers and on their behalf told Harty that the three of us would be wearing our Nike boots since we had a right to do so and a failure to honour the Nike contract would have adverse financial consequences.

Harty replied, "Oh well, if that's the case, they can't play." DOJ replied, "Well, that's your call; there is nothing further I can do."

In the meantime, Josh, Jeff and I had knocked on the door, unaware of the words Harty had just spoken. He turned to us, smiled and said, "Everything's fine, you're playing. All the best." It was brinkmanship!

I ended up packing three pairs of boots in my kit that evening: my Nike boots, a pair of Mizuno boots and a pair of blacked-out Mizuno boots. When it came down to it, it was my call which ones I'd play in. But it was hardly the sort of question I needed weighing on my mind during the countdown to a test match. One thing that helped was that Harty and Mike told Jeff, Josh and me that if the board directed them to drop us, they would resign. Whether that was ever going to be the case, I don't know, but that's what they told us. It was good to have at least some official support.

The epilogue to the whole absurd situation is that, in time, Nike came to an agreement with the NZRFU. This agreement meant that we switched to Mizuno boots halfway through the subsequent tour of South Africa – Nike had granted a moratorium on condition that discussions be continued. Eventually there was a further agreement between Nike and the NZRFU that meant we would stay in Mizuno boots until the end of 1998.

If you read the newspapers, you'll know it was reported that, at best, Nike had negotiated "an arrangement" by which they would become the next sponsor of the rugby union – that was understood to be the reason they generously allowed us to wear Mizuno boots. At worst, there was believed to be an understanding that they would be the preferred bidder. A relatively short time later the NZRFU signed an exclusive boot deal…with adidas.

Today, two years on, I'm still affected by the whole mess. My NZRFU contract expires on December 31 this year. At the same time, I'll still have a contractual obligation to Nike. With the NZRFU having secured an exclusive boot deal with adidas, I'm going to have legal difficulties finalising a new contract because the fact of the matter is I'm still contracted to one of adidas' rivals.

It raises the question: why did the NZRFU allow the pre-existing sponsorship clause in the first place? Well, travel round the world a bit and you'll soon see that the All Blacks are the odd men out. You only have to look at the big soccer teams in England to see that while there will always be an official team footwear sponsor, individual players maintain their own sponsorship deals. Official team sponsors get to leverage the team profile and brand for all its worth, that's what they pay for, but individuals remain free to negotiate their own professional contracts. So, while Company A might be the official team footwear sponsor, the players can still wear Company B boots. It's the same in America.

I think the NZRFU clause might have been a recognition of this, an acknowledgement that in embracing professionalism they should move away from enforcing a "team sponsor" to allowing their new professionals to negotiate their own professional contracts. But instead they're going the other way.

There are significant implications for the All Blacks. First, the number of "official NZRFU sponsors" is increasing all the time. Given the expectation that players will not endorse or promote any rivals to these official sponsors, it means that we're very restricted in terms of finding our own endorsement contracts – especially if the NZRFU has already covered the market.

Secondly, under the terms of the NZRFU contract, players must give their time each year to do a certain amount of endorsement work for the NZRFU's official sponsors. Players must do this for nothing. The union's answer to that is that we're not "doing it for nothing", we're getting our money for playing rugby and that money comes from the sponsors. That's all very well, but it means that a lot of players get overexposed in the process – they can't go out and get their own contracts because prospective companies will say we're too well known for doing such-and-such for a competitor or whomever.

What's more, a player is only paid if he is selected to play. That means that if you're not selected, even though you're not being paid, you still have an obligation to go and do endorsements for the NZRFU!

Hopefully this sort of unfairness will be worked out over the next few years, but it illustrates the monumental leap in thinking we had to make as we crossed the blurred line from amateur to professional in 1995. So the WRC was a very important chapter for us, in the final analysis. Without the WRC experience, it's unlikely players would have had the nous to even ask the NZRFU for something as standard (in other sports) as player insurance or to stand up for their rights on other issues. It was Derek Dallow of Davenports, then acting for the WRC, who first taught me what to look for in a contract. Both my own lawyer, David Jones, and John Hart would further train me as a professional – Harty very quickly organised seminars for us when he became New Zealand's first coach of the pro era. But there's no doubt about it, the WRC did wonders for New Zealand rugby and for the players at a critical time in our history. They really hauled everyone, players and unions, into the professional era. Not only that, but they brought them up to speed quicker than might have happened otherwise.

Having said that, in hindsight I'm very happy with the direction in which our rugby's gone. I'm glad we signed with the NZRFU in the end. There have been teething problems, sure, but the union came up to speed in most areas, particularly with better insurance clauses, better guarantees, better incentives. We've been allowed to work pretty closely with the NZRFU board, who I think have far outstripped other rugby unions' boards in the way they've adjusted to professionalism.

I also believe that Tri-nations and Super 12 rugby was the better choice for rugby. At the time, of course, we didn't know that. We had no way of comparing the SANZAR concept with the WRC dream; they were both embryonic. But the way it's worked out, I have no doubt we went the right way in the end. It's been great for the game – and we kept the tradition of the silver fern alive.

10

Behind Every Good Team

When you hang around in the All Blacks as long as I have, you get to be introduced to a mixture of team officials. With my international career spanning amateur and professional eras, it would be unfair to draw comparisons. But it is fascinating to illustrate some of the different traits they exhibited.

As a lock, I considered I was extremely fortunate to have the great Colin "Pinetree" Meads – Tree, as we called him – as as my manager in 1994 and 1995. If that wasn't bonus enough, we were joined in 1995 by another legend, Brian Lochore, who filled the role of campaign manager at the third World Cup with distinction.

Meads' greatest attribute obviously was that, with few exceptions, no matter what the challenge was, or where, he'd been there, done that. However, one experience which was unique, even to the great Pinetree, was our visit during the 1995 tour of Italy and France to Catania in Sicily… Mafia territory.

A greater challenge for Pinetree than getting his boys safely out of the land of the mafioso was transporting the touring party of 30-plus from Bologna, following the international against Italy, to Toulon in France.

Pinetree's Italian wasn't up to much, but he reckoned he had the transport arrangements under control… until we arrived at Bologna Airport early on the Sunday morning to discover there were no reservations in the system for any rugby team from New Zealand. A plane which might have taken some of us had already departed. The next one had enough spare seats to take less than half our team. And that was it for that particular Sunday.

You don't get to be as famous as Pinetree if you're not resourceful. Out

Fotopacific

Colin Meads

came the gold Visa card. He glowered at the gentleman behind the check-in counter. "Please arrange a charter flight to Toulon for the other fifteen players," he ordered. "For today!" The attendant was undoubtedly more familiar with soccer celebrities than overseas rugby players but he seemed to sense that Colin Meads was not a man to be trifled with. "I will see what I can arrange," he said. Fifteen minutes later he reported back. Yes, two small planes would be available in approximately four hours. "Thank you very much," said manager Meads. "You are very welcome," replied the relieved airport official.

Meads had a huge regard for Laurie Mains' coaching ability, particularly his technical skill with the forwards. He would write in the foreword to Laurie's biography, that he was "a brilliant technical coach of forward play… who managed to touch the right cog at training. He was an innovator all the way."

Because of Laurie's talents, Colin seldom intruded into coaching issues. He would offer words of encouragement at team meetings, more to remind us of the traditions associated with the black jersey than anything specifically tactical. But there was one famous exception which followed our dismal showing against France at Toulouse on that '95 tour. We'd had to contend with a gale-force wind which was the equal of anything I've ever encountered at Athletic Park (and that's saying something!). After all that we'd achieved during the year, it was extremely disappointing to lose to the French, particularly as we'd wanted to round out Laurie's coaching term on a high.

The first opportunity for the management to address the players in the wake of the defeat was at a team meeting at Nancy the following afternoon. Normally Pinetree would be reticent on such occasions, but after Laurie had outlined the arrangements for the next few days, Pinetree stood up and addressed us.

He started from the top and told it straight. He said he was greatly disappointed to see an All Black team play as poorly as we had at Toulouse. Where was our commitment? It was an embarrassment, he told us, to see an All Black pack worked over by the French as we had been.

He fixed his beady stare upon Tim Barry, the Steinlager representative who'd been involved in all our meetings to that point. Never, in his day, was a sponsorship person privileged to attend team meetings. Whereupon he kicked him out, which was an obvious shock to Laurie. Tree continued. He accused Laurie of getting soft on the players and blamed himself for not seeing it. Most of the players by this stage had their stares fixed firmly on the floor. I doubt anyone was looking at Tree. He concluded by reminding us how proud he had been every time he'd pulled on an All Black jersey.

When he then asked Laurie to leave the meeting, we wondered what was coming next. It transpired he'd finished his tirade. Now he was dealing with the appointment of the next All Black coach. Asking us to write down our individual preference for coach, he said he would take them along to the next board meeting of the NZRFU. I'd have to say the players were rather shell-shocked at this unexpected request. Most did as requested, however. Tree collected them all, and that was that. Whether the players' selections were ever made known to the union, I've no idea. Personally, I didn't feel it was up to us to choose our new boss.

Tree was a mighty manager because he'd been such a great player and had achieved legendary status. He'd first pulled on the All Black jersey in 1957, 10 years before I was born, but wherever we went, he was instantly recognised and probably signed as many autographs as most All Blacks (although definitely not as many as Jonah Lomu!).

He would regularly attend trainings but never intrude, respecting Laurie's authority as the coach. Where he was valuable to Laurie was if he thought the players were getting full of themselves. He had a marvellous way of bringing you back to earth. "That's your bloody job," he'd say to anyone who gave the impression he was looking for a degree of praise. "That's what you're here for – now get on with it!"

Tree was the ultimate team man. He was authoritative but, remembering his own days as an All Black, he also respected the wishes of the team. If the majority of the players wanted something he personally was opposed to, he would accede to their wishes. It takes a big man to do that. The most famous occasion that Tree yielded to team pressure was in Sydney following the Bledisloe Cup match in 1995 when the players effectively hijacked the bus en route to the test dinner. Our mission was a meeting with one of the WRC bosses – at his home in Botany Bay - to hear their proposals. Tree (and Laurie) wouldn't have a bar of it and remained steadfastly on the bus. As the manager, Tree was in an invidious situation but, not without some misgivings I'm sure, he permitted democracy to rule.

Many people might regard Colin Meads as gruff and rather uncommunicative, but once relaxed with friends around him, he transforms into a wonderful raconteur. We'd while away many an hour on tour listening with fascination to Tree relating tales from his days as an All Black involving legendary opponents like Willie John McBride, Martin Pelser, Nick Shehadie and Frik du Preez. Tree wasn't big into small talk, but as a teller of tales there was never a manager like him, not in my experience any way.

My first manager back in 1989, John Sturgeon, with whom I developed a warm, lasting friendship, was a contradiction in terms – a West Coaster who doesn't drink. There aren't too many of them! He and Alex "Grizz" Wyllie had a tremendous relationship, once Grizz got over what must have been a shock at discovering that his All Black "partner" was a teetotaller, because Grizz's capacity to put away alcoholic beverages is legendary.

Grizz was a sole coach from 1988 through until John Hart was introduced as his partner in the run-in to the World Cup in 1991. This meant he shouldered a massive work schedule, and while he appeared to thrive on it, there were moments of tension, shall we say bumps in the road, along the way. That's when Sturge would jump in and calm the grizzled one. Often after a dressing down from Sturge, Grizz would sulk for a while, but he always understood who was running the tour. Sturge was the boss. The buck stopped with him and if Grizz was behaving in a manner unacceptable to him, he sure let him know. They had some furious rows at times, none of which I can ever recall Grizz winning.

Sturge had this classic saying which he'd trot out when everything was going well: "She's 22-carat." It tickled my fancy, so I sort of picked it up and it became the "in" phrase between Sturge and me. "G'day, Sturge, how are things going?" "Twenty-two carat, Kamo. Twenty-two carat." When he uttered that, you knew the good ship All Black was sailing a true course.

It's traditional that on the morning of an All Black game, you go to the manager's room where he has your jersey, shorts and socks waiting for you. It was always a special event going to Sturge's room where he would have the gear meticulously laid out on his bed. He'd have an encouraging word for everyone. If you wanted to engage in conversation, he was the perfect listener or adviser, as required. If you preferred silence, he'd shut up.

He was like a father to me and the other young guys on my first tour, to Wales and Ireland in 1989, which was important because the senior players weren't spending a lot of time with the newcomers. When I went to collect my gear for my debut against Cardiff, I nervously inquired of Sturge how he was. "Twenty-two carat, Kamo. Twenty-two carat." It was the first time I'd heard that term. It was reassuring, in a West Coast kind of way.

If we thought we knew all about Sturge, we were in for a shock at Bayonne during the French tour in late 1990. The boys had taken a beating from Cote Basque and were pretty disconsolate in the dressing room, four days out from the first test. Sturge suddenly burst into song. It was an old West Coast ballad that Sturge had learnt from his grandfather. It was a song inspired by, of all things, tripe. Sturge, with a more than adequate voice, gave us three verses and three hearty renditions of the chorus. The players were entranced and gave him a thunderous reception when he finished. It was a side of Sturge we'd never seen before but it had the effect of jelling the team together. It certainly took everyone's mind off what could have been a depressing defeat. Naturally, there were endless requests for Sturge to perform again, but he was a reluctant singer and I think he only ever broke into song on one other occasion, at a team social. Grizz, I should add, was never moved to sing, which was probably a blessing for all of us.

Most of us presumed that Sturge's song-burst was entirely impromptu but it turned out Alan Whetton was behind the dressing-room recital. The previous night Sturge had accompanied several of the Dirty Dirties to a restaurant in Bayonne where AJ had initiated a competition – to sing the oldest song they knew.

Simon Mannix had delivered *"I'm Forever Blowing Bubbles"* which would have been worth the price of admission on its own! Sturge, not to be outdone, trundled out his tripe song which not only won hands down but had the guys rolling about with laughter. AJ was determined the rest of the team should hear Sturge's song, and it was he who called everyone to attention in the changing room the following night.

In Argentina in 1991 many of the hotel telephone operators had extremely limited grasps of English, as a consequence of which it was often sheer luck if calls from our partners back in New Zealand were ever connected to the right room. More often than not, the calls would be routed through to manager Sturgeon's room. He never minded. He'd chat for up to 20 minutes to our partners, then wander down to our rooms and assure us the lawns were mowed, the mortgage was paid and the wife/partner had just had her hair done!

A few nights before the All Blacks tackled Canada in Lille in a quarter-final match at the 1991 World Cup, Sturge decided it was time to vary the meal arrangements. We'd seen enough of hotel dining rooms, he said, and requested three of the younger guys, Craig Innes, John Timu and Walter Little, arrange a suitable restaurant in the northern French city. He gave them a reasonable allocation of funds and told them to set it up.

They dutifully reported back that they had located the ideal venue. But it was high class. The players would be required to wear dinner suits and bow ties. And they'd need some more funds.

"Jeez," said Sturge, "she must be up-market. Okay, you guys deserve it." And dug deeper into his wallet.

There were universal moans when it was announced number ones were required to be worn at dinner that evening. And there was chaos when, upon assembly in the team room, Richard Loe and Graham Purvis began pulling everyone's bow ties out. Eventually, order was restored and we piled on the bus and headed for what was obviously going to be the ritziest joint in Lille.

You can imagine the reactions of the players and manager Sturge when we pulled up outside McDonald's. The guys had reserved the entire third floor, including the kids' area. It was quite a sight, formally attired All Blacks thrashing about in the playpen and whizzing down the slides. All part of the World Cup preparation! I'm not sure whether the guys cut out all of Sturge's meal allocation that night but there were a serious number of hamburgers and milk shakes consumed!

Sturge began organising an annual charity game in Greymouth in 1992, his fifteen against the West Coast. He'd invite a group of All Blacks down and it reflects the regard the players held for him that, barring broken legs, no one ever declined the invitation. The match was always organised for February or March when the weather was invariably fine; in fact, I've never been to the West Coast when it rained. Can you believe that? Sturge would get us involved in promotional activities with the locals kids, then he and Mary would host us at his home, where he has assembled a mighty trophy room and where you can scoff whitebait fritters till you're ready to explode. The game's always on the Saturday and you fly home on the Sunday. An experience never to be missed.

Sturge was a mighty players' manager, someone who created a tightness within the team. If he had a shortcoming as a manager it was possibly in his understanding of the requirements of the media. The All Blacks were shown up in the matter of public relations at the World Cup in 1991 but that was largely because the Australians, being proactive, had involved a media liaison person, Greg Campbell, who took all the media pressure off his management. Poor Sturge as the manager was responsible for everything. His first priority was always the players and if something had to be sacrificed, it was the press. He must view the present setup, where Jane Dent handles all the All Blacks media communications, with a degree of envy. Back in 1991, Sturge had to handle everything.

After the disappointments at the '91 World Cup, there was a complete clean-out at the top. Alex Wyllie gave way to Laurie Mains as coach, Peter Thorburn and Earle Kirton were new selectors and Sturge's successor as manager was Neil Gray, a farmer from Morrinsville who'd operated as a liaison officer with several overseas touring teams. The system that yielded All Black manager status to Neil in 1992 – it being mandatory then for the manager to be a member of the national council – wouldn't work now in the professional era. However, Neil was a loyal, hard-working manager who arrived with great intentions.

He had several homespun sayings which he repeated regularly. One was that he would never write a book, that he'd take all his stories to the grave. As an extremely punctual person, he consistently reminded us that "five minutes lost in the morning is two hours lost at night"; another philosophical utterance was that we should "always take the lift because the stairs will kill you"; and he assured us that we could tour the world on "please" and "thank you". It's probably as well he's intending to take his stories to the grave because I think a book of The Sayings of Manager Neil would have a limited shelf life.

Neil Gray

Neil had a passion for rugby and as a rural person reminded us regularly in 1992, which was New Zealand rugby's centennial season, that the game was of the heartland. We weren't just playing for the major centres but for the whole of New Zealand. Before every test he wished us well on behalf of all New Zealand.

In 1993 it became increasingly obvious that there had been a serious fallout between Neil as the manager and Laurie Mains as the coach. Although they were never openly hostile, you could tell in their body language that they were not functioning as a unit. And when your manager and coach are not in sync, it flows right down through the team. Because Neil and Laurie weren't functioning, it placed extra pressure on Sean Fitzpatrick as the captain who became the link man and had to deputise for them on occasions. As a consequence of this, Sean's play suffered. At times when we wanted to slot in some extra lineout work, Sean, whose throwing was such a critical component, was required elsewhere.

In the tight environment of a touring team, it was easy to pick up Neil and Laurie's antipathy towards each other. I know Laurie felt Neil was too quick to fraternise with the alickadoos when we were touring overseas. Certainly, 1993 was a challenging year for the man from Morrinsville.

The challenge of any management is how they respond to crises, and ours probably didn't fare too well in the closing couple of weeks of the tour of England and Scotland. Their decision which caused an uproar back in New Zealand, and certainly didn't have the wholehearted backing of the touring party, was to involve Mike Brewer as a reserve against England and the Barbarians at the expense of Liam Barry. Neil was privy to the discussions between Laurie and NZRFU chairman Eddie Tonks before the announcement was made. As the manager, he had the power to overrule Laurie who, in his defence, believed he was operating in the best interests of the team. Neil didn't countermand Laurie but was later critical of the decision.

When television replays of the England international showed that Jamie Joseph, our flanker, had injudiciously stamped on Kyran Bracken's foot (with sufficient force to put him out of rugby for a month), the management imposed a suspension which ruled him out of the Barbarians game. Although millions of viewers had witnessed Joseph's indiscretion on television, our management decided the matter would be dealt with "in house". There was no press statement, which was the more bizarre because the All Blacks now had their own press liaison officer, Ric Salizzo. Jamie simply wasn't chosen for the Barbarians game, leaving the press to draw their own conclusions. Neil, as the manager, should have insisted on issuing a press statement.

There was no possibility of Neil and Laurie working together for another year. At the end of 1993, Neil was replaced by Colin Meads.

The fourth manager during my term in the All Blacks was Mike Banks, who took up the reins in 1996 when John Hart became coach, thus becoming the first manager of rugby's professional age. Banko, as he became known, is a former Manawatu fullback with a corporate background. He runs several pubs in the Manawatu and Wanganui regions and is a member of the nine-man board administering New Zealand rugby.

Early in 1996 they set up a seminar for the country's leading players at the Waipuna Lodge in Auckland entitled *"Professionalism – The Way Ahead"*. The players were addressed by lawyers, accountants, media people (including Paul Holmes), even Rikki Ellison, the New Zealander who'd made good in American Football. He spoke to us on what it means to be a professional sportsman.

Their next important initiative was the introduction of the All Black mentor scheme. With the advent of professionalism, they realised it was vitally important to preserve the value of the All Black jersey. To promote this, a selection of the nation's greatest players, covering all positions, were chosen to act as mentors. As a lock, mine was Andy Haden. He's the individual I would turn to if I ever needed advice or encouragement.

It was an important development. One can see how competitors in other professional sports are driven entirely by success and money. The greatest motivational weapon in New Zealand rugby, however, remains the black jersey. The mentor scheme helps strengthen that bond, keeping today's players in touch with the heroes of the past.

Banko, or WBM (world's best manager) as some of the guys have dubbed him, has brought organisation to a new level within the team. Our job is to play, train and meet our promotional commitments. His job is to oversee everything else.

During 1996 and 1997, the All Blacks played 22 internationals at 17 different venues in five countries and Banko drop-kicked a goal (from the 22) at every venue, from Wellington to Wembley, Dunedin to Dublin, Melbourne to Manchester. He's taken only one shot at each ground and hasn't yet missed. WBM's drop-kicking prowess is seen as a good omen. I guess we're in trouble if he ever misses!

Banko is a meticulous organiser. For example, in June the All Blacks were issued with a brochure providing not only assembly and travel details for all seven internationals coming up, but a comprehensive description (and photo) of each hotel, along with phone and fax numbers. Not only are the players thus fully briefed, but our partners and families know exactly what's going on.

Mike Banks

Fotopacific

The workload of an All Black manager has probably almost doubled since Sturge was boss back in the 1980s. Therefore, the modern-day manager has necessarily got to be more organised. Mind you, the present management has now expanded to an extraordinary degree. There's almost one management person for each two players. At the first training session following the 1998 All Black trial, the team bus carried 24 players, a manager, three coaches, two selectors, a doctor, a physiotherapist, a trainer, a media liaison person and a sponsorship liaison manager.

Banko was lucky to survive his first test, against the Western Samoans at Napier in 1996. That was when Jeff Wilson, Josh Kronfeld and myself declared we would wear Nike boots instead of Mizunos from the official boot supplier. We had nothing against the official product but the NZRFU, in its haste to get all the players signed in 1995, had accepted the Nike contracts which Jeff, Josh and myself held. Our contracts were specific – they entitled us to wear Nike boots as All Blacks. While the NZRFU was threatening us with suspension, we knew we were on strong legal ground. It was an anxious time for Banko who was caught in the crossfire. He and Harty threatened to resign if the NZRFU suspended us. Fortunately, after a series of meetings, a compromise was agreed upon allowing us to wear the Nike gear at Napier. But Jeff, Josh and I took both sets of boots along to McLean Park just in case!

Two of the most valuable members of the All Black squad are Doc and

Abo – John Mayhew, the doctor, and David Abercrombie, the physiotherapist. Both were involved when I first entered the All Black scene in 1989. They dropped out for a while but were recalled by John Hart. They would have few peers in international rugby.

Doc was effectively a second manager back in Sturge's day. On the tour of Wales and Ireland in '89 there would be consistently two or three dinners a week requiring All Black management presence. Sturge couldn't handle all of them, so Doc would often deputise for him.

That wasn't the only area where he went beyond the call of duty. As a former lock for the Northcote senior team – his brother David was an All Black trialist – he was often in demand at trainings, making up the numbers. On many occasions I've packed down against the match pack in combination with Doc's bony frame. He jumped in a few lineouts too. We never called on Abo for training sessions. He was too short!

Of course, Doc's primary role was as the doctor, dispensing pills and lotions and, on more occasions that any of us would have preferred, demonstrating rare skill in stitching players back together, more often than not in the less than perfectly hygienic surroundings of the dressing room.

There is a good story going round about Doc. After the All Blacks' game at Tucuman during the 1991 tour of Argentina, a player was required to give a urine sample. Murphy's Law determines that you can never urinate when you have to, so he was sitting around for ages becoming increasingly frustrated, particularly when the team bus was shortly to depart. It's imperative that local officials monitor drug testing carefully, but that night their vigilance was almost nonexistent. So when Doc wandered by, on his way to the toilet, he was offered the utensil to be filled. He obliged and, once they had located the official who was supposed to be observing, handed in the sample, to the satisfaction of all. It's a frightening story to relate because you like to believe that established procedures are rigidly adhered to with drug testing and what was contrived that night is not possible. "They" returned a negative test which would have happened anyway. It was laughed off, but drug-test security should never be that lax. Doc, of course, vehemently denies this story.

My first association with Abo was at a Northern Zone game at Takapuna in 1989. With Northland, the "physio" was a general dogsbody who also doubled as baggageman and masseur. He probably had limitations when it came to repairing a torn muscle, but he was wonderfully soothing as a rubber-down. When I approached Abo and asked, "Any chance of a rub-down?" I was a bit taken aback when he replied, "No, not really." The boy from Northland was a little naive, you understand, and didn't appreciate that in the big smoke a "physio" was precisely that, a fully-qualified physiotherapist, a specialist in sports medicine. You wanted a rub-down, you made your own arrangements.

I quickly came to appreciate that Abo was not only vastly better qualified than the more basic masseurs I'd been accustomed to, but as a physiotherapist he's the best. He explains your injuries in layman's terms and if it's a major, he knows the procedures to follow. Having been associated with the All Blacks for so long, he knows most of our bodies intimately now. The classic example of this was in Melbourne in 1997 when Sean Fitzpatrick, his knee having swollen alarmingly during the match at Ellis Park, was referred to an orthopaedic surgeon who gloomily advised him he would never play rugby again. Fitzy wasn't hugely impressed with that verdict so reported back to Abo and asked what the alternative was. Abo set to work. The combination of Fitzy's grim determination and Abo's intimate knowledge of his knee meant that the All Black captain, knee heavily strapped, survived 80 minutes of action at the MCG, his 89th test outing.

During 1989 and 1990, Doc and Abo's "surgery" became a great place for the boys to congregate and chill out when on tour. Rather than sit around your hotel or watch endless videos, Doc and Abo's became the "in" gathering place. A delightful custom that developed on Friday evenings was the sipping of port. No, we didn't knock back endless bottles of the stuff; in fact, I don't think I was ever offered a second glassful. Doc and Abo never poured you more than one drink which was a great nightcap. You'd sit and chat for a while, then head for bed. The port, combined with enjoyable conversation, had a pleasantly soporific effect. I always slept wonderfully well on those Friday nights. The port sessions were discontinued when Doc and Abo dropped out of the All Black scene during the Laurie Mains era and, no, they haven't been revived in the professional era.

Doc and Abo's – it sounds like an American bar and, in a sense, it served the same purpose – was where the guys could sound off if something was bugging them. As a consequence, the medical twosome

Dr. John Mayhew (Doc.)

David Abercrombie (Abo)

became an important link between the players and the management. It was where you went if you were frustrated with something. Rather than confront the manager or coach directly, which was always a daunting option, you could bounce your concerns off Doc and Abo. If you were off beam, they would enlighten you there and then. But if you had a justifiable beef, you knew they would subtly convey your sentiments to management without having your identity revealed. Like anything, life's so much more uncomplicated once you understand the system!

A lot of All Blacks owe a huge indebtedness to Doc and Abo, not only for their medical expertise but for their compassion and personal understanding. Their contribution to New Zealand rugby since the late 1980s has been massive. Abo's the guy who makes the initial assessment of players who limp off, or are carried off, with muscle damage. His strength is in being able to quickly sum up the extent of an injury and to recommend the correct treatment. He would never do anything to jeopardise a player's future. Players are naturally impatient, desperate to return to action. Today more than ever players know that their long-term careers can be put at risk by coming back from injury too early. Abo, in his placid, expert way, will let you know exactly where you stand. And you don't return to action – not for the All Blacks, anyway – until he says so. He's only got one shortcoming that I can pinpoint – he doesn't do rub-downs!

Media liaison officers are a modern phenomenon. The Australians were the first nation to come up with one, Greg Campbell proving a smash hit at the 1991 World Cup. By the next World Cup in South Africa just about everyone had an MLO and now, amazingly, they are to be part of all 20 nations' official squads for Wales in 1999.

The All Blacks have had two MLOs – Ric Salizzo, who was associated with Laurie Mains' teams from 1992 to 1995, and Jane Dent, who came on the scene with John Hart in 1996. Ric didn't have an easy assignment, in light of Laurie's natural animosity towards the press. Actually, Laurie wasn't against all journalists, just those he felt criticised rugby and/or his teams unreasonably. Laurie was such a passionate, honest rugby soul he couldn't understand why anyone would want to write disparagingly about any aspect of the game. He could be easily baited at press conferences and so it was in Laurie's and the team's interests for him to be left alone to focus on his role as coach, which happened brilliantly at the World Cup in South Africa when Brian Lochore, as campaign manager, fronted up at most of the press conferences.

Being an All Black doesn't qualify you to handle interviews or appear on television. Players need grooming, in all senses, and Ric was the first person to offer advice on this important, modern aspect of sport.

Ric had been around the All Black camp for a number of years – making videos with his business partner John Kirwan – before his MLO appointment; indeed, he had picked up the nickname of Number 31. He was an unofficial member of the touring party long before media liaison officers were considered.

There was an element of surprise, I guess, when we learned that Ric's successor was a woman, television presenter Jane Dent, but it's hard to worthily explain all that she's achieved. It's not easy being a lone female among up to 40 rugby players but Jane has handled it brilliantly. The players now have a clear understanding of the requirements of the various sections of the media, from journalists to radio people to television interviewers. Instead of an us-and-them mentality, which used to exist, there's now an excellent camaraderie between players and press, which is to the benefit of everyone.

With John Hart's encouragement, and Jane's organisation, the current All Blacks have been projected brilliantly on television and through the papers. The public now has a much better perception of the players.

The remaining member of the official All Black squad, 1997 and 1998 vintage anyway, is Richard Fry, the sponsorship liaison manager. He ensures we fulfil our obligations to the NZRFU on behalf of all sponsors, which is vitally important in view of the substantial input from corporates these days. He also helps out when the All Blacks are overseas as an assistant manager.

Richard has another important role. As the most proficient golfer in the party (and, incidentally, my partner in endless matches against John Hart and Sean Fitzpatrick) it's his duty to arrange course bookings and the hire of clubs when we're touring. Golf has become the All Blacks' "other" sport. When I first came on the scene, Grant Fox was one of the few dedicated golfers, but because it wasn't a game that appealed to Laurie Mains, it wasn't encouraged. That's not a criticism of Laurie – golf simply didn't rate with him.

John Hart, in contrast, is a most capable golfer and in no small measure because of his enthusiasm the game has become the All Blacks' spare-time activity. Whenever we announce a golf outing, usually about 80 per cent of the players get involved. Frank Bunce has been one of the few nongolfers, he and Bull Allen. On the occasions it's compulsory, Frank usually takes responsibility for the drinks trolley.

Golf gets you out in the fresh air, it's relaxing and entertaining, although, as any regular player would acknowledge, it's not necessarily stress free. I'm the tournament director and, thanks to Jeff Crowe, the former New Zealand cricket captain who now organises golf tours, I've established a handicap system that is fair to all. It's based on the ISTAS point-scoring system and ensures the burglars don't win every time. Sometimes we indulge in match play and at other times we use the Ambrose system (where the guys operate in teams and have the option of hitting the best ball for each stroke).

We've been fortunate to play on some of the finest courses in the world. Fancourt near George in South Africa, a 36-hole resort course, would be one of the nicest and we've clubbed our way around three or four Gary Player-designed courses in South Africa. The climate is so great there, you can virtually guarantee to play any time.

I've walked on the famous old course at St Andrew's in Scotland and down the famed 18th hole at Pebble Beach, while Sean and I once spent four hours during the world match play championships at Wentworth in England. We stood for about 15 minutes watching this player practising his bunker shots, unaware of his identity, although we were close enough to shake hands with him. We finally asked another spectator who he was. To our embarrassment, it turned out to be the great German player Bernhard Langer.

The best golfer among the All Blacks is probably Andrew Mehrtens, with Robin Brooke the biggest hitter. Fitzy was showing promise till his knee caved in.

11

No Two Coaches are the Same

The important thing to appreciate about coaches is that no one knows it all. And anyone who thinks he does is a fool. I've been privileged to operate under some of the best-qualified coaches in the game and yet when I needed advice on tackling – because no one had taught me the mechanics of tackling in my early years – I turned to Frank Bunce. In fact, I've approached Frank on several occasions because when it comes to tackling, he's the best.

John Hart won international acclaim as a coach, yet as a technician he wouldn't rank with Laurie Mains. Hart's strength, brilliantly exemplified in 1996 and 1997, was as an organiser and man-manager who harnessed the best available talent and co-ordinated it expertly. He had Ross Cooper and Gordon Hunter as assistants in those years, replacing them with Wayne Smith and Peter Sloane in 1998.

None of us ever stops learning. What I say to kids is listen to everyone because you never know where the next valuable tip will come from. Weed out what is not relevant to you. No one knows it all and the smart coaches, like John Hart, bring in experts to advise on individual skills.

As an All Black, I've operated under three coaches since my elevation to international status – Alex Wyllie, Laurie Mains and John Hart. You couldn't get three more different personalities. If they were wines, one would be a white, one a red and the other a bubbly.

I'd had little contact with Grizz Wyllie prior to my All Black selection in 1989 because I'd missed the intake for the New Zealand Colts trials and therefore had had almost no association with any of the New Zealand selection panel. I certainly knew of Grizz who had achieved legendary status in Canterbury and who had obviously been a formidable player in his day. Sid

Fotopacific

Alex Wyllie

Going, who'd toured with him back in the 1970s, had related some fascinating tales of Grizz, painting him larger than life.

I was apprehensive initially because of his image as a tough guy but I found him really likeable, quite unlike the image painted of him. He was open to new training ideas and was prepared to listen. He also had a good handle on when guys needed to rest, which is important when you're touring. And he was a visionary. Although Jim Blair is probably remembered for his innovative fitness training methods with Auckland, it was Grizz who first involved him in rugby, with his great Canterbury Ranfurly Shield team of the early 1980s.

He was probably the first coach to use the interchange system, too, getting Zinzan Brooke onto the field for Mike Brewer, who was ostensibly injured, at a critical stage of the test against France at Nantes in 1990.

Warren Gatland, a teacher when he toured Wales and Ireland with the All Blacks in 1989, came up with this game his kids had taught him, called Jail. Grizz saw the benefits of it and it became our alternative training option, usually pitting the backs against the forwards. You establish square goals in front of the two sets of goalposts and place a ball in the middle of each one. The object is to get inside the other team's zone, steal the ball and deliver it to your zone. If you're tagged in the opposition half, you go to jail where you have to do push-ups or burpees or similar. If you lose possession or drop the ball, all the players in the opposition half have to go to jail. It was a fun game which we'd often play for two hours, to the bemusement of the locals. They'd come along to observe the latest training methods of the best team in the world, to find them playing a kids' game for two hours!

Grizz was big into live training sessions, 15 players against 15. He believed you trained hard and played hard, which was a good attitude. He wasn't technically proficient, although he knew what he wanted in the scrum. As a lineout specialist, I cannot ever recall receiving any personal tuition from him and he essentially left Grant Fox to organise the backs. He was insistent on the basics being done well – accurate throwing to the lineouts, low, solid scrums, speed to the rucks and accurate passing.

He got involved at trainings and enjoyed bawling out players who were giving less than a hundred or who weren't performing to his satisfaction. If it was your turn to be picked on, you just had to grin and bear it. We never trained on Sundays on that '89 tour, which was appreciated. The midweekers would usually go for a morning run but there was never an organised practice. He was good at monitoring when the players needed rest.

Passion played a huge part in Grizz's preparation. You were never in any doubts about what the black jersey meant or the sacrifices of those who'd gone before. That passion overflowed at times and could leave you bruised. Grizz obviously didn't know his own strength because his favourite way of greeting good buddies was to whack you in the ribs. An early victim was manager John Sturgeon who had to account to his wife for all the bruising around his body. "The next time he went to whack me," said Sturge, "I grabbed his arm, whipped it behind him and said, 'Don't you ever do that again!' It fixed him."

The first inkling that Grizz, who had operated as a sole coach from his appointment in 1988, was stressed came in Argentina in 1991. He'd obviously had a bad night and he put us through a hell session for no obvious reason, just ran us into the ground. Then in the announcement of the second test line-up he bracketed all four props – Steve McDowell and Richard Loe, the established test pair, with Lawrence Hullena and Graeme Purvis – which was an unusual thing to do. As we advanced from the dressing room to the training ground, Richard Loe said, "Brackets? I thought they were what you sat bookshelves on!"

When it was announced midway through 1991 that John Hart would be assisting Grizz, it seemed to be a sensible arrangement. Like Grizz, Harty was a hugely successful coach at representative level and I felt the two would be great together. I was wrong. We were at a stage where we were not going any further under Grizz, and Hart's fresh input could have helped lift us to win the World Cup. Without knowing the history of the pair, I believed it would be an ideal formula.

The success of the All Blacks in 1996 and 1997 was the shared responsibility concept, with Hart co-ordinating the coaching talents of Ross Cooper, Gordon Hunter, Wayne Smith and Peter Sloane. It could have, and should have, worked like that in 1991. But it didn't. Grizz plainly resented Hart's intrusion into *his* team, which wasn't helped by John having a close association with the Auckland guys and some really tight relationships with a couple of them.

That they were incompatible became increasingly obvious at team meetings. They were not remotely in sync. Their emphases were dramatically different and their training styles a million miles apart. They almost seemed to be in competition, which is not the way to mould a team to win the World Cup. I don't suggest that their antagonism was the sole reason we lost the

World Cup, but it certainly had a bearing.

At the end of the day, there were no winners. The All Blacks were bundled out of the World Cup and the NZRFU rejected Wyllie as a selector and Hart as the coach for 1992. It was time, the national body determined, for a fresh start.

Which opened the way for Laurie Mains. He would take the All Blacks through to the third World Cup. As with Grizz three years earlier, I really knew nothing about him, except that he had excellent credentials, having played fullback for the All Blacks and Otago and then coached Otago through to NPC glory.

It was an exciting, refreshing time for the All Blacks with a new coach, a new manager (Neil Gray), a new captain (Sean Fitzpatrick) and a lot of new challenges in New Zealand's centenary season. A bucketload of new players forced their way into the test squad and Mains set about rebuilding the All Blacks as a world force.

I understood where Laurie was coming from initially. He stressed that rugby was a running game and therefore we should run to get fit. He rejected the Jim Blair approach of preparing for a rugby season in the gymnasium. In Laurie's book, gym work complemented the aerobic fitness developed through running. With new trainer Martin Toomey monitoring our progress meticulously, Laurie pushed the All Blacks to levels of fitness most of them, I'm certain, had never believed were possible. It made for a stimulating season – a great series against the Wallabies in Australia and an unbeaten sweep through South Africa culminating in an historic test victory on Ellis Park.

Unfortunately, the momentum build-up in '92 wasn't sustained over the next two seasons, partly because with no mid-season tours Laurie wasn't able to promote the same fitness levels, but also because of the unsettling number of changes the selection panel kept making.

From a player's viewpoint, there was no obvious direction. Individuals weren't prepared to take chances because the feeling was if they made mistakes, they'd be dropped. Laurie's suspicions of the media rolled over onto the players and we became unsmiling giants. He was so intense and it impacted on his players, which was a tragedy really because we'd produced our best rugby in 1992 when we were all relaxed.

Laurie dropped me in 1993 after the first Lions test. It came as a thunderbolt. There was no phone call or warning – I learned via the radio like any rugby supporter in the land. When we assembled in Wellington on the Tuesday – I was still involved as a reserve – I talked to Laurie and Peter Thorburn. They said I hadn't got involved enough in the first test at Lancaster Park, so I asked what more could I have done. Laurie replied that I hadn't taken enough kickoffs. Now that was interesting because the way we trained meant Robin Brooke always stood infield from me at kickoffs. At Christchurch the Lions had consistently used short kickoffs, which meant the ball was always going to Robin. Was I supposed to have changed the battle plan?

I was simply another victim of their revolving-door policy. It seemed they were determined to try as many combinations as possible and while this may have been fruitful in the end, it was certainly unsettling at the time. After 26 consecutive test appearances, it hurt suddenly being wrenched out like that. It was a valuable experience, I'll concede, because it made me appreciate how much being there meant to me. I was ferociously determined it wasn't going to happen again.

On matters of leisure, Laurie and I didn't see eye to eye. He was not a keen golfer and didn't encourage the game among his players. In fact, he patently discouraged it. During the Scottish tour of 1993 several of us had the opportunity to play at the old St Andrew's links, one of the most famous courses in the world. Laurie thwarted our plans by calling an extra training run. We were in Scotland to play rugby, I know, but it was a shame to miss such an opportunity. I refused to let Laurie's bloody-mindedness completely win the day, so I asked to be driven to the course late that afternoon and walked down the 18th fairway.

Laurie Mains

Fotopacific

Laurie developed various fascinations with nutrition which again impacted on the team. He warned us off steaks, convinced that red meat made you lethargic, and he also ruled McDonald's out of bounds. All that did was make the hamburger freaks deceitful. Trying to tell people like Inga Tuigamala they can't have a Big Mac is like suggesting to Grizz Wyllie he should only drink lemonade on tour. Laurie freaked out in France in 1995 when he found Jonah Lomu had polished off a dozen eggs at one breakfast sitting. He surely didn't think we would all try and emulate such a monumental feat, but he declared eggs off limits. The consequence of this was that there were a lot of players arriving early at breakfast and hiding eggs under their toast.

Laurie was at his best in 1995. The trial-and-error process of the previous two years had finally thrown up 26 players capable of winning the World

Fotopacific

John Hart

Cup and Laurie whipped everyone into shape at the Taupo and Christchurch camps. The introduction of Brian Lochore as a campaign manager freed him to focus on coaching and he flourished in the role. He'd had a vision for New Zealand rugby which we gave full expression to in South Africa. Tragically, after his players had been stricken with what we can only presume was food poisoning 48 hours out from the final, the greatest prize in rugby eluded him, albeit by the narrowest of margins.

Technically, he was the best coach I ever encountered, one of the few who could give precise directions to me as a lineout jumper. Most coaches operate on the pretext that you're an expert in your own role and take it from there. Laurie was specific in what he wanted every player to achieve and he was able to convey his requirements without pressures that could make you nervous. Previously, I'd had to turn to people like Murray Pierce to talk through the specifics of lineout play.

With the advent of professionalism, John Hart was the perfect appointment as coach in 1996. Ross Cooper, who'd been Laurie's assistant to France the previous year and who many saw as the heir apparent, would have been an appropriate choice had rugby remained amateur. But the professional era demanded a professional coach, and Harty was the man.

He did the job brilliantly until the team came horribly unstuck in 1998, significantly after the departure of Sean Fitzpatrick, Zinzan Brooke and Frank Bunce. The layman can only judge Hart on the All Blacks' onfield performances which through 1996 and 1997 were mightily impressive, with two Tri-nations triumphs, two Bledisloe Cup successes, a famous first series win in South Africa and an unbeaten sweep through the UK. For a player like myself, touring with the All Blacks in '96 and '97 under Hart was like being on a month-long man-management and motivation seminar.

Harty's coaching style is all about shared leadership, with everyone buying into the game plan. He gives responsibility to his players who organise how they want to operate. Harty's then on hand to oversee matters at training. Loyal to his players and demanding loyalty in return, he surrounds himself with the best, from coaches to the medical team to the press liaison officer.

The tight five in control against the Springboks at Cape Town in 1996. Olo Brown is about to run onto my pass.

John Selkirk

Matt Dowd

It was so important for us to beat the Australians in 1995 after failing
to win the World Cup. Hence my delight at the final whistle after our
34-23 win in Sydney.

John Selkirk

It's not every president who wears a rugby jersey, but South Africa's
Nelson Mandela did for the World Cup final at Ellis Park in 1995. It
helped inspire his team to a famous win.

Niels Schipper

The Chiefs didn't meet everyone's expectations in 1998, but we did defeat the eventual champions the Canterbury Crusaders in our opening game at Albany.

This was it. All Black teams had been striving since 1928 to win a series on South African soil. There was plenty to celebrate when we finally managed it at Pretoria in 1996

John Selkirk

A perfect day for Janine and I. Our wedding in Fiji, November 1996.

What else could you call a horse owned by this bunch but Tight Five? I'm one of the five owners, along with Olo Brown, Sean Fitzpatrick, Craig Dowd and Robin Brooke

Ian Jones Collection

If the Tri-nations trophy we were presented with at Cape Town in 1996 seems disproportionately large, it's because it was constructed in inches instead of centimetres. It was replaced with a more appropriately sized trophy the next season

John Selkirk

Jeez, Zinny, you've got no show of winning this lineout! Why don't you beat it back to No 8 where you belong?

He's a meticulous organiser who helps the players understand their commercial and media responsibilities.

Hart inherited an All Black team that had produced rugby of often sublime quality in 1995, refining it on and off the field. While in action the team revealed enormous character and grit in coming back from several no-win situations (such as at Suncorp Stadium and Cape Town); away from the field Hart gave the All Blacks a new voice. He expanded people's skills so that in newspaper and television interviews they portrayed themselves favourably.

In contrast with Laurie, who delivered precise instructions to players about what he wanted, John vests responsibility in the individuals. We organise how we want to run our particular phase of the game and John oversees everything. Having said that, you've got to turn up at Harty's training sessions alert and sharp because he is demanding. In every aspect of play, he'll single out one player who's got to lead. It might be Craig Dowd in the rucks, the hooker (previously Fitzy, now Anton Oliver) in the scrums, myself at lineout time. He's a believer in individuals taking a part of the game and owning it. In this environment I've seen players grow amazingly because they've suddenly become leaders.

It's still important to have technicians fine-tuning your game. Even at the highest level some players are deficient in particular skills. Examples are Frank Bunce and Eroni Clarke who aspired to All Black status without ever being able to kick. My shortcoming when I arrived at top level was in not being able to tackle effectively. It wasn't easy to find a coach who could demonstrate the ideal technique. The best teacher turned out to be Frank, the man who couldn't kick. But, boy, can he tackle. Just ask some of the celebrities who've had to oppose him over the years – players like Tim Horan, Jason Little and Will Carling. I went back to Frank several times and now regard myself as a proficient tackler. Not a ferocious, cut-'em-in-half cruncher like Frank himself but someone who isn't going to let the team down when a saving tackle needs to be made.

Peter Sloane was brought into work with the forwards in 1998 and proved especially valuable. Having "been there, done that" - as a hooker who played 16 times for the All Blacks and 147 times for Northland - Peter is a skilled, hands-on coach, one who understands the mechanics of scrums, rucks and lineouts. The potency of the All Black scrum against the Springboks in Durban, when Carl Hoeft, Royce Willis and Isitolo Maka were introduced, was a tribute to his coaching skills.

When John Hart did finally arrive as All Black coach, it was eight years after he'd first sought the position. He'd been beaten to the punch by Grizz Wyllie in 1988 and then become a victim of the disaster that was the New Zealand World Cup challenge four years later. As mentioned, one of his first initiatives was the mentor scheme, which paired Robin Brooke and I off with Andy Haden. I wasn't immediately blown away with the prospect of working with big Andy because in my seven years in the All Blacks he'd never once made contact with me and he'd been a sharp critic of the All Blacks during both Grizz and Laurie's reigns. I wondered what would make a former All Black turn on his own team like that. Anyway, as a longtime supporter of Harty, he became an outstanding mentor and we have developed a close relationship. Since early 1996 we've talked regularly on lineout play and he's offered a lot of suggestions that have really made me think.

The John Hart era began in Napier, first with a trial, which the shadow test team won 72-18, and then with the first international in New Zealand under lights, against Western Samoa, a game we took out 51-10. We were essentially the same combination Laurie had brought together in 1995, with Christian Cullen at fullback ahead of Glen Osborne and Scott McLeod at second-five for an injury-troubled Walter Little.

It was at Napier that the awesome foursome golfing school was established – Richard Fry and me against John Hart and Sean Fitzpatrick. We would play on many courses around the world for varying sums. Richard had the tightest handicap, three, Fitzy and I were both on 15 and Harty was a couple more than that. It was a pastime that would bring us a lot of entertainment and a lot of laughs and provide useful pocket money for Richard and me.

On the Monday after the Napier test, our boot row was resolved at a meeting between Nike officials and the NZRFU. It was agreed that Jeff, Josh and I would play in Mizuno boots for the remainder of the season. I think the most relieved person was Mike Banks who hadn't been looking forward to submitting a resignation so early in his tenure!

If ever there was a case of deja vu, it was the Scottish international at Carisbrook. Apart from the fact it was my 50th international, not my first, everything was a spooky repeat. We trained in bitterly cold weather during the week but it was pleasantly fine on match day, we wore white jerseys again and Damian Cronin was still in the opposition. Not only that but I scored another try in the same spot as 1990. It was virtually in the same square metre of grass. Naturally, I was a target for the media again. Six years previously I'd described the satisfaction of my test debut; now I was talking as a veteran of 50 tests. I reminded the journalists that some of them were the ones who'd insisted I was too skinny to succeed in international rugby. "I'm still here and you're still here," I told them. "So we must all be doing all right!"

The guys marked the occasion by presenting me with a Swedish fishing reel. They'd given JK (John Kirwan) a surfboard when he hit the half-century and Zinny benefited by a gas barbecue. Fitzy was shouted a holiday in Fiji.

The Scots made the huge mistake at Carisbrook of throwing all their men on Jonah, as a consequence of which Cully (Christian Cullen) ran riot, scoring four tries. We'd put 51 on them at Murrayfield in 1993, now we careered on to 63 points. There was never any chance of us extending that record at Eden Park because a northeasterly storm meant playing conditions were about as miserable as they could possibly be.

Hart's philosophy was falling easily on everyone's shoulders. His ideas for the 15-man game were not dissimilar to Laurie's but he insisted that the more expansive we wanted to be, the tighter the forwards had to play. We trained hard, essentially with Laurie's ideals and disciplines, but John was cranking us up to another level.

Operating against Western Samoa and Scotland is one thing, but taking on the Wallabies and the Springboks, who rank as rugby's super powers along with ourselves, is something quite different. It's no longer enough to merely perform well in the basics, the scrums, the lineouts and at kickoffs. In Tri-nations matches you have to step up another level – give 110 per cent, not 80.

It's a shame the facilities at Athletic Park are so abysmal, because the stadium itself is one of the finest in the world, offering great atmosphere and always an excellent surface. On my previous visit to the capital, our changing room plunged into darkness when the solitary light bulb burnt out. In '96, for the opening Tri-nations encounter against the Wallabies, the changing room was flooded because it had rained all week. I can understand why the Wallabies were less than enthusiastic about playing there. The winds whistled up from the Antarctic all week and the Athletic Park changing rooms are about as bleak as you can imagine. It would be pretty unsettling for someone from a tropical climate like Queensland accustomed to modern facilities.

Still, it was the same for both teams and I'm sure we triumphed because we were better focused, for which John Hart can take much of the credit. We could have screened ourselves from the elements by training indoors or gone searching for the best-drained surface in Wellington or Lower Hutt. None of that. We trained in the mud and rain all week. When the appalling conditions persisted on the Saturday, we were physically and mentally prepared for them; in fact, we might have struggled to adapt to a hard surface and dry ball. Throughout the week, Hart's focus was on ball retention. He'd run with us and throw the ball into the slushiest areas. "Your ball, Olo!" or "This one for you, Kamo!" would be the call. Despite the fact it was like mud wrestling, you were expected to secure the ball and set it as the remaining forwards drove over you. Athletic Park on match day was simply a re-creation of what we'd been practising all week. We blew the Aussies away, winning 43 to 6, an astonishing result. That scoreline on a balmy day would have been unlikely; in the inclement conditions that existed it was almost unbelievable. Fifty thousand dollars were invested on the pick-the-score option at the TAB and not one person selected 43-6.

In such horrible conditions it's vital to be focused. You've got to want to play. Maybe the Wallabies didn't want to, but we certainly did and we turned on one of the best performances I've been privileged to be involved in.

Ball retention into the wind was sensational and someone said it was almost 25 minutes before we made our first mistake. As our confidence grew, so did our defence strengthen. Once we'd scored the tries that would ensure the victory, it became a fresh objective to keep Australia tryless. Over a period of about 15 minutes, they threw everything at us without once breaching our goal line. We took our defence to a new level that day, directly involving the tight forwards. Until then, the loosies and the midfielders had been largely responsible for containing the enemy, with the remaining team members tackling only when specifically required. But at Athletic Park that afternoon, it was a whole team effort. The involvement of the tight five freed up the loosies and the backs to operate wider.

We weren't delivering passive tackles either. They were aggressive tackles, aimed at driving the opposition back. It was the introduction to the All Blacks of a defensive mindset.

When the Australians rebounded from their demolition in Wellington to defeat the South Africans in Sydney, there were predictions of another record victory for us against the Boks at Lancaster Park. Far from that, we were fortunate to escape with a 15-11 win, all our points coming from Andrew Mehrtens' boot in a game that focused attention strongly on scrummaging.

The Springboks caught us by surprise in the scrums. Our (legitimate) procedure at scrum time was: hit, hold, ball in, push. But the Boks, whose tactics had the passive approval of the referee, Scotsman Ray Megson, simply went hit, push. It had a most unsettling effect on us, because their scrum was advancing by the time the ball left the halfback's hands. Some critics interpreted these events as a weakness in our scrum, but we were victims of clever strategy by the Springboks who were taking advantage of the referee's leniency. Another referee would have pinged them at the first scrum.

The All Black team of 1993 or 1994 may never have recovered but we were more streetwise by 1996, more composed. We talked through what was happening and adjusted our technique to combat their aggressive approach. It made for some pretty explosive impacts, which isn't recommended because it is downright dangerous. But if the referee wasn't going to enforce the law, we had to make our own arrangements.

Wherever Mr Megson operated in his playing days, it plainly wasn't in the front row. It's obvious he had little appreciation of why scrums collapse. Late in the game he penalised the Springboks after a scrum collapsed 25 metres out in front of our goalposts. It was a critical decision because we led only 12-11 at the time. The Springbok management went hostile about it, and while I don't go to bat for the opposition, I could understand their frustration on that occasion.

The Springboks were on attack and their scrum had pressured us for much of the game. Why the hell would they want to collapse one in front of our posts? Referees have got to think beyond the square at times. An attacking team is not suddenly going to pull a scrum down.

In the 250-plus games I've appeared in at first-class level, I can honestly state I've never once gone into a scrum with a mindset of collapsing. I'm prepared to concede that a weak scrum being shunted towards its own goal line might try and prevent the inevitable by pulling the scrum down, but in general play, when two strong packs are opposing each other, a collapse is more likely to be caused by loose gripping, loose footing or a bad hit when the front rows come together. A referee can't just presume one team is offending. In crucial encounters such as test matches, you can't have referees guessing who might be responsible for a collapsed scrum. Those decisions can make the difference between winning and losing in a tight game.

In lineouts, if a jumper has been going up all afternoon and making two-handed takes but suddenly can't get off the ground, the referee is justified in being suspicious of the other team. That's why I say referees have to think beyond the square. In the same way, a team with strong forwards isn't suddenly going to collapse a scrum in an attacking situation.

Forwards appreciate referees who lucidly explain from the start what they want when the front rows come together. It's exasperating to have a referee who plainly has little understanding of what's going on in the scrums dishing out penalties for the sake of them. Especially these days when a team can rake off 40 metres from a penalty and get the throw-in to ensuing lineout. A team can be seriously penalised for effectively doing nothing.

There was a second important lesson for the All Blacks to come out of the Christchurch international. When we studied the video replays of Andre Joubert's try – the game's only try, created for him by my opposite Mark Andrews – we realised we were overcommitting forwards to rucks. On this particular occasion, as we all sprinted to the ruck, the Springboks left forwards out in the backline and seriously outnumbered us when they spun the ball. Defensively, we were caught short.

If scrums and rucks were a worry in Christchurch, the lineout certainly wasn't. We killed 'em, thanks to Fitzy's pinpoint throwing to Robin and myself and the expert support play of our colleagues. This was, of course, the first season in which the revolutionary new lineout laws applied, permitting jumpers to be, not lifted as many initially believed, but supported in the air. My supports, who were totally reliable, were Zinny and Craig Dowd.

We'd won at Lancaster Park without tries but better things were to come, although we left our run desperately late in the rematch against the Wallabies in Brisbane. This was a more confident, revitalised Aussie team, relishing the warmer climate and superior facilities of Suncorp Stadium.

The Wallabies played most of the quality rugby and deserved to be ahead 22-9 with two-thirds of the game expired. But what the Brisbane experience demonstrated was that our All Black team possessed great composure. There was no panic, no despair. There was, instead, a sense of calm. Under Fitzy's urgings, we appreciated that we needed to start making things happen. We needed field position, which we hadn't achieved, from which the points would start to flow. That is precisely what happened.

At 22-25, Fitzy called for a massive final effort from the forwards, and particularly the tight five. Mehrts levelled the scores with a 50-metre penalty goal and, after we'd withstood a strong assault from the Wallabies, he let fly with a huge 22-metre drop-out.

After 79 minutes of furious action, there was justification, if we'd been searching for it, to ease back and allow the match to dwindle to a conclusion. But our guys chased Mehrts' kick as if their lives depended on it. The reward was a scrum on halfway, our put-in, after we nailed Ben Tune and forced a turnover.

A dropped goal was an obvious option, and that apparently was what Wallaby captain John Eales was anticipating. But the call as we prepared to lock into the final scrum was University, a move we'd practised but never put into effect on match day. Although University was a move schemed by and essentially for the backs, the forwards had a critical part to play. Its effectiveness relied on the forwards piling in behind Zinzan Brooke and securing swift ruck ball after Zinny had committed the first-five and the openside flanker by picking up and driving powerfully from the scrum.

The move unfolded like clockwork and there was justice in the fact that Frank Bunce scored the winning try after he'd earlier been the victim of an amazing punching outburst by Michael Brial. It was ludicrous that Brial could stay on the field after indulging in such blatant hitting.

I've rarely experienced such emotion, such joy, amongst the All Blacks as when Frank scored that try. We'd had the confidence as a team to go for the knock-out blow, and we'd achieved it. Winning virtually guaranteed us the Tri-nations title.

I introduced a new jump to my lineout repertoire that afternoon in Brisbane and it worked sensationally well for 40 minutes, till the Australians cottoned on to what was happening. Normally, I jumped directly opposite John Eales, one of the most accomplished exponents in the game. At Brisbane, I shuffled back four or five paces on our throw so that I was effectively jumping against Daniel Manu, who presented me with no opposition at all. It meant we secured heaps of quality two-handed ball from well back in the lineout. This was ball Michael Jones usually gathered, but my shuffling back freed him up as a loose forward, with obvious advantages.

Our Awesome Foursome unwound on the Coolum golf course the next day. It was a serious challenge match, with Fitzy, Harty, Richard Fry and myself each depositing $A100 at the pro shop. I'm pleased to report that Richard and I secured a memorable victory on the 17th green, as a consequence of which we purchased snazzy looking Hyatt Regency polo shirts after picking up our winnings.

As we jetted off to South Africa for our eight-match tour, player numbers had swollen to 36 and with management the tour party now numbered 45. I must say, when we assembled for the first time, in Brisbane, the size of our group was overwhelming. But it was a master stroke taking two complete teams along, freeing the test squad from midweek commitments – a famous first.

With the frequency and intensity of internationals these days and with the prizes so much higher, it's important to be able to rest between games. I encountered former New Zealand cricketer John Parker on one of my school visits and he said one of the most important lessons he'd absorbed during his international career was how to relax away from the playing field. If you were given two days off, he said, make sure you took advantage of them. They weren't for training. Wise words.

In South Africa, where we played four test matches on successive Saturdays, the two days we were given off after each international were precious to us. Sunday, when we invariably travelled, involved nothing more than a pool session and perhaps a spa, while Monday, for me and a good few others, was golf day. South Africa is a marvellous country for golfers because of its almost faultless winter climate. It's not like touring the UK or New Zealand where you need to monitor the weather forecast before booking a tee-off time.

I rarely sighted a rugby ball on a Monday during that trek through South Africa, but I belted dozens of golf balls around an impressive array of courses from George to Johannesburg.

Our first port of call in South Africa was a stunner – Plettenburg Bay, a fabulous holiday retreat on the southern coast, the ideal place to unwind after the arduous journey through from Australia. We had two or three days of relaxation before focusing on rugby, which presented opportunities for surfing, fishing and, funnily enough, golfing. The 36-hole Gary Player-designed Fancourt course at nearby George remains one of the finest I have played.

For team-building purposes, the management divided the 36 players into four teams – North Otaba, the Purfs, Big Mex and No Bull. North Otaba, in case you've forgotten, was the province the then chairman of the NZRFU, Richie Guy, once credited "Scott" Bunce as belonging to in a memorable All Black team announcement.

One of our first activities was to construct two scrum machines and two ruck machines. For this purpose, each group was under the masterly guidance of one of the team's builders. Little did we appreciate the competitive nature of Sean Fitzpatrick and Zinzan Brooke who, late at night, crept into the workroom and not only spent time assembling their own ruck machine but absconded with a large bolt from a "rival" scrum machine. Craig Dowd and his Purfs were becoming mightily perplexed the next day, until the bolt was found in Zinzan's pocket!

That kind of set the tone for the tour. I'm not sure if team building was the winner on that occasion. It certainly established a deadly rivalry between the Purfs and North Otaba over the next month. We pursued a lot of fun-filled activities, climaxing in a talent quest which North Otaba won under the inspired leadership of Eric Rush.

The Cape Town international was a rarity for a contest between the All Blacks and the Springboks because technically there was nothing at stake. We already had the Tri-nations series sewn up, while our three-test series didn't kick off for another week. In those circumstances it would have been easy to lose focus, but that was where John Hart came into his own. Every game in 1996 was, to him, a one-off contest. We never looked beyond the next game. In the past, All Black teams had possibly lost sight of the immediate test by being too desperate to win the series. John had broken our 1996 season down into 10 individual challenges.

Obviously, we didn't want to present any psychological advantages to the South Africans, who were at that stage being prepared by Andre Markgraaff, but it seemed we were doing precisely that as we fell behind 18-6 after a lack-lustre opening 30 minutes. However, in contrast to Christchurch, our scrum was dominant and there was a confident air within the team. As in Brisbane, we maintained our composure and began to take the game to the Springboks.

Once we gathered momentum in the second half, we were unstoppable. South Africa remained static on 18 while we piled on 23 points to record a most emphatic victory. We were beginning to regard Newlands as one of our favourite grounds, following on from the unforgettable display there against England at the World Cup. Cape Town is an awesome city and Newlands has an awesome feel to it, truly one of the great rugby stadiums of the world.

Phil Kearns, the former Wallaby skipper who was in the grandstand at Cape Town, was full of praise for our forward performance. "The All Black scrum was completely dominant," he wrote. "They gave a clinical performance in the final 40 minutes. I would love to see the All Black scrum against the

Argentinians – at the moment they are the best in the world."

All the pressure was now on the Springboks. Captain Francois Pienaar was out of the series with a displaced vertebra, loosehead prop Os du Randt, who we understood had departed the field with concussion, told a journalist he'd gone off because he was "fed up" (presumably with the hiding he was getting from Olo Brown) and James Small received a reprimand for nightclubbing in the lead-up to the test.

We blinked when we were presented with the new Tri-nations trophy down on the field because it was grotesquely large. Sean did uncommonly well to lift it, while in the dressing room Christian Cullen jumped inside it. It was large enough to bath in. Then the truth was revealed – the trophy maker had misread the instructions and constructed it in inches, not centimetres! So our name is the only one on that trophy.

During our stay in Cape Town, where I roomed with Robin Brooke, we observed these five guys in the Newlands Hotel car park dressed up as nuns, with numbers one to five on their backs. We laughed. "Probably Kiwis," I commented. When I next got into conversation with Con Barrell he revealed that several of them were from my home town, Kamo! (The five were Andrew Golightly, John Peterson and Fraser Moores from Kamo, Andrew Hall from Wanaka and Richard Doocey from Christchurch.) They were sensationally distinctive. More than once while we were standing to attention for the

Amazing who (or should that be what?) bobbed up in the crowd at Cape Town in 1996 – five Kiwi blokes dressed as nuns. The five were Andrew Golightly, John Peterson, Fraser Moores, Andrew Hall and Richard Doocey.

national anthems during the tour I spotted them in the crowd. They were invited into corporate tents and had a great time.

During 1996 we introduced a Friday custom. It was our mental preparation day, one when we didn't train. But we always went to the test venue for a Walk in the Park. We'd spend 10 minutes in the changing room, where you'd find your seat and generally get a feel for the place. A lot of the players were experiencing Newlands and King's Park and Ellis Park for the first time and Friday was therefore an important bonding opportunity for them. We'd then walk around the ground and "feel" the venue where the next afternoon we would be putting our bodies on the line. Every stadium has its own atmosphere, even with no spectators present, and Friday afforded us the opportunity to breathe it into our nostrils. On that '96 adventure, Fitzy usually called us together out in the middle of the stadium and offered a few suggestions, something to muse over for the next 24 hours. Instead of rushing back to our hotel, we would then call at a cafe or restaurant for coffee or tea and scones. Very British, we always thought, and delightfully relaxing. The Friday outing would conclude with a stroll, through the town or city, or sometimes along the beach. Back at the hotel, we'd retreat to our rooms for a snooze or quiet read through until the early evening captain's meeting.

My room-mate in Durban was to be Craig Dowd. We stepped out of the lift together on the 19th floor of the Crowne Plaza Hotel to find our electronic key wouldn't operate. All the other players' keys worked, but not ours. Nineteen floors below, I was assured they did not have a spare key. But there would be an attendant who would let us in. In theory, fantastic; in practice, useless. When the attendant finally turned up – he'd obviously been home for dinner – his master key didn't work either. The door was somehow secured from the inside. Not to worry, he assured us, whereupon he entered the room next door. Craig and I watched in morbid fascination as he eased himself out onto a ledge inches wide and shuffled along – 19 stories up – to our window. We finally took possession of our room, almost an hour after our team-mates and in a somewhat shell-shocked state.

If we were going to create history and take out a series in South Africa, winning the first test in Durban – where the Springboks had lost only once in 15 tests, and that in 1933 – was absolutely critical. No team had ever come from behind to win a series in South Africa. And we certainly didn't want to be relying on victory at Ellis Park in the tour finale to create such a piece of history. No, we wanted the series signed and sealed after Pretoria.

We suffered a setback when Andrew Mehrtens, who'd been averaging 16 points a test during 1996, suffered cartilage damage in training and had to be flown to Johannesburg for surgery. His replacement, Simon Culhane, boasted pretty mean credentials himself: four test outings for 97 points.

That we won at King's Park, 23-19 after a torrid battle in the best traditions of New Zealand-South Africa internationals, owed not a little to an audacious tactical substitution – substitutions hadn't been approved by the IRB at that stage – by Springbok coach Andre Markgraaff. With 10 minutes remaining, he "pulled" lock Hannes Strydom and sent on Kobus Wiese, later insisting Strydom was injured.

Well, Markgraaff was left to rue that strategic ploy, not us. The Springboks were feeding to an attacking scrum when Wiese joined the action. Seeing him coming, we decided we'd do to the Boks what they'd done to us in Christchurch – produce a concerted heave as the ball was coming in. Poor Kobus didn't have time to compose himself before the scrum of which he was now part began retreating. In their desperation to retrieve the situation, the Boks offended and we escaped from a tricky situation through a penalty.

Sean Fitzpatrick said at the press conference afterwards that that scrum was "the turning point of the game. It certainly wasn't a good time to be making a tactical substitution."

Our determination to focus only on the game at hand proved challenging when we arrived in Pretoria because every call back home and the hundreds of faxes we received reminded us of the fact that we were just one victory away from creating history. We tried to shut that out, to not concern ourselves with the big picture – just concentrate on the next game, as we'd been doing all season. We did, however, take encouragement from the many All Blacks who'd battled determinedly to win in South Africa and who were now wishing us well.

Loftus Versfeld was at the opposite end of the spectrum to Athletic Park where our major test campaign had begun. We were at 6000ft, not sea level. The temperature was 25 deg C, not 9 deg. We had sun in our eyes, not rain squalls. We sweated profusely – we certainly didn't shiver. And 98 per cent of the crowd were roaring for the Springboks, not us.

We produced some of our mightiest rugby of the year during the first half, including two fabulous counterattacking tries, to open up a 21-8 advantage. Against any other opponent, we might have felt secure. But we knew that in their desperation the Springboks would come back strongly.

As the second half unfolded, the heat, the altitude and the physicalness of the Boks began to take their toll. It was apparent our energy levels were beginning to run low. And the enemy had all but wiped out the deficit. Now it was 24-23.

In effecting a tackle with about 15 minutes to play, I finished up with my leg pinned under a South African player. As the forwards blew over me, the top half of my leg twisted and I felt pain in my knee and ankle ligaments. In 56 previous test outings I'd never once had to exit early. Now, in arguably my most important test, I was limping towards the sideline… with the series in the balance.

I swear it was far more nerve-racking sitting with the reserves than being out in the middle. Alongside Bull Allen, I was living the drama without being able to do anything about it. Jon Preston, who'd won the nickname of The Cleaner after the character in *Pulp Fiction*, was keeping us ahead with penalty goals, having replaced Simon Culhane.

Doc Mayhew was rushing around delivering a hundred messages from John Hart. It was almost too much to bear. Life had been far less frenzied out in the middle!

Then Zinny dropped his goal. Oh, the relief. So different from his "pot" against England in the World Cup. That one provided light-hearted relief, even made us laugh in the middle of an international. Although we now applauded Zinny's heroics, there was no laughing this time. The Boks were still within a converted try of saving the game.

How long can five minutes take? The Springboks threw everything at us. Our guys were out on their feet but never stopped tackling. Both teams were calling on their last resources because there was so much at stake. I have never experienced such tension in rugby in my life.

Then finally M'sieur Patrick Robin blew his whistle for full time and we had won. The series was ours. The players were so exhausted, some of them had trouble getting to their feet. The Dirty Dirties, who at that moment were more excited about the achievement than those on the pitch, burst into a haka. Their contribution to the campaign had been just as great as the players. Only 15 can take the field, but the back-up boys have an equally important role to play.

It was only when we were in the changing room that the true significance of the victory began to sink in. Radio New Zealand's Graeme Moody reflected what I guess the whole of New Zealand was feeling at that moment. Moods had a smile from ear to ear. " Fantastic, guys," he declared. "After 70 years, you guys have finally done it – beaten the bastards at home. Awesome!" Awesome indeed. We'd been too scared to contemplate the victory in case we stumbled. But now we'd done it. Euphoria was setting it. It was time to celebrate.

It was probably a shame from the All Blacks' viewpoint that the tour didn't finish at Pretoria. We had the Bledisloe Cup and the (huge) Tri-Nations trophy in the bag and we'd accomplished our major objective of winning a series in South Africa. These was little left to strive for, save for the satisfaction of completing a five-nil whitewash of the Springboks in one season.

The finale at Ellis Park was a lesson to all, including the management. The lesson was never to underestimate a team like South Africa and never to allow your preparation to drop below 100 per cent intensity. A lot of the guys

Olympix

Ellis Park represented the only blot on the All Blacks' vintage season of 1996, as is reflected on the faces of Andrew Blowers and myself. I came off with 30 minutes to play.

were flat after the Pretoria performance – hardly surprising in light of the energies they'd expended – and some were carrying the odd injury. I was still suffering knee and ankle soreness and, I guess if we'd been true to each other, I possibly should not have played.

Such is John Hart's loyalty, he stuck to the same fifteen when he probably would have been wiser to have introduced some fresh legs for our seventh major international in eight weeks.

Ellis Park is an intimidating place for an overseas player. It's effectively the South Africans' home ground and when full to capacity, as it was in 1996, the spectators seem to hover over you. We'd allowed ourselves to relax so much in that final week that at one stage we trailed the Springboks 32-8 and were on course for a record loss. It speaks volumes for the guys' spirit and determination that we came back to 32-22, finishing all over them.

No one seemed to notice that defeat when we arrived home. New Zealanders were going dotty because we'd taken out the series, achieved what had eluded the teams of 1928, 1949, 1960, 1970 and 1976. We were national heroes. It was amazing the progress rugby had made, in the eyes of the public, in the five years since the debacle at the 1991 World Cup. No recriminations this time, just plaudits.

News Media

12

Something Completely Different

After eight seasons travelling the world with the All Blacks, I thought I'd taken in all the major rugby stadiums. Then came 1997 and in rapid succession I got to play internationals at three test venues where New Zealand rugby players had never set foot before – Melbourne Cricket Ground, Old Trafford and Wembley.

I guess it demonstrates the growing international stature of the All Blacks that all three matches were sell-outs. I'm sure no more than 5000 spectators had ever attended an All Blacks game in Melbourne, but in late July the MCG – the winter home of Australian Rules – packed in 90,100 people for our Bledisloe Cup and Tri-nations encounter with the Wallabies. It would be interesting to know what percentage of the crowd understood the complexities of rugby. It was estimated that about 50,000 of those in attendance were dedicated Rules followers, for whom lineouts, rucks and scrums were probably thoroughly bewildering. They knew to cheer for the team in green and gold, but unfortunately they were always trailing the team in black!

Four months later a capacity 55,000 fans crammed Manchester United's home ground, Old Trafford, in Manchester to watch us play England, while the following Saturday 78,000 filled Wembley, the venue of soccer and league's championship finals, for our clash with Wales.

It was fascinating to experience these different venues and to compare them with the great rugby stadiums of the globe. The All Blacks' first taste of the MCG was on the Friday night, just over 24 hours before kickoff. Even without a single person in the vast stands, there existed an unbelievable atmosphere. As a player, it was a case of being in the right place at the right time. On previous visits to Melbourne, the All Blacks had been quartered in third-rate hotels and played at modest grounds like Olympic Park. We were living at the Centra Hotel and performing in front of one of the largest audiences ever to attend a rugby game anywhere in the world. Even though the field at the MCG was set at an odd angle to the stands, as a player you felt at one with the massive crowd. It was one of my great sporting experiences playing there.

Old Trafford was another notable first. We were honoured to play at the famous stadium because the ground is oversubscribed for every game Manchester United plays there. Wouldn't the North Harbour Rugby Union cherish that situation, knowing that North Harbour Stadium was sold out for every home game, even before the season kicked off!

We were given authority to train on the ground on the Friday, a decision I'm sure the head groundsman didn't subscribe to. He cringed every time we set a scrum. The difference between Old Trafford and most rugby grounds around the world is that there was no hump in the middle. It was dead flat, like a billiard table. An international-sized rugby field only just fits into Old Trafford. The crowd is extremely close on both sides and the deadball areas are short.

Wembley is a much larger stadium, more accustomed to staging football matches, but of the league variety. There's a quaint tradition which has to be observed prior to kickoff, one which is foreign to rugby players. You don't run out onto the field. You walk out in an orderly fashion. That's after the two teams have lined up in the tunnel, shoulder to shoulder. The captains then lead their teams out behind the ball boys. You don't run until you are on the playing surface. That's the uniqueness of Wembley.

Of the 78,000 fans who watched us play, they estimate almost 50,000 of them journeyed across the Severn River Bridge from Wales, which must have given a hell of a boost to the toll collection that week. The Welsh proved they can sing just as lustily away from Cardiff Arms Park. Such was the passion in their singing, I felt more emotion when their national anthem was booming out than I did our own!

The major rugby grounds of the world all have their own distinctive characteristics, features which spring to mind whenever you hear the name of the ground mentioned.

Some people wonder why England's home matches are listed as being at Twickenham, not London. Well, there's a good reason for that – Twickenham isn't in London. It's about 30 kilometres due west of the great city, in Middlesex. The great tradition which has developed there, fitting of the upper classes – because in England rugby is their game – are the boot parties in the car parks. You'd lose count of the Rolls-Royces, Bentleys, Jaguars and like which pepper the parks, out of the boots of which Twickenham's dignitaries sip their wines and sample their picnic hampers before and after the rugger. Rugger at Twickers is how it is. It's not unusual to find Jeeves preparing lunch at the car and having everything laid out when his crew return after the final whistle.

As a player, my lasting impression is how immaculate everything is at Twickers. The turf is mowed with precision, there's usually a red carpet laid out, upon which a member of the Royal Family is introduced to both teams, and under the grandstand there appear to be countless immaculately attired officials monitoring everything. As an All Black, you know you're not doing particularly well if the spectators burst into *"Swing Low Sweet Chariot".*

A sweet, delightfully English feature of the Twickenham changing rooms are the baths. Of basic porcelain, there are seven of them, each about six feet long and quite wide. Three players can get in them, sitting crossways. They're empty when you go out to play but filled by the time you return. There's a lot to be said for a good soak when your body is battered and bruised.

Cardiff Arms Park, which is where I made my All Black debut, can be a shade unnerving when you first arrive at the ground. Usually, there's almost no one there! In dramatic contrast to Twickenham, which is a train ride (or a Rolls-Royce journey, if you're a genuine Twickers member) out of London, the Arms Park is slap bang in the middle of Cardiff. Like, if you're staying at the Angel Hotel, it's further to the Post Office than it is to the rugby ground. So when the All Blacks used to step onto the hallowed turf an hour before kickoff, most of the fans were still quaffing their last ales in the local pubs. They're not big into curtainraisers in Wales, and most of those attending the game wouldn't take up their seats until about 15 or 20 minutes before kickoff.

Cardiff is famous for its singing. While our audiences mumble their way through *"God Defend New Zealand"* or maintain a steely glare as though they personally are about to engage in 80 minutes of desperate rugby activity, the Welsh throw themselves into their national anthem with unbelievable intensity and passion. I'm sure the authorities view video replays afterwards and anyone not singing wholeheartedly is struck off the ticket list for the next international.

They are undertaking an incredibly ambitious project at Cardiff. As I write this, the grand old stadium has been completely torn down and is to be replaced with an amazing new construction with an all-seat capacity of 73,500. It will be the only stadium in the UK with a retractable roof. With luck, it will be ready for the opening of the 1999 Rugby World Cup which Wales is hosting. The International Board isn't taking any chances though – it has made alternative arrangements to stage the final at Twickenham or in Paris if the construction company doesn't finish the project on time.

Lansdowne Road Stadium in Ireland is a little like Cardiff in that because of its proximity to the centre of Dublin the fans prefer to partake of a Guinness or two in a nearby cafe or bar and delay their arrival at the ground as late as possible. I'll never forget my first outing on the ground, for the All Blacks against Leinster in 1989. When I joined the players out in the middle about an hour before kickoff, the stands were almost deserted. I wondered if we'd got the match day wrong!

The novel feature of Lansdowne Road is that the railway station is literally under the grandstand. If you're coming to the game by train, it's a gentle stroll from your carriage to your seat. Unlike the Welsh, the Irish prefer to do their singing at halftime. You'll often hear the strains of *"Molly Malone"* as you sit in the changing room getting your instructions for the second half.

The unique aspect of Murrayfield, which is as close to the centre of Edinburgh as Eden Park is to Auckland, is that because of Scotland's harsh winter climate there is an "electric blanket" under the turf, to melt the ice and snow which occur there not infrequently in winter.

Unfortunately, when the All Blacks played there in 1993 there was a "hole" in one side of the ground where a grandstand had been demolished, as a consequence of which the place lost much of its atmosphere.

Their anthem, the *"Flower of Scotland"*, is probably the most inspirational of all the national anthems of the major rugby playing countries.

When you play in Paris, getting to the venue is usually as breathtaking as anything that transpires in the game itself. That's because you always have a police motorcycle escort who, with lights aflashing, give the impression they are actually trying to lose the visiting team, rather than guide them through the busy streets to the stadium.

The Latin temperament reveals itself wherever you play in France or Italy. Noise is paramount. They let off firecrackers, produce shrill whistling whenever the visiting goalkicker is lining up a shot, boo the referee wholeheartedly and don't hesitate to pelt the players with, at best, oranges and, at worst, beer or soft-drink cans. French supporters are extremely passionate and like to express themselves.

Sadly, the Parc des Princes, where we produced one of our most rousing performances on the 1995 tour, has been closed down as a rugby venue and all future internationals will be staged at the all-new Paris North Stadium which was opened in 1998 in time for the Soccer World Cup. While the facilities will undoubtedly be among the finest in the world, the spectators will remain boisterous and highly excitable.

The major stadiums in South Africa are all distinctive. The one great benefit all the major rugby centres have over Europe is climate. While rugby is still a winter game, any resemblance between the climates of Johannesburg and Durban and the major European destinations is purely coincidental. It doesn't rain for the three months of Johannesburg's winter, while in the rugby season in Cardiff it doesn't stop!

Cape Town is the exception in South Africa. It has a climate more like New Zealand's with winter rain, sometimes so persistent that Newlands can churn up and produce mud scrambles. For all that, Newlands is one of my favourite grounds. The view outside the ground, of the majestic Table Mountain, is awe-inspiring. Newlands inside is enclosed on all four sides by sheer grandstands, putting the crowd right there with you. Newlands has a rich tradition and somehow you sense that when you play an international there.

King's Park in Durban, where I played my first game in South Africa, against Natal in 1992, probably has a greater atmosphere outside the stadium than in it. That's because the fans take advantage of Durban's fabulous tropical climate – it's usually about 25 deg C and intensely humid when you play there – to enjoy barbecues before and after the rugby. The aroma from hundreds, probably thousands of barbecues is quite overwhelming. At Twickenham, they indulge themselves similarly but need fur-lined coats and/ or thermals to brace themselves against the climate; at Durban, most people are in light, short-sleeved shirts and many in shorts.

Ellis Park in Johannesburg and Loftus Versfeld in Pretoria, which, remarkably, are only 50 kilometres apart, are two of a kind. You can be sure when you play at those stadiums in winter the sky will be blue, the temperature warm, the grass more brown than green and – in contrast to European venues – there will be curtainraisers. Very likely a whole cluster of curtainraisers, often kicking off at about 10.30 in the morning.

Ellis Park, more than Loftus Versfeld, is intimidating because it is so vast. There's also a lot of security to pass through entering and leaving the grandstand. For players, the novel feature of Ellis Park is the long, dark tunnel you pass through from the changing rooms before emerging into the brightness of the stadium.

While the Melbourne Cricket Ground has been the preferred venue for All Black tests in Australia in 1997 and 1998, partly to promote rugby in Victoria but obviously also because of the massive financial take – 90,000 in Melbourne brings in a hell of a lot more than 40,000 in Brisbane – the rugby stadiums I'm more familiar with across the Tasman are Ballymore and the Sydney Football Stadium.

The uniqueness of Ballymore lies in the grass – couch, which is really spongy. Eighty minutes flat out there and you become leg weary. The grass also has a cushioning effect on rugby balls, which don't bounce as much.

Brisbane's climate is tropical and the often intense humidity finds out a lot of overseas players, especially those from colder climates. The dressing rooms there are quite small and can become stiflingly hot. I always remain in a light T-shirt until a few minutes before taking the field.

It's a ground with great atmosphere. The Four X Hill is quite something, akin to Bay 13 at the MCG, always chocker with vocal Queensland or Wallaby fans, which makes for a lot of fun and entertainment. In typical Australian fashion, there's a large bar under the grandstand, adjoining the changing rooms, which means the players skim the bar patrons as they prepare to run out onto the field. More than once I've declined a can of beer as I readied myself for action.

Ballymore is a wonderful rugby asset, but because of its limited capacity (about 24,000), internationals are now being staged at Suncorp Stadium. On the only occasion I played there, the All Blacks came from 9-22 down to win, so I've got pretty fond memories of the place!

I've always enjoyed my visits to Sydney with the All Blacks, as much because of where we've been quartered – initially at Manly and more recently at Coogee Bay, both with spectacular beaches. People always seem to be swimming, even in midwinter.

For matches at the Sydney Football Stadium, the bus always parks outside, leaving the players to walk approximately 200 metres through the crowd to gain access, which is unusual among major sports stadiums.

The SFS has large changing rooms, from where you walk through a long tunnel to the ground. I played my first night test there in 1994. Night rugby works well in Australia because of their superior climate. Playing rugby at night in New Zealand can be a risky business. At best, there's always a dew which leaves the ball slippery.

SFS is a player-friendly ground with ideal facilities. The crowd is close which creates a nice atmosphere and being a sole-purpose football ground, there is no grassless cricket block in the middle, as used to exist at the Sydney Cricket Ground.

The Wallabies were the world champions in the making, and playing like it, when I first started travelling across the Tasman as an All Black. Four of my first five internationals in Australia were lost. Fortunately, since 1995, I've been on the winning side. Long may it continue!

The test grounds of New Zealand all have their special features. A Carisbrook test is a whole week happening. The game takes over Dunedin, vibrant university city that it is, creating a marvellous atmosphere. From the moment you arrive at Dunedin Airport, you feel rugby in the air. Dunedin is about spirited young people enjoying themselves, face painting, fun and laughter, a rugby occasion. It's more than Dunedin's test – it's the deep south's test, attracting thousands of fans from Southland, Central Otago and beyond.

They make a weekend of it. While Dunedin takes a lot of ribbing about its climate, there hasn't been a wet-weather test at Carisbrook since 1983. The All Blacks always look forward to their visits to Dunedin.

Being a sole-purpose rugby ground – of which there are few in New Zealand – Athletic Park always presents a near impeccable playing surface. No bare, muddied cricket-pitch zone in the middle, just lush grass from goalposts to goalposts. Rather like Dunedin, rugby tests seem to electrify the whole city. Fly into Wellington on the eve of a major rugby international and you immediately sense it's a special occasion. Unfortunately, the Athletic Park facilities are arguably the worst of any major rugby stadium on the globe, being dark, cold and dingy. And Wellington's notorious wind can reduce contests to battles against the elements as much as the enemy. I know Sean Fitzpatrick preferred not to win the toss on windy days in Wellington, hating to make the decision over whether to go with the gale or into it. From the year 2000, Wellington's rugby focus will switch from Athletic Park to the smashing new stadium near the railway station. I know the sentimentalists fought hard to retain Athletic Park, claiming it created a very special atmosphere for rugby matches, which is correct. But I doubt any of those fighting the fight ever had to prepare themselves mentally for an important match in those depressing concrete dressing rooms.

Lancaster Park is another ground where the player facilities are in need of an upgrade and I understand that's on the drawing board. The distinctive aspect of Christchurch is that the spectators are so hugely parochial towards their Canterbury players. It's not something that happens in Auckland, Wellington (where admittedly they've produced few All Blacks in my time) or Dunedin. At those venues, you sense the crowd is right behind the men in black. At Lancaster Park, the greater support is for the local heroes, the Marshalls, Mehrtens, Blackadders and Mayerhoflers. It probably has a lot to do with the domination of New Zealand rugby by Auckland through the 1980s. Canterbury rugby went through a real trough and the fans fell away. Now that the red and blacks are back, stronger than ever it seems, the support is massive. It doesn't bother the other All Blacks that the locals are getting the support. The crowd's enthusiasm brings out the best in everyone.

Eden Park is a superb stadium which seems to bring out the best in Auckland teams and, because Auckland has tended to dominate test selections certainly during my time in the national team, the All Blacks as well. The only test the All Blacks have dropped at Eden Park in two decades was to France in 1994 when Philippe Saint-Andre's men swept the length of the field for the matchwinner a minute from time. Eden Park presents outstanding facilities and invariably an ideal surface on which to operate. Auckland doesn't have the intimacy of Dunedin or Wellington obviously because of its size (after all, one third of New Zealand's population does live within its boundaries) but thousands of rugby fans flock to the city for rugby internationals. The night before a test there are usually half a dozen major rugby dinners happening around the city.

Taking their cue from Twickenham, the Auckland administrators have installed a spa bath in the changing room which has been much appreciated, and well used, by the All Blacks.

An exciting new test venue in 1997 was my home ground, North Harbour Stadium at Albany. After the humble surroundings North Harbour representatives had endured from 1985 at Onewa Domain, Albany represented the ultimate in modern facilities. And like Athletic Park, not having to share with cricket means the turf is always in impeccable order. Some people see Albany as being slightly remote, but as the Massey University campus and the massive new shopping complex develop, Albany will become a thriving centre with the stadium the focal point.

The All Blacks' 1997 campaign began at Albany, with a night test against Fiji. The remarkable feature of the selection was that the same eight forwards who had played all 10 internationals the previous season – Zinzan Brooke, Josh Kronfeld, Michael Jones, Robin Brooke, Ian Jones, Olo Brown, Craig Dowd and Sean Fitzpatrick – were together again. Considering the physical demands of rugby at the highest level and the fact that Zinny, Michael, Robin, Fitzy and myself had all clicked over 30, this was nothing short of miraculous, a tribute to the conditioning skills of Martin Toomey and revitalising talents of medics Doc and Abo and coach John Hart.

The Awesome Eight wouldn't progress beyond Albany, sadly. Michael Jones came to grief in a tackle and for the second time in eight years was rushed to the Mater Hospital for major surgery on his knee. As in 1989, a combination of modern medical techniques and Michael's unshakeable personal faith would see him defy the odds and (eventually) return to rugby action.

Michael's injury cast a pall over our victory, but there was general satisfaction with our 71-5 victory, highlighted by Jeff Wilson's five tries. It was hard to tell whether Goldie was a left winger or a right winger, because he alternated all night and scored tries down both flanks.

We approached the test against the Argentinians in Wellington with some apprehension because we knew they possessed big forwards and indulged in power scrummaging. They had the former All Black coach Grizz Wyllie along as a technical advisor and we figured he'd be alerting them to our individual frailties.

Well, for the second year in a row at Athletic Park we performed beyond everyone's expectations. The previous season we'd put 43 points on the Wallabies; this time we hit 93 against the Pumas. It was one of those magical days where everything we attempted came off. We even had Zinny placing centring kicks for his brother Robin to score.

Humbled on the field the Pumas might have been, but they had the last word. They challenged us at something they were incredible good at – singing. We contemplated putting up a representative until we heard Omar Hasan's magnificent deep, opera voice. We surrendered at that stage.

The rematch a week later was at Hamilton's Rugby Park, another fresh test venue. Damp conditions and a determined opposition, playing to keep the score down, meant we laboured at times, but still notched up nine tries and 62 points, leaving us well primed for the Tri-nations series.

As in 1996, we'd broken the season down to a series of one-off tests. The Wallabies were our challenge in Christchurch and it was decided we would attack them through the scrum, as a consequence of which our focus throughout the entire week was on scrummaging. We put in some huge grunt sessions, mostly under Ross Cooper's guidance. What you find is that if you concentrate on one aspect of your play, it flows on to the playing field. Which is what happened at Lancaster Park.

The Wallabies under Greg Smith came to town confident of a bold showing, having won their previous 13 matches, but we demoralised them in the scrums. We even managed a tighthead and a pushover try, rare events in internationals between major nations these days. Smith conceded that his team had found our scrum "too much to cope with for a whole game".

Then it was the long trek through to South Africa to tackle the Springboks in Johannesburg. Winning at Lancaster Park is one thing, taming the Boks at Ellis Park quite another. We'd stumbled there in the World Cup final and again in 1996 which obviously gave the men in green a psychological advantage.

Mind games matter in these crunch encounters. The first thing our management did was change our accommodation. We abandoned the hotel where we'd stayed in 1995 and 1996 at Sandton. Nothing personal against the hotel (although Laurie Mains is still suspicious of what was added to the tea and coffee for the midday meal on the Thursday prior to the World Cup final). It's just that that hotel was associated with two losses. So we pitched our tent in Pretoria, 50 kilometres up the road. That was after four days' rest and recreation at Sun City where golf had a higher priority than rugby.

We were, to all intents and purposes, out of the Ellis Park game after 30 minutes. We'd believed the advance publicity about flyhalf Jannie de Beer, that he'd control the game with his tactical kicking. Wrong, wrong, wrong. He controlled the game, all right… by running. Before we knew it, the Springboks had opened up a 23-7 advantage and we were in serious trouble.

There were countless good excuses for losing that game, not least being the departure soon after halftime of Sean Fitzpatrick, the first sign that his knee was packing up. We'd earlier lost Tana Umaga and replaced him on the wing with Alama Ieremia, a specialist midfielder. Just being 16 points down at Ellis Park would have psyched most teams out, including probably the All Blacks of 1993 and 1994. But the team of '97 possessed immense resolve, the capacity to remain calm under pressure and to pace itself and stay the full 80 minutes. We knew we possessed individuals who could turn any game round – we just needed to give them the opportunity.

One of those individuals, arguably the greatest gamebreaker in rugby, happened to be wearing the No 14 jersey, Jeff Wilson. Just when we needed him most, he created two tries – scoring one himself, the other going to Carlos Spencer – and suddenly we were right back in the game at 19-23.

After ageless Frank Bunce had scored one of the great individual test tries, the game became a goalkicking duel between Spencer and de Beer, till it was 32-all. We'd have taken the draw and run at that stage. But the drama continued. Carlos landed his final kick while de Beer struck the upright at the other end. We'd won, beating the Ellis Park bogey. It ranks as one of the greatest games I've ever been involved in, a test that had everything.

One of the negatives of the Tri-nations competition in 1997 was the poor scheduling of the matches. The Wallabies copped the worst deal, having to travel from Dunedin to play their final game at Pretoria seven days later. That involved a massive amount of travel. Our journey from Johannesburg to Melbourne was almost as arduous. Pulling out of Pretoria on the Sunday morning, we eventually checked into the Centra Hotel in Melbourne 32 hours later at 1am Tuesday.

An Australian Rules writer came along to watch us train on the Wednesday afternoon and wrote glowingly of the intensity of the session and of our "professionalism". He noted we rejected the available excuses of jetlag and tiredness as we went diligently about our job.

That was the week of Fitzy's knee which had blown up like a balloon by the time we arrived in Melbourne. A surgeon he referred it to assured him he would never play rugby again. Fitzy didn't fancy that prognosis, so limped back to Abo and asked him to do his best. Having observed the swelling 48 hours previously, we were surprised when Fitzy turned up at training on the Thursday and even more amazed when he stripped and joined us for the workout. His presence certainly gave the whole team a boost. I'm sure he must have been experiencing considerable pain but he never once complained. That's Fitzy.

This was the game that worried John Hart most. The Wallabies were fresh while we were travel wearied and struggling to readjust to a fresh time zone. Perhaps if the game had been in Sydney or Brisbane, the home advantage might have swung things Australia's way. But in a weird way, Melbourne was almost a neutral venue. Of the 90,000 who attended, some 50,000 were Australian Rules fans, few of whom would have understood the niceties of the game, and up to 25,000 were Kiwis, more than half of whom had travelled across the Tasman specially for this historic occasion. We went into the game positively, determined to produce a strong 80-minute effort. We didn't want to lose and fall back on excuses. The All Black attitude, as exemplified by Laurie Mains and John Hart, is that there are no excuses for losing.

With more magic from Goldie (Jeff Wilson) and Buncey, we pulled off a surprisingly comfortable victory, 33-18, having the game in safe keeping by halftime. Plainly the Australian officials hadn't anticipated us winning because they didn't have the Bledisloe Cup ready for handing over. Having already won in Christchurch, the Cup was ours, but the Aussies were reluctant to hand it across. Goodness knows why. Anyway, after we'd hung about on the field for 10 minutes, an Aussie official located the trophy and the presentation was made. We wanted to show it off because of all the Kiwis present, to acknowledge their support. I'm sure if the boot had been on the other foot, the award ceremony wouldn't have been overlooked.

Our final two domestic tests in '97 brought victories over the Springboks at Eden Park and the Wallabies at Carisbrook, but in these games a disturbing trend began to emerge, our giving away soft tries when well ahead. We let the Boks come back from 50-21 to 55-35 and the Wallabies, more spectacularly, from 36-nil to 36-24. We weren't doing the 80-minute thing and were plainly relaxing our defence once comfortably ahead. Our second-half efforts meant the gloss came off both wins. The fans probably went home from Eden Park satisfied, for the All Blacks had never previously put a half-century of points on the Springboks, but I know there was a mass of disgruntled followers after we'd lost the second half 24-nil to the Wallabies in Dunedin. We had them on toast at halftime but failed to put them away.

Notwithstanding those second-half hiccups, it was enormously satisfying to complete a second Tri-Nations series without defeat. The trophy was on hand for the presentation at Carisbrook, the new trophy, that is. The one Fitzy received this time looked like a miniature compared with the original which had inadvertently been shaped on a scale of inches instead of centimetres.

Our test record after Carisbrook was eight wins out of eight with 55 tries scored and 17 conceded. We'd won a series against Argentina, retained the Tri-nations title and had beaten the Wallabies three out of three. Pretty impressive stuff, yet there was an element of dissatisfaction because we had failed to shut out the Springboks and the Wallabies in our final two games.

It has to be something in the New Zealand psyche that causes us to relax when we're comfortably ahead. The best of the All Blacks is always seen when the team's backs are to the wall… 16 points down against the Springboks at Ellis Park, 13 points down against the Wallabies at Brisbane, beaten by the Lions at Athletic Park. In those situations, the resolve of the All Blacks is an awesome weapon. Tradition is always on the New Zealand rugby player's side. He knows he is expected to win and no matter what the situation on the scoreboard, he can win.

When England toured New Zealand in 1998 there were 16 leading players unavailable, for a variety of reasons. When New Zealand toured the UK seven months earlier, there was not one top-flight player who declined the invitation. Even Jonah Lomu was there, and after the horrendous drug programme he'd been on to repair the debilitating kidney disease that had struck him down at the beginning of the year, he probably should have been left behind. It's the difference between players being contracted to the national body (as in New Zealand) as compared with players holding contracts with individual clubs (as in the UK).

No incumbent All Black would dare stay behind for personal reasons, unless they were matters of life or death, because he wouldn't want to give the opportunity to a rival to establish himself in his position.

As on the South African expedition the year before, we took 36 players to the UK, the "extra" team taken along to handle the midweekers, three of which were in England and one in Wales.

We actually ended up with an international against Ireland in Dublin, which is novel on a tour of Wales and England. Ireland wasn't featuring until the NZRFU agreed to a second test against England (at Old Trafford). That stirred the Irish. If you can play two tests against England, you can manage one against us, they insisted. Hard to argue against that logic. And Ireland is such a delightful country to visit. So it became a tour of Wales, England and Ireland… if you can call five days in a country a tour.

When the English media dropped in to see us for the first time in London, they obviously expected to find plenty of rugby balls. They saw none. But they did see lots of timber and nails and several hammers. The All Blacks were constructing ruck and scrum machines, building them once again to the team's personal specifications. Was this the New Zealand rugby team, wondered the journalists, or the New Zealand carpentry team?

If the Irish could force an extra game into the itinerary, so could the All Blacks. Coach Hart was concerned that the original fixture list had his first fifteen playing the international in Dublin first up. That was a bit severe, he decided, so he requested a warm-up game. Which led to us playing the Welsh club champion, Llanelli, at Stradey Park, famous for being where the All Blacks last lost to a Welsh team, 25 years previously. There wouldn't be a repeat in

1997. We outgunned them 81 points to 3, scoring 13 tries. Only the lightweight Reebok ball, which caused consternation among the goalkickers, saved the home side from conceding close to a century of points. Captaining the All Blacks at Llanelli was not Sean Fitzpatrick (whose knee was now a major source of concern), not Zinzan Brooke (who was abandoning New Zealand rugby to play for London Harlequins), not Taine Randell (regarded by many as the heir apparent) but someone who had rarely led a side in his entire career, Justin Marshall.

The logic for appointing Justin to deputise for Sean seemed to be that his form was on a high and that halfback was an excellent position from which to captain a team. The management plainly wanted to give Taine time to concentrate on his play as a loose forward and Zinny presumably wasn't entertained because, with his All Black career rapidly coming to a close, there was a possibility he wouldn't be used in every international. As it turned out, he played all the tests, bringing up his 100th game for New Zealand in the tour finale at Twickenham. Zinny thrives on captaincy and it would have been a fitting way to round out his career.

In hindsight, elevating Justin to the captaincy probably wasn't the smartest decision. He did the best job he could, but his own play suffered. And after half a dozen seasons under super-cool Fitzy, who remained unruffled under the greatest provocation, it came as a jolt to have our new skipper twice marched 10 metres at Twickenham for challenging the referee in less than diplomatic terms.

The disappointment of the tour was spending only five days in Ireland. Many of the players regard the Emerald Isle as their favourite destination, so a midweeker at Cork or Limerick would have been hugely popular, but it wasn't to be.

The one thing you could guarantee was that Ireland – at this point coached by Brian Ashton, who'd taken over from the deposed Kiwi Murray Kidd and who would soon be sacked himself – would come at us with great ferocity. Reputations count for nothing with the Irish and until the about the 30th minute we were on the back foot. Two tries by Keith Wood had the Irish ahead 15-11. Fortunately, we scored the next 52 points!

England proved a doughtier opponent at Old Trafford the following weekend, although our 25-8 winning scoreline represented a record winning margin for the All Blacks in England. A fellow you couldn't help but notice among the opposition was Richard Cockerill who was all bravado, eyeballing Norm Hewitt during the haka and playing up to the crowd. Nothing wrong with that, I suppose, if you're good enough to deliver, but it surprises me a player would inflict such expectations upon himself. Better to say nothing and deliver heaps, I believe. That's the New Zealand way. The most aggressive part of his play was the pushing and shoving he indulged in after the whistle.

It was a great occasion being at Old Trafford, and beating England on its home soil was something I had not experienced before. We were a shade bemused as we wended our way towards the changing room after the final whistle to find the English team performing a lap of honour. We were assured later they were merely thanking the rugby people of the north of England for supporting them. Sure looked like a lap of honour to the All Blacks!

By the time we got through to London to prepare for the Welsh international at Wembley in the last week of November, many of the players had been effectively playing rugby nonstop for nine months. Coach John Hart was obviously mindful of this when we embarked on yet another training session on the Thursday, this time at the British Airways Sports Field at Heathrow.

After 15 minutes of warm-up, Hart brought us together for team training. We'd been going no more than one minute, when he ordered a stop and asked us to gather round him. "Are you ready to play against Wales?" he asked Christian Cullen. The answer was yes. "Are you ready to play against Wales?" he asked Jeff Wilson. He answered in the affirmative also. Hart continued, posing the question to each of the 15 test players. Everyone answered yes.

"Righto, then," said Hart. "We're ready to play against Wales. That'll do for today." And with that, training concluded. Our one-minute team run was enough for us to do the business against Wales, 42 points to 7. Fitzy, with 91 test appearances behind him, had the unique experience of sitting on the reserves bench… and getting the call-up as a tactical substitute 15 minutes into the second spell. Norm Hewitt was the only person who didn't seem to appreciate the swap and was subsequently reprimanded by management for ungracious behaviour.

Our final score against Wales was a dropped goal from you-know-who… Zinzan Brooke. Our rugby had become a bit ragged in the final stages, so Zinny decided to straighten matters out, as only he can. Overseas fans express amazement that a forward can drop goals, but Zinny used to practise them endlessly at training and right through his formative years he was always his team's goalkicker. He used to take great umbrage whenever anyone expressed amazement that a forward should be drop-kicking goals. The backs didn't have exclusive rights on drop-kicks, he insisted – "I practise them as much as they do."

The focus was very much on Zinny in our tour finale at Twickenham. It was his 100th and last appearance for the All Blacks in a celebrated career dating back to the 1987 World Cup.

We had everything to play for at Twickenham. There was the memory of the 1993 loss , Zinny's farewell and we were striving for an unbeaten record in 1997. We'd achieved so much – the other 11 tests had all been won handsomely – and we didn't want to let ourselves down.

Maybe our focus was on going home. It was now December and summer was just around the corner. And perhaps we were so carried away with Zinny's big occasion… winning in style, and all that… that we forgot about the enemy.

We were seriously adrift at halftime, 23-9 down. It was Ellis Park all over again. If we were thinking about our return home, that scoreline certainly provided the wake-up call we needed. We actually played some tremendous rugby in the second half and if we'd grabbed all our chances we'd have won comfortably. But in the end we had to settle for a 26-all draw which was bloody disappointing. In a sense, a draw represented a loss to us.

Perhaps we should have used our interchange bench better. Who knows? What we did know was that we'd lost our last test in 1996 and drawn our last test in 1997. Bearing in mind that our last test in 1999 will, hopefully, be the World Cup final, it's something John Hart and the All Blacks need to address.

The English couldn't do a lap of honour – they'd already done that at Old Trafford. It's not something New Zealanders indulge in, being the undemonstrative lot we are. We're more concerned with assessing our mistakes than celebrating our successes. I'm not sure it's the most desirable trait, but it's how we are. Goldie started showing emotion after scoring tries but copped so much flak he gave it away. We've gone back to being unsmiling giants. That's how the nation seems to prefer us

Niels Schipper

13

South to Harbour

North Harbour, the union that adopted me in 1994 when I made the break with Northland, was in many ways a paradox. Despite being the country's youngest union, in 1995 it claimed more representatives in the All Black World Cup squad (eight) than any other. Yet it also possessed the most humble home stadium of any first division union. Onewa Domain, Harbour's "home" for 12 seasons from its formation in 1985, was nothing more than a club facility. I recall a Transvaal player, whose home stadium was the magnificent Ellis Park, one of the world's finest test venues with a capacity of 75,000, looking around Onewa after arriving for a Super 10 fixture and saying, "This is obviously the training ground – where do we play the match?" He looked quite shocked upon being informed that, no, *this* was the ground where Transvaal would be doing battle with North Harbour.

In 1997, North Harbour would celebrate the opening, at Albany, of one of the smartest and best-equipped stadiums in the country, but until then we all had to make do with the Takapuna club's facility at Onewa which was often a source of ridicule and controversy, particularly during the first season I was involved, '94.

Having been allocated a match against the touring French team, the North Harbour officials decided to hire Eden Park for the game. It was a beautiful day, a large crowd attended and Harbour made history by fashioning a spectacular win.

When later in the season the high-flying Harbour team blasted aside Canterbury in the semi-final, it became eligible for a home final. The NZRFU suggested a more appropriate venue than Onewa should be used and the

Ode to the Kamo Kid

It's time for the poets to wax lyrical,
tis the hour to drink the kegs dry,
For our women to go all hysterical,
and 20-stone props start to cry.

Cos the flag's at half-mast up in Kamo,
and the mood in the city's all black.
Things are miserable down on the farm - o,
Jonesy, please - why won't you come back?

We know you've got reasons for leaving,
and you're proud to be born Cambridge Blue.
But your leaving is leaving us grieving.
Without you, just what will we do?

It'll feel really weird watching telly,
when we're needing five points just to tie.
And Keith Quinn says 'the big lock from MILFORD
has scored in the corner a try!

At the outset they said you were scrawny,
and wouldn't stand up to the Test.
But we backed you to outjump those brawny,
slow meatheads, - who thought they were best.

You've become now a quite famous person,
keeping all of the north in the news.
Remember, when you kissed Elle McPherson? We
were standing right there in your shoes.

You're a Kauri grown mighty in stature,
who has never forgotten his roots.
The thing we admire most is that ya,
never got too damn big for your boots.

Haere ra, then, o spring-heeled gazelle,
keeping one jump ahead as you go.
Whoever's jersey you wear, fare thee well,
We'll still hail the Kid from Kamo.

-Steve Challis

Auckland union offered Eden Park which would have meant home advantage for Auckland. This time the Harbour officials dug their toes in. The final, they insisted, would be played at Onewa Domain. Which it was. Harbour had the right to stage the showpiece of the NPC and took up the challenge, which the players appreciated.

Auckland was accustomed to being in the NPC final but this was the first time the young upstart from across town had challenged its status. And as often happens with neighbouring factions, the game turned into a dogfight. Nike, North Harbour's apparel sponsor, has always been aggressive in its marketing and maintained that reputation by erecting deliberately provocative signs and billboards which the Auckland players and their supporters could see as they drove towards Takapuna.

There were skirmishes among the spectators even before kickoff, while the main feature degenerated into a snarly, ugly battle from which All Blacks Eric Rush, Harbour, and Robin Brooke, Auckland, were sent off with several others being cited. The NZRFU judicial committee handed out mass suspensions, while the council ruled that for future NPC finals it would reserve the right to select the venue. Obviously, it didn't consider Onewa Domain appropriate for New Zealand representative rugby's showpiece.

North Harbour is still an extremely young union, being only 13 years old, which is nothing compared with the likes of Auckland, Wellington, Canterbury and Otago which have all celebrated their centenaries. Even my old union Northland dates back to 1920.

Harbour is still finding its feet in terms of tradition and in establishing a style of play. In the early years Harbour developed a lot of free spirits, players like Frano Botica, Iain Woods, Scott Pierce, Paul Feeney and Walter Little. They developed an adventurous spirit which, in a sense, came to epitomise Harbour rugby.

As the game became more professional, this attitude sometimes rebounded on North Harbour. At crucial stages when Harbour teams needed to knuckle down, the team's free spirit would be in the ascendancy. You ignore the basics at your peril and too often that was Harbour's downfall. Having said that, the Harbour team of '94, which was the one I slotted into, produced rugby of often breathtaking quality. We twice won on Eden Park, against France and, in a famous first, against Auckland, we beat Transvaal and narrowly missed out on the Super 10 final at Durban, we demolished Canterbury by 59 points to 27 in the NPC semi-final and foundered only against Auckland's magnificent forward pack, led by those titans Sean Fitzpatrick and Zinzan Brooke, in the final. At the end of it all, Brad Meurant was named the New Zealand coach of the year and North Harbour fielded accolades galore. We were unquestionably the glamour team of the season with half the side in the All Blacks.

News Media

Richard Turner, North Harbour's captain in 1994... a flamboyant character with a novel attitude to training.

Unfortunately, North Harbour, having made gigantic progress in an extremely short time, thereafter began to slip back. A lot of it had to do with the preparation. There's a free and easy life style on the North Shore which manifested itself in the representative team. This may change now that Buck Shelford, a no-nonsense man if ever there was one, has taken over. But because Shore players have never wanted for much, I always felt there was a lack of steel about the team. When victories needed to be ground out, Harbour often sought the easier option, and lost.

The team has certainly featured some flamboyant characters, not least the man who captained that fine side of '94, Richard Turner, popularly known as Pod. He was a big man with a novel attitude to training. He'd do the team work, the scrums, the lineouts and the rucks with us, but when Peter White, Harbour's trainer, called the guys together to discuss fitness drills, Richard would listen for a while, shake his head and walk off. Remarkably, this was accepted. Richard was one of the cafe set, a man-about-town who seemed to conduct most of his business by mobile phone from his favourite cafes and bars. Pod loved the media and they loved him. He used them to his advantage – he could speed-dial most of them on his mobile phone! He was everything that was good and bad about North Harbour, an amusing entertainer who mixed well with the corporates but who had a bad attitude towards training, and Brad Meurant accepted it. If he'd ever got himself even 90 per cent fit, he could have been a sensational player. His timing of the tackle was second to none and many a dashing opponent has been left flattened on the turf wondering what it was that hit him. Richard is now in Milan. Whatever he's up to, he'll be enjoying himself, with a cup of laté amid the fashionable people.

Brad Meurant was very much a players' coach, certainly when the players were of a North Harbour mindset. Brad, always with a cigarette lit (until he dramatically gave up in 1996), was a bloke's bloke, who blended a rare mix of egos together and, certainly in '94, came up with an uncommonly good team. His team couldn't have achieved a lot more that season, apart from the two major goals which eluded him – reaching the Super 10 final and winning the NPC.

Long-serving front rowers Ron Williams and Graham Dowd and first-five Warren Burton, complemented by the current All Blacks when they were around, implemented the game plan which Brad in his cool way oversaw.

Because rugby was still amateur and because Brad, as a plumber, was struggling to pay the bills, he resigned as Harbour coach and took himself (and his family) off to East London in South Africa where he coached one of the less glamorous provincial teams, Border.

His successor at North Harbour was Chas Ferris who'd been coaching New Zealand Maori, not without considerable success. But there were ominous signs as Harbour tailed the field this time in the Super 10.

Our campaign opened with a trip to South Africa. After a comfortable warm-up victory against Western Transvaal at Potchefstroom, we faced Transvaal at Ellis Park. They were out for revenge, having been comprehensively put away at the Wembley of the south, Onewa Domain, the previous season. Chas Ferris' son Myles, a prop, played this game, in which one of his roles was to provide a block for the jumpers at lineout time. Late in the game, with us holding a narrow lead, Transvaal prepared to throw to a lineout on our 22. I became aware that there was no one between myself and Mark Weedon, the other jumper. Myles Ferris was missing. I looked around and saw him across the touchline with his boot off, receiving treatment for a blister. Transvaal, seizing the opportunity, threw in, drove through the gap where the prop should have been and scored the matchwinning try.

In such critical situations, blisters can wait. At least, that's always been my attitude on the rugby field. You're there to support your 14 team-mates. The team wasn't happy about that at all, and with the player involved being the coach's son, it did nothing for morale.

Chas sought to implement a different culture into the team. He assured us that if we wanted to be better people we should learn Maori. All our team calls should be in Maori. And we should number off in Maori. An interesting innovation, at the opposite end of the spectrum from Brad Meurant's laid-back attitude. It went down like a lead balloon with most of the Harbour players.

The loss to Transvaal was the start of an ill-fated season. We did manage to beat Auckland at Onewa Domain, a result which, in the context of the rest

Niels Schipper

It's not only Frank Bunce who can throw well-timed passes to the left. Action from an NPC encounter against King Country in 1996.

of the season, represented a minor miracle, but we didn't win a single game in the Super 10 and bowed out at the semi-final stage of the NPC with an embarrassing 60-26 loss to Auckland. Harbour's record for the year was nine wins, nine losses and two draws.

Midway through the NPC, a summit conference was called to discuss Chas' performance. Frank Bunce, Ant Strachan and myself as players met with president Peter Lamont, chief executive officer Grant Elley and Harbour's foundation coach Peter Thorburn.

There was a strong move to dump him, there and then, which I resisted. I wasn't that happy with Chas as a coach but I was adamant that firing your coach halfway through an NPC campaign wasn't in the best interests of the team or the union. Chas stayed and his team, boasting eight All Blacks, won enough matches to scrape into the play-offs. The players didn't have the desire to kick on at that stage and we suffered our biggest NPC loss.

The team seldom realised its potential that season which was a major disappointment for the fans after the achievements of '94. We possessed an exciting backline, but backs are only as good as the quality ball which gets delivered to them. Although we secured our share of lineout ball, our scrum was never more than adequate and was rudely dealt to by Auckland in the semi-final. It's a problem that has carried through to today with Harbour – the slick, talented backs being frustrated for want of quality possession.

One season in South Africa was enough for Brad Meurant and he was back in town for '96, in swift succession being appointed coach of both North Harbour and the new Waikato Chiefs Super 12 franchise. It should have been the start of a big, bright coaching career for Brad. But he failed to produce the goods.

Brad's mistake, I believe, was that he tried to coach the same way he had in 1994. But the scene had changed. Rugby was now professional, demanding professional attitudes. Brad was still coaching like an amateur.

Under Brad, North Harbour developed a style probably suitable for the NPC, although his team had lost to Otago and Taranaki before the bevy of All Blacks reported for duty following the triumphant tour of South Africa.

At the first (Tuesday) training session, we All Blacks tried to implement tactics and concepts we'd been using, with spectacular success, at international level and which we genuinely felt would bolster Harbour's chances of success. It was, I appreciate now, bewildering for the guys who'd been diligently operating back home under Brad. Several of the changes revolved around the lineout – using a flanker as halfback, employing an offensive defence and varying the lifting technique.

Unfortunately, we didn't have the wholehearted support of the non-internationals, with the result that the Ranfurly Shield challenge against Waikato in Hamilton became something of a disaster. We were badly beaten in the lineouts because we had some people operating on one game plan and others on another.

Brad as the coach should have been more authoritative. In his laid-back way, he left the forwards to it when he should have taken decisive action. Either the team adopted the All Black pattern or it didn't. At Hamilton, we weren't committed one way or the other.

It was natural for Brad to want to utilise his All Black talent at the earliest possible opportunity, but for those of us who'd been involved in the tests in South Africa, a fortnight's break to freshen would have been a marvellous tonic. Frank Bunce, Walter Little, Glen Osborne and myself were coming off the euphoria of a historic series win on South African soil, a series which had drained us physically and mentally.

We were probably more of a disruption than a help and, not surprisingly, Harbour experienced a jumbled NPC campaign, finishing a dismal eighth, ahead of only King Country which was relegated. Not only was it the first time Harbour had failed to make the play-offs but the Ranfurly Shield eluded us even though Harbour featured in three – yep, three – challenges in the space of six weeks, at New Plymouth, Hamilton and Auckland. It was a shame Harbour didn't fare better because Brad had had such a great year in '94, but professionalism had caught him out. He needed to be more organised and stamp his authority.

Needing a new coach for 1997, Harbour surprisingly didn't promote its B team coach, Wayne Pivac, who took off to Northland, or seek an outsider; it recalled the man who'd helped launch the union back in 1985, taken it from humble third division status to premier ranks and guided the representative team's fortunes for seven seasons before becoming an All Black selector, Peter Thorburn.

Thorbs came back with only one objective, to develop the player resources of the Harbour union. He'd started Harbour with local talent and was determined to promote that policy in 1997. Rent-a-player wasn't Thorbs' way. He saw that as providing only short-term solutions. Harnessing your own union's talent was the way to guarantee a sound future.

I was standing among the media when Thorbs introduced his '97 Harbour squad at a promotional function at Albany. "I hope they are supplying us with photos of these guys," commented one journalist, "because I've never heard of half of them."

Thorbs had to endure a lot of criticism over his approach in '97. His team really needed a seasoned tighthead prop, a thinking No 8 and an experienced first-five to run the backline. But Thorbs was grimly determined that his team would survive with 15 players with Made In North Harbour stamped on their backsides. Survive Harbour did, although it has to be said that Thorbs personally went through purgatory in the final couple of weeks of the competition. After his team had dropped five in a row, Harbour eked out a 7-6 win over Southland in Invercargill only because Simon Culhane hit the uprights from point blank range in the final minute, then held on for a 21-16 win over Taranaki at Albany after surviving 11 consecutive five-metre scrums in the dying stages.

As in 1996, we All Blacks were coming off another strenuous, but also successful, campaign and again found it difficult readjusting from the ultra-professional All Black scene to the semiprofessional situation at North Harbour. Harbour, with its limited resources, has never had the luxury of offering its internationals a holiday while the batteries recharged. No, if you arrived home on a Monday, you were expected to be at training on the Tuesday. Things were better in '97, however, because Thorbs had kept his All Blacks well briefed on developments and, in contrast to Brad, was emphatic on what tactics would be employed. Everyone responded to Thorbs' enthusiasm.

I'd had to introduce myself to a lot of the guys at early training sessions. They were a rawboned lot, some of whom hadn't even been age-grade representatives. Not only were they absolute greenhorns as rep players, they didn't even know the basic role of a duty boy or even know about a number call. They were eager but as green as grass.

What impressed me was how they developed from naive newcomers to a group of guys who really gutsed it out in those critical late-season clashes against Southland and Taranaki. Critics who only judge a side on where it sits on the table had a field day with North Harbour in '97. On pure results – four games won and 10 lost – sure, the '97 season was a disaster, but in terms of building for the future, it achieved plenty, for which Thorbs can take a bow. I hadn't had a lot to do with him previously. He was an All Black selector, of course, when Laurie Mains was coaching but his direct involvement with Harbour teams had ended in 1991. His enthusiasm and philosophies were something I took to. Guys like Thorbs should never be lost to North Harbour or New Zealand rugby. As well as being a great analyst of rugby, he dispenses sound business advice. He is ideally equipped to become a mentor for aspiring young players.

Having achieved what he set out to do, Thorbs stepped aside and now Buck Shelford comes in. He was uncompromising as a player and the guys remember him for that. Now he's got to transfer those qualities into his coaching role. The union's new chief executive officer Doug Rollerson, an exuberant and dynamic individual – as he was when he represented the All Blacks in the early 1980s – complements Buck perfectly. Together, they should get Harbour moving forward strongly again.

Harbour is still young and growing. It's now got a home at Albany, the equal of anything in international rugby. The facilities are outstanding. What North Harbour hasn't got, of course, is a Super 12 franchise. Those who have, have stolen a march on the others because they train for and play to a similar pattern to that which they use in the NPC. You can see that with Auckland, Canterbury and Otago, where the coaches and the players are essentially the same. North Harbour does not have that luxury.

Harbour has spent three years bonding with Waikato in the Chiefs (formerly Waikato Chiefs) franchise. Now, it seems, the make-up of the two most northern franchises will change, with Harbour joining forces with Auckland and Northland to make up the Auckland Blues and Counties-Manukau moving south to link with Waikato, Bay of Plenty and King Country in the Chiefs.

When the Super 12 was first mooted three years ago, there was talk that North Harbour would combine with Auckland, which was logical, both being based in the same city. But at that stage, the two unions were supplying more than half the All Black squad and it was felt that together they would be too strong. So Harbour was combined with Waikato and the other Coronation Shield districts.

There was initial bickering over whether the franchise should be centred on Hamilton or Albany. Obviously, there was some resentment among Harbour fans when Waikato got the nod. It was also apparent that the relationship between the officials of the two unions was strained, which filtered down and naturally impacted on the players.

Although the North Harbour and Waikato players got on individually well enough, subconsciously there existed a them-and-us mentality. What disappointed me was how the Waikato supporters would boo players from outside areas, the worst example being when Leon Macdonald, drafted from Canterbury, came on as a replacement for local hero Ian Foster this year. That was a sure sign that a lot of people still hadn't come to grips with the Super 12 concept.

It hasn't been easy amalgamating the two styles of Waikato and North Harbour, but Ross Cooper achieved success in 1998. After three years, the players and unions have now bonded strongly. If the NZRFU is going to split the franchises, it has to do it now, because given another year, it would be too strong a base to dismantle.

14

Fit for Anything

Although they've been playing rugby in New Zealand for well over 100 years, some things haven't changed. It's always been 15 to a side, 40 minutes each way, scrums and lineouts to restart play, with the grafters in the pack and the speedsters on the wing. And some players have always been fitter than others.

With the advent of professionalism, fitness, particularly for the elite players, has become a science, with personal fitness levels monitored with meticulous precision. But it wasn't always like that. Rugby being the staunchly amateur game that it was for so long, fitness was largely left to the individual. Indeed, it's only in the 1990s that fitness trainers have been taken on board by national rugby teams.

My own career provides a graphic example of the developments made in training over the past couple of decades and emphasises how much of the early fitness work by rugby players, certainly in the 80s, was hit or miss.

When I first started turning up for representative practices, it was a case of being in the best shape possible. How fit you were depended entirely on how you'd prepared yourself personally. Because Northland was such a far-flung province, the coach never had the time to focus on fitness work. He was preoccupied with developing team work. So it was over to the individual to get himself fit. I weighed only about 98kg when Danny O'Shea first selected me for Northland, although I never appeared in the programme weighing less than 101kg. That always mystified me because no one ever asked me what my weight was. Perhaps Garry Frew, who edited the programme, felt sorry for me!

Competitive swimming had given me a great fitness base and also an understanding of the need for self-discipline in training. You have to be extremely disciplined to swim countless lengths of the pool, starting at 6am, most mornings of the week. It indoctrinated me into the need to train daily.

When I was first whistled up for Northland rugby sessions, I had the body of a swimmer – extremely lean with wide shoulders. No wonder John Hart dubbed me "stringbean" when he first sighted me. I was a rugby player with a swimmer's body at the time.

My general fitness improved dramatically after I teamed up with Mike Barry in 1988. The son of 1960s All Black Kevin Barry, Mike had preceded me into the Northland team, as a hooker, by a year. We established a vigorous training regime which benefited us both mightily.

It was great to have a training partner with the same motivation. I never trained on my own again, always with Mike. And, boy, did we punish ourselves. Before Laurie Mains introduced me to his killer 150s, we used to do 400 metre repetitions. For ball skills, we'd make each other catch up-and-unders. You didn't finish till you'd safely fielded 10 in a row. We really used to dig it in pre-season.

Our workouts were generally at the Kensington Oval and a shy little kid, aged about 12 or so, who lived nearby used to wander across and assist by kicking balls back to us and operating the stopwatch. He never ran with us because he was a bit young, but he was always enormously enthusiastic. His name was Mark Robinson. Nine years later he was playing alongside me in the All Blacks!

It was Bill Kini, the masseur with the Kamo team but more famous as a Commonwealth Games and six times New Zealand heavyweight boxing champion, who introduced me to cross training. Every Sunday morning a group of six to 10 of us, which used to include Con Barrell, would meet at Bill's. He introduced us to the methods which took him to the top as a boxer. For a part of the morning we'd have the boxing gloves on, sparring. After tossing medicine balls about he'd then have us skipping, an exercise totally unfamiliar with most modern-day rugby players, I would imagine.

Bill was the manager of a brick works and often we'd assemble there. He'd make us shovel sand, from one side of the pit to the other, then back again. He would then make us sprint with a giant rubber band holding us back. And he had a fun obstacle course which involved climbing over fences and crawling through pipes. We loved it, which is the best way to develop your fitness. What we were doing was far removed from the gym-based work the players in Auckland were assigned, but it was having essentially the same effect.

Whangarei has always been blessed with sportsmen of outstanding calibre.

Another was my next-door neighbour in Kamo, Brian Maunsell, a former New Zealand hockey representative, who managed the Kensington Fitness Centre. He first introduced me to the machines with which I would become very familiar once I graduated to the All Blacks and came under the influence of the fitness trainer, Jim Blair. Maunsell explained how the machines had benefited him more specifically than generally.

This fascinated me because the Jim Blair philosophy was slightly at odds with my own feelings which didn't fully crystallise themselves until Laurie Mains took over the All Blacks in 1992. Laurie's approach, which I guess was a mix of his own beliefs and the findings of the man he would introduce as the All Black trainer, Martin Toomey, was that rugby was a running game and that only running adequately prepared you for it.

The Blair doctrine was adopted wholeheartedly by Auckland, and in the period through until the World Cup campaign in 1991, when New Zealand rugby was dominated by Auckland, it also became the All Black doctrine. His approach was far more gym-based than what I had been taught and believed in.

However, Jim was the first trainer I'd come across who provided fitness-based tests for players and who demonstrated how we could therefore monitor our fitness levels. These preceded the beep test, which I'd first encountered in Glasgow during the New Zealand Youth team's tour of Scotland in 1988. Glasgow, funnily enough, was Jim Blair's home city. Martin Toomey introduced beep testing to the All Blacks in 1992 and until recently it remained the norm for fitness testing, but has now been replaced by the three-kilometre run.

There were endless postmortems and evaluations of the All Blacks after we crashed out of the 1991 World Cup which we were confidently expected to win... well, certainly by the people back in New Zealand. A sequence of 50 games without defeat, which Alex Wyllie's team had managed from 1987 to 1990, not unnaturally had our supporters full of expectations. One of the conclusions some (including Laurie Mains) reached, as to why we failed, was that we weren't the fittest team at the tournament.

When Mains succeeded Wyllie in '92, he set about rectifying that. Martin Toomey, who had helped Laurie prepared the Otago representative team, was introduced as his fitness adviser, later to become the All Blacks' official trainer, a position he holds to this day.

Another huge influence on my career was Keith Roberts, also from Northland, whose specialty was the track and, in particular, sprint work. We first started working together around 1992. Three years later, Laurie Mains would help utilise his considerable talents in preparing the All Blacks for the World Cup campaign. An ex-player, he is a tremendous guy, deeply religious and utterly dedicated to whatever he turns his mind to. He still sends me a fax before every test. Wonderfully original faxes they are too, usually with famous quotations. A typical example was the fax he sent before the Springbok test in Wellington this year: "Be a yardstick of quality. Some people aren't used to an environment where excellent is expected."

Keith taught me how to run properly. How to improve my times by seconds simply by getting me to use my legs and arms in the correct fashion. He improved my sprinting ability unbelievably. Keith was involved in training the Northland league team and he and Jason Mackie, a New Zealand league representative, had this refreshing attitude. Everyone was welcome, whether you were a league player or not. It really brought the codes together. Obviously, that's more easily achieved in a small place like Whangarei than in a major city, but it was to the benefit of sport as a whole in Northland. In the past couple of years Keith has been involved as the fitness trainer with the Wellington Hurricanes Super 12 team.

When I moved south to link with North Harbour in 1994, I came in contact with Peter White, Harbour's trainer, who ran the Browns Bay Health Club and who directed me towards weights to boost my upper-body strength. I weighed around 101kg when I came to North Harbour, which is what I wanted to weigh. I'd heard all the arguments for and against me bulking up, but I'd previously decided I preferred to be 101kg and mobile rather than 110 to 115kg and sluggish.

Under Peter's guidance I put a lot of work into the weights. As my weight increased, so did my strength. I'm now at 106kg, my heaviest ever, but I'm comfortable with that because my strength has increased by almost 40 per cent.

I'm lucky in that I can eat almost anything and never put on weight. Jim Blair once did a blood test on me. There are three ways food can show in your blood – as muscle, as fat or not at all. I'm in the third category. It doesn't matter what I eat – obviously within reason – it makes absolutely no difference to my metabolism.

The method of determining All Blacks' true fitness, from 1992 until 1995, was the beep test, appreciated by few and detested by many. It was Laurie Mains' measuring stick when he took over in '92. If you flunked it, you were obliged to go away and train yourself into the dust before Laurie and his fellow selectors would seriously consider you for national selection. It's one of the reasons Olo Brown didn't play the centenary tests in '92 – his beep-test reading was too poor. There were a few others in that category, including Inga Tuigamala, whose beep-test reading at the '92 trials in Napier was a shocker, but Laurie (and his fellow coach Earle Kirton) decided to risk him immediately because of his obvious value as an impact player.

If you've never had the thrill of taking a beep test, which is always conducted indoors, what happens is you sprint across a defined 20-metre area, turn and run back, crossing the line each time ahead of the beep. As the beeps quicken, so does your speed. Your reading relates to the number of beeps before you collapse in a heap. There is an acceptable level for different positions within the team. Obviously, threequarters are expected to hit a much higher number than the tight five. Locks were expected to achieve around 120 beeps. My best, achieved in 1995 when I was preparing for the World Cup, was 140.

In 1995, when Laurie Mains was at his most zealous, the fitness testing was extended to include the bench press (where you were expected to hoist 70 per cent of your body weight 20 times), the leg press (working 120 per cent of your body weight 20 times), the bench pull (60 per cent of your body weight 20 times) and the bicep curl (40 per cent of your body weight, also 20 times).

From day one, my greatest bugbear, for an obvious reason, was the bench press – because my arms were too long. It was all very well for muscle men like Norm Hewitt to lift massive amounts. Their arms were short. I had to hoist the weights so much further.

The reason Laurie focused on the bench press was because he could see

Proving that there's more than one use for tackle bags on the training field.

that the players of South Africa, Australia and France possessed greater upper-body strength than us. We needed to bulk up. The consequence of all this was that many of the players, myself included, developed quite different body shapes, becoming much bulkier across the chest and shoulders. Peter White, who assisted Laurie and Martin Toomey at the World Cup camps in '95, was a huge help back at his gym in guiding me through weight programmes.

In 1995, Laurie phased out the beep test, replacing it with the three-kilometre run, which may not have been appreciated by everyone but certainly suited me, because I was a runner. The cut-off time you had to beat was 15 minutes. I think everyone made it at the World Cup camps in '95, although some like Jonah Lomu, Waisake Sotutu and Mark Cooksley had nothing to spare. First man home in every three-kilometre run, until Caleb Ralph set staggering new standards in 1998, was always Jon Preston who usually completed the distance in a shade over 10 minutes. My best time was 11m 25s.

Martin Toomey

Fotopacific

It has become a tactical race. In the early days, we used to hare off at breakneck speed, hit the wall and endure great agonies through the last couple of laps. We've learnt to pace ourselves better and finish strongly.

In 1997, Marty Toomey modified the strength testing, which he felt was rather severe. Rather than relating the weights to a percentage of body weight, there is now a set table. Locks bench press 90kg, bench pull 77.5kg and do 50kg on the bicep curl. The leg press has been dropped altogether.

Marty has wielded a huge influence on the All Blacks over the past four years and the team's achievements, not least in the thrillers at Ballymore, Newlands and Ellis Park when we've demonstrated stamina and resolve in coming from a long way behind, owe a lot to his masterly conditioning.

Marty was based at the University of Otago in Dunedin but in 1997 moved to Auckland to be closer to the bulk of the players. He's become a personal friend... and even gives rub-downs! He understands the need to introduce variety into training, recognising that anything too repetitive can become monotonous.

I enjoy running and am fortunate to have several appealing courses near where I live on Auckland's North Shore. I can run along Milford beach, take myself around Lake Pupuke or, if I fancy some hill work, strike out towards Brown's Bay. Whenever I'm back in Whangarei I call on Keith Roberts and we always fit in some track work at Kensington Park.

Training became more enjoyable for me when I moved from Whangarei to Auckland because there was so many more training partners available. Suddenly I appreciated there were a lot of North Harbour guys with similar goals to myself. With the advent of Super 12, pre-season training with Chiefs players has become a team-building exercise. In a group situation, if you're having a shit day, you get pulled along by the others. I hark back to some of my earlier summers in the north when, if I was having a shit day, I had to deal with it myself. Training's so much more invigorating in a team environment.

The physical requirements to play rugby at the highest level have changed considerably since I first arrived on the senior scene. It was back in the mid-80s that rugby first began to be played at pace for 80 minutes. Gradually, strength was allied to speed until now, to operate at Super 12 and international level, it's essential for players to have speed, strength, agility and vast reserves of energy.

The commitment to fitness among southern hemisphere nations is what is allowing us to play a more expansive game. When play roars on to a fourth, fifth or sixth phase, that's when northern hemisphere players are found out. They don't play that continuity game back home, so negate it by killing the ball as frequently as possible.

We're now seeing impact players on the bench with different body shapes to the starting fifteen – fellows like New Zealand's Isitolo Maka, Australia's Willie Ofahengaue and South Africa's Bobby Skinstad. These guys are introduced to the action usually between the 50th and 60th minutes to inject a fresh dynamism into their sides. Previously, there was a reassurance in the knowledge that the other 29 guys in any given fixture were tiring at the same rate as yourself. But now you have to contend with these 120kg, fired-up monsters exploding onto the scene in the second half, hell bent on creating as much damage as they can. These guys can change the course of a game. Their preparation and fitness requirements are quite different from the rest of the squad.

A lock in 1988 was required to perform at maximum capacity in an international match for 75 per cent of the game. He hit the scrums, the lineouts and the rucks but generally didn't do a lot in between. Now, however, he's required to commit himself to 100 per cent of the game. Besides the set pieces, he's expected to be involved in every ruck, to read the game and have the ability and confidence to run and operate with the backs, as well as make tackles. Today, he's part of the first line of defence, expected to execute turnover tackles.

Ten years ago, training for a tight forward was 80 per cent gym work and 20 per cent aerobic training with no speed work. Now it's 50-50 with heaps of speed work.

Don't conclude from this that rugby has ceased to be a game for all body shapes. That's always been one of the special qualities of the sport. Whether you were short and fat, tall and thin, fast or slow, there was always a position for you in rugby. That still applies, although obviously to survive at the elite level now players are required to be super sportsmen.

Nutrition has been an item on the All Black agenda since 1995. Generally, if you follow a healthy New Zealand lifestyle and eat sensibly, you're okay. I personally have never sought a lot of advice on nutrition. Having said that, I've made use of the various food supplements and carbohydrate drinks that provide energy bursts. The popular energy drink amongst the All Blacks, introduced in 1997, is called Growling Dog. Every time you drink it, you're supposed to follow the ritual and growl like a dog. Taken 20 minutes prior to kickoff, it supposedly helps energise you during the match.

Twenty years ago, the All Blacks used to guzzle beer after a match. These days, you'd be lucky to see one bottle of beer consumed in our dressing room, even though our major sponsor is Steinlager. When you're dehydrated after a game, the last thing you need is alcohol. With tests being played every weekend these days, the best drink is water. Lots of it. A quiet beer or a glass of wine complements dinner nicely but alcohol is largely reserved until the final test or the Super 12 or NPC play-offs are over.

One of the special strengths of the All Blacks, who as individuals are always striving to improve, is the ability of the tight five to Up the Tempo at any given stage of a game. Throughout my time as an international, it was something the All Blacks always had up their sleeve. We would Up the Tempo to try and shrug off a tenacious opponent. The classic times to put it into effect were in the 10 minutes before and the 10 minutes after halftime.

Our increasing the tempo doesn't mean we've been operating in casual mode till then. What it does mean is that we began stringing more phases together at a higher rate of knots. We speed up the lineouts by throwing in quicker, whether the opposition is ready or not, we get the ball into and out of scrums faster, we blow over rucks and try not to allow any static ball. We don't commit every forward to every ruck, some holding back for the next one. The object in upping the tempo is to move the big men in the opposition wide as frequently as possible to tire them out.

There have been a couple of classic examples when our increasing the tempo has impacted dramatically on matches. One was at Newlands in 1996. After half an hour, the Springboks, who'd started strongly, held a decisive advantage but in the 10 minutes either side of halftime we secured the victory.

Increasing the tempo is done in 10-minute phases, relevant to the scoreboard. Basically, we break the game down into eight 10-minute segments. We visualise it as eight 10-minute bursts of energy rather than an 80-minute slog, usually with different people taking responsibility for driving the others on during each particular segment.

Another occasion when we turned on the pressure 10 minutes before halftime, with tangible results, was at Ellis Park last year. We didn't panic when we found ourselves 23-7 down against the Springboks, just called for an up-tempo effort in the 10 minutes before the interval. In that period we scored two tries to come right back into the game. And, of course, we went on to record a famous victory.

It's not always left to the captain to decide the appropriate time to lift the tempo. Take Sean Fitzpatrick, for example, a hooker with his head stuck in every scrum. His "eyes" were Zinzan Brooke. Zinny, who had a marvellous "feel" for a game, would often sense when the opposition were feeling the pressure and therefore know the precise moment to turn the heat up.

One of the oddities of the All Blacks in recent seasons has been a tendency to ease off, completely unintentionally, in the final quarter when games have been in safe keeping. The most obvious illustration of this was the '97 test at Carisbrook when the Wallabies were allowed to come back from 0-36 at halftime to 24-36. That was the extreme example, but there were other occasions when we failed to finish off teams after having them on the ropes. I don't ever recall a command to up the tempo when we were 25 points ahead. Essentially, in that situation you preserve your energy for the next game.

Powerful teams like the All Blacks – or, say, the great Auckland team of the 80s – often maintain a holding pattern during the opening 20 or 25 minutes while fired-up opponents expel their passion and energy, mindful they cannot sustain it. The Irish are the classics of this kind. If they ever introduced 30-minute test matches, the Irish would be unbeatable. They invariably start to lose their zing 10 minutes out from halftime.

Southern hemisphere nations know how to pace themselves better. When All Black sides take on the likes of Ireland, Wales and Scotland, it's not so much a case of us upping the tempo as them losing their vitality, usually inside 30 minutes.

World Cup tournaments place a fresh set of demands upon coaches and fitness trainers. In South Africa in '95 we played three tests in eight days and six over four weeks, a far more rigorous schedule than on a normal tour. Players need to be aerobically fit for a World Cup because recovery is all important.

The best development in modern times is the decision to allow countries to take 36 players on overseas tours. The game being so much more physically demanding on top internationals now, it's important they be allowed time to rest between test matches which, these days, usually fall on successive Saturdays.

The pattern for a frontline player now is to play the test on a Saturday, have Sunday and Monday off, train Tuesday to Thursday and play again the next Saturday. In days gone by, you'd often be a reserve or, worse, have to play, on the Tuesday. It was physically and mentally draining.

It's terribly important for test players to have a complete break for at least a couple of days after a major international. I remember talking with John Parker, the former New Zealand cricketer who now runs Sport Waikato. He said that as a professional, the more he played, the more he needed to rest. It's a philosophy I've adopted. Rugby is so dominant in our lives that opportunities for time off are to be treasured. There's little point on your rest day in turning up at a club game or going to the gym. A day off is a day off.

Peaking is a trendy word, one I first encountered when I was a swimmer. However, it was a hell of a lot easier to peak for one race in the pool or one championship meeting than it is to meet the "peak" requirements of coaches, the public and the media as a professional rugby player. The critical games when a frontline player supposedly needs to peak during the rugby season would number four or five in Super 12, every test match (which in 1998 numbered seven) and another four or five in the NPC. That's about 17 games in '98, spread over eight months. If the All Blacks are touring, you can add in another handful of "peak" times.

So-called peaking for rugby is about sustaining a quality level of performance, which you endeavour to improve on for the major games – the Super 12 play-offs, tests against South Africa and Australia and selected other fixtures.

I believe a tight forward needs to maintain a constant level of performance, one he's personally happy with. Early season, it's about concentrating on lineouts, scrums and kickoffs. As the internationals approach, it's about doing the extra yards. In 1998, the two tests against England were, for the tight five, about re-establishing yourself as an All Black and developing combinations and patterns that would pay off in the all-important Tri-nations internationals.

It hasn't been easy for All Blacks to carry their form over into the NPC which, in 1997 and 1998, has kicked off about three weeks before the international season has concluded. I think the NPC, so worthily sponsored by Air New Zealand, is a fabulous competition. The making of it was the introduction of the play-off system in 1992, because prior to that once a team had suffered a couple of losses, it was out of the running.

With the demands of the Super 12 and test play, it's a huge ask on the top-flight players expecting them to reproduce their best for their NPC teams in September and October. It's especially tough on a union like North Harbour. Having been operating in a fully professional environment, the All Blacks find it difficult to readjust to the semiprofessional situation. Nothing to do with attitude, but consider this: the internationals have been training daily as All Blacks, usually in the morning, sometimes in the afternoon. Back at Albany, the guys who've been shoring up the team in their absence but who are semiprofessionals, most with jobs, want to train in the evenings. How do you compromise? Not easily. The one lot are reluctant to take time off work, the others find it hard to readjust to training at dinner time in damp, murky conditions. It's a hard blend.

Another graphic example of the problems came after the All Blacks had created history by winning a series against the Springboks in South Africa in 1996. Before the euphoria had subsided, Harbour's All Blacks fronted up at representative training and set about preparing for the upcoming NPC fixture. It quickly became apparent the lineout tactics Harbour had been using were completely at odds with what we'd been using in South Africa. In hindsight, I'd have to say that unwisely we tried to make tactical changes which, not surprisingly, not all the Harbour guys bought into. As a result, it was a muddled campaign for North Harbour. We would have been better left out of it, or given a couple of weeks to sell our ideas. In 1997, when Peter Thorburn was the coach and having learnt from the previous year's experience, we didn't push our ideas too quickly. The lesson from all that was that NPC coaches have got to be mindful of the mental state of the All Blacks and their level of fatigue, and the All Blacks in turn have got to know not to try and force their ideas on the home-town boys in one session.

Niels Schipper

15

Dream Teams

One of the best features of writing a book is that you can appoint yourself a selector. A sole selector. Not only of New Zealand but of the world.

Of course, my teams will never lose because they will never take the field. But, oh, if they could. Wouldn't it be marvellous if we could blend the best players of the 80s with those of the next decade.

Well, in my book, anything's possible. I'm going to select a New Zealand team and an international team to play the Millennium super series. After training at the Kamo Recreation Ground, where thousands of locals will give them the encouragement they need, they will play three tests – at Eden Park in Auckland, Newlands in Cape Town and Lansdowne Road in Dublin.

My 10 seasons in the All Blacks and the several invitations to represent the UK Barbarians have afforded me the opportunity of playing alongside and against many of the game's greatest players.

Fortunately, a lot of the most dynamic individuals in my time have worn the black jersey, like myself. I wouldn't have fancied trying to tackle Jonah Lomu when he was at his explosive best in 1995 or even John Kirwan six years earlier.

In selecting my fabulous fifteens, I have considered only performances in my time. This has naturally counted against individuals like John Gallagher and Buck Shelford who produced their finest rugby, I believe, before I arrived on the international scene.

With the international selection, I have given preference to players who have influenced the outcome of matches I have been involved in or posed a major threat. You're making an impact when the opposition spend time

Niels Schipper

Frank Bunce and Walter Little... masterly midfield combination.

discussing how to negate your effectiveness. And there have been a few of those, of which David Campese is an outstanding example.

So here we go. With no apologies to anyone, the Jones boy's selections.

THE MIGHTY ALL BLACKS

Fullback: Christian Cullen.

In the modern game, speed is essential and with Cully and Goldie, we'd have it in abundance. Cullen threatens the opposition with every touch of the ball. Only four players have bettered 20 test tries for New Zealand. Cullen had chalked up 23 in 23 outings, a phenomenal achievement. He's a proven last line, a committed footballer, a joy to watch. I'd have to say that seeing young guys like Christian emerge, with all his skills, certainly boosted my enthusiasm.

Wingers: John Kirwan and Jeff Wilson.

I've gone for JK ahead of Jonah Lomu because he maintained his world-class standards over a longer period. He was the first of the big, strong wingers, something you didn't see a lot of in 1989, when I entered the international arena. He could stand in tackles seemingly forever, allowing players to run off him. There were heaps of tries scored off JK, if he didn't score them himself. Rather like Jonah, he attracted a lot of attention which often eased the pressure on the players around him. He was a real encourager and motivator, a great person to have on tour.

When I first joined the All Blacks, the team's security blanket was Grant Fox. No matter how desperate the situation, you always knew Foxy would save the day. Jeff Wilson, Goldie to everyone, is becoming a little like that. It's not so easy to dictate the play from out on the wing, but it's amazing how many times Goldie turns a game with a vital try. He possesses so much pure skill and enthusiasm and enjoys being involved. His attributes are different to JK's but they'd complement each other perfectly, JK the setter-up, Goldie the finisher.

Centre: Frank Bunce.

For six seasons, Frank has been the steel in the All Black backline, the equal of any opponent. He's unsettled many teams and intimidated a lot of famous opponents with his thunderous tackling. His defence was unquestioned and he had a great ability to get the ball away in almost any situation. The wings always saw a lot of action when Frank was playing. And let's face it, apart from Bloemfontein in 1995, he didn't miss a test from 1992 to 1997. He achieved a masterly midfield liaison with Walter Little.

Second-five: Walter Little.

Walter and Frank. It's the Laurel and Hardy scenario – you can't really have one without the other. They teamed together mightily. Walter was, and still is, a stepper and a much underrated defender. A lot has been made of Frank's defence, but Walter is a great tackler also. He makes more breaks than most midfielders, possessing an uncanny ability to step through tackles. He and Foxy didn't hit if off too well in 1989-90 but they will have resolved those differences by the time the Millennium series takes place.

First-five: Grant Fox.

Any All Black team I played in when Grant Fox was in the No 10 jersey, I was confident would win. He was the matchwinner so many times, a cool, calculating footballer who approached rugby contests rather like others would a chess match. He would control the game through his kicking ability. Not that I'm suggesting we would play 10-man rugby, but all teams operate best when they're rolling forward. Foxy showed in 1992 under Laurie Mains that he could change his tactical approach. Everything he did on a rugby field he accomplished with pinpoint accuracy. Naturally, he's our goalkicker.

Halfback: Graeme Bachop.

The greatest attribute of the kid from Canterbury was his distribution skill. We'd supply him with plenty of ball off the top of the lineout and Bach would ignite the backline. Those skills were recognised at an early age, with Bach being rushed from New Zealand Colts straight into the All Blacks in 1987 before he'd represented Canterbury. Laurie Mains thought enough of him to bring him back from Japan for the '95 World Cup campaign. A player with a cool head, Bach always remains calm in crises.

Number eight: Zinzan Brooke.

It wasn't easy choosing between Zinny and Buck Shelford, but Buck misses out because his best rugby, I feel, was played in the years before I came into the All Blacks. Zinny was a remarkable footballer, with exceptional skill levels. He was Fitzy's eyes on the paddock and possessed a rich capacity to read the opposition's play in the build-up to a major game. There wasn't much Zinny couldn't do on a football field, and if all else failed he'd drop-kick a goal. The most competitive individual I've ever encountered, he flourished when the going was toughest. It would be a

News Media

Zinzan Brooke and Michael Jones... legendary loosies.

toss-up between Zinny and Frank Bunce to find the more punishing tackler.

Flankers: Michael Jones and Alan Whetton.

Michael Jones gets the nod as an openside flanker ahead of Josh Kronfeld, really because of who he is. To come back from those two major knee operations is so inspirational. No one runs better lines than Michael and from his teachings the whole pack would benefit. He's an uncanny support player and we'd use him as a jumper at the back of the lineout, which is one of his special strengths. Michael was an awesome opensider in his early days, a player who consistently Did the Damage.

I've gone for Alan Whetton because he's such a valuable lineout jumper and because no one patrolled the blindside better than him. I also need my No 6 to be an aggressive tackler, one who will force turnovers and help us get the ball going forward. AJ will fill that role admirably. He was a champion grafter in his day which is what you wanted in a blindside flanker. It's a position combining the talents of both a tight and a loose forward. AJ would be the team's social director.

Locks: Gary Whetton and Robin Brooke.

Gary Whetton, or Gee Dub as he was known, was one of the first truly athletic locks on the world scene. With his speed and ball skills, he would complement Robin Brooke brilliantly. He could dominate the lineout and have the athleticism to be involved in general play. He would suit today's game perfectly and his experience would be of immense assistance to Fitzy.

Like Frank Bunce in the backline, Robin Brooke would bring steel to the pack. A totally uncompromising individual, he gets in and does the work, allowing the team to surge forward. One of his special strengths is gathering the ball from restarts, which is so vital. When you've just scored, it's important to consolidate by securing the ball and getting straight back down into enemy territory. Robin's the man for that role. As a former sevens player, he can run and pass like a back. He'd be a sensation in broken play as we cultivate our 15-man game.

Props: Steve McDowell and Olo Brown.

When I came on to the scene in 1989, Steve McDowell was the prototype All Black front rower – explosive, powerful in the scrum and valuable in the lineout. In those days, lifting (or supporting, to be accurate) wasn't permitted but Steve was the jumpers' ally as a block. And he was also good at driving around the front of the lineout. He was another with outstanding ball skills who would be ideally suited to the modern game.

Olo Brown's got to be there for his sheer scrummaging ability and because any game is based around the set pieces. The scrum is the most confrontational zone in rugby and therefore you need confrontational props, of which Olo is the most outstanding example in my time at the top. Whenever he goes looking for work around the field, he's devastating. One of the great satisfactions in rugby is to be in a scrum that shunts a vaunted opponent back. In no small measure thanks to Olo, I've enjoyed that experience on many occasions.

Hooker: Sean Fitzpatrick.

It would be impossible for me to select another hooker because Sean has completely dominated the No 2 jersey throughout my career as an international. But he'd be my man, regardless. He's the most competitive on-field All Black I've played with (which is saying something when Zinny's in the side), being possessed of an uncompromising attitude and great mental toughness. In my time, the more professional rugby became, the better Fitzy enjoyed it. He was the ultimate hooker and, naturally, he's my captain.

The unlucky ones: Jonah Lomu, Andrew Mehrtens, Justin Marshall, Buck Shelford, Josh Kronfeld and Richard Loe.

In this category, I'm listing players who deserve to be selected but who have missed out because truly outstanding individuals have won appointment ahead of them.

Sean Fitzpatrick... the ultimate hooker.

Jonah Lomu, who loses out to John Kirwan, is the ultimate impact player who took the world by storm in 1995. Throughout that year, he injected himself into the game with unbelievable impact, becoming rugby's No 1 personality. I'm sure glad he was on our side at the World Cup. His sheer size and strength – at 118kg, he was the heaviest member of our World Cup squad by 5kg – allowed him swat hapless opponents aside.

Andrew Mehrtens is definitely unlucky to miss out, but Foxy's one of a kind. Mehrts has many of Foxy's skills – a massive punt, the ability to read a game and determine the attack. He's got more speed than Foxy and consequently runs more but he probably lacks some of Foxy's precision. Mehrts would be chairman of the entertainment and games committee and, of this lot, my golfing partner.

Justin Marshall is in many ways a modern-day version of Nick Farr-Jones. Strong with the ability to bolt through gaps, he complements the loosies wonderfully. His contribution to New Zealand's series win in South Africa in '96 was massive. We took the direct route up the middle a lot and Justin would just grab the ball and explode through the Bok defences.

You had to admire Buck Shelford's never-say-die approach. He led by example, in life and in rugby. His attitude stirred the players around him and built passion as an All Black. He was an inspiring captain to have when I entered the international scene in 1989, although unfortunately, as a greenhorn, I only got to play under him twice on that tour of Wales and Ireland. As a true Maori warrior, who better to lead our haka.

Josh Kronfeld is probably the first player most modern-day coaches would want to select. His special strength, under the modern laws, is to create turnover ball from aggressive tackling. He's the key to success for a lot of teams these days. He learnt a lot from Michael Jones and incorporated all into his own play. He's the original terrier to breakdowns.

Richard Loe is not only a great character and a hell of a guy, but he has the rare ability to play on both sides of the scrum equally effectively. He didn't succeed through text book technique but through sheer strength, which was the hallmark of his play. He was the protector of the lineout, his big mitts upsetting many an opponent. There was no more effective mauler in my time.

Coach: John Hart, with Laurie Mains assisting.

I stand accused of ridicule by pairing these two together, because their distaste for each other is well documented. However, this exercise is about giving the best players the best coaches. Which is why I'd go for Harty and Laurie. As the manager (I've got to be involved somewhere - I'm not missing out on this magnificent occasion), I'd relieve them of all extraneous duties. Harty wouldn't have any input into events beyond the training pitch and the game while Laurie would be kept a safe distance from the media. With Harty's motivational input, restricted to two speeches a week, and Laurie's technical know-how, they'd be an awesome combination. And I'd be a contender for the Nobel Peace prize for getting them to work together! We couldn't undertake such an important mission without Doc and Abo as the medical team.

THE REST OF THE WORLD

Fullback: Serge Blanco (France).

It wasn't so much what Serge Blanco achieved against the All Blacks in my time, as the threat he posed. We knew what he was capable of and prepared accordingly. He could set any game alight with his running from fullback. The All Black planners always devised strategies to shut him down. An interesting person, he captained the French against us in the 1990 series over there. He would thrive in the modern game.

Wingers: David Campese (Australia) and James Small (South Africa).

It seemed there wasn't an Australian team touring overseas from the early 80s to the mid-90s that didn't have Campo on board. A free spirit, he lost a few games for the Wallabies because of his eagerness to attack from any situation, but, by God, he won a few, too, including – and I recall it with a tear in my eye – the semi-final at Dublin in 1991. Campo was respected immensely by New Zealanders, and vice versa. He loved playing against the All Blacks. He could tear a game apart with half a chance and was probably at his peak during that '91 World Cup.

James Small isn't everybody's favourite individual and he had a knack of getting himself into strife with officialdom. But he was a champion winger, confrontational and a mighty finisher. New Zealanders loved him for his competitiveness; indeed, if he'd played in New Zealand, he would probably have been a bigger hit than he was in South Africa. The manner in which he contained Jonah Lomu was one of the key factors behind the Springboks beating us in the '95 World Cup final.

Centre: Philippe Sella (France).

You don't get to play 110 test matches – hell, that's 35 more than I've managed and I've been going for a decade – without being a truly exceptional footballer. There was always a mystique about French backs, exemplified by Sella who could rip a game wide open. He had electrifying pace, an eye for a gap, solid defence and, obviously, amazing resilience. The confrontation between Bunce and Sella – both players at their peak – would be the ultimate in centre play.

Second-five: Tim Horan (Australia).

Horan broke into international rugby a couple of months before me. His big break came in the Bledisloe Cup game at Eden Park in August 1989 after

Col Whelan

Nick Farr-Jones and David Campese (showing off the Bledisloe Cup which we let them have in 1992).

Bob Dwyer audaciously plucked him out of the Queensland B team. This was the game in which Dwyer also introduced two other "unknowns", Phil Kearns and Tony Daly, to his test line-up. Such bravery. He was rewarded by winning the World Cup two years later. Horan has acceleration and a keen eye for a gap. He's a bootlace tackler and would complement Sella beautifully in midfield.

First-five: Michael Lynagh (Australia).

Lynagh changed the course of rugby history by scoring a try two minutes from time in the '91 World Cup quarter-final against Ireland in Dublin. You can spend a long time contemplating developments had Lynagh, who orchestrated those dramatic final few minutes in Dublin, not rescued his team from a desperate situation. But that was Lynagh, a cool, calculating and highly accomplished footballer who, not unlike Foxy, controlled the game. He kept the ball in front of his forwards and they loved him for that. He had the audacity to score more test points than Foxy.

Halfback: Nick Farr-Jones (Australia).

For a while in the early 1990s I was getting sick of hearing Nick make winning test speeches; indeed, it wasn't until he finally retired that the All Blacks started to win again. He'd captain the international side, the obvious choice being such an astute footballer and intelligent thinker. There would be a lot to handle on and off the field with the international side, and he'd handle it all with consummate ease. He was a big halfback for his day and a threat whenever he ran. He was also one of the first tackling halfbacks, rather like a fourth loosie, in the mould of Joost van der Westhuizen and Justin Marshall.

Number eight: Abdel Benazzi (France).

A giant of a man: in fact, one of the biggest players I ever opposed. Wonderfully adaptable, he could play in all three loose positions and at lock. An explosive runner, he was a huge threat with ball in hand and created major problems for the All Blacks in 1990 and 1994. Came within a couple of inches of scoring the matchwinning try in the World Cup semi-final against the Springboks at Durban in 1995.

Flankers: Andre Venter (South Africa) and Ben Clarke (England).

Venter only came into the Springbok team when Francois Pienaar pulled out but has been enormously impressive. He's a big man with speed, probably the biggest specialist openside flanker at international level, and big men with speed do greater damage than small men with speed. A former South African sevens representative, he can operate with the backs although his greatest impact is around rucks.

Abdelatif Benazzi picks up Stephen Bachop on the way through.

Richard Hare, Visual impact pictures

Clarke made a huge impact against the All Blacks in 1993, first with the Lions on their tour Down Under and then in the international which we lost to England at Twickenham. He's a hard grafter who plays an essentially tight role but possesses a lot of speed, being deceptive for a big man. England has phased him out in recent years, which surprises me. He's a player who would have had a long career at top level in New Zealand.

Locks: John Eales (Australia) and Martin Bayfield (England).

Such has been Eales' impact in recent years that a fair percentage of the All Blacks' planning before a match against Australia has been on how to nullify him, which in turn would lead to the taming of the Wallaby pack. He's a magnificent athlete who does a lot of damage around the field. I enjoy jumping against him because he's a classical leaper like myself, in that we believe in contesting the ball in the air, not on the ground. Where we differ is that he believes he's a goalkicker.

In choosing Bayfield, I realise I'm nominating two middle lineout specialists, but both are capable of adapting to whatever role is required of them. Bayfield was one of the better performers among the '93 Lions and at 2.08m (and 115kg) is probably the tallest player I ever jumped against. He performed well in the lineouts and we found him a real handful in '93, particularly at Wellington when he played a major part in the Lions' victory. Win the set pieces, win the game – the Lions proved that at Athletic Park.

Props: Nick Popplewell (Ireland) and Christian Califano (France).

Richard Linton, Visual Impact Pictures

John Eales demonstrating his lineout mastery.

Popplewell would be the loosehead specialist, a player with genuine ability at scrum time. His other strength, well demonstrated in New Zealand with the '93 Lions, was with ball in hand running at the opposition. The Irish haven't won a lot of test matches in the 90s, but with Popplewell there, they've always tested opponents in the scrums.

I've chosen Califano as a tighthead, even though he's been specialising at loosehead in recent times. But he packed down on the tighthead side against us in

'94 when the French achieved their historic series win against us. He's worked hard on his ball skills and was one of the sensations of the last Five Nations championship.

Hooker: Phil Kearns (Australia).

I've appreciated his no-nonsense approach. I used to listen in on his verbal battles with Fitzy and he gave as good as he got. He never allowed himself to be intimidated and he never backed down. Phil entered the international scene at the same time as me in '89 and was probably at his peak during the World Cup in 1991 and in the seasons immediately after that. He's done remarkably well to battle back from a series of serious leg injuries. We might have to work on his lineout throwing. We used to call him Lightning – because he never hit the same spot twice!

The unlucky ones: Gavin Hastings (Scotland), Emile Ntamack (France), Craig Chalmers (Scotland), Tim Rodber (England), Olivier Roumat (France) and Ewen McKenzie (Australia).

Hastings was hugely popular in New Zealand and probably produced his best performance in Scotland's brave effort at Eden Park in 1990. Two massive penalty goals from his own half almost brought an upset win. We needed Foxy's deadly accurate boot to rescue us. Gavin's specialty was the kick-and-chase which could unsettle the best defences.

Ntamack was a smash hit on the 1994 New Zealand tour, a big winger which the All Blacks weren't accustomed to. He ran baffling lines and carved us up on several occasions. He also played a big hand in France's victory in the wind at Toulouse (his home ground) in 1995.

I first encountered Craig Chalmers in a curtainraiser at Murrayfield in 1988. He was playing for Scotland U21 and I was in the New Zealand Youth team. We met afterwards and have been firm friends ever since. He's played more than 50 tests for Scotland and always performed creditably, more often than not with his forwards under pressure.

England shut us down in the Twickenham test in '93 and one of the people responsible was Rodber. Because we didn't have any backs who could kick, we ran too often and people like Rodber gobbled us up. He's big, strong and a most effective tackler.

Another of the seriously big opponents I encountered in the early 1990s was Roumat. A giant of a man, he was a tremendous athlete and a neat guy. We had a couple of classic conversations in pidgin English during the '90 tour. He was a most accomplished middle lineout jumper.

McKenzie was one of the heroes of Australia's successful World Cup campaign in 1991. Prior to that, the All Blacks had had the edge in scrummaging, but not that year. And one of the reasons was McKenzie. He developed his game and became an effective runner with the ball.

Coach: Ian McGeechan.

McGeechan has a great understanding of the game and of New Zealand rugby and he'd be the ideal person to mould this international side. "Geek" has an excellent record overseas and wouldn't be daunted by the assignment.

THE MILLENNIUM SERIES

After training at Kamo Rec, the first international would be at Eden Park, the home of New Zealand rugby. A 2.30 kickoff on a sunny Auckland afternoon would ensure a capacity crowd and a sparkling game of rugby which the mighty All Blacks would win to go one-up in the series.

The teams would then move to South Africa for the international at Newlands. The rains won't have arrived, so the field will be in perfect order. Table Mountain would be looking a picture. The passionate South African crowd would be supporting the world team because they would want to see the All Blacks beaten. But the test would end in a draw.

The decider would be at Lansdowne Road in Dublin, a fitting finale because it's a venue spectators enjoy. So do the All Blacks, who'd be happy to travel there for an international every year. The game would kick off at 2pm before it got dark. The Irish would support whichever team had the ball and would cheer the eventual victory by the All Blacks.

Everyone would then adjourn to Leeson Street to celebrate a great festival of rugby, superbly refereed by Australian Peter Marshall. Well, we had to have a southern hemisphere referee, didn't we!

16

Me and the Judiciary

As the 1998 season kicked off, my fact file revealed that I had played in excess of 250 first-class fixtures over 10 seasons. And not once in that time had I been required to appear before the NZRFU judicial committee. To my extreme discomfort, I would finish up calling on them twice in four months.

The first incident occurred in the Chiefs game against Wellington Hurricanes under lights at Hamilton's Rugby Park. As I advanced into a ruck, I clipped Jason O'Halloran, who was on the ground. The doctor's report described a half-centimetre long wound that required one stitch. Although there was a lot of blood at the time, Jason, bandaged, returned to the field after treatment.

I telephoned Jason the next morning and said, "Sorry, mate, the ball was there, I went for it – it happened." He accepted my apology.

That afternoon I was officially cited by the NZRFU citing commissioner Steve Hinds, himself a former representative lock, which meant, at my own expense, I had to fly to Wellington on the Monday for a judicial committee hearing. Steve Gilbert, the Chiefs manager, accompanied me. The committee comprised Bruce Squire QC as chairman, former NZRFU councillor Mattie Blackburn and a third person whom I haven't been introduced to yet and who remained silent throughout the entire hearing.

Unlike a court of law, where you're innocent until proven guilty, at a judicial hearing you're basically guilty unless you can prove you're innocent. I explained to the committee the nature of the game, that it was a ruck situation and that there was no malicious intent. The committee obviously wasn't impressed with my explanation of events and dealt me a four-week suspension.

No one condones a boot to the head in rugby, but it was genuinely accidental, so I was extremely disappointed to receive such a hefty penalty. In the professional era, suspensions cost more than time on the field, they cost large amounts of money. My salary from the NZRFU was stopped for a month. What I didn't appreciate was that the suspension was extended from three weeks to four because the Chiefs had a bye in that period. While that might seem a logical development in a purely rugby-playing sense, it cost me another week's pay. What the committee failed to appreciate, I believe, is that as a professional player, I was still required to train and do promotional activities. The bye, in that sense, was irrelevant.

When I read the press release concerning the inquiry, I was intrigued to read the final paragraph: "Prior to the hearing Jones elected to publicly release details of his answer to the citing complaint and the matter received extensive coverage in both the print and electronic media. We do not know whether Jones was advised to take that step or did so of his own volition, nor do we know what promoted it, although we have our own views. In the absence of evidence clarifying those matters, we confine ourselves to the observation that similar steps taken by players appearing before the judicial committee in future are unlikely to have advantageous consequences for them, as was the case in this instance."

I strongly resented those comments. They implied that I had sought to influence the outcome of the hearing by "going public", that my call to Jason was for publicity purposes. I had phoned Jason because I felt guilty about what had happened. When the media then contacted me, I told them I had phoned Jason and apologised. I did not call a press conference and orchestrate my own publicity. If I interpret Bruce Squire's words right, he's saying players guilty of incidents involving a citing shouldn't apologise.

My experience at rugby union headquarters that Monday was one of the least pleasant of my entire career. I was certain I didn't want to go through that gruelling process again. Unfortunately, lightning was to strike twice in 1998. Following the All Blacks' opening test encounter of the season, against England at Dunedin, a game involving some of the most blatant, niggly, off-the-ball incidents I'd ever experienced, I was cited again. My citing came in the wake of the far more sensational ordering off of English lock Danny Grewcock for kicking All Black hooker Anton Oliver in the head in a collapsing scrum. I suspect the English management, adopting a tit-for-tat mentality, was behind my citing, although the complaint was officially laid by one of the NZRFU citing commissioners David Gray. I was accused of "carelessly treading on England player G. Roundtree's upper body, appearing to make contact with his head". I presume the player referred to as G Roundtree was actually Graham Rowntree, the English loosehead prop.

What happened was that Jonah Lomu was tackled by two English players and our pack drove in over them, with Rowntree falling on to our side of the ruck. As I linked with a team-mate in driving into the ruck, I was blown over the top of the ruck. There was nowhere to put my feet except on his chest. As I tried to regain my balance, my foot caught under his scrum cap and came in contact with his head. There was nothing deliberate in my actions. It was one of those hectic ruck situations where circumstances largely determine where your feet finish up.

At least I didn't have to fly to Wellington this time. The inquiry was conducted in Dunedin the day following, the judicial committee comprising Terry Willis, an Australian lawyer, who acted as an independent chairman, former All Black Doug Bruce and Dunedin lawyer NRW Davidson.

Unlike the Wellington judicial meeting, where I felt like the accused from the moment I came before the committee, events in Dunedin were a true rugby judicial hearing. The atmosphere was more relaxed, the meeting as formal as it needed to be, with everyone expected to tell the truth.

Referee Wayne Erickson explained that while he did not see the incident at the time, he had viewed it on video and believed it constituted "a classical New Zealand rucking formation". If he had witnessed it on the field, he would not have taken any action, he said.

My actions constituted legitimate rucking, the committee determined. So this time, there was no penalty imposed. I was free to continue playing, an immense relief.

They are worrying times being exposed to the judicial system, whether you're in the right or the wrong. And I'm lying one-all at the moment. Apart from the financial cost of defending yourself, which admittedly didn't apply after the test in Dunedin, there is the discomfort of having the incidents highlighted by the media and often blown out of proportion. Some of the UK media were insisting my sin was as great as Danny Grewcock's. How they arrived at that conclusion, I don't know, because what Grewcock did wasn't captured on television or video. And the judicial committee found the two incidents dramatically different. Grewcock was suspended for five weeks while I was exonerated.

It isn't just the player who suffers when you are summoned to appear before the judiciary. I know in my situation my wife, Janine, and my parents were worried sick. What about the commissioner who cited me at Dunedin? Does he receive a black mark or a penalty when the judicial committee decided I was innocent of the charge? While I condone all attempts to keep rugby clean, I can't stress strongly enough how important it is for commissioners to be 100% certain of their facts before citing a player. Even though a player might be found not guilty of the charge, there's still a stigma attached to appearing before the judiciary.

In concluding this book, it's timely, I feel, to take a step back and assess where the All Blacks are at, a little more than 12 months out from the fourth World Cup.

In 1995, the All Blacks under Laurie Mains were a good team, bordering on greatness. But although we set the world alight with our new-age approach we didn't (for whatever reason you care to promote, food poisoning or the brilliant defence of the Springboks) win the World Cup. That was the difference between being a good team and a great team. In 1996, when John Hart took over, we became a *great* team because we broke through for a famous series victory in South Africa. Great teams pull off the big ones - series victories against the odds and World Cups. In 1997, we reverted to being a good team again. Sure, we won the Tri-nations series undefeated, but we'd already accomplished that the previous season and there were several rather unconvincing performances. We certainly ended the domestic season on an anti-climactic note by conceding 24 points in the second half against the Wallabies at Carisbrook after establishing an overwhelming halftime lead of 36-nil. And, of course, the year's finale produced a 26-all draw with England at Twickenham.

Those blemishes appeared rather insignificant in the context of two years of stunningly successful All Black rugby. Or so I thought as I worked on the bulk of this manuscript through the summer of 1997-98. But now, in September 1998, as I review a catastrophic international season in which we dropped five consecutive tests to Australia and South Africa, plummeting from top ranking in the world to a clear third, I would suggest that the '97 blips were symptomatic of faults developing within the organisation.

First, however, it must be acknowledged that the All Blacks were forced to embark on a rebuilding phase when three legends of the game dropped out - Sean Fitzpatrick, with his wonky knee, Zinzan Brooke, who sought a more gentlemanly level of play with Harlequins in England, and Frank Bunce, who couldn't resist the alluring option of rounding out his career in the south of France. Collectively, they'd appeared in 205 test matches, three remarkable individuals who injected leadership, inspiration and tactical guidance into the team.

Although New Zealand with its powerful infra-structure traditionally has talented players coming through to plug the gaps, it was always going to take some time before we could operate to the same level of efficiency as when we had Fitzy and Zinny and Buncey on board. They brought mana, experience and clear thinking to the field. Fitzy's strength was his composure in the tighter matches when he ordered his team to play the percentages. Test match rugby demands a test match approach in his book. You're not out there to entertain or to gamble in tests. When Fitzy was at the helm, you kicked the goals, you played for position and if the scores were close, you grafted out the victory.

Zinny's onfield exploits are well known but it was his calculated input as we prepared for internationals that made him so valuable as far as his colleagues were concerned. He had an innate ability to anticipate opponents' tactics. Many's the time Zinny has analysed a game in advance, enabling us to scuttle enemy plans, to their frustration. It would have been interesting to know what Zinny would have deduced before the opening international in the '98 Tri-nations series at Melbourne because the Aussies - who've been rather predictable in recent years - did a lot of things we didn't anticipate. While we went for quick ball off the top of the lineout, they took every lineout ball in and drove.

Frank Bunce was an intimidating force in our backline. Over the years, the Aussies genuinely feared him, I know. With that element of fear in their minds, it gave Buncey that split second longer to operate. His opponents were half thinking Frank, half thinking off-loading the ball. If you can put doubt into the mind of an opponent, the game's half won.

New Zealand has consistently been the trend setter. In 1987, when we took out the first World Cup, we led the world in fitness. Eventually, and it took a while, the world caught up. Then in 1995 we bolted clear again, even though our example was lessened somewhat because we lost to the Springboks, albeit after extra time, in the World Cup final. Supreme fitness was again a factor, the All Blacks under Mains introducing a spectacular, free-flowing game based on quick rucks and ball off the top of the lineout. Again the world has caught up and, I declare with a tear in my eye, in the case of South Africa and Australia, on performances in 1998, they have overtaken us.

So why did the mighty All Black machine not function to anywhere near capacity in 1998? Why did some of the leading players become disillusioned? Why did John Hart stand accused of over-controlling the players?

Let's take the last issue first. When John Hart arrived on the All Black scene in 1996, he was an inspiration. He introduced elements of his corporate background with Fletchers, ensuring a smooth transition from amateurism to professionalism for the now generously recompensed All Blacks. He surrounded himself with experts. We were a mean team. As a coach, he wasn't as hands-on as Laurie Mains had been, but he oversaw his assistants (Ross Cooper and Gordon Hunter through 1996 and 1997) and delivered impressive motivational speeches usually on the Fridays and Saturdays before the big matches. That was the pattern in 1996 and it worked well.

In February this year John organised a seminar for the players at Wairakei.

It would have been ideal, I believe, for serious businessmen. For me, it was inappropriate. We sat through hours of key-note addresses from professional people, all formally attired. Personally, I took little out of the seminar that would have helped me as a rugby player. It probably had merit if you were focusing on your career after rugby, but it wasn't what we as All Blacks were all about. Our mission in '98 was to retain the Bledisloe Cup and Tri-nations title. Almost nothing at Wairakei prepared us for that. Instead, it set the trend for the corporatisation of the All Black team.

By September, in the wake of the five test defeats when some commentators and critics, and a share of NZRFU board members, it seemed, were calling for John Hart's head, there were urgent reviews of the All Black set-up taking place. Both team manager Mike Banks and the director of NZRFU services Bill Wallace were travelling the country soliciting comment from players in a bid to try and establish how a once mighty team had come so seriously unstuck.

Upon reflection, it's a shame a similar review didn't take place late in 1997, after that successful season. Not unnaturally, I guess, everyone sat back and wallowed in another series of outstanding victories. Coach Hart undoubtedly assessed the players, but it would have been of considerable value to the NZRFU, I'm sure, if the players had been canvassed for opinion on the coach and the management at the time.

A concern that would have surfaced, emanating from the tour of the UK, was that the players felt they were being over organised, to the point of being cloistered. There were too many meetings, to start with, but the greater concern was that the meetings were getting longer, from 30 to 60, sometimes to 90, minutes. Rugby players hate meetings. They're sportsmen, happiest when they're out expressing themselves at training or in match situations.

Moving 36 players and a support crew of 13 or 14 around the UK is a major exercise, for sure, and manager Banks deserves a medal for accomplishing it with an absolute minimum of hitches. However, if you canvassed the players, you would undoubtedly find most of them felt the venture became monotonous. Besides the excess of meetings, everything was too regimented. Speaking as a test player, we trained at the same times every week, played golf on the same days, dined out on the same evenings and went off limits to the media, our families, the public usually from about 48 hours out from the Saturday game. I wonder whether it's not time to review what has become a tradition with the All Blacks of shutting themselves off from the world from Thursday on, in the countdown to internationals. If it's for the best, okay; if not, it should be re-assessed.

Most players are quite relaxed the day before and on the morning of a big game. Why shouldn't we be allowed to wander the streets, take a coffee and chat to our family and, if we prefer, the supporters? Media interviews, which are organised through the media liaison person (Jane Dent since 1996), would be optional. Personally, I wouldn't be averse to chatting to a journalist on a Friday morning.

It would be a pleasant distraction. At present, however, the All Blacks are a complete no-go zone from the Thursday which makes me think perhaps we are taking ourselves just a little too seriously. After all, we train intensely to express ourselves as footballers. Are we only permitted to do that when the referee blows his whistle?

John Hart is a most capable coach, in my opinion, as his record through 1996 and most of 1997 demonstrated but we started running into problems when his focus became too diverse. As a pure coach, he's extremely talented but he tried taking on too much with the All Blacks and should have looked to delegate more. I hark back to the World Cup in 1995 and remember how Laurie Mains flourished when Brian Lochore came on board as a campaign manager and relieved him of extraneous duties, most notably dealing with the media. That's what John could have done with in 1998, a campaign manager, freeing him up to concentrate on his most important role, coaching the team.

The All Blacks have enough time and talent to regroup and peak for the World Cup in Wales in 1999, and I'm confident we can triumph. But whoever the coach is, it's imperative he concentrates on his primary role, coaching the team.

Career Statistics

statistics compiled by Geoff Miller, Hamilton

Name:	I.D. (Ian) Jones
Born:	17.04.67 at Whangarei
Physical:	1.98m; 105kg
Educated at:	Kamo High School
Team position:	Lock
Club:	East Coast Bays

FIRST CLASS CAREER (to 1 August 1998)

TEAM	PERIOD	GAMES	TRIES	POINTS
North Harbour	1994-97	42	6	30
North Auckland	1988-93	66	10	42
New Zealand	1989-98	100	14	65
NZ Trials	1989-98	9	1	5
North Zone	1989	1		
NZ Barbarians	1989-96	3		
UK Barbarians	1990-96	6	1	5
North Island	1995	1	2	10
Harlequins	1995	1		
Chiefs	1996-98	30	3	15
Total		259	37	172

GENERAL

- Has the unusual distinction of having played more games and scored more tries for New Zealand than for any other team.
- Second most capped All Black.
- Has played more test matches (75) than any other lock in the history of the game.
- Became the ninth All Black to play 100 matches for New Zealand when he took the field against Australia at Christchurch in 1998. The others are: Colin Meads, Ian Kirkpatrick, Bryan Williams, Bruce Robertson, Andy Haden, Gary Whetton, Sean Fitzpatrick and Zinzan Brooke.
- His partnership with Robin Brooke (46 matches together after Christchurch) is a world record for a locking combination. If they had played all seven tests in 1998, they would have established a world record for any combination in test rugby (currently 47 held by Australians Nick Farr-Jones and Michael Lynagh).
- Jones and Springbok Mark Andrews shared the world record of nine test tries by a lock. Although Andrews had a few matches at No 8, all his tries have been scored from lock.
- Great-grandson of "Bunny" Finlayson, who played 36 times for the All Blacks between 1925 and 1930.
- His three tries scored for the Waikato Chiefs against NSW Waratahs in 1996 were the most scored by a lock in a first-class game for nearly 30 years - and represented the first triple for a Chiefs player in the Super 12.